366 DAYS

of World War II

by Richard F. Binder

ISBN-10: 0988407957

ISBN-13: 978-0-9884079-5-4

TABLE OF CONTENTS

LIST OF ILLUSTRATIONS

ACKNOWLEDGMENTS

This book could not exist without the efforts of thousands of people I'll never meet but to whom I shall be ever grateful: historians, photographers, and researchers who have devoted millions of hours to recording and trying to explain the worst conflict humanity has ever known—and especially the veterans who by sharing their memories of that conflict have helped the rest of us to understand just a little of what it was like.

I wish to express my appreciation to many of my Facebook friends, who encouraged me to transfer my writing from Facebook to a less evanescent medium, and to the late Elaine Maddox, whose postings on Facebook moved me to undertake the project that eventuated in the publishing of this book.

I also appreciate beyond words the inexhaustible patience of Barbara, my beloved wife, who for an entire year put up with my insistence on making my daily Facebook postings before taking care of such trivialities as breakfast and the email that is the lifeblood of my fountain pen business, and the generosity of my daughter Kate, who does this sort of thing for a living and has edited, designed, and composited this book free of charge.

AUTHOR'S NOTE

I conducted my research for this book entirely on the Internet. Using principally the timelines at Wikipedia and the World War II Database, I chose incidents to include and then sought multiple sources that I could compare and crosscheck to verify the accuracy of the statements I would present. Sources included personal memoirs and diaries; unit logs and histories; databases of submarines and of ship sinkings; photographs; contemporaneous newspapers, histories, and other documents (many of which I found in Google Books); and more. Not infrequently, there were disagreements between sources; when these situations arose, I considered "majority rule" but placed greater weight on where and when the various sources originated. I am quite certain that this book is not free of error, but I am also sure that whatever errors do exist are few and minor.

Given the pervasive nature of the Internet, there is no practicable way for me to track down the copyright holders, if any, of the photographs in this book, which were all taken during World War II and on which the copyrights, if any, may or may not have expired decades ago. If I have trodden upon anyone's intellectual-property toes, I offer my apologies.

PREFACE

At the Tehran Conference in late 1943, Joseph Stalin said to Winston Churchill in response to the latter's protest that opening a second front in France prematurely would result in an unjustified loss of tens of thousands of Allied soldiers, "When one man dies it is a tragedy; when thousands die it's statistics."

Every day for one year, from 6 June 2013 to 5 June 2014, I posted a brief historical article on Facebook, a project I undertook to honor the men and women who fought and died during World War II and, I hoped, to raise awareness of why the war was fought and how terrible it was. For my entries I chose a variety of events, from those concerning the death or survival of one man or woman to those about the deaths of thousands. This book is a compilation of those entries, just as I posted them except that I have revised a few words or phrases for clarity; corrected a few errors; added personal names in a few entries; and moved the final entry, from 6 June 2014, to the beginning and rewritten it to become this preface. Because 2014 was not a leap year, there was no entry for February 29 in the Facebook diary. I have added an entry for that date in this book. I hope you will find these pages stimulating and informative.

When I started the project, I planned to write just a short "squib" every day. That plan was soon derailed by a desire to say more, to make the entries more personal, more vivid. Thus, after the first few weeks, the average length of an entry grows somewhat—and, in some instances, rather significantly. For this reason, I have added some footnotes, primarily supplementing the shorter entries in the earlier portions of the book.

During the course of the war, approximately sixty-five million people were killed. Let's put some perspective on that incomprehensible statistic. On 11 September 2001, the four airplanes hijacked by al Qaeda and used as guided missiles killed two thousand nine hundred ninety-six people including the 19 hijackers. In World War II, that many people were killed *every two and a half hours, every day, for six years.*

Courageous men and women around the world left their homes and their families, and millions of them gave their very lives, to put a stop to what Winston Churchill called "a monstrous tyranny, never surpassed in the dark and lamentable catalogue of human crime." Most of them do not consider themselves heroes. If they talk about it at all (which many are still not willing to do), they will say they were just doing their jobs—doing what had to be done. In the U.S.A., these self-effacing heroes are dying of old age at the rate of more than one thousand per day. Please don't let them die unremembered and unthanked. Consider supporting the non-profit Honor Flight Network.

www.honorflight.org

COMPARISON OF OFFICER RANK TITLES, U.S. AND GERMAN

In this book, instead of Anglicizing German rank titles, I have chosen to retain the usages of the *Wehrmacht*. The following listing will assist you in relating a given German rank to its approximate U.S. equivalent.

In the listing, naval (*Kriegsmarine*) titles are presented above army (*Heer*) titles. This arrangement is not intended to imply any superiority of actual rank. The *Waffen*-SS, primarily to distinguish itself from the *Heer*, created its own rank hierarchy; thus, the listing includes ranks for the *Kriegsmarine*, the *Heer*, and the SS.

U.S. Rank	German Rank
Fleet Admiral General of the Army	*Großadmiral* *Generalfeldmarschall* *Volksmarschall*
Admiral General	*Generaladmiral* *Generaloberst* *Oberstgruppenführer*
Vice Admiral Lieutenant General	*Admiral* *General* *Obergruppenführer*
Rear Admiral Major General	*Vizeadmiral* *Generalleutnant* *Gruppenführer*
Commodore Brigadier General	*Konteradmiral* *Generalmajor* *Brigadeführer*
Captain Colonel	*Kapitän zur See* *Oberst* *Standartenführer*
Commander Lieutenant Colonel	*Fregattenkapitän* *Oberstleutnant* *Obersturmbannführer*

U.S. Rank	German Rank
Lieutenant Commander	*Korvettenkapitän*
Major	*Major*
	Sturmbannführer
Lieutenant	*Kapitänleutnant*
Captain	*Hauptmann*
	Hauptsturmführer
Lieutenant Junior Grade	*Oberleutnant zur See*
First Lieutenant	*Oberleutnant*
	Obersturmführer
Ensign	*Leutnant zur See*
Second Lieutenant	*Leutnant*
	Untersturmführer

JUNE						
S	M	T	W	T	F	S
..	..	..	..	1	2	3
4	5	6	7	8	9	10
11	12	13	14	15	16	17
18	19	20	21	22	23	24
25	26	27	28	29	30	..
..	..	..	..	..	..	..

TUESDAY
6
JUNE

JULY						
S	M	T	W	T	F	S
..	..	..	..	..	..	1
2	3	4	5	6	7	8
9	10	11	12	13	14	15
16	17	18	19	20	21	22
23	24	25	26	27	28	29
30	31	..	..	..	..	..

1944

Beginning at 0630 on 6 June 1944, Allied forces under the command of General Dwight D. Eisenhower executed an amphibious landing on the beaches of Normandy in France: Americans at beaches code-named Utah and Omaha, British at Gold and Sword, Canadians at Juno, and a small contingent of Free French with the British at Sword. American and British airborne troops who had landed during the night took and held key bridges and causeways to hinder German reinforcement efforts and aid the amphibious troops' advance off the beaches. Thus began the Allied assault on Hitler's vaunted *Festung Europa.*[1]

---

1. There are still no complete casualty figures for 6 June 1944, the first day of the invasion. As of this writing, the U.S. D-Day Museum has confirmed 4,414 Allied dead (2,499 Americans, 1,915 Commonwealth and French troops) and approximately 6,000 wounded or missing. Axis casualties, including *Osttruppen* (Eastern European troops, either conscripts or volunteers), are unknown but have been estimated to have been between 4,000 and 9,000.

		THIS MONTH				
			JUNE			
S	M	T	W	T	F	S
..	1	2	3	4	5	6
7	8	9	10	11	12	13
14	15	16	17	18	19	20
21	22	23	24	25	26	27
28	29	30	..	..	..	..
..	..	..	..	..	..	..

SUNDAY
7
JUNE

1942

		NEXT MONTH				
			JULY			
S	M	T	W	T	F	S
..	..	..	1	2	3	4
5	6	7	8	9	10	11
12	13	14	15	16	17	18
19	20	21	22	23	24	25
26	27	28	29	30	31	..
..	..	..	..	..	..	..

On 7 June 1942, troops of the Japanese 301st Independent Infantry Battalion invaded the Aleutian island of Attu. Operation AL,[2] which also included the invasion of the island of Kiska a day earlier, was the first invasion of American soil since the War of 1812, and it gained strategic control of the North Pacific for the Japanese.[3] One American, the radio operator Foster Jones, was killed, and one Attuan woman was shot in the leg; Jones' wife and 42 other Attuans (including the wounded woman) were captured. Japanese losses are not known, but personal memoirs mention one or two troops who were killed.[4]

---

2. Two-letter Japanese operation names are the character sequences used in coded transmissions; they are not words having a meaningful relationship to the operations themselves.

3. Widely thought to have been nothing but a diversion to draw American attention away from the 4 June Japanese attack on Midway, the Aleutian occupation had potentially serious implications: it would hamper American attempts to invade Japan from the north while making it easier and less risky for Japan to attack Alaska or the continental United States.

4. Controversy raged over Jones' death. Official Japanese records and some Attuans' personal memoirs state that he slit his own wrists; but other Attuans, including Mike Lokanin, who buried the body, said that the Japanese tortured Jones in an unsuccessful attempt to extract the location of his radio and then killed him. Jones' body was exhumed in 1948 and found to have been shot through the head. His wife Etta, the schoolteacher, did have cuts on her wrists but survived.

THIS MONTH						
JUNE						
S	M	T	W	T	F	S
..	..	1	2	3	4	5
6	7	8	9	10	11	12
13	14	15	16	17	18	19
20	21	22	23	24	25	26
27	28	29	30	..	..	..
..	..	..	..	..	..	..

TUESDAY

8

JUNE

1943

NEXT MONTH						
JULY						
S	M	T	W	T	F	S
..	..	..	..	1	2	3
4	5	6	7	8	9	10
11	12	13	14	15	16	17
18	19	20	21	22	23	24
25	26	27	28	29	30	31
..	..	..	..	..	..	..

On 8 June 1943, Japanese forces began their evacuation of Kiska in the Aleutians after having lost Attu to American forces in a bloody campaign during May. The evacuation was completed on 28 July, and American forces landed unopposed on 15 August.

JUNE

S	M	T	W	T	F	S
..	1	2	3	4	5	6
7	8	9	10	11	12	13
14	15	16	17	18	19	20
21	22	23	24	25	26	27
28	29	30	..	..	..	..
..	..	..	..	..	..	..

TUESDAY
9
JUNE

JULY

S	M	T	W	T	F	S
..	..	..	1	2	3	4
5	6	7	8	9	10	11
12	13	14	15	16	17	18
19	20	21	22	23	24	25
26	27	28	29	30	31	..
..	..	..	..	..	..	..

1942

On 9 June 1942, German troops obliterated the Czech village of Lidice as reprisal for the killing of Reinhard Heydrich, who had been appointed as the chief officer to implement the Final Solution to the Jewish Question. The village was razed to the ground and burned. All adult males were killed, and all but a handful of the women and children were sent to concentration camps, where they were also killed.

THIS MONTH									NEXT MONTH					
JUNE									JULY					
S	M	T	W	T	F	S			S	M	T	W	T	F	S
..	..	..	..	1	2	3			..	..	..	..	..	..	1
4	5	6	7	8	9	10			2	3	4	5	6	7	8
11	12	13	14	15	16	17			9	10	11	12	13	14	15
18	19	20	21	22	23	24			16	17	18	19	20	21	22
25	26	27	28	29	30	..			23	24	25	26	27	28	29
..	..	..	..	..	..	..			30	31	..	..	..	..	..

SATURDAY
10
JUNE

1944

On 10 June 1944, German *Waffen*-SS troops murdered 642 men, women, and children in the French town of Oradour-sur-Glane, as reprisal for local Resistance activities.

		JUNE								JULY				
S	M	T	W	T	F	S		S	M	T	W	T	F	S
..	..	..	..	..	..	1		..	1	2	3	4	5	6
2	3	4	5	6	7	8		7	8	9	10	11	12	13
9	10	11	12	13	14	15		14	15	16	17	18	19	20
16	17	18	19	20	21	22		21	22	23	24	25	26	27
23	24	25	26	27	28	29		28	29	30	31	..	..	..
30	..	..	..	..	..	..		..	..	..	..	..	..	..

THIS MONTH

NEXT MONTH

TUESDAY
11
JUNE

1940

On 11 June 1940, as German forces approached the city, the French government declared Paris an open city to prevent its destruction and removed itself to Tours.

THIS MONTH						
JUNE						
S	M	T	W	T	F	S
..	..	..	..	1	2	3
4	5	6	7	8	9	10
11	12	13	14	15	16	17
18	19	20	21	22	23	24
25	26	27	28	29	30	..
..	..	..	..	..	..	..

MONDAY
12
JUNE
1944

NEXT MONTH						
JULY						
S	M	T	W	T	F	S
..	..	..	..	..	..	1
2	3	4	5	6	7	8
9	10	11	12	13	14	15
16	17	18	19	20	21	22
23	24	25	26	27	28	29
30	31	..	..	..	..	..

On 12 June 1944, American aircraft carriers commenced air strikes on the Mariana Islands, including Saipan, preparing for the invasion that was to follow. Control of the Marianas would provide the B-29 bases the Americans would need to bring Japan to surrender.

		THIS MONTH				
			JUNE			
S	M	T	W	T	F	S
..	..	..	..	1	2	3
4	5	6	7	8	9	10
11	12	13	14	15	16	17
18	19	20	21	22	23	24
25	26	27	28	29	30	..
..	..	..	..	..	..	..

TUESDAY
13
JUNE
1944

		NEXT MONTH				
			JULY			
S	M	T	W	T	F	S
..	..	..	..	..	..	1
2	3	4	5	6	7	8
9	10	11	12	13	14	15
16	17	18	19	20	21	22
23	24	25	26	27	28	29
30	31	..	..	..	..	..

On 13 June 1944, Germany launched the first V-1 attack on England. Hitler viewed the use of these pilotless flying bombs, which were known as *Vergeltungswaffen* (retribution[5] weapons, not vengeance weapons as most English accounts call them) and which were the progenitors of today's cruise missiles, as requital for Allied attacks on Berlin, and he vowed that they would bring England to its knees.

---

5. *Retribution* is punishment that is morally right and fully deserved, in contrast to *vengeance*, which can simply mean "getting even."

THIS MONTH								SATURDAY	NEXT MONTH						

JUNE

S	M	T	W	T	F	S
1	2	3	4	5	6	7
8	9	10	11	12	13	14
15	16	17	18	19	20	21
22	23	24	25	26	27	28
29	30	..	..	..	..	..
..	..	..	..	..	..	..

SATURDAY
14
JUNE

1941

JULY

S	M	T	W	T	F	S
..	..	1	2	3	4	5
6	7	8	9	10	11	12
13	14	15	16	17	18	19
20	21	22	23	24	25	26
27	28	29	30	31	..	..
..	..	..	..	..	..	..

On 14 June 1941, the United States, not yet a combatant, froze all German and Italian assets in the U.S. Two days later, the government ordered that all German and Italian consulates in the United States be closed, their staffs to leave the country by 10 July.

		THIS MONTH				
			JUNE			
S	M	T	W	T	F	S
..	..	..	..	1	2	3
4	5	6	7	8	9	10
11	12	13	14	15	16	17
18	19	20	21	22	23	24
25	26	27	28	29	30	..
..	..	..	..	..	..	..

THURSDAY
15
JUNE

		NEXT MONTH				
			JULY			
S	M	T	W	T	F	S
..	..	..	..	..	..	1
2	3	4	5	6	7	8
9	10	11	12	13	14	15
16	17	18	19	20	21	22
23	24	25	26	27	28	29
30	31	..	..	..	..	..

1944

On 15 June 1944, U.S. Marine and Army forces commanded by Lieutenant General Holland Smith invaded the island of Saipan. The battle lasted until 9 July, leaving 2,949 Americans dead and 10,464 wounded; Japanese losses were 24,000 killed, 5,000 suicides, and 921 captured. 22,000 Japanese civilians also died, mostly by suicide under encouragement from Emperor Hirohito, whose message promised them special status in the afterlife.

THIS MONTH

JUNE

S	M	T	W	T	F	S
..	1	2	3	4	5	6
7	8	9	10	11	12	13
14	15	16	17	18	19	20
21	22	23	24	25	26	27
28	29	30	..	..	..	..
..	..	..	..	..	..	..

TUESDAY

16

JUNE

NEXT MONTH

JULY

S	M	T	W	T	F	S
..	..	..	1	2	3	4
5	6	7	8	9	10	11
12	13	14	15	16	17	18
19	20	21	22	23	24	25
26	27	28	29	30	31	..
..	..	..	..	..	..	..

1942

On 16 June 1942, two Allied convoys bound for Malta (Operation HARPOON from Gibraltar and Operation VIGOROUS from Alexandria) suffered heavy losses while German aircraft continued to pound the island itself. Operation HARPOON arrived in Malta, but four of its six merchant ships had been sunk, and one of the two remaining had lost part of its cargo as a result of striking a mine. Late in the day, Operation VIGOROUS was cancelled, the convoy returning to Alexandria.

THIS MONTH						
JUNE						
S	M	T	W	T	F	S
..	..	..	..	..	..	1
2	3	4	5	6	7	8
9	10	11	12	13	14	15
16	17	18	19	20	21	22
23	24	25	26	27	28	29
30	..	..	..	..	..	..

MONDAY
17
JUNE
1940

NEXT MONTH						
JULY						
S	M	T	W	T	F	S
..	1	2	3	4	5	6
7	8	9	10	11	12	13
14	15	16	17	18	19	20
21	22	23	24	25	26	27
28	29	30	31	..	..	..
..	..	..	..	..	..	..

On 17 June 1940, Junkers Ju 88 aircraft from II. *Gruppe/Kampfgeschwader* 30 bombed and sank the Cunard liner RMS *Lancastria* off St Nazaire, France. The ship had embarked an unknown number of civilian refugees and military personnel, far in excess of its listed capacity of 2,200 including a crew of 375. At least 4,000 lives, and probably hundreds more, were lost, the worst-ever loss of life in the sinking of a single British ship and also the greatest death toll for U.K. forces in a single engagement during World War II.

THIS MONTH												NEXT MONTH					

THURSDAY

18

JUNE

1942

JUNE						
S	M	T	W	T	F	S
..	1	2	3	4	5	6
7	8	9	10	11	12	13
14	15	16	17	18	19	20
21	22	23	24	25	26	27
28	29	30	..	..	..	..
..	..	..	..	..	..	..

JULY						
S	M	T	W	T	F	S
..	..	..	1	2	3	4
5	6	7	8	9	10	11
12	13	14	15	16	17	18
19	20	21	22	23	24	25
26	27	28	29	30	31	..
..	..	..	..	..	..	..

On 18 June 1942, the United States placed the Manhattan Project under the direction of Major General Leslie Groves of the U.S. Army Corps of Engineers, marking the beginning of a scientific approach to the development of nuclear weapons. Three new cities would grow around the centers of the project in Oak Ridge, Tennessee; Los Alamos, New Mexico; and Hanford, Washington.

		THIS MONTH									NEXT MONTH				

THIS MONTH

JUNE

S	M	T	W	T	F	S
..	..	..	..	1	2	3
4	5	6	7	8	9	10
11	12	13	14	15	16	17
18	19	20	21	22	23	24
25	26	27	28	29	30	..
..	..	..	..	..	..	..

MONDAY
19
JUNE

NEXT MONTH

JULY

S	M	T	W	T	F	S
..	..	..	..	..	..	1
2	3	4	5	6	7	8
9	10	11	12	13	14	15
16	17	18	19	20	21	22
23	24	25	26	27	28	29
30	31	..	..	..	..	..

1944

On 19 June 1944, the two-day Battle of the Philippine Sea began. This engagement, the largest carrier-on-carrier battle in history, destroyed the Imperial Japanese Navy's capacity for large-scale carrier actions. American advantages in pilot and crew training and tactics, technology, and ship and aircraft design, which the Japanese could not match over the course of the war, resulted in a hugely lopsided outcome despite Admiral Raymond Spruance's cautious approach to the battle. Three Japanese fleet carriers and two oilers were sunk,[6] and three more carriers were damaged. One American battleship[7] received damage; no American ships were lost. American pilots shot down 550–650 Japanese aircraft against a loss of 123, a result they referred to as the Great Marianas Turkey Shoot.

---

6. Fleet carriers *Shōkaku*, *Hiyō*, and the newly commissioned *Taihō* (Vice Admiral Jisaburō's flagship and the first Japanese carrier to have an armored flight deck) went to the bottom.

7. USS *South Dakota* took a 250-kg bomb on the main deck that killed 24 men and injured 27 but did not disable the ship.

THIS MONTH						
JUNE						
S	M	T	W	T	F	S
..	..	..	..	..	..	1
2	3	4	5	6	7	8
9	10	11	12	13	14	15
16	17	18	19	20	21	22
23	24	25	26	27	28	29
30	..	..	..	..	..	..

THURSDAY
20
JUNE

1940

NEXT MONTH						
JULY						
S	M	T	W	T	F	S
..	1	2	3	4	5	6
7	8	9	10	11	12	13
14	15	16	17	18	19	20
21	22	23	24	25	26	27
28	29	30	31	..	..	..

On 20 June 1940, as the German *Blitzkrieg* was rolling across northern France, the battered French government, already having fled to Tours and then Bordeaux, sought an armistice with Italy to stop Mussolini's invasion of southern France. The invasion was a debacle in any case, with the Italians losing 631 men killed, 2,361 wounded, 616 missing, and 2,000 disabled by frostbite. The French lost 40 men killed, 84 wounded, and 150 missing.

		JUNE				
S	M	T	W	T	F	S
..	..	..	..	..	1	2
3	4	5	6	7	8	9
10	11	12	13	14	15	16
17	18	19	20	21	22	23
24	25	26	27	28	29	30
..	..	..	..	..	..	..

THIS MONTH

THURSDAY
21
JUNE

1945

NEXT MONTH

		JULY				
S	M	T	W	T	F	S
1	2	3	4	5	6	7
8	9	10	11	12	13	14
15	16	17	18	19	20	21
22	23	24	25	26	27	28
29	30	31	..	..	..	..
..	..	..	..	..	..	..

On 21 June 1945, Allied forces completed the defeat of the Japanese on Okinawa. The Japanese commander, Admiral Minoru Ota, had committed ritual suicide on 17 June for his failure to defend the island. Casualties for the Allies numbered 12,513 killed, 38,916 wounded, and 33,096 non-combat losses; Japanese forces lost about 95,000 killed and more than 7,400 captured. Civilian deaths are estimated to have been as high as 150,000.

THIS MONTH						
JUNE						
S	M	T	W	T	F	S
1	2	3	4	5	6	7
8	9	10	11	12	13	14
15	16	17	18	19	20	21
22	23	24	25	26	27	28
29	30	..	..	..	..	..
..	..	..	..	..	..	..

SUNDAY
22
JUNE
1941

NEXT MONTH						
JULY						
S	M	T	W	T	F	S
..	..	1	2	3	4	5
6	7	8	9	10	11	12
13	14	15	16	17	18	19
20	21	22	23	24	25	26
27	28	29	30	31	..	..
..	..	..	..	..	..	..

On 22 June 1941, more than four million Axis troops, mostly Germans, invaded the Soviet Union in *Fall* (Operation, literally "case") *Barbarossa*, a three-pronged offensive along a 1,800-mile front. The operation was aimed at taking Leningrad and Moscow to destroy the Soviet Union and gain *Lebensraum* (living space) for Germany, and capturing the oilfields of the Caucasus to provide needed petroleum for Hitler's war effort. At the outset, Joseph Stalin, desperate to preserve the Molotov-Ribbentrop treaty[8] until preparation for a planned Soviet invasion of Germany could be completed, issued orders that his forces were not to fire on the advancing enemy.[9]

---

8. Officially called the Treaty of Non-aggression between Germany and the Union of Soviet Socialist Republics, the treaty was signed by Soviet Foreign Minister Vyacheslav Molotov and German Foreign Minister Joachim von Ribbentrop on 23 August 1939.

9. The intended Soviet invasion, code-named Operation THUNDERSTORM and planned by Marshal Georgiy Zhukov, was originally scheduled for 12 June 1941. Preparation efforts failed to meet the deadline, and Stalin delayed the date to 15 July. On 22 June, Foreign Minister Vyacheslav Molotov broadcast news of the German invasion and called for a victorious Patriotic War. Not until 3 July did Stalin echo Molotov's call to arms in an address to the Soviet people. By that time, the Soviets had lost 800,000 men; 4,000 aircraft; 21,500 field guns; and 11,800 tanks against German losses of 80,000 men; 850 aircraft; and 400 field guns and tanks.

THIS MONTH | NEXT MONTH

JUNE						
S	M	T	W	T	F	S
..	..	1	2	3	4	5
6	7	8	9	10	11	12
13	14	15	16	17	18	19
20	21	22	23	24	25	26
27	28	29	30	..	..	..
..	..	..	..	..	..	..

WEDNESDAY
23
JUNE

JULY						
S	M	T	W	T	F	S
..	..	..	..	1	2	3
4	5	6	7	8	9	10
11	12	13	14	15	16	17
18	19	20	21	22	23	24
25	26	27	28	29	30	31
..	..	..	..	..	..	..

1943

On 23 June 1943, American and Australian forces continued Operation CARTWHEEL, the "island hopping" drive northward toward Rabaul, with landings in the Trobriand Islands (north of the eastern end of New Guinea), where they established a staging base with a hospital and two airstrips on the island of Kiriwina. The Japanese had not occupied the Trobriands, and the landings were unopposed.

THIS MONTH							MONDAY	NEXT MONTH						

JUNE

S	M	T	W	T	F	S
..	..	..	..	..	..	1
2	3	4	5	6	7	8
9	10	11	12	13	14	15
16	17	18	19	20	21	22
23	24	25	26	27	28	29
30	..	..	..	..	..	..

MONDAY
24
JUNE

1940

JULY

S	M	T	W	T	F	S
..	1	2	3	4	5	6
7	8	9	10	11	12	13
14	15	16	17	18	19	20
21	22	23	24	25	26	27
28	29	30	31	..	..	..
..	..	..	..	..	..	..

On 24 June 1940, the French government, having signed an armistice with Germany two days earlier, signed an armistice with Italy. At 0135 hours the next morning, 25 June, French representatives suffered the humiliation of being compelled to sign the official papers of surrender to Germany in the same railroad car that had hosted Germany's signing of the armistice that ended World War I.[10]

10. Despite the inclusion of a sentence in the preamble reading as follows (translated by Ulrich H. Rudofsky), "However, Germany does not have the intention to use the armistice conditions and armistice negotiations as a form of humiliation against such a valiant opponent," the railroad car was removed from a museum established in 1927 and placed on the exact spot in the Compiègne Forest where it had sat on 11 November 1918.

THIS MONTH

JUNE

S	M	T	W	T	F	S
..	1	2	3	4	5	6
7	8	9	10	11	12	13
14	15	16	17	18	19	20
21	22	23	24	25	26	27
28	29	30	..	..	..	..
..	..	..	..	..	..	..

THURSDAY
25
JUNE

NEXT MONTH

JULY

S	M	T	W	T	F	S
..	..	..	1	2	3	4
5	6	7	8	9	10	11
12	13	14	15	16	17	18
19	20	21	22	23	24	25
26	27	28	29	30	31	..
..	..	..	..	..	..	..

1942

On 25 June 1942, General Dwight D. Eisenhower arrived in London to assume command of American forces in Europe. By November, he would be given overall command of Operation TORCH, the Allied landing in French North Africa. He then commanded Operation HUSKY, the invasion of Sicily, and was named Supreme Commander Allied Expeditionary Force (SCAEF) for the Battle of Normandy.

JUNE						
S	M	T	W	T	F	S
..	..	..	..	1	2	3
4	5	6	7	8	9	10
11	12	13	14	15	16	17
18	19	20	21	22	23	24
25	26	27	28	29	30	..
..	..	..	..	..	..	..

MONDAY
26
JUNE

1944

JULY						
S	M	T	W	T	F	S
..	..	..	..	..	..	1
2	3	4	5	6	7	8
9	10	11	12	13	14	15
16	17	18	19	20	21	22
23	24	25	26	27	28	29
30	31	..	..	..	..	..

On 26 June 1944, Allied forces under the command of Major General Joseph "Lightning Joe" Lawton Collins captured the Fort du Roule in Cherbourg, France, ending the Germans' organized defense of the city. Two days later, *Generaloberst* Friedrich Dollmann, the German commander, died; it is not clear whether his death was due to a heart attack or was suicide by poison. Cherbourg, located at the northern tip of the Cotentin Peninsula, is an important seaport. Thoroughly wrecked by the Germans, the harbor was nevertheless restored to full usability by mid-August.

THIS MONTH

		JUNE				
S	M	T	W	T	F	S
..	1	2	3	4	5	6
7	8	9	10	11	12	13
14	15	16	17	18	19	20
21	22	23	24	25	26	27
28	29	30	..	..	..	..
..	..	..	..	..	..	..

SATURDAY
27
JUNE

NEXT MONTH

		JULY				
S	M	T	W	T	F	S
..	..	..	1	2	3	4
5	6	7	8	9	10	11
12	13	14	15	16	17	18
19	20	21	22	23	24	25
26	27	28	29	30	31	..
..	..	..	..	..	..	..

1942

On 27 June 1942, Convoy PQ-17, the war's first joint Anglo-American naval operation under British command, set sail from Hvalfjord, Iceland, bound for Arkhangelsk (Archangel), Russia, with supplies for Soviet troops. During the week beginning on 2 July, Convoy PQ-17 was subjected to a series of heavy daylight attacks by German aircraft and submarines. On 4 July, the covering naval force, Task Force 39, was withdrawn, and the merchantmen were ordered to scatter. The Germans took full advantage of the situation; in all, the convoy lost 24 of its 35 merchant ships, and 153 merchant sailors' lives. U.S. Admiral King, already distrustful of the British, perceived the horrendous losses of 4 July as the result of British bungling and immediately thereafter withdrew TF 39 from the Atlantic, sending it to the Pacific.

The Soviet Union did not believe so many ships could be lost in one convoy and openly accused the Western Allies of lying. Despite the help provided by the *matériel* delivered, PQ-17 actually worsened Soviet–Western relations over the short term, with the Soviets never acknowledging the efforts of Allied merchant seamen or the sailors in either nation's navy.

	THIS MONTH					
		JUNE				
S	M	T	W	T	F	S
1	2	3	4	5	6	7
8	9	10	11	12	13	14
15	16	17	18	19	20	21
22	23	24	25	26	27	28
29	30	..	..	..	..	..
..	..	..	..	..	..	..

SATURDAY
28
JUNE

1941

	NEXT MONTH					
		JULY				
S	M	T	W	T	F	S
..	..	1	2	3	4	5
6	7	8	9	10	11	12
13	14	15	16	17	18	19
20	21	22	23	24	25	26
27	28	29	30	31	..	..
..	..	..	..	..	..	..

On 28 June 1941, *Fall Barbarossa* continued with German forces commanded by *Generalfeldmarschall* Fedor von Bock encircling about 300,000 Red Army troops under General of the Army Dmitry Pavlov near Minsk and Białystok. The Battle of Białystok-Minsk closed on 3 July with the Germans having lost 276 aircraft and an unknown number of troops, while Soviet losses came to 341,073 men killed or captured, 76,717 men wounded, and 4,799 tanks, 9,427 guns, and 1,669 aircraft destroyed.

		THIS MONTH													NEXT MONTH		

		JUNE				
S	M	T	W	T	F	S
1	2	3	4	5	6	7
8	9	10	11	12	13	14
15	16	17	18	19	20	21
22	23	24	25	26	27	28
29	30	..	..	..	..	..
..	..	..	..	..	..	..

SUNDAY
29
JUNE
1941

		JULY				
S	M	T	W	T	F	S
..	..	1	2	3	4	5
6	7	8	9	10	11	12
13	14	15	16	17	18	19
20	21	22	23	24	25	26
27	28	29	30	31	..	..
..	..	..	..	..	..	..

On 29 June 1941, Finish and German troops launched *Unternehmen Silberfuchs* (Operation SILVER FOX), a plan calling for a three-pronged attack under the overall command of *General der Infanterie* Nikolaus von Falkenhorst. The target was the vital port city of Murmansk, control of which was key to supply operations in the region. The plan called for attacks from Finnish and Norwegian territory. It ultimately failed, leaving Murmansk in the hands of the Soviets, who continued to use it throughout the war. Axis forces lost 21,501 Germans and approximately 5,000 Finns killed or wounded; Soviet losses are not known.

THIS MONTH						
JUNE						
S	M	T	W	T	F	S
..	..	..	..	..	..	1
2	3	4	5	6	7	8
9	10	11	12	13	14	15
16	17	18	19	20	21	22
23	24	25	26	27	28	29
30	..	..	..	..	..	..

SUNDAY
30
JUNE

1940

NEXT MONTH						
JULY						
S	M	T	W	T	F	S
..	1	2	3	4	5	6
7	8	9	10	11	12	13
14	15	16	17	18	19	20
21	22	23	24	25	26	27
28	29	30	31	..	..	..
..	..	..	..	..	..	..

On 30 June 1940, a *Luftwaffe* reconnaissance pilot, *Hauptmann* Reinhard Liebe-Piderit,[11] *Staffelkapitän* of 3.(F)/123, landed at Guernsey's deserted airfield and discovered that the Channel Islands had been partially evacuated. He reported his findings, and a small force of *Luftwaffe* ground troops under *Major* Albrecht Lanz was flown to the island in Junkers Ju 52 transports, thereby pre-empting the regular army, the *Wehrmacht Heer*. Inspector William Sculpher of the Guernsey police delivered to *Major* Lanz a note explaining that the islands had been demilitarized and declared open islands (in hope of preventing their ruination by an assault). Two days earlier, unaware of the demilitarization, the *Luftwaffe* had bombed island harbors, killing 44 people. By 1 July, German occupation was complete, and construction began on fortresses and gun emplacements that were to become part of Hitler's Atlantic Wall.

---

11. Frequently misidentified as "*Hauptmann* (no first name) Liebe-Pieteritz."

TUESDAY

1

JULY

\	JULY					
S	M	T	W	T	F	S
..	..	1	2	3	4	5
6	7	8	9	10	11	12
13	14	15	16	17	18	19
20	21	22	23	24	25	26
27	28	29	30	31	..	..
..	..	..	..	..	..	..

\	AUGUST					
S	M	T	W	T	F	S
..	..	..	..	..	1	2
3	4	5	6	7	8	9
10	11	12	13	14	15	16
17	18	19	20	21	22	23
24	25	26	27	28	29	30
31	..	..	..	..	..	..

1941

On 1 July 1941, Finish and German troops launched *Unternehmen Polarfuchs* (Operation ARCTIC FOX), a campaign against the Soviet Union's northern defenses at Salla, Finland, the northernmost of the three prongs of *Unternehmen Silberfuchs,* whose timetable had begun two days earlier.

THIS MONTH							TUESDAY	NEXT MONTH						
JULY							**2**	AUGUST						
S	M	T	W	T	F	S		S	M	T	W	T	F	S
..	1	2	3	4	5	6	JULY	..	..	..	..	1	2	3
7	8	9	10	11	12	13		4	5	6	7	8	9	10
14	15	16	17	18	19	20		11	12	13	14	15	16	17
21	22	23	24	25	26	27		18	19	20	21	22	23	24
28	29	30	31	..	..	..		25	26	27	28	29	30	31
..	..	..	..	..	..	..		..	..	..	..	..	..	..

1940

On 2 July 1940, Hitler ordered his military staff to prepare plans for the invasion of Britain, code named *Unternehmen Seelöwe* (Operation SEA LION). The plan called for achieving air and naval superiority by the destruction of the Royal Air Force and Royal Navy, after which ground forces would land from ships and barges. After German forces failed to achieve either of the prerequisites, Hitler postponed *Seelöwe* indefinitely, and the plan was never resurrected.

THIS MONTH						
JULY						
S	M	T	W	T	F	S
..	1	2	3	4	5	6
7	8	9	10	11	12	13
14	15	16	17	18	19	20
21	22	23	24	25	26	27
28	29	30	31	..	..	..
..	..	..	..	..	..	..

WEDNESDAY
3
JULY

NEXT MONTH						
AUGUST						
S	M	T	W	T	F	S
..	..	..	..	1	2	3
4	5	6	7	8	9	10
11	12	13	14	15	16	17
18	19	20	21	22	23	24
25	26	27	28	29	30	31
..	..	..	..	..	..	..

1940

On 3 July 1940, amid fears that the French fleet would fall into German hands and not knowing that Hitler had decided to tread lightly in that area lest he anger the Vichy French enough that they would continue fighting, the Royal Navy surrounded the French fleet at the port of Mers-el-Kébir at Oran, Algeria, and delivered an ultimatum from Churchill: sail to Britain, sail to the United States, or scuttle your ships in the next six hours. Upon learning that the French were temporizing while they tried to rush troops to Oran, Churchill ordered his commanders to attack. Within 90 minutes, three battleships were put out of action. Five destroyers and one battleship escaped. French losses were 1,297 dead.

THIS MONTH						
JULY						
S	M	T	W	T	F	S
1	2	3	4	5	6	7
8	9	10	11	12	13	14
15	16	17	18	19	20	21
22	23	24	25	26	27	28
29	30	31	..	..	..	..
..	..	..	..	..	..	..

WEDNESDAY

4

JULY

1945

NEXT MONTH						
AUGUST						
S	M	T	W	T	F	S
..	..	..	1	2	3	4
5	6	7	8	9	10	11
12	13	14	15	16	17	18
19	20	21	22	23	24	25
26	27	28	29	30	31	..
..	..	..	..	..	..	..

On 4 July 1945, General Douglas MacArthur announced that the Philippines had been liberated. The campaign to liberate the island nation had begun more than eight months earlier, on 20 October 1944, with landings on the beaches of Leyte. U.S. losses were about 14,000 killed and 48,000 wounded; the Japanese suffered 336,000 killed and 12,000 captured. It is significant to note that it was a common Japanese practice simply to shoot personnel too badly wounded to return to duty rather than to expend medical care on saving their lives.

THIS MONTH								MONDAY	NEXT MONTH						

JULY

S	M	T	W	T	F	S
..	..	..	..	1	2	3
4	5	6	7	8	9	10
11	12	13	14	15	16	17
18	19	20	21	22	23	24
25	26	27	28	29	30	31
..	..	..	..	..	..	..

MONDAY
5
JULY

1943

AUGUST

S	M	T	W	T	F	S
1	2	3	4	5	6	7
8	9	10	11	12	13	14
15	16	17	18	19	20	21
22	23	24	25	26	27	28
29	30	31	..	..	..	..
..	..	..	..	..	..	..

On 5 July 1943, German forces under the command of *Generalfeldmarschall* Erich von Manstein launched *Unternehmen Zitadelle* (Operation CITADEL), beginning the Battle of Kursk. The aim of the operation was to pinch off a Red Army salient that had been created in the aftermath of Stalingrad. A Soviet counteroffensive launched on 12 July and commanded by Marshall Georgiy Zhukov took only four days to stall the Germans and convince Hitler to terminate *Unternehmen Zitadelle*, but fighting for the salient lasted until 23 August and included the Battle of Prokhorovka, the largest armored engagement of World War II. The Battle of Kursk ended in a decisive Soviet victory, and the initiative on the eastern front never returned to the Germans.

THIS MONTH						
JULY						
S	M	T	W	T	F	S
..	..	..	..	..	..	1
2	3	4	5	6	7	8
9	10	11	12	13	14	15
16	17	18	19	20	21	22
23	24	25	26	27	28	29
30	31	..	..	..	..	..

THURSDAY
6
JULY

NEXT MONTH						
AUGUST						
S	M	T	W	T	F	S
..	..	1	2	3	4	5
6	7	8	9	10	11	12
13	14	15	16	17	18	19
20	21	22	23	24	25	26
27	28	29	30	31	..	..
..	..	..	..	..	..	..

1944

On 6 July 1944, American Marines on the island of Saipan slaughtered approximately 4,300 Japanese troops attacking in the largest "Banzai" charge of the war. In a *Banzai* charge, the attacking troops simply ran pell-mell at the enemy *en masse,* taking no advantage of cover.[1] Entrenched defenders, especially when armed with machine guns, could wreak havoc on their attackers while suffering few or no losses themselves. Japanese officers, armed only with pistols and their samurai swords, were in the van and were usually killed almost immediately, leaving their troops with no leadership.

---

1. *Bushido,* the code of the samurai, taught that it was honorable to die in battle while allowing oneself to be captured was the ultimate, inexpungible dishonor. Thus, *Banzai* charges, usually executed as a last resort, were an acceptable way to commit honorable suicide in order to prevent capture.

THIS MONTH						
JULY						
S	M	T	W	T	F	S
..	..	1	2	3	4	5
6	7	8	9	10	11	12
13	14	15	16	17	18	19
20	21	22	23	24	25	26
27	28	29	30	31	..	..
..	..	..	..	..	..	..

MONDAY
7
JULY

NEXT MONTH						
AUGUST						
S	M	T	W	T	F	S
..	..	..	..	..	1	2
3	4	5	6	7	8	9
10	11	12	13	14	15	16
17	18	19	20	21	22	23
24	25	26	27	28	29	30
31	..	..	..	..	..	..

1941

On 7 July 1941, under an agreement with the Icelandic government, the 1st United States Marine Brigade (The 1st Division with additional forces) arrived in Iceland to reinforce British and Canadian troops there as the first step in an American hemisphere defense plan titled INDIGO. U.S. Army troops followed, and the Marines, as well as the British and Canadians, were entirely relieved in the spring of 1942.

THIS MONTH						
JULY						
S	M	T	W	T	F	S
..	..	1	2	3	4	5
6	7	8	9	10	11	12
13	14	15	16	17	18	19
20	21	22	23	24	25	26
27	28	29	30	31	..	..
..	..	..	..	..	..	..

TUESDAY
8
JULY

NEXT MONTH						
AUGUST						
S	M	T	W	T	F	S
..	..	..	..	..	1	2
3	4	5	6	7	8	9
10	11	12	13	14	15	16
17	18	19	20	21	22	23
24	25	26	27	28	29	30
31	..	..	..	..	..	..

1941

On 8 July 1941, forces of Germany's Army Group North, under the command of *Generalfeldmarschall* Wilhelm Ritter von Leeb, isolated Leningrad from the rest of the Soviet Union and set the stage for an extended siege that would begin in September.

THIS MONTH												NEXT MONTH					
JULY												**AUGUST**					

SUNDAY

9

JULY

1944

JULY						
S	M	T	W	T	F	S
..	..	..	..	..	..	1
2	3	4	5	6	7	8
9	10	11	12	13	14	15
16	17	18	19	20	21	22
23	24	25	26	27	28	29
30	31	..	..	..	..	..

AUGUST						
S	M	T	W	T	F	S
..	..	1	2	3	4	5
6	7	8	9	10	11	12
13	14	15	16	17	18	19
20	21	22	23	24	25	26
27	28	29	30	31	..	..
..	..	..	..	..	..	..

On 9 July 1944, British forces under the command of General Sir Bernard Montgomery captured the northern half of Caen, France, and the neighboring Carpiquet Airfield. The original Allied plan for Operation OVERLORD had recognized Caen as a strategically critical point and had called for its capture on 6 June, but strong resistance by German troops under *Generalfeldmarschall* Erwin Rommel prevented the British from securing the objective at that time. Fighting for Caen would continue until 18 July, when the British finally liberated the remainder of the city. The Allies lost more than 50,000 men killed, wounded, or missing; German losses are not known. By that time, Caen was several miles behind the front line, but the fighting there had tied down four German corps, including critical armored divisions, preventing their deployment against upcoming American operations.

			JULY			
S	M	T	W	T	F	S
..	1	2	3	4	5	6
7	8	9	10	11	12	13
14	15	16	17	18	19	20
21	22	23	24	25	26	27
28	29	30	31	..	..	..
..	..	..	..	..	..	..

THIS MONTH

WEDNESDAY
10
JULY

NEXT MONTH

		AUGUST				
S	M	T	W	T	F	S
..	..	..	..	1	2	3
4	5	6	7	8	9	10
11	12	13	14	15	16	17
18	19	20	21	22	23	24
25	26	27	28	29	30	31
..	..	..	..	..	..	..

1940

On 10 July 1940, German forces attacked Allied shipping in the English Channel, beginning the Battle of Britain. Subsequent attacks against Royal Air Force aircraft, aerodromes, and supply facilities continued almost daily until 31 October in a massive attempt to destroy the RAF as a prelude to the invasion of Britain (*Unternehmen Seelöwe*). Ultimately a failure, the offensive cost the Germans 2,698 pilots and crew dead, 967 captured, 638 missing, and 1,887 aircraft destroyed, against British losses of 544 pilots dead, 422 wounded, and 1,547 aircraft destroyed.

	THIS MONTH															NEXT MONTH				

SUNDAY

11

JULY

1943

	JULY					
S	M	T	W	T	F	S
..	..	..	..	1	2	3
4	5	6	7	8	9	10
11	12	13	14	15	16	17
18	19	20	21	22	23	24
25	26	27	28	29	30	31
..	..	..	..	..	..	..

	AUGUST					
S	M	T	W	T	F	S
1	2	3	4	5	6	7
8	9	10	11	12	13	14
15	16	17	18	19	20	21
22	23	24	25	26	27	28
29	30	31	..	..	..	..
..	..	..	..	..	..	..

On 11 July 1943, the Ukrainian Insurgent Army carried out the bloodiest single day during nearly two years of ethnic cleansing in part of Nazi-occupied Ukraine, attacking 167 villages and killing 80%–90% of the ethnic Poles living in the region. The atrocities were carried out indiscriminately and without restraint. Norman Davies, author of *No Simple Victory,* wrote: "Villages were torched. Roman Catholic priests were axed or crucified. Churches were burned with all their parishioners. Isolated farms were attacked by gangs carrying pitchforks and kitchen knives. Throats were cut. Pregnant women were bayoneted. Children were cut in two. Men were ambushed in the field and led away."

THIS MONTH						
JULY						
S	M	T	W	T	F	S
..	..	..	..	1	2	3
4	5	6	7	8	9	10
11	12	13	14	15	16	17
18	19	20	21	22	23	24
25	26	27	28	29	30	31
..	..	..	..	..	..	..

MONDAY
12
JULY

1943

NEXT MONTH						
AUGUST						
S	M	T	W	T	F	S
1	2	3	4	5	6	7
8	9	10	11	12	13	14
15	16	17	18	19	20	21
22	23	24	25	26	27	28
29	30	31	..	..	..	..
..	..	..	..	..	..	..

On 12 July 1943, nearly 3,000 German tanks commanded by *Obergruppenführer-SS* Paul Hausser and *SS-Brigadeführer* Theodor Wisch engaged more than twice their number of Soviet tanks under Chief Marshal Pavel Rotmistrov, Colonel General Mikhail Katukov, and others in the Battle of Prokhorovka, the largest tank battle in history. German tanks were far superior in armor and firepower to their Soviet counterparts; one SS tank destroyed 22 Soviet tanks in less than an hour. But the Soviets had by then rebuilt their air force. Soviet air power evened the odds somewhat, proving that a tank on a plain, like a battleship on the sea, was easy prey for aircraft against which it could not be defended. There remains much disagreement over loss figures; however, it is clear that the Battle of Prokhorovka, while a tactical victory for the Germans, was a strategic loss for them because the *Wehrmacht* was less able than the Red Army to recover from the losses of men and *matériel* sustained in the fighting.

THIS MONTH						
JULY						
S	M	T	W	T	F	S
..	..	..	..	1	2	3
4	5	6	7	8	9	10
11	12	13	14	15	16	17
18	19	20	21	22	23	24
25	26	27	28	29	30	31
..	..	..	..	..	..	..

TUESDAY
13
JULY

NEXT MONTH						
AUGUST						
S	M	T	W	T	F	S
1	2	3	4	5	6	7
8	9	10	11	12	13	14
15	16	17	18	19	20	21
22	23	24	25	26	27	28
29	30	31	..	..	..	..
..	..	..	..	..	..	..

1943

On 13 July 1943, a Japanese "Tokyo Express" troop reinforcement force of one light cruiser and five destroyers under the command of Rear Admiral Shunji Isaki won a tactical victory over an Allied force of three light cruisers and 10 destroyers under the command of Rear Admiral Walden Ainsworth in the battle of Kolombangara, in the Solomon Islands. The Japanese lost 482 lives, their cruiser sunk with nearly its whole complement, including Admiral Isaki, and one destroyer sunk. The Allies lost 89 lives, one destroyer sunk, and all three cruisers[2] heavily damaged and out of action, two for several months and one never returning to action during the war. The Japanese were able to land 1,200 combat troops at their base on Kolombangara, but the Allied force had prevented an attack on the U.S. Marines on the island.

---

2. USS *Honolulu*, USS *St. Louis*, and HMNZS *Leander* were damaged; *Leander* was under repair for a year and never returned to action during the war.

THIS MONTH

		JULY				
S	M	T	W	T	F	S
1	2	3	4	5	6	7
8	9	10	11	12	13	14
15	16	17	18	19	20	21
22	23	24	25	26	27	28
29	30	31	..	..	..	..
..	..	..	..	..	..	..

SATURDAY
14
JULY

1945

NEXT MONTH

		AUGUST				
S	M	T	W	T	F	S
..	..	..	1	2	3	4
5	6	7	8	9	10	11
12	13	14	15	16	17	18
19	20	21	22	23	24	25
26	27	28	29	30	31	..
..	..	..	..	..	..	..

On 14 July 1945, Italy, a member of the Axis until its surrender in September 1943, declared war on Japan.

JULY

S	M	T	W	T	F	S
..	..	1	2	3	4	5
6	7	8	9	10	11	12
13	14	15	16	17	18	19
20	21	22	23	24	25	26
27	28	29	30	31	..	..
..	..	..	..	..	..	..

TUESDAY
15
JULY

AUGUST

S	M	T	W	T	F	S
..	..	..	..	..	1	2
3	4	5	6	7	8	9
10	11	12	13	14	15	16
17	18	19	20	21	22	23
24	25	26	27	28	29	30
31	..	..	..	..	..	..

1941

On 15 July 1941, as part of the Lend-Lease agreement with Great Britain, the United States Navy established Naval Station Argentia in Newfoundland, commissioning the base on 28 August as a base for convoy protection, coastal patrol, and antisubmarine aircraft, both land-based and seaplanes. In the spring of 1942, the U.S. Army and the Royal Navy established bases at Argentia, and in the spring of 1943 a 7,000 ton floating drydock was installed there, along with a ship repair facility. Argentia served throughout the war as a major transfer station for Allied personnel, aircraft, and ships.

THIS MONTH						
JULY						
S	M	T	W	T	F	S
1	2	3	4	5	6	7
8	9	10	11	12	13	14
15	16	17	18	19	20	21
22	23	24	25	26	27	28
29	30	31	..	..	..	..
..	..	..	..	..	..	..

MONDAY
16
JULY

NEXT MONTH						
AUGUST						
S	M	T	W	T	F	S
..	..	..	1	2	3	4
5	6	7	8	9	10	11
12	13	14	15	16	17	18
19	20	21	22	23	24	25
26	27	28	29	30	31	..
..	..	..	..	..	..	..

1945

On 16 July 1945, the United States Army detonated the world's first nuclear device, code named TRINITY, at the new White Sands Proving Ground. The TRINITY device, nicknamed the "Gadget," used the plutonium-implosion design that was also used for "Fat Man," the bomb later to be dropped on Nagasaki, Japan. The engineers decided to test this design first because they were not sure that it would work. (They were confident that the gun-type design they had developed for their uranium bomb would work.)

THIS MONTH													NEXT MONTH

JULY

S	M	T	W	T	F	S
..	..	..	1	2	3	4
5	6	7	8	9	10	11
12	13	14	15	16	17	18
19	20	21	22	23	24	25
26	27	28	29	30	31	..
..	..	..	..	..	..	..

FRIDAY
17
JULY

AUGUST

S	M	T	W	T	F	S
..	..	..	..	..	..	1
2	3	4	5	6	7	8
9	10	11	12	13	14	15
16	17	18	19	20	21	22
23	24	25	26	27	28	29
30	31	..	..	..	..	..

1942

On 17 July 1942, the United States began a campaign to convince Britain that the Allies should launch an invasion of mainland Europe in 1942. The British pushed back, arguing that they were not ready and that at that time the Allies could do more harm to the overall Axis effort by attacking in the Mediterranean. The eventual outcome was the creation of Operation TORCH, the November 1942 invasion of French North Africa.

THIS MONTH						
JULY						
S	M	T	W	T	F	S
..	1	2	3	4	5	6
7	8	9	10	11	12	13
14	15	16	17	18	19	20
21	22	23	24	25	26	27
28	29	30	31	..	..	..
..	..	..	..	..	..	..

THURSDAY
18
JULY

NEXT MONTH						
AUGUST						
S	M	T	W	T	F	S
..	..	..	..	1	2	3
4	5	6	7	8	9	10
11	12	13	14	15	16	17
18	19	20	21	22	23	24
25	26	27	28	29	30	31
..	..	..	..	..	..	..

1940

On 18 July 1940, in response to the 3 July destruction of the French fleet at Mers-el-Kébir by the Royal Navy, the Vichy French government authorized a bombing raid on Gibraltar by aircraft based in Morocco. The raid produced little damage but did kill three people and wound 11.

			JULY			
S	M	T	W	T	F	S
..	..	1	2	3	4	5
6	7	8	9	10	11	12
13	14	15	16	17	18	19
20	21	22	23	24	25	26
27	28	29	30	31	..	..
..	..	..	..	..	..	..

THIS MONTH

SATURDAY
19
JULY

NEXT MONTH

			AUGUST			
S	M	T	W	T	F	S
..	..	..	..	..	1	2
3	4	5	6	7	8	9
10	11	12	13	14	15	16
17	18	19	20	21	22	23
24	25	26	27	28	29	30
31	..	..	..	..	..	..

1941

On 19 July 1941, the "V sign," displayed most notably by Sir Winston Churchill over a grin decked with his trademark cigar, was unofficially adopted as the Allied victory signal, together with the four-note motif of the first movement of Beethoven's Symphony No. 5. The four musical notes, three short and one long, mimic the International Morse Code letter V, and it became common practice for radio stations to play the symphony after an Allied victory about which details could not be announced in the press for security reasons.

THIS MONTH						
JULY						
S	M	T	W	T	F	S
..	..	..	..	..	..	1
2	3	4	5	6	7	8
9	10	11	12	13	14	15
16	17	18	19	20	21	22
23	24	25	26	27	28	29
30	31	..	..	..	..	..

THURSDAY
20
JULY

1944

NEXT MONTH						
AUGUST						
S	M	T	W	T	F	S
..	..	1	2	3	4	5
6	7	8	9	10	11	12
13	14	15	16	17	18	19
20	21	22	23	24	25	26
27	28	29	30	31	..	..
..	..	..	..	..	..	..

On 20 July 1944, a briefcase bomb brought by *Oberst* Claus von Stauffenberg detonated during a conference in Hitler's headquarters at the *Wolfsschanze* (Wolf's Lair) near Rastenburg, East Prussia, demolishing the conference room and killing three officers and one assistant. Von Stauffenberg had left the room to answer a strategically timed telephone call. Because the briefcase had been pushed out of the way behind a table leg, probably by *Oberst* Heinz Brandt, one of the doomed officers, Hitler was shaken up but otherwise suffered only singed clothing and a perforated eardrum. The assassination attempt was part of a plot named *Unternehmen Walküre* (Operation Valkyrie), whose ultimate object was to overthrow the Nazi regime; but once it was certain that Hitler had survived, quick action by loyal officers brought down the coup. Reprisals against the conspirators and their families resulted in 4,980 deaths, including *Generalfeldmarschall* Erwin Rommel's forced suicide by cyanide, and 7,000 arrests.[3]

---

3. Children of those arrested were taken from their families and forcibly adopted into new homes so that they would grow up as good Aryans, without the stain of their parents' names.

THIS MONTH						
JULY						
S	M	T	W	T	F	S
..	..	..	..	..	..	1
2	3	4	5	6	7	8
9	10	11	12	13	14	15
16	17	18	19	20	21	22
23	24	25	26	27	28	29
30	31	..	..	..	..	..

FRIDAY
21
JULY

1944

NEXT MONTH						
AUGUST						
S	M	T	W	T	F	S
..	..	1	2	3	4	5
6	7	8	9	10	11	12
13	14	15	16	17	18	19
20	21	22	23	24	25	26
27	28	29	30	31	..	..
..	..	..	..	..	..	..

On 21 July 1944, after six days of naval and aerial bombardment, U.S. Marines under the command of General Roy "Jiggs" Geiger landed on Guam, the largest of the Mariana Islands. The island had not been so strongly fortified as Saipan and Tinian, the other Marianas, but there was a large Japanese garrison commanded by Lieutenant General Takeshi Takashina, and the fighting was heavy and desperate. Takashina was killed on 28 July, and Lieutenant General Hideyoshi Obata assumed command until organized Japanese resistance ended and Guam was declared secure on 10 August. The next day, Obata committed ritual suicide. The Marines lost 1,747 dead and 6,053 wounded; in contrast, the Japanese suffered more than 18,000 deaths, and 485 Japanese troops were captured. A few Japanese soldiers held out in the jungle, and the last of them was not found until 1972.[4]

---

4. Shōichi Yokoi was a sergeant in the Imperial Japanese Army. When American forces captured Guam, he and nine other soldiers went into hiding. Seven of the ten eventually moved away, leaving only three in the region. These men separated but visited each other until the other two died in a 1964 flood. On 24 January 1972, two local men discovered Yokoi in the jungle. Thinking he was in danger, he attacked them, but they subdued him and returned him to civilization.

THIS MONTH						
JULY						
S	M	T	W	T	F	S
..	..	..	..	1	2	3
4	5	6	7	8	9	10
11	12	13	14	15	16	17
18	19	20	21	22	23	24
25	26	27	28	29	30	31
..	..	..	..	..	..	..

THURSDAY
22
JULY

NEXT MONTH						
AUGUST						
S	M	T	W	T	F	S
1	2	3	4	5	6	7
8	9	10	11	12	13	14
15	16	17	18	19	20	21
22	23	24	25	26	27	28
29	30	31	..	..	..	..
..	..	..	..	..	..	..

1943

On 22 July 1943, the city of Palermo, Sicily, with its harbor and the surrounding areas all but destroyed by Allied bombing, fell to a provisional corps assembled at the direction of Lieutenant General George Patton and commanded by Major General Geoffrey Keyes. The city's fall led Benito Mussolini's political opponents, soured by the long and costly war, to oust him from power two days afterward, and one day later King Victor Emmanuel III had him arrested.

THIS MONTH

	JULY					
S	M	T	W	T	F	S
..	..	..	..	..	..	1
2	3	4	5	6	7	8
9	10	11	12	13	14	15
16	17	18	19	20	21	22
23	24	25	26	27	28	29
30	31	..	..	..	..	..

SUNDAY
23
JULY

1944

NEXT MONTH

	AUGUST					
S	M	T	W	T	F	S
..	..	1	2	3	4	5
6	7	8	9	10	11	12
13	14	15	16	17	18	19
20	21	22	23	24	25	26
27	28	29	30	31	..	..
..	..	..	..	..	..	..

On 23 July 1944, 629 aircraft of the Royal Air Force participated in an overnight bombing raid on the German city of Kiel, the first major air raid on a German city since April and the heaviest single RAF raid of the war. Kiel was a major naval base and a shipbuilding center engaged in the production of submarines, and much of the city's local industry was manned by slave labor. Decoy raids were often used to lure German air defenses away from the real raiders, and on this night the *Luftwaffe* fell for the trick. Without fighter cover, Kiel suffered major damage. There was no running water for three days, public transportation did not operate for eight days, and gas service was out for nearly three weeks.

JULY						
S	M	T	W	T	F	S
..	..	..	..	..	..	1
2	3	4	5	6	7	8
9	10	11	12	13	14	15
16	17	18	19	20	21	22
23	24	25	26	27	28	29
30	31	..	..	..	..	..

MONDAY
24
JULY

1944

AUGUST						
S	M	T	W	T	F	S
..	..	1	2	3	4	5
6	7	8	9	10	11	12
13	14	15	16	17	18	19
20	21	22	23	24	25	26
27	28	29	30	31	..	..
..	..	..	..	..	..	..

On 24 July 1944, in what would be an aborted start to Operation COBRA, the U.S. breakout from the Normandy beachhead, U.S. aircraft that failed to receive the abort order mistakenly bombed the U.S. Army's 30th Division near Saint Lô, France, killing 35 and wounding 131, prompting the Assistant Division Commander, Brigadier General William K. Harrison, to remark, "As a fiasco, this operation was a brilliant achievement." Saint Lô, by the time operations in its area were finished, was about 95% destroyed; Irish writer Samuel Beckett called it "the Capital of the Ruins." One American soldier was heard to remark, "We sure liberated the hell out of this place."

JULY						
S	M	T	W	T	F	S
..	..	..	..	..	..	1
2	3	4	5	6	7	8
9	10	11	12	13	14	15
16	17	18	19	20	21	22
23	24	25	26	27	28	29
30	31	..	..	..	..	..

THIS MONTH

TUESDAY
25
JULY

1944

NEXT MONTH

AUGUST						
S	M	T	W	T	F	S
..	..	1	2	3	4	5
6	7	8	9	10	11	12
13	14	15	16	17	18	19
20	21	22	23	24	25	26
27	28	29	30	31	..	..
..	..	..	..	..	..	..

On 25 July 1944, Operation COBRA, the U.S. sweep southward and westward from the Normandy beachhead, got underway one day late, again with an aerial bombardment as a prelude. This time the bombardment blasted the enemy so severely that roughly 70% of the German troops were killed, wounded, or so knocked about that they were mentally incapable of action. Sadly, bombs again landed on American positions, and the 30th Division took more casualties from the USAAF than from the enemy on any day in the war, losing 111 killed and 490 wounded. Among the dead was Lieutenant General Lesley McNair, a staff officer with no combat experience who was visiting from Washington and had—despite Eisenhower's repeated warnings—foolishly issued orders including himself in the complement of the 30th Division. McNair was the highest-ranking Allied officer killed during the war.

JULY

S	M	T	W	T	F	S
..	..	1	2	3	4	5
6	7	8	9	10	11	12
13	14	15	16	17	18	19
20	21	22	23	24	25	26
27	28	29	30	31	..	..
..	..	..	..	..	..	..

AUGUST

S	M	T	W	T	F	S
..	..	..	..	..	1	2
3	4	5	6	7	8	9
10	11	12	13	14	15	16
17	18	19	20	21	22	23
24	25	26	27	28	29	30
31	..	..	..	..	..	..

SATURDAY
26
JULY

1941

On 26 July 1941, U.S. President Franklin D. Roosevelt ordered all Japanese assets in the United States seized in response to the Japanese occupation of French Indochina. The Japanese had invaded French Indochina in 1940 as part of the ongoing Second Sino-Japanese War, in order to block China's importation of arms via the *Chemins de Fer de L'Indo-Chine et du Yunnan* (Indo-Chinese-Yunnan Railroad), which connected Haiphong and its harbor, in French Indochina, with Kunming, in China's Yunnan Province. After fighting lasting only a few days, the Japanese had reached an agreement with the pro-Axis Vichy French that allowed the Japanese to occupy the northern half of the country, thereby creating the blockade they desired.

JULY

S	M	T	W	T	F	S
..	..	..	..	..	..	1
2	3	4	5	6	7	8
9	10	11	12	13	14	15
16	17	18	19	20	21	22
23	24	25	26	27	28	29
30	31	..	..	..	..	..

THURSDAY
27
JULY

1944

AUGUST

S	M	T	W	T	F	S
..	..	1	2	3	4	5
6	7	8	9	10	11	12
13	14	15	16	17	18	19
20	21	22	23	24	25	26
27	28	29	30	31	..	..
..	..	..	..	..	..	..

On 27 July 1944, fighting for the strategically located Narva Isthmus in Estonia began as Soviet forces attacked to recapture the isthmus. The Battle of the Tannenberg Line, as it was called, would continue for two full weeks. The Germans' "*Narwa*" detachment, consisting of 22,500 men, comprised 25 Estonian infantry battalions (most of whom had been impressed) along with 24 Dutch, Danish and Flemish ones; artillery, armored, engineering, and special units were mostly Germans. The Soviets' Leningrad Front numbered 136,800 troops. The Soviet operation ultimately failed. Axis records list about 2,500 killed or missing and 7,500 wounded, along with six tanks destroyed. Soviet losses were reported to be about 35,000 killed or missing and 135,000 wounded or sick, plus about 160 tanks.

THIS MONTH						
JULY						
S	M	T	W	T	F	S
..	..	1	2	3	4	5
6	7	8	9	10	11	12
13	14	15	16	17	18	19
20	21	22	23	24	25	26
27	28	29	30	31	..	..
..	..	..	..	..	..	..

MONDAY
28
JULY

NEXT MONTH						
AUGUST						
S	M	T	W	T	F	S
..	..	..	..	..	1	2
3	4	5	6	7	8	9
10	11	12	13	14	15	16
17	18	19	20	21	22	23
24	25	26	27	28	29	30
31	..	..	..	..	..	..

1941

On 28 July 1941, Japanese troops occupied southern French Indochina but allowed the pro-Axis Vichy French to continue to administer Vietnam. The Vichy French also agreed to the establishment of Japanese bases in Indochina.

<table>
<tr><td colspan="7">THIS MONTH</td></tr>
<tr><td colspan="7">JULY</td></tr>
<tr><td>S</td><td>M</td><td>T</td><td>W</td><td>T</td><td>F</td><td>S</td></tr>
</table>

S	M	T	W	T	F	S
..	..	..	..	..	..	1
2	3	4	5	6	7	8
9	10	11	12	13	14	15
16	17	18	19	20	21	22
23	24	25	26	27	28	29
30	31	..	..	..	..	..

SATURDAY
29
JULY

NEXT MONTH

AUGUST

S	M	T	W	T	F	S
..	..	1	2	3	4	5
6	7	8	9	10	11	12
13	14	15	16	17	18	19
20	21	22	23	24	25	26
27	28	29	30	31	..	..
..	..	..	..	..	..	..

1944

On 29 July 1944, Operation COBRA was in full swing as American troops captured the city of Coutances, about eight miles from the western coast of the Cotentin Peninsula, during the predawn hours. The ultimate goal of the operation was to escape Normandy and capture Breton ports, such as Brest, for use as supply channels; but in the weeks following the operation's launching, it was determined that these ports were too far from the front lines to be of use, and no Allied ships berthed there during the war. The operation was nonetheless a great success, as it led to the destruction of Germany's Army Group West in what became known as the Falaise Pocket.

THIS MONTH						
JULY						
S	M	T	W	T	F	S
1	2	3	4	5	6	7
8	9	10	11	12	13	14
15	16	17	18	19	20	21
22	23	24	25	26	27	28
29	30	31	..	..	..	..
..	..	..	..	..	..	..

MONDAY
30
JULY

NEXT MONTH						
AUGUST						
S	M	T	W	T	F	S
..	..	..	1	2	3	4
5	6	7	8	9	10	11
12	13	14	15	16	17	18
19	20	21	22	23	24	25
26	27	28	29	30	31	..
..	..	..	..	..	..	..

1945

On 30 July 1945, Imperial Japanese Navy submarine *I-58* torpedoed the American cruiser USS *Indianapolis,* which was on a course for Australia after having delivered the critical components of two atomic bombs to Tinian Island in the Marianas. Of 1,199 personnel aboard, approximately 300 went down with the ship, which sank in only 12 minutes.

Because *Indianapolis* was operating under radio silence, the Navy did not know where the ship was or that she had sunk. The remaining 900 crew, crammed into too few lifeboats with almost no food or water, suffered exposure, dehydration, and persistent shark attacks as they floated without rescue for four days until they were discovered by a Navy aircraft on routine patrol. There were only 316 survivors.

Operating under orders to "zigzag at his discretion, weather permitting," *Indianapolis* had been sailing on a straight course. Captain Charles McVay, who survived the sinking, was courtmartialed, and despite testimony from the captain of *I-58*, Commander Mochitsura Hashimoto, that zigzagging would have made no difference, McVay was convicted of "hazarding his ship by failing to zigzag." He was exonerated, posthumously, in 2000; weighed down by grief and shame, he had suicided in 1958.

THIS MONTH								THURSDAY	NEXT MONTH						
JULY									AUGUST						
S	M	T	W	T	F	S		**31**	S	M	T	W	T	F	S
..	..	1	2	3	4	5			..	..	..	..	..	1	2
6	7	8	9	10	11	12			3	4	5	6	7	8	9
13	14	15	16	17	18	19		JULY	10	11	12	13	14	15	16
20	21	22	23	24	25	26			17	18	19	20	21	22	23
27	28	29	30	31	..	..			24	25	26	27	28	29	30
..	..	..	..	..	..	..			31	..	..	..	..	..	..

1941

On 31 July 1941, Japanese ships in Sukumo Bay allegedly sighted two darkened cruisers approaching the Bungo Channel, which runs roughly east to west between the Pacific Ocean and Seto Inland Sea, from the east; the vessels supposedly disappeared to the south behind a smoke screen when challenged. In an apparent attempt at provocation to assume the moral high ground in ongoing negotiations over U.S. exports to Japan, the Japanese delivered a falsified formal protest to U.S. Ambassador Joseph Grew in Tokyo, describing the purported incident and claiming that the putative intruders were American ships trespassing in Japanese territorial waters. The next day, the United States embargoed all oil and gasoline exports to Japan, virtually ensuring that war would come between the two countries.[5]

---

5. According to writer Robert Stinnett, White House records show that earlier in 1941 U.S. President Roosevelt, pursuing a policy of provoking war with Japan, had initiated Action D, a series of naval sorties into Japanese waters and that the 31 July incident marked the third and last of these missions.

AUGUST						
S	M	T	W	T	F	S
..	..	1	2	3	4	5
6	7	8	9	10	11	12
13	14	15	16	17	18	19
20	21	22	23	24	25	26
27	28	29	30	31	..	..
..	..	..	..	..	..	..

TUESDAY
1
AUGUST

1944

SEPTEMBER						
S	M	T	W	T	F	S
..	..	..	..	..	1	2
3	4	5	6	7	8	9
10	11	12	13	14	15	16
17	18	19	20	21	22	23
24	25	26	27	28	29	30
..	..	..	..	..	..	..

On 1 August 1944, U.S. forces completed the capture of Tinian in the Mariana Islands. (Saipan was captured on 9 July, and the battle for Guam would rage until 10 August.) The Battle of Tinian had pitted 30,000 U.S. Marines against 8,810 Imperial Japanese soldiers and marines. American casualties numbered 328 killed and 1,571 wounded; the Japanese lost 8,010 killed and 313 captured. In 1945, Tinian became home to the 509th Composite Bomb Group, which would deliver the death blow to the Japanese military regime.

<table>
<tr><td colspan="7" align="center">THIS MONTH</td></tr>
<tr><td colspan="7" align="center">AUGUST</td></tr>
</table>

THIS MONTH

AUGUST

S	M	T	W	T	F	S
1	2	3	4	5	6	7
8	9	10	11	12	13	14
15	16	17	18	19	20	21
22	23	24	25	26	27	28
29	30	31	..	..	..	..
..	..	..	..	..	..	..

MONDAY
2
AUGUST
1943

NEXT MONTH

SEPTEMBER

S	M	T	W	T	F	S
..	..	..	1	2	3	4
5	6	7	8	9	10	11
12	13	14	15	16	17	18
19	20	21	22	23	24	25
26	27	28	29	30	..	..
..	..	..	..	..	..	..

On 2 August 1943, at about 0200 hours, while traveling at a high rate of speed on its return to Rabaul from Vila, Kolombangara, after offloading supplies and soldiers, Japanese destroyer *Amagiri* rammed and sank an Elco-built U.S. Navy motor torpedo boat. The boat's crew had less than 10 seconds after spotting the destroyer in the moonless night before it struck amidships and split the wooden boat in two. The surviving crew placed their lantern, shoes, and nonswimmers on a floating timber from the wreck and swam with it for four hours until they reached a tiny island 3.5 miles distant without interference from sharks or crocodiles. The boat's commanding officer towed an injured crewman by clenching the man's life jacket in his teeth. After reaching the island, he then swam another 2.5 miles to two other islands in search of food and water and then led the crew to yet another island, where they found coconut trees and fresh water. They were rescued six days later. The commander of *PT-109* was Lieutenant (Junior Grade) John Fitzgerald Kennedy, who in 1960 became the 35th president of the United States.

THIS MONTH						
AUGUST						
S	M	T	W	T	F	S
..	..	1	2	3	4	5
6	7	8	9	10	11	12
13	14	15	16	17	18	19
20	21	22	23	24	25	26
27	28	29	30	31	..	..
..	..	..	..	..	..	..

THURSDAY
3
AUGUST

1944

NEXT MONTH						
SEPTEMBER						
S	M	T	W	T	F	S
..	..	..	..	..	1	2
3	4	5	6	7	8	9
10	11	12	13	14	15	16
17	18	19	20	21	22	23
24	25	26	27	28	29	30
..	..	..	..	..	..	..

On 3 August 1944, Allied forces under the command of General Joseph "Vinegar Joe" Stilwell, including three divisions of the New China Army, which had been trained to American standards, and the 5307th Composite Unit, better known as Merrill's Marauders, captured Myitkyina Airfield, in northern Burma. After a stubborn months-long defense, Major General Mizukami Genzu had withdrawn his forces, members of the Imperial Japanese Army's 18th Division, leaving a rearguard of 187 sick men and taking his own life in accordance with orders that he defend the airfield to the death. The capture of Myitkyina made it possible for the Allies to reopen the Burma Road, which was the critical supply line from the Indian subcontinent to China.

THIS MONTH						
AUGUST						
S	M	T	W	T	F	S
..	..	1	2	3	4	5
6	7	8	9	10	11	12
13	14	15	16	17	18	19
20	21	22	23	24	25	26
27	28	29	30	31	..	..
..	..	..	..	..	..	..

FRIDAY
4
AUGUST

NEXT MONTH						
SEPTEMBER						
S	M	T	W	T	F	S
..	..	..	..	..	1	2
3	4	5	6	7	8	9
10	11	12	13	14	15	16
17	18	19	20	21	22	23
24	25	26	27	28	29	30
..	..	..	..	..	..	..

1944

On 4 August 1944, as they approached the Germans' last defensive line in Italy, the Gothic Line, Allied troops, principally British and Commonwealth units under the command of Field Marshal Sir Harold Alexander, liberated Florence. To hinder the Allied advance, the retreating Germans destroyed the bridges along the Arno River; but at the last moment Carlo Steinhäuslin, a Florentine who was serving as consul in Florence for 26 countries, persuaded *Generalfeldmarschall* Albert Kesselring not to blow up the last of the bridges, the *Ponte Vecchio* (the "Old Bridge," built *c.* 995 and most recently rebuilt after a flood in 1345), because of its historical value. Instead, the Germans used mines to destroy an equally historic area directly to the south of the bridge, including part of the *Corridoio Vasariano,* an elevated enclosed passageway built in 1564 to connect the *Palazzo Vecchio* with the *Palazzo Pitti* via the Uffizi Gallery and the *Ponte Vecchio.*

THIS MONTH						
AUGUST						
S	M	T	W	T	F	S
..	..	1	2	3	4	5
6	7	8	9	10	11	12
13	14	15	16	17	18	19
20	21	22	23	24	25	26
27	28	29	30	31	..	..
..	..	..	..	..	..	..

SATURDAY
5
AUGUST

1944

NEXT MONTH						
SEPTEMBER						
S	M	T	W	T	F	S
..	..	..	..	..	1	2
3	4	5	6	7	8	9
10	11	12	13	14	15	16
17	18	19	20	21	22	23
24	25	26	27	28	29	30
..	..	..	..	..	..	..

On 5 August 1944, more than 540 Japanese prisoners of war escaped from No. 12 Prisoner of War Compound, near Cowra, in New South Wales, Australia, where were housed some 6,000 POWs, including some civilians. During the ensuing manhunt, four Australian soldiers and 231 Japanese soldiers died, while 108 prisoners were wounded. All of the surviving escapees were captured and returned to prison. An inquiry into the breakout, found that many of the dead had committed suicide or been killed by other prisoners, and many of the wounded had suffered self-inflicted wounds. Two of the dead Australians were posthumously awarded the George Cross, Britain's highest military or civilian honor (equal with the Victoria Cross, but awarded in cases where purely military honors would not be appropriate).

THIS MONTH						
AUGUST						
S	M	T	W	T	F	S
..	..	..	1	2	3	4
5	6	7	8	9	10	11
12	13	14	15	16	17	18
19	20	21	22	23	24	25
26	27	28	29	30	31	..
..	..	..	..	..	..	..

MONDAY
6
AUGUST
1945

NEXT MONTH						
SEPTEMBER						
S	M	T	W	T	F	S
..	..	..	..	..	..	1
2	3	4	5	6	7	8
9	10	11	12	13	14	15
16	17	18	19	20	21	22
23	24	25	26	27	28	29
30	..	..	..	..	..	..

On 6 August 1945, at approximately 0815 hours, *Enola Gay*, a B-29 Super-fortress piloted by Colonel Paul Tibbets and named for his mother, dropped the first nuclear weapon ever used in combat on the military stronghold city of Hiroshima, Japan. The city had not been attacked prior to this mission so that the effects of the bomb on an undamaged city could be observed.

The bomb, nicknamed "Little Boy," was a gun-type uranium device, in which a six-foot-long "cannon" fired a hollow U-235 cylinder six inches in diameter at a second piece of U-235 shaped as a plug to fill the cylinder. The conjoining of the two pieces of uranium, at an altitude of 1,868 feet, created a critical mass, setting off a blast equal to that from approximately 16,000 tons of TNT. The blast flattened virtually everything within a mile of the hypocenter (the spot directly beneath the blast) except about

50 reinforced concrete structures, and it partially damaged structures as far as five miles away.

The explosion immediately killed approximately 66,000 people and injured another 69,000. The final death toll was something greater than 100,000. Contrary to popular belief, the bomb did not vaporize people's bodies; the fireball did not reach ground level.

THIS MONTH						
AUGUST						
S	M	T	W	T	F	S
..	..	..	..	..	..	1
2	3	4	5	6	7	8
9	10	11	12	13	14	15
16	17	18	19	20	21	22
23	24	25	26	27	28	29
30	31	..	..	..	..	..

FRIDAY
7
AUGUST
1942

NEXT MONTH						
SEPTEMBER						
S	M	T	W	T	F	S
..	..	1	2	3	4	5
6	7	8	9	10	11	12
13	14	15	16	17	18	19
20	21	22	23	24	25	26
27	28	29	30	..	..	..

On 7 August 1942, the U.S. 1st Marine Division, under the command of Major General Alexander Vandegrift, began Operation WATCHTOWER, the first U.S. offensive of the war, by landing on Guadalcanal and the smaller islands of Tulagi and Florida in the Solomon Islands chain. The Japanese had landed on Guadalcanal a month earlier to construct an airbase; U.S. strategic planners concluded that allowing the completion of that base would imperil Allied transportation lines to Australia. The Marines quickly took control of the airbase, naming it Henderson Field and finishing it for use by Allied aircraft; but they did not soon evict the Japanese defenders from the island. The Guadalcanal Campaign would continue until 9 February 1943, resulting in an American victory that left 7,100 Allied dead and four captured, 29 ships sunk, and 615 aircraft destroyed. The Japanese lost 31,000 dead, 1,000 captured, 38 ships sunk, and 680–880 aircraft destroyed, but were able to evacuate 10,652 men.

THIS MONTH

AUGUST

S	M	T	W	T	F	S
..	..	..	1	2	3	4
5	6	7	8	9	10	11
12	13	14	15	16	17	18
19	20	21	22	23	24	25
26	27	28	29	30	31	..
..	..	..	..	..	..	..

WEDNESDAY
8
AUGUST

NEXT MONTH

SEPTEMBER

S	M	T	W	T	F	S
..	..	..	..	..	..	1
2	3	4	5	6	7	8
9	10	11	12	13	14	15
16	17	18	19	20	21	22
23	24	25	26	27	28	29
30	..	..	..	..	..	..

1945

On 8 August 1945, after seeing that the United States was about to bring Japan to its knees, the Soviet Union declared war on Japan, launching its Manchurian Strategic Offensive Operation about an hour after issuing the declaration. The operation included an invasion of the Kuril Islands, which the Japanese had been evacuating in anticipation of the Soviet attack, for the purpose of acquiring the islands for the Soviet Union. Soviet sovereignty over the Kuriles was never recognized, but Russia today remains in control of the northern part of the islands.

THIS MONTH						
AUGUST						
S	M	T	W	T	F	S
..	..	..	1	2	3	4
5	6	7	8	9	10	11
12	13	14	15	16	17	18
19	20	21	22	23	24	25
26	27	28	29	30	31	..
..	..	..	..	..	..	..

THURSDAY
9
AUGUST

NEXT MONTH						
SEPTEMBER						
S	M	T	W	T	F	S
..	..	..	..	..	..	1
2	3	4	5	6	7	8
9	10	11	12	13	14	15
16	17	18	19	20	21	22
23	24	25	26	27	28	29
30	..	..	..	..	..	..

1945

On 9 August 1945, at approximately 1102 hours, *Bock's Car*, a B-29 Super-fortress piloted by Major Charles Sweeney, dropped the second of the two nuclear weapons used in World War II. Poor visibility over the primary target, the city of Kokura, made it necessary to switch to the alternate target, Nagasaki, which was the location of the Mitsubishi-Urakami Ordnance Works, producer of Type 91 torpedoes (the type used in the attack on Pearl Harbor).

The bomb, nicknamed "Fat Man," was an implosion-type plutonium device like the one tested in mid-July, in which a subcritical sphere of Pu-239 was placed inside a wrapper of chemical explosive. Detonation of the wrapper at an altitude of 1,650 feet compressed the plutonium sphere sufficiently to create a critical mass, setting off a nuclear blast equal to approximately 21,000 tons of TNT.

The explosion immediately killed approximately 70,000 people and injured another 75,000. The torpedo factory, which was almost exactly at the hypocenter, was destroyed along with most of the northern end of the city; but because Nagasaki was located on uneven ground instead of a flat plain, the total damage was less than that at Hiroshima despite the second bomb's greater power.

According to figures developed by U.S. experts before the bombs were used, the deployment of these two weapons, as horrendous as it was, would save probably 20,000,000 military and civilian lives that would have been lost in Operation DOWNFALL, the planned invasion of the Japanese homeland—and very probably saved the Japanese nation from eradication.

THIS MONTH

		AUGUST				
S	M	T	W	T	F	S
..	..	1	2	3	4	5
6	7	8	9	10	11	12
13	14	15	16	17	18	19
20	21	22	23	24	25	26
27	28	29	30	31	..	..
..	..	..	..	..	..	..

THURSDAY
10
AUGUST
1944

NEXT MONTH

		SEPTEMBER				
S	M	T	W	T	F	S
..	..	..	..	..	1	2
3	4	5	6	7	8	9
10	11	12	13	14	15	16
17	18	19	20	21	22	23
24	25	26	27	28	29	30
..	..	..	..	..	..	..

On 10 August 1944, American troops liberated the former American territory of Guam. 36,000 American Marines and soldiers had engaged 22,000 Japanese troops; U.S. losses were 1,747 dead and 6,053 wounded, while Japanese casualties numbered more than 18,000 killed and 485 captured. With all of the Mariana Islands in American hands, Guam, Tinian, and Saipan islands were turned into a major air and naval center for attacks against the Japanese homeland.

THIS MONTH									NEXT MONTH					
AUGUST									SEPTEMBER					

SUNDAY

11

AUGUST

1940

S	M	T	W	T	F	S
..	..	..	..	1	2	3
4	5	6	7	8	9	10
11	12	13	14	15	16	17
18	19	20	21	22	23	24
25	26	27	28	29	30	31
..	..	..	..	..	..	..

S	M	T	W	T	F	S
1	2	3	4	5	6	7
8	9	10	11	12	13	14
15	16	17	18	19	20	21
22	23	24	25	26	27	28
29	30	..	..	..	..	..
..	..	..	..	..	..	..

On 11 August 1940, during the successful Italian invasion of British Somaliland (begun on 3 August), the five-day Battle of Tug Argan began. To avoid encirclement as Italian forces under Lieutenant General Carlo De Simone took one after another of the six hills on which British troops commanded by Major-General Reade Godwin-Austen had established their defensive positions, Godwin-Austen withdrew his remaining forces after dark on 15 August.

THIS MONTH						
AUGUST						
S	M	T	W	T	F	S
..	..	..	..	..	..	1
2	3	4	5	6	7	8
9	10	11	12	13	14	15
16	17	18	19	20	21	22
23	24	25	26	27	28	29
30	31	..	..	..	..	..

WEDNESDAY
12
AUGUST

NEXT MONTH						
SEPTEMBER						
S	M	T	W	T	F	S
..	..	1	2	3	4	5
6	7	8	9	10	11	12
13	14	15	16	17	18	19
20	21	22	23	24	25	26
27	28	29	30	..	..	..
..	..	..	..	..	..	..

1942

On 12 August 1942, with fighting on the increase as the Germans approached Stalingrad, Churchill informed Stalin during a conference in Moscow that the Western Allies would not be invading Europe in 1942. The Russians had been crying out to the Western Allies to open a "second front" to divert some of the Germans' resources away from the eastern front, but the British and Americans had considered their overall capabilities and realized that they were not yet prepared to execute an invasion of the continent.

THIS MONTH													NEXT MONTH						

AUGUST

S	M	T	W	T	F	S
..	..	..	..	1	2	3
4	5	6	7	8	9	10
11	12	13	14	15	16	17
18	19	20	21	22	23	24
25	26	27	28	29	30	31
..	..	..	..	..	..	..

TUESDAY
13
AUGUST

SEPTEMBER

S	M	T	W	T	F	S
1	2	3	4	5	6	7
8	9	10	11	12	13	14
15	16	17	18	19	20	21
22	23	24	25	26	27	28
29	30	..	..	..	..	..
..	..	..	..	..	..	..

1940

On 13 August 1940, *"Adler Tag"* (Eagle Day), Hermann Göring's *Luftwaffe* launched *Adlerangriff* (Eagle Attack), a concerted two-week assault on British coastal airfields in preparation for the invasion planned as *Unternehmen Seelöwe* (Operation SEA LION). *Adler Tag* was delayed one day by weather; *Adlerangriff* had been scheduled to begin on 12 August, and on that day fighter-bomber aircraft from *Erprobungsgruppe* 210 had attacked four of England's coastal radar stations, disabling three of them for less than six hours. The raids showed that British radars would be difficult to destroy, and the Germans failed to follow up on either the radars or their supporting infrastructure. Some German historians mark *Adler Tag* as the beginning of the Battle of Britain, which conventional histories consider to have begun on 10 July with aerial battles over the English Channel.

THIS MONTH						
AUGUST						
S	M	T	W	T	F	S
..	..	1	2	3	4	5
6	7	8	9	10	11	12
13	14	15	16	17	18	19
20	21	22	23	24	25	26
27	28	29	30	31	..	..
..	..	..	..	..	..	..

MONDAY
14
AUGUST

NEXT MONTH						
SEPTEMBER						
S	M	T	W	T	F	S
..	..	..	..	..	1	2
3	4	5	6	7	8	9
10	11	12	13	14	15	16
17	18	19	20	21	22	23
24	25	26	27	28	29	30
..	..	..	..	..	..	..

1944

On 14 August 1944, inadequate communication between General Sir Bernard Montgomery and General Omar Bradley prevented their forces from closing the "mouth" of a pincer movement around the town of Falaise, France. This monumental SNAFU allowed perhaps 40,000 troops of *Generalfeldmarschall* Günther von Kluge's Army Group B, consisting of the Seventh and Fifth Panzer Armies, to escape eastward from the Falaise Pocket. Even so, the Germans lost more than 60,000 men killed or captured, along with massive amounts of *matériel*.

THIS MONTH						
AUGUST						
S	M	T	W	T	F	S
..	..	..	1	2	3	4
5	6	7	8	9	10	11
12	13	14	15	16	17	18
19	20	21	22	23	24	25
26	27	28	29	30	31	..
..	..	..	..	..	..	..

WEDNESDAY
15
AUGUST
1945

NEXT MONTH						
SEPTEMBER						
S	M	T	W	T	F	S
..	..	..	..	..	..	1
2	3	4	5	6	7	8
9	10	11	12	13	14	15
16	17	18	19	20	21	22
23	24	25	26	27	28	29
30	..	..	..	..	..	..

On 15 August 1945, the Japanese people heard the voice of their emperor for the first time in history as Emperor Hirohito issued a radio broadcast ordering the government of Japan to accept the non-negotiable terms laid out in the Allies' Potsdam Declaration. (He made no explicit mention of surrender.) He had recorded the broadcast one or two days earlier. During the night before the broadcast aired, an unsuccessful coup, led by Imperial Japanese Army Major Kenji Hatanaka, had been launched by military and right-wing diehards who wanted to prevent the surrender by capturing the recording and overthrowing the government. On the morning of 15 August, the recording was smuggled out of the Imperial palace in a laundry basket full of women's underwear. Because the Allies' terms had not required unconditional surrender of everything Japanese, but only that of Japan's armed forces, Hirohito retained his position as emperor.[1]

---

1. After the coup was put down, Major Hatanaka and co-conspirator Lieutenant Colonel Jiro Shiizaki shot themselves in the plaza fronting the imperial palace.

THIS MONTH								MONDAY	NEXT MONTH						
AUGUST								**16**	SEPTEMBER						
S	M	T	W	T	F	S		AUGUST	S	M	T	W	T	F	S
1	2	3	4	5	6	7			..	..	..	1	2	3	4
8	9	10	11	12	13	14			5	6	7	8	9	10	11
15	16	17	18	19	20	21			12	13	14	15	16	17	18
22	23	24	25	26	27	28			19	20	21	22	23	24	25
29	30	31	..	..	..	..			26	27	28	29	30	..	..
..	..	..	..	..	..	..			..	..	..	..	..	..	..

1943

On 16 August 1943, in response to a German announcement of mass deportations from the Białystok ghetto, Polish Jews launched an uprising in an attempt to break the German siege and allow as many Jews as possible to escape deportation by fleeing into the nearby Knyszyński Forest. Equipped with only 25 rifles and about 100 pistols, and having only very limited supplies of ammunition, the 300 to 500 insurrectionists had no chance against the overwhelming force of the Germans, and the leaders committed suicide when they ran out of ammunition. The planned deportations went ahead without any delay. Approximately 10,000 Jews were herded onto trains bound for Treblinka, Majdanek and Auschwitz. Approximately 1,200 children were sent to Theresienstadt, later to be sent on to Auschwitz.

THIS MONTH						
AUGUST						
S	M	T	W	T	F	S
..	..	..	..	..	..	1
2	3	4	5	6	7	8
9	10	11	12	13	14	15
16	17	18	19	20	21	22
23	24	25	26	27	28	29
30	31	..	..	..	..	..

MONDAY
17
AUGUST

1942

NEXT MONTH						
SEPTEMBER						
S	M	T	W	T	F	S
..	..	1	2	3	4	5
6	7	8	9	10	11	12
13	14	15	16	17	18	19
20	21	22	23	24	25	26
27	28	29	30	..	..	..
..	..	..	..	..	..	..

On 17 August 1942, the U.S. Army Air Forces' 97th Bomb Group, part of the Eighth Air Force, flew America's first heavy bomber raid in Europe. Twelve B-17 Flying Fortresses, escorted by Spitfires of the RAF, inflicted heavy damage on the Sotteville railroad marshaling yards at Rouen, France, while six other B-17s made a diversionary run along the French coast. Although U.S. A-20 bombers had earlier executed raids over Europe, this raid was the first test of the USAAF's Precision Bombing Doctrine, which called for pinpoint targeting of industrial and military objectives and avoidance of civilian populations. All of the B-17s returned safely, and the USAAF deemed the raid a qualified success. The British were not impressed, saying that the Americans were trying things at which they, the British, had already failed, and that the Americans would make the same mistakes the British had made.

THIS MONTH						
AUGUST						
S	M	T	W	T	F	S
..	..	..	..	..	..	1
2	3	4	5	6	7	8
9	10	11	12	13	14	15
16	17	18	19	20	21	22
23	24	25	26	27	28	29
30	31	..	..	..	..	..

TUESDAY
18
AUGUST

1942

NEXT MONTH						
SEPTEMBER						
S	M	T	W	T	F	S
..	..	1	2	3	4	5
6	7	8	9	10	11	12
13	14	15	16	17	18	19
20	21	22	23	24	25	26
27	28	29	30	..	..	..
..	..	..	..	..	..	..

On 18 August 1942, nine members of the Ukrainian soccer team Start were arrested and tortured by the Gestapo, charged with being NKVD members. Two more players were arrested later. German assertions notwithstanding, Ukrainian citizens believed that the players were actually arrested for having defeated Flakelf, a squad of German soldiers, by a score of 5–3 in a game played on 9 August, after having been warned that they could not win and should consider the consequences before attempting to do so. (Start had previously beaten seven straight Axis opponents, including Flakelf on 6 August.) The 9 August game became known popularly and in official Soviet histories as the Death Match. One of the arrested players, Mykola Korotkykh, died under torture. Another, Oleksander Tkachenko, was shot during an alleged escape attempt. The rest were sent to the Syrets labor camp, where four were executed in February 1943. It is unquestionably true that these 11 players were arrested, but it is doubtful that the reason for their arrest was their victory on the soccer field.

THIS MONTH													
AUGUST							WEDNESDAY	NEXT MONTH					
							19	SEPTEMBER					

AUGUST						
S	M	T	W	T	F	S
..	..	..	..	..	..	1
2	3	4	5	6	7	8
9	10	11	12	13	14	15
16	17	18	19	20	21	22
23	24	25	26	27	28	29
30	31	..	..	..	..	..

WEDNESDAY
19
AUGUST

SEPTEMBER						
S	M	T	W	T	F	S
..	..	1	2	3	4	5
6	7	8	9	10	11	12
13	14	15	16	17	18	19
20	21	22	23	24	25	26
27	28	29	30	..	..	..
..	..	..	..	..	..	..

1942

On 19 August 1942, at 0500 hours, British and Canadian forces launched Operation JUBILEE, an amphibious raid on Dieppe, France. The raiders came under intense fire from German defenders under *Generalfeldmarschall* Gerd von Rundstedt, and the raid turned into a disaster. Of the 6,086 men who managed to get ashore, 3,623 were killed, wounded, or captured, most of them Canadians. The Royal Navy lost one destroyer sunk, 33 landing craft destroyed, and 550 men killed or wounded; and the Royal Air Force lost 100 aircraft and 62 men killed, 30 wounded, and 17 captured. The Germans lost 311 men killed and 280 wounded, and the *Luftwaffe* lost 48 aircraft. The Allied failure at Dieppe provided painful lessons that almost certainly made the difference between success and failure three months later in North Africa and two years later in Normandy.[2]

---

2. It was not revealed until decades later that the Dieppe raid had actually accomplished its triple objectives of deceiving the Germans as to the timing and location of any potential Allied invasion of Europe; of discovering how good German radar was by retrieving certain key components of the Germans' most up-to-date radar unit, which was installed at Dieppe; and of then destroying that radar unit.

THIS MONTH						
AUGUST						
S	M	T	W	T	F	S
..	..	..	..	..	..	1
2	3	4	5	6	7	8
9	10	11	12	13	14	15
16	17	18	19	20	21	22
23	24	25	26	27	28	29
30	31	..	..	..	..	..

THURSDAY
20
AUGUST

NEXT MONTH						
SEPTEMBER						
S	M	T	W	T	F	S
..	..	1	2	3	4	5
6	7	8	9	10	11	12
13	14	15	16	17	18	19
20	21	22	23	24	25	26
27	28	29	30	..	..	..
..	..	..	..	..	..	..

1942

On 20 August 1942, nineteen Grumman F4F Wildcat fighters of VMF-223, led by Major John L. Smith, and twelve Douglas SBD Dauntless dive bombers of VMSB-232, led by Lt. Colonel Richard Mangrum, flew from the deck of America's first escort carrier, the USS *Long Island,* and landed at Guadalcanal's Henderson Field, which had been repaired and made operational, and was kept in almost continual operation thereafter, by U.S. Navy Seabees.[3] These thirty-one warplanes, the first contingent of what became known as the Cactus Air Force (from CACTUS, the U.S. military's code name for Guadalcanal), conducted combat missions on the next day. They were instrumental in the Guadalcanal campaign and went on to compile a distinguished war record.

---

3. The name "Seabee" derives from CB, the initial letters of Construction Battalion. The Seabees' motto is "Can do. With willing hearts and skillful hands, the difficult we do immediately; the impossible takes a bit longer."

THIS MONTH						
AUGUST						
S	M	T	W	T	F	S
..	..	1	2	3	4	5
6	7	8	9	10	11	12
13	14	15	16	17	18	19
20	21	22	23	24	25	26
27	28	29	30	31	..	..
..	..	..	..	..	..	..

MONDAY
21
AUGUST

NEXT MONTH						
SEPTEMBER						
S	M	T	W	T	F	S
..	..	..	..	..	1	2
3	4	5	6	7	8	9
10	11	12	13	14	15	16
17	18	19	20	21	22	23
24	25	26	27	28	29	30
..	..	..	..	..	..	..

1944

On 21 August 1944, the Washington Conversations on International Peace and Security Organization, better known as the Dumbarton Oaks Conference, opened at Dumbarton Oaks, a historic mansion in Washington, DC. The conference, called to implement paragraph 4 of the Moscow Declaration of 1943, which recognized the need for a postwar international organization to succeed the League of Nations, formulated the structure of the United Nations. Among those participating were the British Permanent Under-Secretary of State for Foreign Affairs, Sir Alexander Cadogan; the Soviet Ambassador to the United States, Andrei Gromyko; the Chinese Ambassador to the United Kingdom, Wellington Koo; and U.S. Undersecretary of State Edward R. Stettinius, Jr., each of whom chaired his respective delegation. Stettinius chaired the conference, and U.S. Secretary of State Cordell Hull (1871–1955) delivered the opening address. The conference occurred in two phases because the Soviets refused to meet face to face with the Chinese. When Cadogan had to return to London after the first half of the conference, the British ambassador to the United States, E. F. L. Wood, 1st Earl of Halifax, assumed leadership of the British delegation.

THIS MONTH						
AUGUST						
S	M	T	W	T	F	S
..	..	..	1	2	3	4
5	6	7	8	9	10	11
12	13	14	15	16	17	18
19	20	21	22	23	24	25
26	27	28	29	30	31	..
..	..	..	..	..	..	..

WEDNESDAY
22
AUGUST
1945

NEXT MONTH						
SEPTEMBER						
S	M	T	W	T	F	S
..	..	..	..	..	..	1
2	3	4	5	6	7	8
9	10	11	12	13	14	15
16	17	18	19	20	21	22
23	24	25	26	27	28	29
30	..	..	..	..	..	..

On 22 August 1945, as the Soviet Union's Manchurian Strategic Offensive Operation was rolling through the Japanese-occupied countries of Asia, its first major victory saw the surrender of the Kwantung Army of the Imperial Japanese Army, under General Otsuzo Yamada, in Manchuria. The Soviet offensive, consisting of a massive pincer movement around all of Manchuria, executed on the west by the Transbaikal Front, under Marshal Rodion Y. Malinovsky, and on the east by the 1st Far Eastern Front, under Marshal Kirill A. Meretskov, was the largest campaign of the 1945 Soviet–Japanese War. The Japanese forces, comprising some 1,217,000 troops, lost 83,737 killed and 640,276 taken prisoner (including General Yamada); Soviet losses were only 9,726 killed or missing out of 1,685,500, and 24,425 wounded. Civilian Japanese settlers suicided *en masse* as the Soviets approached, with mothers being compelled to kill their own children before taking their own lives or being killed by their own soldiers. The Japanese considered this defeat to be the worst in their entire military history.

THIS MONTH												NEXT MONTH					

SUNDAY

23

AUGUST

1942

AUGUST						
S	M	T	W	T	F	S
..	..	..	..	..	..	1
2	3	4	5	6	7	8
9	10	11	12	13	14	15
16	17	18	19	20	21	22
23	24	25	26	27	28	29
30	31	..	..	..	..	..

SEPTEMBER						
S	M	T	W	T	F	S
..	..	1	2	3	4	5
6	7	8	9	10	11	12
13	14	15	16	17	18	19
20	21	22	23	24	25	26
27	28	29	30	..	..	..

On 23 August 1942, German forces launched massive attacks against Stalingrad, on the west bank of the Volga, as part of *Fall Blau* (Case Blue), the continuation of 1941's *Fall Barbarossa*. The Germans considered Stalingrad to be a potentially defensible city along the route of their planned advance to capture the oilfields of the Caucasus, without which Germany's war effort would be severely hampered. The Soviets had advance warning of the impending attack and had moved virtually all the city's grain, cattle, and railroad rolling stock to the east bank of the river, where it would be safe.

Generaloberst Wolfram Freiherr (Baron) von Richthofen's *Luftflotte 4*, the most powerful single air formation in the world, opened the Battle of Stalingrad by dropping approximately 1,000 tons of bombs that reduced much of the city to rubble—which later had a major effect on the course of the battle for Stalingrad.

Hitler became obsessed with taking the namesake city of his bitter enemy Stalin, and the battle raged for more than five months, until 2 February 1943, when Soviet armies surrounded the Germans in the city and forced the capitulation of some 90,000 troops commanded by Friedrich von Paulus, whom Hitler had just promoted to the rank of *Generalfeldmarschall* in the vain expectation that he would suicide rather than allow himself to become the first German field marshal ever to be taken captive. The final toll showed German losses of approximately 850,000 killed, missing, or wounded, 900 aircraft destroyed, and 1,500 tanks and 6,000 artillery pieces lost. (Counted among the missing were 107,000 captured troops, of whom only about 6,000 returned alive from Soviet prison camps.) Soviet losses numbered approximately 1,150,000 killed, missing, or wounded (including some 40,000 civilians), 2,769 aircraft destroyed, and 4,341 tanks and 15,728 artillery pieces lost.

THIS MONTH						
AUGUST						
S	M	T	W	T	F	S
..	..	..	..	..	..	1
2	3	4	5	6	7	8
9	10	11	12	13	14	15
16	17	18	19	20	21	22
23	24	25	26	27	28	29
30	31	..	..	..	..	..

MONDAY
24
AUGUST

1942

NEXT MONTH						
SEPTEMBER						
S	M	T	W	T	F	S
..	..	1	2	3	4	5
6	7	8	9	10	11	12
13	14	15	16	17	18	19
20	21	22	23	24	25	26
27	28	29	30	..	..	..
..	..	..	..	..	..	..

On 24 August 1942, a U.S. carrier force commanded by Vice Admiral Frank Jack Fletcher discovered and engaged a Japanese carrier force under Vice Admiral Chūichi Nagumo in the two-day Battle of the Eastern Solomons, the second major naval battle fought between the two countries as part of the American campaign to secure Guadalcanal and its strategically critical airbase, Henderson Field. The Japanese mission was probably an attempt by the Japanese Combined Fleet to assist aerial forces from Rabaul in neutralizing Henderson Field, but it may instead have been a decoy so that other Japanese ships could approach the U.S. naval forces undetected. The outcome of the battle saw the Japanese losing the light carrier *Ryūjō*, the destroyer *Mutsuki*, the transport *Kinryu Maru*, and 75 aircraft with many aircrew, and also taking heavy damage to the light cruiser *Tone* and the seaplane tender *Chitose*. Total Japanese deaths were about 290. The Americans lost 20 aircraft, suffered serious damage to the fleet carrier *Enterprise*, and lost about 90 lives. There was no clear winner, but the battle is considered to have been an American tactical and strategic victory because it delayed resupply of the Japanese troops on Guadalcanal, and more importantly because of the number of virtually irreplaceable trained carrier aviators the Japanese lost.

THIS MONTH						
AUGUST						
S	M	T	W	T	F	S
..	..	1	2	3	4	5
6	7	8	9	10	11	12
13	14	15	16	17	18	19
20	21	22	23	24	25	26
27	28	29	30	31	..	..
..	..	..	..	..	..	..

FRIDAY
25
AUGUST

1944

NEXT MONTH						
SEPTEMBER						
S	M	T	W	T	F	S
..	..	..	..	..	1	2
3	4	5	6	7	8	9
10	11	12	13	14	15	16
17	18	19	20	21	22	23
24	25	26	27	28	29	30
..	..	..	..	..	..	..

On 25 August 1944, *General der Infanterie* Dietrich von Choltitz, the German military governor of Paris, surrendered his garrison to the French Forces of the Interior (*Forces françaises de l'intérieur,* the FFI) under General Philippe

Leclerc, ending the six-day Battle of Paris. Hitler had issued instructions that Paris "must not fall into the enemy's hand except lying in complete debris," but von Cholditz disobeyed his orders and turned the city over in good condition except for the relatively minor damage that was done during the battle itself. Upon learning that Paris had fallen, Hitler demanded of *Generaloberst* Alfred Jodl, his chief of staff, "Is Paris burning? Jodl, I want to know... is Paris burning? Is Paris burning right now, Jodl?" Von Choltitz later claimed that he had disobeyed orders because he "knew that Hitler was insane." Although the French still insist that this was a fabrication, transcripts of telephone conversations he had with his superiors support his statement.

THIS MONTH								MONDAY		NEXT MONTH						
AUGUST								**26**		SEPTEMBER						
S	M	T	W	T	F	S				S	M	T	W	T	F	S
..	..	..	..	1	2	3		AUGUST		1	2	3	4	5	6	7
4	5	6	7	8	9	10				8	9	10	11	12	13	14
11	12	13	14	15	16	17				15	16	17	18	19	20	21
18	19	20	21	22	23	24				22	23	24	25	26	27	28
25	26	27	28	29	30	31				29	30	..	..	..	..	..
..	..	..	..	..	..	..				..	..	..	..	..	..	..

1940

On 26 August 1940, in the midst of the Battle of Britain, British aircraft bombed Berlin for the first time. Unaware that the German bombing of a church in the Cripplegate area of London on the night of 24 August had been an accident, Churchill had ordered that Berlin be bombed as retaliation for that incident. Of the 95 aircraft that Bomber Command sent to bomb Siemensstadt and Berlin's city-center Tempelhof Airport, 81 dropped their bombs in and around Berlin. Despite causing only slight damage, this and subsequent raids on Berlin changed the course of the Battle of Britain, as Hitler ordered *Reichsmarschall* Hermann Göring to bomb cities instead of airfields and air defenses. Because British air defenses were critically close to collapse, Hitler's strategic shift may have saved Britain from defeat.

THIS MONTH						
AUGUST						
S	M	T	W	T	F	S
..	..	..	..	..	1	2
3	4	5	6	7	8	9
10	11	12	13	14	15	16
17	18	19	20	21	22	23
24	25	26	27	28	29	30
31	..	..	..	..	..	..

WEDNESDAY
27
AUGUST

NEXT MONTH						
SEPTEMBER						
S	M	T	W	T	F	S
..	1	2	3	4	5	6
7	8	9	10	11	12	13
14	15	16	17	18	19	20
21	22	23	24	25	26	27
28	29	30	..	..	..	..
..	..	..	..	..	..	..

1941

On 27 August 1941, as fighting in and around Stalingrad raged on, and in the midst of heavy bombing strikes by the *Luftwaffe*, Joseph Stalin appointed Marshal Georgiy Zhukov to be Deputy Commander-in-Chief and sent him to the Southwestern Front to take charge of the defense of Stalingrad. Together with Marshal Aleksandr Vasilevsky, Zhukov planned Operation URANUS, a Red Army counteroffensive that was launched in November and encircled the entire German Sixth Army, commanded at that time by *General* Friedrich von Paulus.

AUGUST

S	M	T	W	T	F	S
..	..	1	2	3	4	5
6	7	8	9	10	11	12
13	14	15	16	17	18	19
20	21	22	23	24	25	26
27	28	29	30	31	..	..
..	..	..	..	..	..	..

MONDAY
28
AUGUST

SEPTEMBER

S	M	T	W	T	F	S
..	..	..	..	..	1	2
3	4	5	6	7	8	9
10	11	12	13	14	15	16
17	18	19	20	21	22	23
24	25	26	27	28	29	30
..	..	..	..	..	..	..

1944

On 28 August 1944, forces of the French First Army under *Général d'Armée* Jean de Lattre de Tassigny accepted the formal German surrender of Marseille and Toulon, in southern France. De Lattre's force, landed on 19 August as part of Operation DRAGOON, split to attack both cities. At Toulon, the defenders, part of the German 19th Army, commanded by *General der Infanterie* Friedrich Wiese, were largely unprepared for the assault, but they fought back vigorously. The French entered the city on 21 August, amid fighting so heavy that de Lattre argued with and then dismissed one of his commanders, taking direct command himself. The remaining German units surrendered on 26 August. At the same time, part of de Lattre's force moved to assault Marseille. The German commander there failed to evacuate the civilian population, a mistake that cost him dearly. Fighting against both the partisans in the city and the troops outside overcame the Germans, and on 27 August most of the city was captured. On 28 August, the official surrender was signed. Taking the two cities cost the French 4,525 casualties, but they captured 28,000 Germans, including the entire surviving force in the Toulon garrison. German engineers had destroyed port facilities in both harbors to deny their use to the Allies.

AUGUST

S	M	T	W	T	F	S
..	..	1	2	3	4	5
6	7	8	9	10	11	12
13	14	15	16	17	18	19
20	21	22	23	24	25	26
27	28	29	30	31	..	..
..	..	..	..	..	..	..

TUESDAY
29
AUGUST

SEPTEMBER

S	M	T	W	T	F	S
..	..	..	..	..	1	2
3	4	5	6	7	8	9
10	11	12	13	14	15	16
17	18	19	20	21	22	23
24	25	26	27	28	29	30
..	..	..	..	..	..	..

1944

On 29 August 1944, Slovak army Lieutenant Colonel Ján Golian launched the Slovak National Uprising, an armed insurrection to overthrow the collaborationist Slovak State of Jozef Tiso. Plans had been formulated beginning in 1943, and they included the relocation of two heavily armed divisions of the Slovak Army and the entire eastern Slovak Air Force to Prešov in northeastern Slovakia to capture the Dukla pass. On 30 August, however, Colonel Viliam Talský and the entire eastern Slovak Air Force flew to a prearranged landing zone in Poland to join the Soviet army, abandoning the two divisions to destruction at Prešov. The Uprising lasted until 28 October, but with the loss of those divisions the outcome was not in doubt; the Germans were victorious. Each side lost about 10,000 casualties; of those on the Slovak side, 5,304 were captured and summarily executed. Partisan guerrilla operations continued until the Soviet army's arrival in 1945.

THIS MONTH

AUGUST

S	M	T	W	T	F	S
..	..	..	..	1	2	3
4	5	6	7	8	9	10
11	12	13	14	15	16	17
18	19	20	21	22	23	24
25	26	27	28	29	30	31
..	..	..	..	..	..	..

FRIDAY
30
AUGUST

1940

NEXT MONTH

SEPTEMBER

S	M	T	W	T	F	S
1	2	3	4	5	6	7
8	9	10	11	12	13	14
15	16	17	18	19	20	21
22	23	24	25	26	27	28
29	30	..	..	..	..	..
..	..	..	..	..	..	..

On 30 August 1940, the so-called Second Vienna Award, which required Romania to hand over Northern Transylvania (including the entire Maramureş and part of Crişana) to Hungary, came into effect. In an effort to maintain peace in the Balkans, the Axis powers had suggested to Hungary and Romania that they solve their differences (ethnic problems exacerbated by the way the countries' boundaries were redrawn by the Treaty of Trianon after World War I) by negotiating with each other. Negotiations started on 16 August 1940 in Turnu Severin, but the talks came to naught, and the Romanian government asked Italy and Germany to arbitrate. The Second Vienna Award was the result. Romania had 14 days to evacuate the territories designated as changing hands and assign them to Hungary. Hungarian troops stepped across the Trianon borders on 5 September. The Regent of Hungary, Miklós Horthy, also participated in the entry. They reached the pre-Trianon border, completing the re-annexation process, on 13 September. The Award aided the Axis powers both strategically and with supplies of war *matériel*, but it strained relations further between Romania and Hungary.

THIS MONTH

AUGUST

S	M	T	W	T	F	S
..	..	1	2	3	4	5
6	7	8	9	10	11	12
13	14	15	16	17	18	19
20	21	22	23	24	25	26
27	28	29	30	31	..	..
..	..	..	..	..	..	..

THURSDAY
31
AUGUST

NEXT MONTH

SEPTEMBER

S	M	T	W	T	F	S
..	..	..	..	..	1	2
3	4	5	6	7	8	9
10	11	12	13	14	15	16
17	18	19	20	21	22	23
24	25	26	27	28	29	30
..	..	..	..	..	..	..

1944

On 31 August 1944, American forces handed over the reins of government in France to troops of the French Forces of the Interior (FFI), who established the Provisional Government of the French Republic (*gouvernement provisoire de la République française*, abbreviated GPRF). It served until the establishment of the Fourth French Republic in 1947. The GPRF began as a tripartite alliance between the French Communist Party (PCF), claiming itself to be the *parti des 75,000 fusillés* ("party of the 75,000 shot"), the French Section of the Workers' International (SFIO, socialist party) and the Christian democratic Popular Republican Movement (MRP). The government's first chairman was *général de brigade* Charles de Gaulle.

THIS MONTH								FRIDAY		NEXT MONTH					
SEPTEMBER								**1**		**OCTOBER**					
S	M	T	W	T	F	S				S	M	T	W	T	F	S
..	..	..	..	..	1	2				1	2	3	4	5	6	7
3	4	5	6	7	8	9				8	9	10	11	12	13	14
10	11	12	13	14	15	16				15	16	17	18	19	20	21
17	18	19	20	21	22	23				22	23	24	25	26	27	28
24	25	26	27	28	29	30				29	30	31	..	..	..	..
..	..	..	..	..	..	..		**SEPTEMBER**		..	..	..	..	..	..	..

1939

On 1 September 1939, with no declaration of war and under a pretext that the Polish army had attacked and killed German soldiers, Nazi Germany introduced the world to a new kind of warfare called *Blitzkrieg*, or "lightning war." (The troops who had been killed were in fact Poles whom the Germans had killed and dressed in German uniforms.)

Beginning at 0445 hours, the *Luftwaffe* launched air strikes against Kraków, Łódź, and Warsaw. At 0450, the battleship *Schleswig-Holstein* opened fire in an unsuccessful attack on the Polish military transit depot in the Free City of Danzig (in German, *Freie Stadt Danzig*; in Polish, *Wolne Miasto Gdańsk*), a semi-autonomous city-state comprising the city of Danzig (Gdańsk) and about 200 smaller towns and villages.

The Free City of Danzig had been created, and aligned in a customs union with Poland, by the Treaty of Versailles that had officially ended World War I. In a speech before the Reichstag, Hitler had insisted, "Danzig ist, und war, eine deutsche Stadt" ("Danzig is, and was, a German city"), falsely claiming that Poland was committing aggression against the Free City and vowing that Germany would speak to Poland in Poland's own language, *i.e.,* bombs. By 0800, troops of the *Wehrmacht Heer* commenced an attack near the town of Mokra.

World War II in Europe had begun, as Great Britain and France surprised Hitler by following through on their respective threats to declare war on Germany if it invaded Poland.

THIS MONTH						
SEPTEMBER						
S	M	T	W	T	F	S
1	2	3	4	5	6	7
8	9	10	11	12	13	14
15	16	17	18	19	20	21
22	23	24	25	26	27	28
29	30	..	..	..	..	..
..	..	..	..	..	..	..

MONDAY
2
SEPTEMBER

1940

NEXT MONTH						
OCTOBER						
S	M	T	W	T	F	S
..	..	1	2	3	4	5
6	7	8	9	10	11	12
13	14	15	16	17	18	19
20	21	22	23	24	25	26
27	28	29	30	31	..	..
..	..	..	..	..	..	..

On 2 September 1940, the governments of Great Britain and the not-yet-belligerent United States signed the Destroyers for Bases Agreement. The U.S. refurbished 50 mothballed American destroyers and delivered them to the Royal Navy in exchange for 99-year rent-free leases on eight British bases in the Western Hemisphere, the bases to be transferred to the U.S. Navy and Army Air Corps. The Agreement contained wording limiting the names the British were permitted to use for the destroyers, and the ships became the Town class, named after British towns whose names were also used for towns in the United States.

THIS MONTH

SEPTEMBER

S	M	T	W	T	F	S
..	..	..	1	2	3	4
5	6	7	8	9	10	11
12	13	14	15	16	17	18
19	20	21	22	23	24	25
26	27	28	29	30	..	..
..	..	..	..	..	..	..

FRIDAY
3
SEPTEMBER
1943

NEXT MONTH

OCTOBER

S	M	T	W	T	F	S
..	..	..	..	..	1	2
3	4	5	6	7	8	9
10	11	12	13	14	15	16
17	18	19	20	21	22	23
24	25	26	27	28	29	30
31	..	..	..	..	..	..

On 3 September 1943, a representative of Italy's prime minister Marshal Pietro Badoglio, newly appointed on orders of King Victor Emmanuel, signed surrender papers ending Italy's status as one of the Axis Powers. The signing was kept secret, with Badoglio and the king both insisting that no such surrender had taken place, until the news broke five days later, with an announcement by General Dwight D. Eisenhower on 8 September.

THIS MONTH						
SEPTEMBER						
S	M	T	W	T	F	S
..	..	..	..	..	1	2
3	4	5	6	7	8	9
10	11	12	13	14	15	16
17	18	19	20	21	22	23
24	25	26	27	28	29	30
..	..	..	..	..	..	..

MONDAY
4
SEPTEMBER

1939

NEXT MONTH						
OCTOBER						
S	M	T	W	T	F	S
1	2	3	4	5	6	7
8	9	10	11	12	13	14
15	16	17	18	19	20	21
22	23	24	25	26	27	28
29	30	31	..	..	..	..

On 4 September 1939, the Royal Air Force launched the first British offensive action of World War II, a raid by 15 Blenheims from No. 110, No. 107, and No. 139 Squadrons and eight Wellingtons from No. 149 Squadron. The targets were the German battleships *Gneisenau* and *Scharnhorst* and the heavy cruiser *Admiral Scheer*, which lay anchored in the Schillig Roads off Wilhelmshaven at the western end of the Kiel Canal. No. 9 Squadron also bombed the same targets later in the day. The day's results were poor, as the RAF lost five Blenheims and two Wellingtons while causing only minimal damage. The *Admiral Scheer* was struck by three bombs that all failed to explode. The most serious damage was to the light cruiser *Emden*, which suffered 11 sailors killed and 30 injured by a Blenheim that crashed into the ship.

THIS MONTH						
SEPTEMBER						
S	M	T	W	T	F	S
..	..	1	2	3	4	5
6	7	8	9	10	11	12
13	14	15	16	17	18	19
20	21	22	23	24	25	26
27	28	29	30	..	..	..
..	..	..	..	..	..	..

SATURDAY
5
SEPTEMBER
1942

NEXT MONTH						
OCTOBER						
S	M	T	W	T	F	S
..	..	..	..	1	2	3
4	5	6	7	8	9	10
11	12	13	14	15	16	17
18	19	20	21	22	23	24
25	26	27	28	29	30	31
..	..	..	..	..	..	..

On 5 September 1942, in the face of superior forces from Australia and the United States, the Japanese high command at Rabaul ordered surviving troops withdrawn from the area around Milne Bay, in Papua. The Battle of Milne Bay, begun on 25 August when Japanese naval troops launched Operation RE against Allied airfields around the bay, did not end officially until 7 September, but this date marks the actual admission of defeat. This was the first outright defeat for Japanese land forces in the Pacific War. The Japanese lost 625 killed and 325 wounded, while the Australians lost 167 killed or missing and 206 wounded and the Americans suffered 14 killed. When the withdrawal order was given, only about 50 Japanese troops were in condition to fight. Australian Corporal John French received the Victoria Cross posthumously for his action in wiping out three Japanese machine gun positions; his body was found in front of the third.

THIS MONTH								WEDNESDAY	NEXT MONTH						

THIS MONTH

SEPTEMBER

S	M	T	W	T	F	S
..	..	..	..	..	1	2
3	4	5	6	7	8	9
10	11	12	13	14	15	16
17	18	19	20	21	22	23
24	25	26	27	28	29	30
..	..	..	..	..	..	..

WEDNESDAY
6
SEPTEMBER

NEXT MONTH

OCTOBER

S	M	T	W	T	F	S
1	2	3	4	5	6	7
8	9	10	11	12	13	14
15	16	17	18	19	20	21
22	23	24	25	26	27	28
29	30	31	..	..	..	..
..	..	..	..	..	..	..

1944

On 6 September 1944, with Allied air forces having gained aerial supremacy and the threat of further German bombing or an invasion deemed highly unlikely, the British government downgraded the night-time blackout to a "dim-out," which allowed lighting to the equivalent of moonlight. A full blackout would be imposed temporarily if an alert was sounded. This change signaled hope of an end to the war, providing a great morale boost to the British population.

THIS MONTH						
SEPTEMBER						
S	M	T	W	T	F	S
1	2	3	4	5	6	7
8	9	10	11	12	13	14
15	16	17	18	19	20	21
22	23	24	25	26	27	28
29	30	..	..	..	..	..
..	..	..	..	..	..	..

SATURDAY
7
SEPTEMBER
1940

NEXT MONTH						
OCTOBER						
S	M	T	W	T	F	S
..	..	1	2	3	4	5
6	7	8	9	10	11	12
13	14	15	16	17	18	19
20	21	22	23	24	25	26
27	28	29	30	31	..	..
..	..	..	..	..	..	..

On 7 September 1940, as it began to appear that the *Luftwaffe* might fail in its mission of destroying the Royal Air Force, German aircraft commenced a campaign of nighttime terror bombing against the cities of Britain. Referred to as the Blitz, the campaign lasted until 21 May 1941. During this period, London was bombed 71 times. (Beginning on 7 September, the city suffered 57 consecutive nights of bombing.) Birmingham, Liverpool, and Plymouth received eight raids each, Bristol six, Glasgow five, Southampton four, Portsmouth three, and eight other cities were hit at least once. The British suffered 40,000–43,000 civilians killed, 46,000 reported injured, and perhaps as many as 93,000 others injured but not reported.

THIS MONTH						
SEPTEMBER						
S	M	T	W	T	F	S
..	..	..	..	..	..	1
2	3	4	5	6	7	8
9	10	11	12	13	14	15
16	17	18	19	20	21	22
23	24	25	26	27	28	29
30	..	..	..	..	..	..

FRIDAY
8
SEPTEMBER

NEXT MONTH						
OCTOBER						
S	M	T	W	T	F	S
..	1	2	3	4	5	6
7	8	9	10	11	12	13
14	15	16	17	18	19	20
21	22	23	24	25	26	27
28	29	30	31	..	..	..
..	..	..	..	..	..	..

1939

On 8 September 1939, the British Government announced that it was reintroducing the convoy system for merchant ships as well as a full-scale blockade on German shipping. The convoy system, developed centuries ago and discarded at the beginning of the age of steam, had been revived successfully in World War I as a response to the then-new threat of submarine warfare. In World War II, the see-saw Battle of the Atlantic was marked by German introductions of new anti-convoy tactics such as Karl Dönitz' *Rudeltaktik* (submarine wolfpack) and the Allies' development of techniques to counter them. The turning point came in mid-1943 with the Allies' development of airborne radar and aircraft with sufficient range to eliminate a coverage hole in the middle of the Atlantic.

THIS MONTH								TUESDAY		NEXT MONTH						

SEPTEMBER

S	M	T	W	T	F	S
..	1	2	3	4	5	6
7	8	9	10	11	12	13
14	15	16	17	18	19	20
21	22	23	24	25	26	27
28	29	30	..	..	..	..
..	..	..	..	..	..	..

TUESDAY
9
SEPTEMBER
1941

OCTOBER

S	M	T	W	T	F	S
..	..	..	1	2	3	4
5	6	7	8	9	10	11
12	13	14	15	16	17	18
19	20	21	22	23	24	25
26	27	28	29	30	31	..
..	..	..	..	..	..	..

On 9 September 1941, forces of Germany's Army Group North, under the command of *Generalfeldmarschall* Wilhelm Ritter von Leeb, commenced an 882-day siege of Leningrad (called "the 900 Days") that cost the lives of 1,042,000 Soviet civilians in addition to 1,017,881 Red Army troops killed, captured, or missing and 2,418,185 wounded and sick. German losses to siege action are unknown, but approximately 141,000 were lost to Soviet offensives. Von Leeb, an old-line Prussian general, did not appreciate having his command managed from afar by Hitler, and in January 1942 asked that he be relieved of command. Hitler replaced him with *Generaloberst* Georg von Küchler, never employing von Leeb again.

THIS MONTH						
SEPTEMBER						
S	M	T	W	T	F	S
..	..	1	2	3	4	5
6	7	8	9	10	11	12
13	14	15	16	17	18	19
20	21	22	23	24	25	26
27	28	29	30	..	..	..
..	..	..	..	..	..	..

THURSDAY
10
SEPTEMBER

NEXT MONTH						
OCTOBER						
S	M	T	W	T	F	S
..	..	..	..	1	2	3
4	5	6	7	8	9	10
11	12	13	14	15	16	17
18	19	20	21	22	23	24
25	26	27	28	29	30	31
..	..	..	..	..	..	..

1942

On 10 September 1942, the Royal Air Force blasted Düsseldorf in a large and effective incendiary raid, paving the way for such horrors as Hamburg and Dresden. By that time, the RAF had perfected its firebombing technique; as Marshal Sir Arthur "Bomber" Harris[1] explained it, "In the early days of bombing our notion, like that of the Germans, was to spread an attack out over the whole night, thereby wearing down the morale of the civilian population. The result was, of course, that an efficient fire brigade could tackle a single load of incendiaries, put them out, and wait in comfort for the next to come along; they might also be able to take shelter when a few high explosives bombs were dropping. ... But it was observed that when the Germans did get an effective concentration, ... then our fire brigades had a hard time; if a rain of incendiaries is mixed with high explosives bombs there is a temptation for the fireman to keep his head down."

---

1. Harris was known to the aircrews of Bomber Command as "Butcher" Harris because of his ready willingness to sacrifice their lives. During the war, 55,573 British and Commonwealth bomber crewmen lost their lives, an appalling 44% of the number who flew in Harris' relentless campaign, whose aim was "the destruction of German cities, the killing of German workers, and the disruption of civilised life throughout Germany."

THIS MONTH

SEPTEMBER

S	M	T	W	T	F	S
..	1	2	3	4	5	6
7	8	9	10	11	12	13
14	15	16	17	18	19	20
21	22	23	24	25	26	27
28	29	30	..	..	..	..
..	..	..	..	..	..	..

NEXT MONTH

OCTOBER

S	M	T	W	T	F	S
..	..	..	1	2	3	4
5	6	7	8	9	10	11
12	13	14	15	16	17	18
19	20	21	22	23	24	25
26	27	28	29	30	31	..
..	..	..	..	..	..	..

THURSDAY
11
SEPTEMBER

1941

On 11 September 1941, U.S. President Franklin D. Roosevelt ordered the United States Navy to shoot Axis vessels on sight under certain circumstances. The order stated that Nazi submarines' "very presence in any waters which America deems vital to its defense constitutes an attack. In the waters which we deem necessary for our defense, American naval vessels and American planes will no longer wait until Axis submarines lurking under the water, or Axis raiders on the surface of the sea, strike their deadly blow—first." Roosevelt probably drafted this order in response to the *Greer* Incident, which occurred on 4 September, when the destroyer USS *Greer*, captained by Commander J. J. Mahoney, became the first American ship to attack a German vessel. The World War I-vintage destroyer depth-charged the Type VIIC submarine *U-652*, commanded by *Oberleutnant zur See* Georg-Werner Fraatz, after the U-boat fired a torpedo that missed the ship by about 100 yards astern. *Greer* was clearly flagged as an American ship; with the U.S. then ostensibly neutral, the ship was therefore not a legitimate target.

THIS MONTH						
SEPTEMBER						
S	M	T	W	T	F	S
..	..	..	..	..	1	2
3	4	5	6	7	8	9
10	11	12	13	14	15	16
17	18	19	20	21	22	23
24	25	26	27	28	29	30
..	..	..	..	..	..	..

TUESDAY
12
SEPTEMBER

NEXT MONTH						
OCTOBER						
S	M	T	W	T	F	S
1	2	3	4	5	6	7
8	9	10	11	12	13	14
15	16	17	18	19	20	21
22	23	24	25	26	27	28
29	30	31	..	..	..	..
..	..	..	..	..	..	..

1939

On 12 September 1939, *Général d'armée* Maurice Gamelin ordered a halt to the French advance into Germany that had begun five days earlier, on 7 September, with a token offensive into the area near Saarbrucken. After advancing only eight miles into lightly defended German territory, the French had been halted on 8 September at the Warndt Forest, which the Germans had mined heavily. The French planned and executed a strategic retreat to the original national boundary, completing their withdrawal on 16 September.

THIS MONTH								FRIDAY	NEXT MONTH						
SEPTEMBER								**13**	OCTOBER						
S	M	T	W	T	F	S			S	M	T	W	T	F	S
1	2	3	4	5	6	7		SEPTEMBER	..	..	1	2	3	4	5
8	9	10	11	12	13	14			6	7	8	9	10	11	12
15	16	17	18	19	20	21			13	14	15	16	17	18	19
22	23	24	25	26	27	28			20	21	22	23	24	25	26
29	30	..	..	..	..	..			27	28	29	30	31	..	..
..	..	..	..	..	..	..			..	..	..	..	..	..	..

1940

On 13 September 1940, the 1st Blackshirt Division of the Italian Army crossed the border between Libya and Egypt, advancing into Egypt. They captured the area around Sidi Barrani and the village of Sollum, together with its small port. The only resistance they faced during this advance was a light British screening force that withdrew as the Italians advanced.

THIS MONTH						
SEPTEMBER						
S	M	T	W	T	F	S
1	2	3	4	5	6	7
8	9	10	11	12	13	14
15	16	17	18	19	20	21
22	23	24	25	26	27	28
29	30	..	..	..	..	..
..	..	..	..	..	..	..

SATURDAY
14
SEPTEMBER

NEXT MONTH						
OCTOBER						
S	M	T	W	T	F	S
..	..	1	2	3	4	5
6	7	8	9	10	11	12
13	14	15	16	17	18	19
20	21	22	23	24	25	26
27	28	29	30	31	..	..
..	..	..	..	..	..	..

1940

On 14 September 1940, Hitler postponed *Unternehmen Seelöwe* (Operation SEA LION, the invasion of Great Britain) until 27 September, which was the last day during September that would offer tides favorable for crossing the English Channel. Three days later, in the face of ever-stiffer British resistance in the air, the postponement became indefinite, and the operation was never carried out. The forces that had concentrated in anticipation of the invasion were diverted to the east for use in *Fall Barbarossa*, the invasion of the Soviet Union, which would begin nine months later, on 22 June 1941.

THIS MONTH						
SEPTEMBER						
S	M	T	W	T	F	S
..	..	..	..	..	1	2
3	4	5	6	7	8	9
10	11	12	13	14	15	16
17	18	19	20	21	22	23
24	25	26	27	28	29	30
..	..	..	..	..	..	..

FRIDAY
15
SEPTEMBER
1944

NEXT MONTH						
OCTOBER						
S	M	T	W	T	F	S
1	2	3	4	5	6	7
8	9	10	11	12	13	14
15	16	17	18	19	20	21
22	23	24	25	26	27	28
29	30	31	..	..	..	..
..	..	..	..	..	..	..

On 15 September 1944, the U.S. 1st Marine Division under Major General William Rupertus landed on the Pacific island of Peleliu, beginning a battle that would rage until 27 November. Peleliu was a hell-hole of an island, hot, humid, and disease ridden, with a rough landscape consisting of jungle foliage on coral so hard that the Marines could not even dig foxholes and took to detonating grenades placed on the ground to blast crude foxholes.

Japanese troops from the 14th Infantry Division, commanded by Colonel Kunio Nakagawa, supplemented by forced laborers from Korea and Okinawa, had crafted a "honeycomb" system of heavily fortified bunkers, caves, and underground positions, and had adopted new tactics. They no longer attempted to stop the invaders at the beaches, and they also abandoned their usually futile *Banzai* charges, instead forcing the Marines into a guerrilla-style battle of attrition.

The Battle of Peleliu remains controversial because the island appears to have had no strategic value despite its capture's being an element of both of the larger plans that the U.S. military considered. Marine and, later, U.S. Army casualties were the highest in any battle of the Pacific war; out of 28,484 troops committed, 1,794 died and 8,010 were wounded or missing. The defenders fought virtually to the last man, losing 10,695 killed and 202 captured out of approximately 11,000 total strength. Colonel Nakagawa committed *seppuku* on 24 November and was posthumously promoted to lieutenant general for his outstanding valor and defensive ability.

THIS MONTH							MONDAY	NEXT MONTH						
SEPTEMBER							**16**	OCTOBER						
S	M	T	W	T	F	S		S	M	T	W	T	F	S
1	2	3	4	5	6	7		..	..	1	2	3	4	5
8	9	10	11	12	13	14	SEPTEMBER	6	7	8	9	10	11	12
15	16	17	18	19	20	21		13	14	15	16	17	18	19
22	23	24	25	26	27	28		20	21	22	23	24	25	26
29	30	..	..	..	..	..		27	28	29	30	31	..	..
..	..	..	..	..	..	..		..	..	..	..	..	..	..

1940

On 16 September 1940, Franklin D. Roosevelt signed into law the Selective Training and Service Act of 1940, also known as the Burke-Wadsworth Bill, introducing the first peacetime conscription in United States history. The Act, which Congress had passed on 1 July, required all men aged 21 to 36 to register for possible conscription. For the first time, it also made provision for conscientious objectors, who would be permitted to serve their country by doing "work of national importance under civilian direction."

THIS MONTH

SEPTEMBER

S	M	T	W	T	F	S
..	..	..	..	..	1	2
3	4	5	6	7	8	9
10	11	12	13	14	15	16
17	18	19	20	21	22	23
24	25	26	27	28	29	30
..	..	..	..	..	..	..

SUNDAY
17
SEPTEMBER
1939

NEXT MONTH

OCTOBER

S	M	T	W	T	F	S
1	2	3	4	5	6	7
8	9	10	11	12	13	14
15	16	17	18	19	20	21
22	23	24	25	26	27	28
29	30	31	..	..	..	..
..	..	..	..	..	..	..

On 17 September 1939, the Japanese 101st, 106th, 6th, 3rd, 13th, and 33rd Divisions attacked Changsha, the provincial capital of Hunan, China. This operation was the first of four battles for Changsha. By 29 September, as the Japanese reached the city's outskirts, the Chinese Nationalist Army, commanded by General Due Yue, had cut the Japanese supply lines, and the Japanese advance petered out, ending on 8 October. Changsha was the first major city that did not fall to the Japanese; because they failed to take the city, the Chinese were able to prevent them from consolidating their occupied territories in southern China.

S	M	T	W	T	F	S
SEPTEMBER						
..	..	1	2	3	4	5
6	7	8	9	10	11	12
13	14	15	16	17	18	19
20	21	22	23	24	25	26
27	28	29	30	..	..	..
..	..	..	..	..	..	..

FRIDAY
18
SEPTEMBER
1942

S	M	T	W	T	F	S
OCTOBER						
..	..	..	..	1	2	3
4	5	6	7	8	9	10
11	12	13	14	15	16	17
18	19	20	21	22	23	24
25	26	27	28	29	30	31
..	..	..	..	..	..	..

On 18 September 1942, German forces attacked the grain elevator in southern Stalingrad in an attempt to rout the 53 Soviet troops holding the fortresslike concrete structure. The Germans threw massive numbers of tanks and infantry at the elevator but were beaten back. Reforming, they attacked again and were beaten off, a total of ten times. With the grain on fire, the cooling water in their machine guns evaporated, and no water to drink, the defenders held on through 18, 19, and 20 September. On the 21st, a German officer delivered an ultimatum: surrender or be blasted flat. The Russians rejected the ultimatum. Andrey Khozyaynov, a sailor serving in the Naval Infantry Brigade, wrote later that the response to the ultimatum was, "Tell all your Nazis to go to hell! You can go back, but only on foot." The Germans finally drove the defenders out, but on their way the Russians stumbled across—and routed—a mortar battery whose food and water proved a welcome relief. In the end, Khozyaynov was the only defender known to have survived; he was captured by SS troops and spent the rest of the war as a POW.

THIS MONTH						
SEPTEMBER						
S	M	T	W	T	F	S
..	1	2	3	4	5	6
7	8	9	10	11	12	13
14	15	16	17	18	19	20
21	22	23	24	25	26	27
28	29	30	..	..	..	..
..	..	..	..	..	..	..

FRIDAY
19
SEPTEMBER

1941

NEXT MONTH						
OCTOBER						
S	M	T	W	T	F	S
..	..	..	1	2	3	4
5	6	7	8	9	10	11
12	13	14	15	16	17	18
19	20	21	22	23	24	25
26	27	28	29	30	31	..
..	..	..	..	..	..	..

On 19 September 1941, the city of Kiev fell to German Army Group South under the command of *Generalfeldmarschall* Gerd von Rundstedt, but fighting to encircle the city continued for another week. The encirclement of Kiev was the largest encirclement in history, trapping 452,700 Red Army soldiers under Colonel General Mikhail Kirponos along with 2,642 guns and mortars, and 64 tanks. By the time the encirclement was fully solidified on 2 October, fewer than 16,000 Soviet troops had escaped. Soviet casualties numbered 616,304 dead or captured and 84,240 wounded. German casualties are not known.

THIS MONTH							WEDNESDAY	NEXT MONTH						

SEPTEMBER

S	M	T	W	T	F	S
..	..	..	..	..	1	2
3	4	5	6	7	8	9
10	11	12	13	14	15	16
17	18	19	20	21	22	23
24	25	26	27	28	29	30
..	..	..	..	..	..	..

WEDNESDAY
20
SEPTEMBER

OCTOBER

S	M	T	W	T	F	S
1	2	3	4	5	6	7
8	9	10	11	12	13	14
15	16	17	18	19	20	21
22	23	24	25	26	27	28
29	30	31	..	..	..	..
..	..	..	..	..	..	..

1939

On 20 September 1939, German submarine *U-27*, commanded by *Kapitän-leutnant* Johannes Franz, fired three torpedoes at the destroyers HMS *Fortune* and HMS *Faulknor*, which were part of a concerted effort to find and sink the U-boat that had been attacking British fishing boats. As had happened six days earlier when *U-39* attempted to sink the carrier *Ark Royal*, all three torpedoes exploded prematurely, doing no damage. The destroyers responded with depth charges, damaging the U-boat sufficiently to force it to the surface. HMS *Fortune* began a ramming attack, but Captain Charles Pizey canceled the action when it became clear that the Germans were surrendering. The U-boat's crew were taken off, and the vessel was then sunk by gunfire, becoming the second German submarine to be sunk in World War II. Before surrendering, Franz managed to inform the U-boat high command of the torpedoes' failure in a radio message sent in that day's Enigma code.

<table>
<tr><th colspan="7">THIS MONTH</th><th></th><th colspan="7">NEXT MONTH</th></tr>
<tr><th colspan="7">SEPTEMBER</th><th></th><th colspan="7">OCTOBER</th></tr>
</table>

S	M	T	W	T	F	S
..	..	..	1	2	3	4
5	6	7	8	9	10	11
12	13	14	15	16	17	18
19	20	21	22	23	24	25
26	27	28	29	30	..	..
..	..	..	..	..	..	..

TUESDAY
21
SEPTEMBER

S	M	T	W	T	F	S
..	..	..	..	..	1	2
3	4	5	6	7	8	9
10	11	12	13	14	15	16
17	18	19	20	21	22	23
24	25	26	27	28	29	30
31	..	..	..	..	..	..

1943

On 21 September 1943, approximately 11,000 men and officers of the Italian 33rd *Acqui* Infantry Division, commanded by General Antonio Gandin, surrendered to the 966th Fortress Grenadier Regiment, under *Oberst* Johannes Barge, on the Greek island of Cephallonia.

On 11 September, eight days after Italy had surrendered to the Allies, Barge had presented Gandin with an ultimatum: continue fighting alongside Axis forces, fight against them, or hand over his troops' guns. Gandin's superiors ordered him to resist the Germans, but the situation was very fluid, and on 13 September Gandin polled his troops. He gave them three options: join the Germans, surrender and be repatriated, or resist the Germans. The overwhelming vote was to resist the Germans.

After eight days of fighting, the Italians surrendered and turned over their heavy weapons. Over the next week, the Germans massacred more than 4,500 of the Italians, and some 3,000 were "lost at sea" during transport. In one place, *Padre* Romualdo Formato recalled, "the Germans went around loudly offering medical help to those wounded. When about 20 men crawled forward, a machine-gun salvo finished them off."

THIS MONTH						
SEPTEMBER						
S	M	T	W	T	F	S
..	..	..	1	2	3	4
5	6	7	8	9	10	11
12	13	14	15	16	17	18
19	20	21	22	23	24	25
26	27	28	29	30	..	..
..	..	..	..	..	..	..

WEDNESDAY
22
SEPTEMBER

1943

NEXT MONTH						
OCTOBER						
S	M	T	W	T	F	S
..	..	..	..	..	1	2
3	4	5	6	7	8	9
10	11	12	13	14	15	16
17	18	19	20	21	22	23
24	25	26	27	28	29	30
31	..	..	..	..	..	..

On 22 September 1943, six British X-class four-man midget submarines executed Operation SOURCE, attacking German warships in northern Norway. HMS *X5* (unofficially named *Platypus* and commanded by Lieutenant "Henty" Henty-Creer), *X6* (named *Piker II* and commanded by Lieutenant Donald Cameron), and *X7* (unofficially named *Pdinichthys* and commanded by Lieutenant Basil Place) took on the battleship *Tirpitz* (anchored in Kjåfjord), damaging her sufficiently that she did not return to action until April 1944. HMS *X9* (commanded by a Lieutenant Martin) and *X10* (unofficially named *Excalibur* and commanded by a Lieutenant Hudspeth of the Royal Australian Naval Volunteers) were to attack the battleship *Scharnhorst* (also in Kjåfjord), but the battleship was engaged in exercises instead of lying at her mooring. HMS *X8* (commanded by a Lieutenant McFarlane of the Royal Australian Navy) was assigned to the heavy cruiser *Lützow* (in Langfjord) but did no damage to the ship. Of the British and Australian personnel, nine were killed and six captured.

THIS MONTH						
SEPTEMBER						
S	M	T	W	T	F	S
..	..	1	2	3	4	5
6	7	8	9	10	11	12
13	14	15	16	17	18	19
20	21	22	23	24	25	26
27	28	29	30	..	..	..
..	..	..	..	..	..	..

WEDNESDAY
23
SEPTEMBER

NEXT MONTH						
OCTOBER						
S	M	T	W	T	F	S
..	..	..	..	1	2	3
4	5	6	7	8	9	10
11	12	13	14	15	16	17
18	19	20	21	22	23	24
25	26	27	28	29	30	31
..	..	..	..	..	..	..

1942

On 23 September 1942, U.S. Marines commanded by Major General Lewis "Chesty" Puller, who is probably the most decorated combat Marine in the history of the Corps, launched an operation to mop up Japanese troops withdrawing after the recent battle of Edson's Ridge on Guadalcanal. In this action, known as the Second Battle of the Matanikau River, Japanese 17th Army troops, under the overall command of Major General Kiyotake Kawaguchi, beat back the Marines in five days of heavy fighting. This action and a third Matanikau battle two weeks later resulted in 156 American deaths and 750 Japanese deaths. The Marines succeeded in the latter operation, greatly hindering Japanese preparations for a late-October attack whose purpose was to destroy Henderson Field, the U.S. airbase on Guadalcanal.

THIS MONTH

SEPTEMBER

S	M	T	W	T	F	S
..	..	..	..	..	1	2
3	4	5	6	7	8	9
10	11	12	13	14	15	16
17	18	19	20	21	22	23
24	25	26	27	28	29	30
..	..	..	..	..	..	..

NEXT MONTH

OCTOBER

S	M	T	W	T	F	S
1	2	3	4	5	6	7
8	9	10	11	12	13	14
15	16	17	18	19	20	21
22	23	24	25	26	27	28
29	30	31	..	..	..	..
..	..	..	..	..	..	..

SUNDAY
24
SEPTEMBER

1939

On 24 September 1939, Soviet aircraft deliberately violated Estonian airspace. Estonia, along with Latvia, Lithuania, eastern Poland, and Bessarabia, had been "assigned" to the Soviet Union by the Molotov-Ribbentrop pact of 23 August, and when Estonian Ambassador August Rei protested to Soviet foreign minister Vyacheslav Molotov in Moscow, the response was a warning that if the Soviet Union did not get military bases in Estonia, it would be forced to use "more radical actions." In the event, some 25,000 Soviet troops were brought into Estonia, and the Soviets used airbases in Estonia to bomb Finland in the 1939–1940 Winter War.

SEPTEMBER

S	M	T	W	T	F	S
..	..	..	1	2	3	4
5	6	7	8	9	10	11
12	13	14	15	16	17	18
19	20	21	22	23	24	25
26	27	28	29	30	..	..
..	..	..	..	..	..	..

SATURDAY
25
SEPTEMBER

1943

OCTOBER

S	M	T	W	T	F	S
..	..	..	..	..	1	2
3	4	5	6	7	8	9
10	11	12	13	14	15	16
17	18	19	20	21	22	23
24	25	26	27	28	29	30
31	..	..	..	..	..	..

On 25 September 1943, in a decisive victory, forces of the Red Army under Generals Andrei Yeremenko and Vasily Sokolovsky (both later promoted to Marshal of the Soviet Union) completed the recapture of Smolensk, a major city about 400 kilometers west of Moscow. The Germans had taken Smolensk in a month-long battle in 1941, part of *Fall Barbarossa*. In the second battle, which had begun on 7 August, the Soviets also retook Roslavi, another important city, advancing a total of 200–250 kilometers. Fighting in the area would continue until 2 October. The Smolensk operation cost the Germans, who were commanded by *Generalfeldmarschall* Günther von Kluge, between 200,000 and 250,000 casualties overall, while the Soviets lost 107,645 killed, missing or captured and 343,821 wounded.

THIS MONTH						
SEPTEMBER						
S	M	T	W	T	F	S
..	1	2	3	4	5	6
7	8	9	10	11	12	13
14	15	16	17	18	19	20
21	22	23	24	25	26	27
28	29	30	..	..	..	..
..	..	..	..	..	..	..

FRIDAY
26
SEPTEMBER

NEXT MONTH						
OCTOBER						
S	M	T	W	T	F	S
..	..	..	1	2	3	4
5	6	7	8	9	10	11
12	13	14	15	16	17	18
19	20	21	22	23	24	25
26	27	28	29	30	31	..
..	..	..	..	..	..	..

1941

On 26 September 1941, the U.S. Naval Command ordered an all-out war on Axis shipping in American waters. The order came 15 days after Franklin D. Roosevelt issued his "shoot on sight" order, in which he instructed American forces to fire upon Axis ships in "any waters which America deems vital to its defense." The Naval Command's order went beyond "shoot on sight"; it instructed all naval vessels and aircraft to carry the war to the Axis by seeking out Axis vessels (specifically submarines) and destroying them, so long as they were found in waters that America deemed necessary for its defense.

THIS MONTH								FRIDAY	NEXT MONTH					

SEPTEMBER

S	M	T	W	T	F	S
1	2	3	4	5	6	7
8	9	10	11	12	13	14
15	16	17	18	19	20	21
22	23	24	25	26	27	28
29	30	..	..	..	..	..
..	..	..	..	..	..	..

FRIDAY
27
SEPTEMBER

OCTOBER

S	M	T	W	T	F	S
..	..	1	2	3	4	5
6	7	8	9	10	11	12
13	14	15	16	17	18	19
20	21	22	23	24	25	26
27	28	29	30	31	..	..
..	..	..	..	..	..	..

1940

On 27 September 1940, in Berlin, German *Führer* Adolf Hitler, Italian foreign minister Galeazzo Ciano, and Imperial Japanese ambassador to Germany Saburō Kurusu signed the Tripartite Pact, promising mutual aid. In English, the pact's preamble reads as follows: "The governments of Germany, Italy and Japan, considering it as a condition precedent of any lasting peace that all nations of the world be given each its own proper place, have decided to stand by and co-operate with one another in regard to their efforts in greater East Asia and regions of Europe respectively wherein it is their prime purpose to establish and maintain a new order of things calculated to promote the mutual prosperity and welfare of the peoples concerned. Furthermore, it is the desire of the three governments to extend co-operation to such nations in other spheres of the world as may be inclined to put forth endeavours along lines similar to their own, in order that their ultimate aspirations for world peace may thus be realized." The term "Axis" had come out of the 1939 Pact of Steel's "Rome-Berlin Axis," and the word was quickly applied to the alliance created by the signing of the Tripartite Pact. The Italian press immediately named the pact "Roberto" from the first syllables letters of the names Roma, Berlin, and Tokyo.

THIS MONTH									THURSDAY		NEXT MONTH					
SEPTEMBER									**28**		**OCTOBER**					

THIS MONTH

SEPTEMBER

S	M	T	W	T	F	S
..	..	..	..	..	1	2
3	4	5	6	7	8	9
10	11	12	13	14	15	16
17	18	19	20	21	22	23
24	25	26	27	28	29	30
..	..	..	..	..	..	..

THURSDAY
28
SEPTEMBER

NEXT MONTH

OCTOBER

S	M	T	W	T	F	S
1	2	3	4	5	6	7
8	9	10	11	12	13	14
15	16	17	18	19	20	21
22	23	24	25	26	27	28
29	30	31	..	..	..	..

1939

On 28 September 1939, German foreign minister Joachim von Ribbentrop and Soviet foreign minister Vyacheslav Molotov signed the German-Soviet Boundary and Friendship Treaty, a secret protocol that was an addendum to the original Molotov-Ribbentrop Pact (signed on 23 August). The new document specified the details of the partition of Poland that had been defined in the original pact and also added Lithuania to the list of countries over which the Soviet Union would assume control.

SEPTEMBER

S	M	T	W	T	F	S
..	1	2	3	4	5	6
7	8	9	10	11	12	13
14	15	16	17	18	19	20
21	22	23	24	25	26	27
28	29	30	..	..	..	..
..	..	..	..	..	..	..

MONDAY
29
SEPTEMBER
1941

OCTOBER

S	M	T	W	T	F	S
..	..	..	1	2	3	4
5	6	7	8	9	10	11
12	13	14	15	16	17	18
19	20	21	22	23	24	25
26	27	28	29	30	31	..
..	..	..	..	..	..	..

On 29 September 1941, SS troops of *Sonderkommando* 4a, commanded by *SS-Standartenführer* Paul Blobel, assisted by other German units and local collaborators, began a two-day operation that ended with 33,771 Jewish civilians dead, murdered in production-line fashion.

The decision had been made to exterminate the entire Jewish population of Kiev, and the place of execution was a ravine called Babi Yar, located outside the city. The people had been instructed by wall posters to come to the ravine to be processed for resettlement; once there, they were herded along a line with individual stations where Ukrainian collaborators divested them of their luggage, their outer clothing, their shoes, their undergarments, their glasses and jewelry, even children's toys. All of these articles were stacked carefully for redistribution to German citizens.

At the end of the line, the Jews were instructed to go to the foot of the ravine and to lie down, making a new layer on top of the bodies of those who had gone before. Members of Police Battalion 45, commanded by *SS-Sturmbannführer* Martin Besser, then went along the line of prone people, shooting each one in the neck with submachine guns.

THIS MONTH						
SEPTEMBER						
S	M	T	W	T	F	S
..	..	1	2	3	4	5
6	7	8	9	10	11	12
13	14	15	16	17	18	19
20	21	22	23	24	25	26
27	28	29	30	..	..	..
..	..	..	..	..	..	..

WEDNESDAY
30
SEPTEMBER

NEXT MONTH						
OCTOBER						
S	M	T	W	T	F	S
..	..	..	..	1	2	3
4	5	6	7	8	9	10
11	12	13	14	15	16	17
18	19	20	21	22	23	24
25	26	27	28	29	30	31
..	..	..	..	..	..	..

1942

On 30 September 1942, the Royal Air Force's No. 71, No. 121, and No. 133 Squadrons, known as the Eagle Squadrons, became active as the 4th Fighter Group's 334th, 335th, and 336th Squadrons, respectively, in the U.S. Army Air Forces. (The order for transfer was signed the day before.) Eagle Squadron pilots were Americans who wanted to fight and, in some cases, had been rejected by the U.S. military as "lacking in intrinsic flying ability." The first Eagle Squadron, No. 71 Squadron, was formed in September 1940 as part of the RAF's buildup during the Battle of Britain and became operational on 5 February 1941. Of the more than 6,700 volunteers who were processed and approved, some 3,000 were brought to the U.K. through the financial generosity of U.S. businessman Charles Sweeny and his associates. Eventually, 244 Americans served in the Eagle Squadrons, losing 77 of their number while claiming 73½ victories.

OCTOBER						
S	M	T	W	T	F	S
..	..	1	2	3	4	5
6	7	8	9	10	11	12
13	14	15	16	17	18	19
20	21	22	23	24	25	26
27	28	29	30	31	..	..
..	..	..	..	..	..	..

TUESDAY
1
OCTOBER

NOVEMBER						
S	M	T	W	T	F	S
..	..	..	..	..	1	2
3	4	5	6	7	8	9
10	11	12	13	14	15	16
17	18	19	20	21	22	23
24	25	26	27	28	29	30
..	..	..	..	..	..	..

1940

On 1 October 1940, in another sign that America was preparing for eventual war, the War Department began a process of separating the nine Corps Areas (geographically based command organizations established in 1921 to perform the administrative and logistical tasks of the various regions of the U.S.) from the four Field Armies established by a plan developed by General Douglas MacArthur in 1932 to replace the "three area, six army" system. The 1940 action transferred tactical command functions to General Headquarters, U.S. Army, separating the field armies from the corps areas. Corps areas were then limited to functioning within U.S. territory as service commands, while the field armies assumed control of all tactical units.

THIS MONTH							THURSDAY	NEXT MONTH					

OCTOBER

S	M	T	W	T	F	S
..	..	..	1	2	3	4
5	6	7	8	9	10	11
12	13	14	15	16	17	18
19	20	21	22	23	24	25
26	27	28	29	30	31	..
..	..	..	..	..	..	..

THURSDAY
2
OCTOBER

1941

NOVEMBER

S	M	T	W	T	F	S
..	..	..	..	..	..	1
2	3	4	5	6	7	8
9	10	11	12	13	14	15
16	17	18	19	20	21	22
23	24	25	26	27	28	29
30	..	..	..	..	..	..

On 2 October 1941, Germany's Army Group Center, commanded by *Generalfeldmarschall* Fedor von Bock, launched *Unternehmen Taifun* (Operation TYPHOON), an all-out offensive designed to capture Moscow. The plan, which committed more than one million men, 1700 tanks, and 14,000 artillery tubes, called for two pincer offensives: one to the north of Moscow against the Kalinin Front by the 3rd and 4th Panzer Armies under *General* Heinz Guderian, to sever the Moscow–Leningrad railway as it closed on Moscow, and another to the south of the Moscow *Oblast*[1] against the Western Front, by the 2nd Panzer Army. As the pincer closed behind the Soviets, the 4th Army would advance directly towards Moscow from the west. Operations were supported by *Luftflotte* 2, under *Generalfeldmarschall* Albert Kesselring.

General Georgiy Zhukov commanded the Soviet forces, constructing three defensive belts and deploying newly raised reserve armies. He also brought troops from the Siberian and Far Eastern Military Districts. Initial fighting resulted in appalling defeats for the Soviets, but eventually they were able to halt the German offensives. Zhukov then initiated a strategic counteroffensive and several smaller-scale offensive operations, forcing the Germans back to their former positions around the cities of Oryol, Vyazma, and Vitebsk and nearly surrounding three German armies in the process.

---

1. An *oblast* is an administrative division in some Slavic countries; there were 21 *oblasti* in the Soviet Union.

THIS MONTH								FRIDAY	NEXT MONTH						

OCTOBER

S	M	T	W	T	F	S
..	..	..	1	2	3	4
5	6	7	8	9	10	11
12	13	14	15	16	17	18
19	20	21	22	23	24	25
26	27	28	29	30	31	..
..	..	..	..	..	..	..

FRIDAY
3
OCTOBER

NOVEMBER

S	M	T	W	T	F	S
..	..	..	..	..	..	1
2	3	4	5	6	7	8
9	10	11	12	13	14	15
16	17	18	19	20	21	22
23	24	25	26	27	28	29
30	..	..	..	..	..	..

1941

On 3 October 1941, in a classic example of bad timing, Mohandas Gandhi urged his followers to begin a passive resistance campaign against British rule in India.

			THIS MONTH							SUNDAY				NEXT MONTH			

OCTOBER

S	M	T	W	T	F	S
..	..	..	..	1	2	3
4	5	6	7	8	9	10
11	12	13	14	15	16	17
18	19	20	21	22	23	24
25	26	27	28	29	30	31
..	..	..	..	..	..	..

SUNDAY
4
OCTOBER

1942

NOVEMBER

S	M	T	W	T	F	S
1	2	3	4	5	6	7
8	9	10	11	12	13	14
15	16	17	18	19	20	21
22	23	24	25	26	27	28
29	30	..	..	..	..	..
..	..	..	..	..	..	..

On 4 October 1942, a small British force comprising 10 men from the Special Operations Executive's (SOE) Small Scale Raiding Force and No. 12 Commando landed on the Channel Island Sark, which had been occupied by the Germans since 4 July 1940. The purpose of the raid, Operation BASALT, was offensive reconnaissance and the capture of German prisoners.

The raiders broke into the house of a local woman, who helpfully told them there were about 20 Germans in a nearby hotel. Closer to her house was a long hut that contained five enlisted Germans but no officers. These Germans' hands were tied, their trouser flies were ripped, and their belts and suspenders were taken so that they had to hold up their trousers with their hands. One of the Germans shouted to alert those in the hotel, and a raider shot him dead.

With fire now coming from the hotel, the raiders took their four prisoners and made for their boat. During their flight, three of the Germans made a break for it; two were shot and one was stabbed to death. Having taken no casualties, the raiders made their escape, taking with them their remaining prisoner and an SOE operative who had been posing as a Polish worker doing forced labor. The local woman declined an offer of transport to England.

It is believed that this raid, which produced much useful information, led to Hitler's issuance of his Commando Order stating that captured Commandos or Commando-type personnel were to be executed immediately instead of being sent to POW camps.

THIS MONTH						
OCTOBER						
S	M	T	W	T	F	S
1	2	3	4	5	6	7
8	9	10	11	12	13	14
15	16	17	18	19	20	21
22	23	24	25	26	27	28
29	30	31	..	..	..	..
..	..	..	..	..	..	..

THURSDAY
5
OCTOBER

NEXT MONTH						
NOVEMBER						
S	M	T	W	T	F	S
..	..	..	1	2	3	4
5	6	7	8	9	10	11
12	13	14	15	16	17	18
19	20	21	22	23	24	25
26	27	28	29	30	..	..
..	..	..	..	..	..	..

1939

On 5 October 1939, Latvian Minister of Foreign Affairs Vilhelms Munters and Soviet Commissar of Foreign Affairs Vyacheslav Molotov signed the bilateral Soviet–Latvian Mutual Assistance Treaty in Moscow. The treaty became effective on 11 October, when ratifications were exchanged in Riga. Ostensibly, it obligated each party to respect the other's sovereignty and independence; but its actual terms allowed the Soviets to establish military bases in Latvia and station about 25,000 troops there, greatly facilitating the Soviet invasion that was to come in June 1940.

THIS MONTH						
OCTOBER						
S	M	T	W	T	F	S
..	..	..	..	..	1	2
3	4	5	6	7	8	9
10	11	12	13	14	15	16
17	18	19	20	21	22	23
24	25	26	27	28	29	30
31	..	..	..	..	..	..

WEDNESDAY
6
OCTOBER

NEXT MONTH						
NOVEMBER						
S	M	T	W	T	F	S
..	1	2	3	4	5	6
7	8	9	10	11	12	13
14	15	16	17	18	19	20
21	22	23	24	25	26	27
28	29	30	..	..	..	..
..	..	..	..	..	..	..

1943

On 6 October 1943, a Japanese force of six destroyers commanded by Rear Admiral Matsuji Ijuin defeated three American destroyers under Captain Frank R. Walker. The Americans were half of a six-destroyer fleet that had been sent to intercept the Japanese, whose actual mission was to extract about 600 ground troops from the island of Vella Lavella, in the Solomons group. The other three American destroyers, commanded by Captain Harold O. Larson, were about 20 miles behind Walker's group. Japanese aerial reconnaissance discovered the Americans but misreported their strength as including four cruisers; this mistake hampered Japanese action and may have saved two of Walker's three ships. USS *Selfridge* and USS *O'Bannon* took heavy damage but survived, while USS *Chevalier* went to the bottom. When Japanese planes spotted Larson's approaching ships, Admiral Ijuin ordered a retreat. American losses, in addition to USS *Chevalier*, were 64 killed, 47 wounded, and 36 missing. The Japanese lost the destroyer *Yugumo*, with Commander Oosako Azuma in command, and 138 lives.

THIS MONTH						
OCTOBER						
S	M	T	W	T	F	S
..	..	..	..	..	1	2
3	4	5	6	7	8	9
10	11	12	13	14	15	16
17	18	19	20	21	22	23
24	25	26	27	28	29	30
31	..	..	..	..	..	..

THURSDAY
7
OCTOBER

1943

NEXT MONTH						
NOVEMBER						
S	M	T	W	T	F	S
..	1	2	3	4	5	6
7	8	9	10	11	12	13
14	15	16	17	18	19	20
21	22	23	24	25	26	27
28	29	30	..	..	..	..
..	..	..	..	..	..	..

On 7 October 1943, troops of the Japanese occupation garrison on Wake Island murdered 98 American civilian workers kept to perform forced labor since the Japanese had taken the island in December 1941. Two days earlier, aircraft from the U.S. aircraft carrier *Yorktown* had raided Wake; fearing an imminent invasion, Rear Admiral Shigematsu Sakaibara ordered the execution of the Americans. Taking the prisoners to the northern end of the island, the Japanese blindfolded them and shot them down with a machine gun. One of the prisoners, whose identity the Japanese did not record, escaped and apparently returned to the site to carve "98 US PW 5-10-43" on a large coral rock near the mass grave in which the victims were hastily buried. When he was recaptured, Sakaibara personally beheaded him. After the war, Sakaibara was tried for and convicted of this and other war crimes, partially on evidence left by subordinates who had written notes incriminating him before suiciding while in American custody. He was sentenced to death, and on 18 June 1947 he died on the scaffold. The invasion that he had feared never materialized.

THIS MONTH						
OCTOBER						
S	M	T	W	T	F	S
..	..	..	1	2	3	4
5	6	7	8	9	10	11
12	13	14	15	16	17	18
19	20	21	22	23	24	25
26	27	28	29	30	31	..
..	..	..	..	..	..	..

WEDNESDAY

8

OCTOBER

NEXT MONTH						
NOVEMBER						
S	M	T	W	T	F	S
..	..	..	..	..	..	1
2	3	4	5	6	7	8
9	10	11	12	13	14	15
16	17	18	19	20	21	22
23	24	25	26	27	28	29
30	..	..	..	..	..	..

1941

On 8 October 1941, the German invasion of the Soviet Union, *Fall Barbarossa*, entered a new stage as 31,000 German soldiers of the redeployed Sixth Army, accompanied by only seven tanks, captured the city of Mariupol from a Red Army force of 136,500 troops with 165 tanks. The Russians were unprepared, as the Soviet Union was still in the process of mobilizing after Stalin's initial refusal to believe that the Germans were going to attack in violation of the Molotov-Ribbentrop Pact. The capture of Mariupol, at the edge of the Sea of Azov, signaled the beginning of the end for Russia—at least in the opinion of Hitler's propaganda machine. "Soviet Russia has been vanquished!" Hitler's press chief Otto Dietrich announced to foreign journalists the next day.

THIS MONTH
OCTOBER

S	M	T	W	T	F	S
..	..	1	2	3	4	5
6	7	8	9	10	11	12
13	14	15	16	17	18	19
20	21	22	23	24	25	26
27	28	29	30	31	..	..
..	..	..	..	..	..	..

WEDNESDAY
9
OCTOBER

NEXT MONTH
NOVEMBER

S	M	T	W	T	F	S
..	..	..	..	..	1	2
3	4	5	6	7	8	9
10	11	12	13	14	15	16
17	18	19	20	21	22	23
24	25	26	27	28	29	30
..	..	..	..	..	..	..

1940

On 9 October 1940, Neville Chamberlain, suffering from terminal cancer, resigned from the House of Commons. Chamberlain had resigned as Prime Minister on 10 June, when the Allies' forced retreat from Norway made it blindingly obvious that the "peace in our time" he had proudly brought home from Munich in 1938 had been only a sham and that appeasement would not stop Hitler. Chamberlain believed that a government supported by all parties was essential, but the Labour and Liberal parties would not join a government with him at its head. He would die exactly a month after leaving Parliament.

THIS MONTH							TUESDAY	NEXT MONTH						
OCTOBER							**10**	NOVEMBER						
S	M	T	W	T	F	S		S	M	T	W	T	F	S
1	2	3	4	5	6	7		..	..	..	1	2	3	4
8	9	10	11	12	13	14	OCTOBER	5	6	7	8	9	10	11
15	16	17	18	19	20	21		12	13	14	15	16	17	18
22	23	24	25	26	27	28		19	20	21	22	23	24	25
29	30	31	..	..	..	..		26	27	28	29	30	..	..
..	..	..	..	..	..	..		..	..	..	..	..	..	..

1939

On 10 October 1939, after a week of back-and-forth discussions with the Soviets and the Germans as well as intense internal debate among Lithuanian leaders, Joseph Stalin and Lithuania's Minister of Foreign Affairs Juozas Urbšys signed the 15-year Soviet–Lithuanian Mutual Assistance Treaty. The treaty gave the Soviets the right to establish military bases in Lithuania and station some 20,000 troops there, ostensibly to protect Lithuania against possible German incursion. (The Soviets' original proposal had been to allow up to 50,000 troops.) Lithuanian territory west of the Šešupė River was to be ceded to Nazi Germany, but the Germans indicated that this was not an urgent matter. In a secret protocol, the historical Lithuanian capital of Vilnius was returned to Lithuania from Poland, which had acquired it as part of the redrawing of boundaries after World War I.

		THIS MONTH				
		OCTOBER				
S	M	T	W	T	F	S
..	..	..	..	1	2	3
4	5	6	7	8	9	10
11	12	13	14	15	16	17
18	19	20	21	22	23	24
25	26	27	28	29	30	31
..	..	..	..	..	..	..

SUNDAY
11
OCTOBER
1942

		NEXT MONTH				
		NOVEMBER				
S	M	T	W	T	F	S
1	2	3	4	5	6	7
8	9	10	11	12	13	14
15	16	17	18	19	20	21
22	23	24	25	26	27	28
29	30	..	..	..	..	..
..	..	..	..	..	..	..

On 11 October 1942, in the Battle of Cape Esperance, a U.S. force of four cruisers and five destroyers under the command of Rear Admiral Norman Scott surprised and intercepted a Japanese force of three heavy cruisers and two destroyers commanded by Rear Admiral Aritomo Gotō. The Japanese force was headed to Guadalcanal to bombard Henderson Field, the American airbase on the island. The Americans sank one Japanese cruiser and one destroyer, heavily damaged another cruiser, mortally wounded Gotō, and forced the rest of Gotō's warships to abandon their mission and retreat. On the same night, a convoy of two seaplane tenders and six destroyers under Rear Admiral Takatsugu Jojima successfully delivered reinforcements to the Japanese force on the island. On the next day, four of Jojima's destroyers went to the aid of the remaining ships from Gotō's force; two of the four destroyers were sunk by aircraft from Henderson Field. The Americans lost one cruiser and one destroyer damaged, one destroyer sunk, and 163 men killed. Of the Japanese engaged, one cruiser and three destroyers were sunk, one cruiser was damaged, approximately 400 men were killed, and 111 men were captured.

THIS MONTH						
OCTOBER						
S	M	T	W	T	F	S
..	..	..	..	..	1	2
3	4	5	6	7	8	9
10	11	12	13	14	15	16
17	18	19	20	21	22	23
24	25	26	27	28	29	30
31	..	..	..	..	..	..

TUESDAY
12
OCTOBER
1943

NEXT MONTH						
NOVEMBER						
S	M	T	W	T	F	S
..	1	2	3	4	5	6
7	8	9	10	11	12	13
14	15	16	17	18	19	20
21	22	23	24	25	26	27
28	29	30	..	..	..	..
..	..	..	..	..	..	..

On 12 October 1943, American aerial forces participating in Operation CARTWHEEL, General Douglas MacArthur's umbrella plan to neutralize the Japanese base at Rabaul, began an extended campaign of bombing against Rabaul itself. Rabaul, on the island of New Britain, was a major base and a staging and supply center for much of Japan's military activity in the southern Pacific. MacArthur's original plan, named ELKTON III, had envisaged capturing Rabaul; but as time went on, it became apparent that capture was not necessary, and the ultimate solution for dealing with Rabaul was to take it out of the war by cutting it off from outside aid or supply. The 1950s documentary TV series *Victory at Sea* referred to this operation as "Rings Around Rabaul."

THIS MONTH						
OCTOBER						
S	M	T	W	T	F	S
..	..	..	..	1	2	3
4	5	6	7	8	9	10
11	12	13	14	15	16	17
18	19	20	21	22	23	24
25	26	27	28	29	30	31
..	..	..	..	..	..	..

TUESDAY
13
OCTOBER

NEXT MONTH						
NOVEMBER						
S	M	T	W	T	F	S
1	2	3	4	5	6	7
8	9	10	11	12	13	14
15	16	17	18	19	20	21
22	23	24	25	26	27	28
29	30	..	..	..	..	..
..	..	..	..	..	..	..

1942

On 13 October 1942, the Newfoundland Railway passenger ferry SS *Caribou*, which ran between Port aux Basques, in the Dominion of Newfoundland, and North Sydney, Nova Scotia, departed North Sydney on one of three weekly SPAB (Sydney–Port aux Basque) convoys, with the minesweeper HMCS *Grandmère* in escort. While in the Cabot Strait in the dark hours of the morning of 14 October, *Caribou* was attacked and sunk by German submarine *U-69*, commanded by *Kapitänleutnant* Ulrich Gräf. As a civilian boat, *Caribou* had passengers aboard, mostly women and children. *U-69* fired one torpedo, whose explosion caused the ferry's boilers to go up, and *Caribou* sank within five minutes, trapping many people belowdecks. A total of 137 people died in the incident, which brought home the fact that the war had reached Canada's home front and was the war's most significant sinking in Canadian waters.

THIS MONTH						
OCTOBER						
S	M	T	W	T	F	S
1	2	3	4	5	6	7
8	9	10	11	12	13	14
15	16	17	18	19	20	21
22	23	24	25	26	27	28
29	30	31	..	..	..	..
..	..	..	..	..	..	..

SATURDAY
14
OCTOBER

1939

NEXT MONTH						
NOVEMBER						
S	M	T	W	T	F	S
..	..	..	1	2	3	4
5	6	7	8	9	10	11
12	13	14	15	16	17	18
19	20	21	22	23	24	25
26	27	28	29	30	..	..
..	..	..	..	..	..	..

On 14 October 1939, six days after beginning her second patrol, German submarine *U-47*, commanded by *Korvettenkapitän* Günther Prien, penetrated the Royal Navy's primary base at Scapa Flow, in Scotland. Although most of the Home Fleet was not at the base at the time, the battleship HMS *Royal Oak* was at anchor there, and *U-47* attacked *Royal Oak* with torpedoes. Her first two salvos did nothing except sever an anchor chain. The submarine's final salvo of three torpedoes struck the British warship, causing severe flooding. The ship took on a list of 15 degrees, flooding her open portholes and increasing the list to 45 degrees. Within 15 minutes of the first explosion, *Royal Oak* sank with the loss of more than 800 men. *U-47* would go on to make a total of nine successful patrols, sinking 30 commercial ships totaling 162,769 tons and one warship of 29,150 tons (HMS *Royal Oak*), and damaging eight commercial ships totaling 62,751 tons and one warship of 10,035 tons. She disappeared on 7 March 1941, on her tenth patrol, and was believed to have been sunk west of Ireland by the British destroyer HMS *Wolverine*.

THIS MONTH								TUESDAY		NEXT MONTH						
OCTOBER								**15**		NOVEMBER						
S	M	T	W	T	F	S				S	M	T	W	T	F	S
..	..	1	2	3	4	5		OCTOBER		..	..	..	..	..	1	2
6	7	8	9	10	11	12				3	4	5	6	7	8	9
13	14	15	16	17	18	19				10	11	12	13	14	15	16
20	21	22	23	24	25	26				17	18	19	20	21	22	23
27	28	29	30	31	..	..				24	25	26	27	28	29	30
..	..	..	..	..	..	..				..	..	..	..	..	..	..

1940

On 15 October 1940, Clarence Addison Dykstra became the first director of the United States Selective Service System that was created by the Selective Training and Service Act of 1940, passed by the U.S. Congress on 16 September. Registration of men aged 21 to 36 began the day after Dykstra's accession. Dykstra served only briefly in this capacity; on 19 March 1941, Executive Order 8716 established the National Defense Mediation Board, whose purpose was to resolve disputes between management and labor in defense industries, and Dykstra became its chairman.

THIS MONTH						
OCTOBER						
S	M	T	W	T	F	S
..	..	..	1	2	3	4
5	6	7	8	9	10	11
12	13	14	15	16	17	18
19	20	21	22	23	24	25
26	27	28	29	30	31	..
..	..	..	..	..	..	..

THURSDAY
16
OCTOBER

NEXT MONTH						
NOVEMBER						
S	M	T	W	T	F	S
..	..	..	..	..	..	1
2	3	4	5	6	7	8
9	10	11	12	13	14	15
16	17	18	19	20	21	22
23	24	25	26	27	28	29
30	..	..	..	..	..	..

1941

On 16 October 1941, as the German army neared Moscow, the Soviet government began decamping eastward to Samara, a city on the Volga River. Stalin, however, remained in Moscow to put up a brave front and show his solidarity with the citizens of the beleaguered city. 250,000 Muscovite women and teenagers, working frantically under the command of General Georgiy Zhukov, the Moscow area commander, excavated trenches and antitank moats around the city, moving almost three million cubic meters (106 million cubic feet) of earth using shovels, buckets, and wheelbarrows, with no help from powered machinery.

THIS MONTH						
OCTOBER						
S	M	T	W	T	F	S
..	..	..	1	2	3	4
5	6	7	8	9	10	11
12	13	14	15	16	17	18
19	20	21	22	23	24	25
26	27	28	29	30	31	..
..	..	..	..	..	..	..

FRIDAY
17
OCTOBER

1941

NEXT MONTH						
NOVEMBER						
S	M	T	W	T	F	S
..	..	..	..	..	..	1
2	3	4	5	6	7	8
9	10	11	12	13	14	15
16	17	18	19	20	21	22
23	24	25	26	27	28	29
30	..	..	..	..	..	..

On 17 October 1941, as a German submarine wolf pack was ravaging Allied Convoy SC-48 near Iceland, the American destroyer USS *Kearny*, DD-432, sent to assist the desperate Canadian defenders, arrived and began dropping depth charges on the U-boats. Early in the midwatch (from midnight to 0400 hours), *U-568* torpedoed the destroyer, tearing a hole in her starboard side. The crew confined flooding to the forward fire room, and the ship escaped the danger zone with power from the aft engine and fire room. She docked in Iceland for temporary repairs before returning to the United States. *Kearny* lost 11 men killed and 22 injured, the first American casualties of the war.

THIS MONTH						
OCTOBER						
S	M	T	W	T	F	S
1	2	3	4	5	6	7
8	9	10	11	12	13	14
15	16	17	18	19	20	21
22	23	24	25	26	27	28
29	30	31	..	..	..	..
..	..	..	..	..	..	..

WEDNESDAY
18
OCTOBER

NEXT MONTH						
NOVEMBER						
S	M	T	W	T	F	S
..	..	..	1	2	3	4
5	6	7	8	9	10	11
12	13	14	15	16	17	18
19	20	21	22	23	24	25
26	27	28	29	30	..	..
..	..	..	..	..	..	..

1944

On 18 October 1944, Adolf Hitler issued an order establishing the *Volkssturm* (literally "people's assault"), a national militia similar to the Home Guard in Britain. All men aged 16 to 60 years who were not already serving in a military unit were immediately conscripted for the *Volkssturm*. Joseph Goebbels and his propaganda machine depicted the *Volkssturm* as an outburst of the people's enthusiasm and will to resist. Morale, sagging after the Normandy invasion and years of Allied bombing, did spark a little; but without uniforms other than a black armband with the words "*Deutscher Volkssturm Wehrmacht*" and a series of silver pips pinned to the wearer's collar to indicate rank, and mostly without real weapons, the overall effect was little. In the Battle for Berlin, 40,000 members of the *Volkssturm* (mainly young boys aged 13–18 and old men) were used as a last-ditch attempt to defend Berlin; as elsewhere, their formations were devastated as many fought to the death rather than allow themselves to be captured by the Soviets.

OCTOBER

S	M	T	W	T	F	S
..	..	1	2	3	4	5
6	7	8	9	10	11	12
13	14	15	16	17	18	19
20	21	22	23	24	25	26
27	28	29	30	31	..	..
..	..	..	..	..	..	..

SATURDAY

19

OCTOBER

1940

NOVEMBER

S	M	T	W	T	F	S
..	..	..	..	..	1	2
3	4	5	6	7	8	9
10	11	12	13	14	15	16
17	18	19	20	21	22	23
24	25	26	27	28	29	30
..	..	..	..	..	..	..

On 19 October 1940, three three-engined Italian SM.82s bombers based on the island of Rhodes flew 3,000 miles to drop several tons of mixed small explosive and incendiary bombs on American-operated British-owned oil refineries near the capital city of Manama in the British Protectorate of Bahrain, damaging some of the plant facilities and setting half a dozen wells and some oil deposits on fire. The fourth plane in the raid lost contact with the other three and dropped its load on other targets in the vicinity of Manama. The raid, which also struck Dhahran in Saudi Arabia but caused little damage there, took the Allies completely by surprise, and all four planes continued unharmed and landed at Zula, Eritrea. Although the raid had done relatively minor damage to its targets, it forced the Allies to upgrade their defenses, further stretching their relatively meager resources.

OCTOBER						
S	M	T	W	T	F	S
1	2	3	4	5	6	7
8	9	10	11	12	13	14
15	16	17	18	19	20	21
22	23	24	25	26	27	28
29	30	31	..	..	..	..
..	..	..	..	..	..	..

THIS MONTH

FRIDAY
20
OCTOBER
1939

NEXT MONTH

NOVEMBER						
S	M	T	W	T	F	S
..	..	..	1	2	3	4
5	6	7	8	9	10	11
12	13	14	15	16	17	18
19	20	21	22	23	24	25
26	27	28	29	30	..	..
..	..	..	..	..	..	..

On 20 October 1939, the Phoney War was settling over Europe. The Phoney War, which lasted until April 1940, was a period during which the Western Allies exerted no major military effort against Germany despite the terms of military alliances by which the United Kingdom and France were obliged to assist Poland. The term "Phoney War" was probably coined by U.S. Senator William Borah of Idaho, who said in September, "There is something phoney about this war." Churchill referred to the period as the Twilight War; British wags called it Der Sitzkrieg ("the sitting war": a play on *Blitzkrieg*), the Bore War (a play on the Boer War), and *drôle de guerre* ("strange/funny war" in French).

The Phoney War quite probably ensured that the next six years would be filled with bloody conflict: Hitler's closest confidant *Generaloberst* Alfred Jodl said at the Nuremberg Trials, "If we did not collapse already in the year 1939 that was due only to the fact that during the Polish campaign, the approximately 110 French and British divisions in the West were held completely inactive against the 23 German divisions"; and *General der Kavallerie* Siegfried Westphal later wrote that if the French had attacked in force in September, the *Wehrmacht* "could only have held out for one or two weeks."

<table>
<tr><td colspan="7">THIS MONTH</td></tr>
<tr><td colspan="7">OCTOBER</td></tr>
</table>

THIS MONTH

OCTOBER

S	M	T	W	T	F	S
1	2	3	4	5	6	7
8	9	10	11	12	13	14
15	16	17	18	19	20	21
22	23	24	25	26	27	28
29	30	31	..	..	..	..
..	..	..	..	..	..	..

SATURDAY

21

OCTOBER

NEXT MONTH

NOVEMBER

S	M	T	W	T	F	S
..	..	..	1	2	3	4
5	6	7	8	9	10	11
12	13	14	15	16	17	18
19	20	21	22	23	24	25
26	27	28	29	30	..	..
..	..	..	..	..	..	..

1944

On 21 October 1944, the Battle of Aachen, begun on 2 October, came to a close as elements of the U.S. First Army, under the command of General Leland Hobbs (30th Infantry Division) and General Clarence Huebner (1st Infantry Division), occupied Aachen, the first major German city to be taken in the push to Berlin. Aachen, which had been fortified as part of Hitler's *Westwall* (known to the Allies as the Siegfried Line), had been evacuated of most civilians, and it was ferociously defended by much-reduced forces of the 246th and 183rd *Volksgrenadier* Divisions, the 49th and 12th Infantry Divisions, and elements of the 1st SS Panzer Division "*Leibstandarte SS Adolf Hitler*," under the overall command of *Oberst* Gerhard Wilck. The Americans had fielded nearly 100,000 men and lost about 5,000 killed, wounded, or missing; the Germans, numbering 13,000 *Wehrmacht* troops and 5,000 men of the *Volkssturm*, lost about the same number of casualties plus about 5,600 troops taken prisoner.

THIS MONTH						
OCTOBER						
S	M	T	W	T	F	S
..	..	..	..	1	2	3
4	5	6	7	8	9	10
11	12	13	14	15	16	17
18	19	20	21	22	23	24
25	26	27	28	29	30	31
..	..	..	..	..	..	..

THURSDAY
22
OCTOBER

NEXT MONTH						
NOVEMBER						
S	M	T	W	T	F	S
1	2	3	4	5	6	7
8	9	10	11	12	13	14
15	16	17	18	19	20	21
22	23	24	25	26	27	28
29	30	..	..	..	..	..
..	..	..	..	..	..	..

1942

On 22 October 1942, British submarine HMS *Seraph*, commanded by Lieutenant Norman "Bill" Jewell, landed a small party in collapsible two-man kayaks called folbots at Cherchel, about 50 miles west of Algiers. The party was led by American General Mark Clark, who at six feet three inches in height was wearing a full set of small bruises on his head from collisions with pipes, valves, and knobs, and who, while embarking into his folbot, got a dunking as the swell dumped the boat. (Clark dried himself off and ousted one of the men from another boat.) The purpose of the mission was to confer with Vichy French officials and Resistance leaders to determine whether the French would fight when the impending Allied invasion of French North Africa, code-named Operation TORCH and scheduled for 8 November, arrived.

THIS MONTH						
OCTOBER						
S	M	T	W	T	F	S
..	..	1	2	3	4	5
6	7	8	9	10	11	12
13	14	15	16	17	18	19
20	21	22	23	24	25	26
27	28	29	30	31	..	..
..	..	..	..	..	..	..

WEDNESDAY
23
OCTOBER

1940

NEXT MONTH						
NOVEMBER						
S	M	T	W	T	F	S
..	..	..	..	..	1	2
3	4	5	6	7	8	9
10	11	12	13	14	15	16
17	18	19	20	21	22	23
24	25	26	27	28	29	30
..	..	..	..	..	..	..

On 23 October 1940, Adolf Hitler met with Generalissimo Francisco Franco at Hendaye, near the Spanish-French border. Uppermost on Hitler's agenda was to convince Franco to bring Spain into the war on the side of the Axis, but Franco let the German dictator down, refusing to become a combatant. While remaining neutral, however, Spain did provide assistance to the Nazis, allowing a strong network of German spies to operate in the country and turning over to the *Abwehr*, the German counterintelligence service, Allied documents and other information that came into Spanish hands. The Allies made use of Spain's pseudo-neutral stance on several occasions, funneling agents (Garbo *et al.*) and disinformation through the country.

THIS MONTH

OCTOBER

S	M	T	W	T	F	S
..	..	..	..	1	2	3
4	5	6	7	8	9	10
11	12	13	14	15	16	17
18	19	20	21	22	23	24
25	26	27	28	29	30	31
..	..	..	..	..	..	..

NEXT MONTH

NOVEMBER

S	M	T	W	T	F	S
1	2	3	4	5	6	7
8	9	10	11	12	13	14
15	16	17	18	19	20	21
22	23	24	25	26	27	28
29	30	..	..	..	..	..
..	..	..	..	..	..	..

SATURDAY
24
OCTOBER

1942

On 24 October 1942, the greater part of Rear Admiral H. Kent Hewitt's Task Force 34, consisting of a number of troop transports, USS *Ranger* and four escort carriers, battleships USS *Massachusetts*, USS *New York*, and USS *Texas*, numerous destroyers, minesweepers, and auxiliary vessels, raised anchor in Casco Bay, Maine, bound for Fedala, Morocco. On the previous day, a smaller transport force had departed from Hampton, Roads, Virginia, for Safi and Mehdia, also in Morocco. Task Force 34, carrying 37,000 troops of the 2nd Armored Division and the 3rd and 9th Infantry Divisions, was the Western Task Force, one of three involved in Operation TORCH, the Mediterranean Theater of Operations' first blooding of American troops, whose D-Day was set for 8 November and whose official mission was to "occupy French Morocco and Algeria with a view to the earliest possible subsequent occupation of Tunisia." The Center Task Force, aimed at Oran, sailed from Britain under Commodore Thomas Troubridge and included the 509th Parachute Infantry Regiment, the 1st Infantry Division, and the 1st Armored Division, totaling 18,500 troops. The Eastern Task Force under Vice Admiral Sir Harold Burrough of the Royal Navy, whose target was Algiers, consisted of two brigades from the British 78th and the U.S. 34th Infantry Divisions, along with Britain's No. 1 and No. 6 Commando units, totaling 20,000 troops.

THIS MONTH						
OCTOBER						
S	M	T	W	T	F	S
1	2	3	4	5	6	7
8	9	10	11	12	13	14
15	16	17	18	19	20	21
22	23	24	25	26	27	28
29	30	31	..	..	..	..
..	..	..	..	..	..	..

WEDNESDAY
25
OCTOBER

NEXT MONTH						
NOVEMBER						
S	M	T	W	T	F	S
..	..	..	1	2	3	4
5	6	7	8	9	10	11
12	13	14	15	16	17	18
19	20	21	22	23	24	25
26	27	28	29	30	..	..
..	..	..	..	..	..	..

1944

On 25 October 1944, the U.S. Navy was caught virtually flat-footed by the Japanese in the Battle off Samar, an island at the northern end of Leyte Gulf in the Philippines. The Japanese had launched a three-pronged attack intending to destroy transport ships supplying troops and *matériel* for the American invasion of the island of Leyte. A Japanese force of capital ships, which the Americans believed to be retreating from an earlier engagement, turned and caught Task Unit 77.4.3 ("Taffy 3") completely by surprise. Taffy 3's few destroyers and destroyer escorts were neither armed nor armored to oppose the Japanese, but they attacked head-on in a desperate attempt to delay the enemy until other American forces could take action. Aircraft from the escort ("jeep") carriers of Taffy 1, 2, and 3 threw everything but the kitchen sink at the Japanese. Taffy 3 lost two jeep carriers, two destroyers, a destroyer escort, dozens of aircraft, and more than 1,000 lives. In exchange, the Americans damaged or sank three Japanese cruisers and wreaked enough havoc to persuade the Japanese commander, Vice Admiral Takeo Kurita, that he was about to become overmatched. He decided to withdraw instead of completing his mission against the invasion transports.

THIS MONTH						
OCTOBER						
S	M	T	W	T	F	S
..	..	..	..	1	2	3
4	5	6	7	8	9	10
11	12	13	14	15	16	17
18	19	20	21	22	23	24
25	26	27	28	29	30	31
..	..	..	..	..	..	..

MONDAY
26
OCTOBER

1942

NEXT MONTH						
NOVEMBER						
S	M	T	W	T	F	S
1	2	3	4	5	6	7
8	9	10	11	12	13	14
15	16	17	18	19	20	21
22	23	24	25	26	27	28
29	30	..	..	..	..	..
..	..	..	..	..	..	..

On 26 October 1942, the U.S. and Imperial Japanese Navies tangled in the Battle of the Santa Cruz Islands, the fourth carrier battle of the Pacific campaign of World War II and the fourth major naval engagement during the strategically important Guadalcanal Campaign, which had begun on 7 August and which lasted until 9 February 1943. The Japanese planned a major ground offensive on Guadalcanal for 20–25 October 1942. To support the offensive, a powerful Japanese carrier force moved into a position near the southern Solomon Islands. On the morning of 26 October, each navy's aerial reconnaissance discovered the other's carrier force. After an exchange of air attacks, the Allied ships were forced to retreat with USS *Hornet* sunk, USS *Enterprise* heavily damaged, one destroyer sunk and two damaged, 81 aircraft lost, and 266 men killed. The Japanese carrier *Zuihō* suffered damage sufficient to render her unable to land aircraft, and *Shōkaku* took serious internal damage. One cruiser was also heavily damaged, several destroyers were somewhat damaged, 99 aircraft went down, and 400 to 500 men were killed. Because most of their losses were among their highly trained and virtually irreplaceable aircrews, the Japanese left the field with a Pyrrhic victory that gave the Americans a long-term strategic advantage despite their losses.

THIS MONTH						
OCTOBER						
S	M	T	W	T	F	S
..	..	..	1	2	3	4
5	6	7	8	9	10	11
12	13	14	15	16	17	18
19	20	21	22	23	24	25
26	27	28	29	30	31	..
..	..	..	..	..	..	..

MONDAY
27
OCTOBER
1941

NEXT MONTH						
NOVEMBER						
S	M	T	W	T	F	S
..	..	..	..	..	..	1
2	3	4	5	6	7	8
9	10	11	12	13	14	15
16	17	18	19	20	21	22
23	24	25	26	27	28	29
30	..	..	..	..	..	..

On 27 October 1941, forces of Germany's Army Group South, commanded by *General* Erich von Manstein, reached Sevastopol in the Crimea. After two failed assaults, von Manstein would elect to besiege the city; his siege would last until 4 July 1942. While Army Group South was engaged in the Crimea, Army Group North's advance on Moscow had been slowed, and in some places stopped entirely, by mud. Although the leading tanks had reached the outskirts of the city by 27 October, the coming of winter had already doomed Germany's hopes of destroying the Soviet Union in 1941.

THIS MONTH							MONDAY	NEXT MONTH						
OCTOBER							**28**	NOVEMBER						
S	M	T	W	T	F	S		S	M	T	W	T	F	S
..	..	1	2	3	4	5		..	..	..	..	..	1	2
6	7	8	9	10	11	12	OCTOBER	3	4	5	6	7	8	9
13	14	15	16	17	18	19		10	11	12	13	14	15	16
20	21	22	23	24	25	26	1940	17	18	19	20	21	22	23
27	28	29	30	31	..	..		24	25	26	27	28	29	30
..	..	..	..	..	..	..		..	..	..	..	..	..	..

On 28 October 1940, Italy's ambassador in Athens, Emanuele Grazzi, handed an ultimatum from Mussolini to Greek Prime Minister Ioannis Metaxas, who was in actuality a dictator. It demanded free passage for Italian troops to occupy unspecified strategic points inside Greece. Although Greece had been friendly and had maintained trade relations with Italy, Metaxas rejected the ultimatum with the words *"Alors, c'est la guerre"* (French for "Then it's war"). He was echoing the will of the Greek people to resist. The Italians apparently expected Metaxas' reply to be in the negative; within hours, they launched their first attacks against Greece from Italian-held Albania to begin the Greco-Italian War. Initially the Greeks prevailed, but Germany intervened on 6 April 1941, transforming the Greco-Italian War into the Battle of Greece and bringing the conflict to a close on 23 April with a victory for the Axis.

OCTOBER						
S	M	T	W	T	F	S
..	..	..	..	1	2	3
4	5	6	7	8	9	10
11	12	13	14	15	16	17
18	19	20	21	22	23	24
25	26	27	28	29	30	31
..	..	..	..	..	..	..

THURSDAY
29
OCTOBER
1942

NOVEMBER						
S	M	T	W	T	F	S
1	2	3	4	5	6	7
8	9	10	11	12	13	14
15	16	17	18	19	20	21
22	23	24	25	26	27	28
29	30	..	..	..	..	..
..	..	..	..	..	..	..

On 29 October 1942, while German troops were massacring some 16,000 Jews in Pinsk, Byelorussia, leading British political figures and clergymen held a public meeting, chaired by the Archbishop of Canterbury, to register their outrage over Nazi Germany's persecution of Jews. Winston Churchill sent a message to be read at the meeting, excoriating Germany. The power of this protest meeting soon had an effect: shortly thereafter, when the Gestapo removed more than 100 Jewish children from a children's home in Brussels for deportation, staff members refused to leave the children and were taken with them to a deportation camp. Protests rained down on the Germans, including one from the secretary-general of the Belgian Ministry of Justice. The Germans returned the children and staff to the home.

THIS MONTH

OCTOBER

S	M	T	W	T	F	S
..	..	1	2	3	4	5
6	7	8	9	10	11	12
13	14	15	16	17	18	19
20	21	22	23	24	25	26
27	28	29	30	31	..	..
..	..	..	..	..	..	..

WEDNESDAY
30
OCTOBER

NEXT MONTH

NOVEMBER

S	M	T	W	T	F	S
..	..	..	..	..	1	2
3	4	5	6	7	8	9
10	11	12	13	14	15	16
17	18	19	20	21	22	23
24	25	26	27	28	29	30
..	..	..	..	..	..	..

1940

On 30 October 1940, in the midst of a hotly contested election campaign, Franklin D. Roosevelt promised to keep American troops out of the war, saying to a crowd in Boston, "I have said this before but I shall say it again and again and again. Your boys are not going to be sent into foreign wars." Newspaper editorials picked up the same spirit of denial. In February 1941, an Iowa paper said, "No one expects the United States Infantry to leave the borders of the United States, even if this country should get into war."

THIS MONTH							FRIDAY		NEXT MONTH						

OCTOBER

S	M	T	W	T	F	S
..	..	..	1	2	3	4
5	6	7	8	9	10	11
12	13	14	15	16	17	18
19	20	21	22	23	24	25
26	27	28	29	30	31	..
..	..	..	..	..	..	..

FRIDAY
31
OCTOBER

NOVEMBER

S	M	T	W	T	F	S
..	..	..	..	..	..	1
2	3	4	5	6	7	8
9	10	11	12	13	14	15
16	17	18	19	20	21	22
23	24	25	26	27	28	29
30	..	..	..	..	..	..

1941

On 31 October 1941, while escorting Convoy HX-156 from Newfoundland to Iceland, the U.S. destroyer *Reuben James,* captained by Lieutenant Commander Heywood L. Edwards, was defending the convoy against a known submarine wolfpack. As she was shielding an ammunition transport from attack, *Reuben James* became the first American ship sunk by hostile action in the war when at about 0525 hours she was attacked by *U-552*, commanded by *Kapitänleutnant* Erich Topp. A torpedo struck the ship forward, setting off a magazine whose explosion blew off her entire bow. The bow section sank immediately, and the remainder of the ship followed it five minutes later. Of the 159 men in *Reuben James'* complement, only 44 survived. Lieutenant Commander Edwards was not among them.[2]

2. Sadly, most of the country ignored the sinking. One who did not was folk singer Woody Guthrie, who immediately after the incident wrote the now famous song "The Sinking of the *Reuben James*":

Tell me, what were their names?
Tell me, what were their names?
Did you have a friend on the good *Reuben James*?

NOVEMBER						
S	M	T	W	T	F	S
..	..	..	..	..	..	1
2	3	4	5	6	7	8
9	10	11	12	13	14	15
16	17	18	19	20	21	22
23	24	25	26	27	28	29
30	..	..	..	..	..	..

SATURDAY
1
NOVEMBER

DECEMBER						
S	M	T	W	T	F	S
..	1	2	3	4	5	6
7	8	9	10	11	12	13
14	15	16	17	18	19	20
21	22	23	24	25	26	27
28	29	30	31	..	..	..

1941

On 1 November 1941, in a clear sign that the U.S. Administration viewed America's imminent entry into the war as inevitable, President Franklin D. Roosevelt announced that the U.S. Coast Guard would thenceforward be under the direction of the U.S. Navy. The Coast Guard, because of its unique mission configuration, operated jointly under the President and the Navy Department, and its transition to full control by the Navy was something that normally would happen only in wartime.

THIS MONTH						
NOVEMBER						
S	M	T	W	T	F	S
..	1	2	3	4	5	6
7	8	9	10	11	12	13
14	15	16	17	18	19	20
21	22	23	24	25	26	27
28	29	30	..	..	..	..
..	..	..	..	..	..	..

TUESDAY
2
NOVEMBER
1943

NEXT MONTH						
DECEMBER						
S	M	T	W	T	F	S
..	..	..	1	2	3	4
5	6	7	8	9	10	11
12	13	14	15	16	17	18
19	20	21	22	23	24	25
26	27	28	29	30	31	..
..	..	..	..	..	..	..

On 2 November 1943, Operation CHERRY BLOSSOM, the Allied campaign to capture the Pacific island of Bougainville, was in its second day. In the dark morning hours, the U.S. Navy's Task Force 39, commanded by Rear Admiral Aaron S. "Tip" Merrill and comprising four light cruisers (CruDiv 12) and eight destroyers (DesDiv 45 and DesDiv 46), engaged a powerful but uncoordinated Japanese force made up of two light cruisers, two heavy cruisers, and six destroyers, assembled from whatever ships were available at Rabaul and dispatched under the command of Admiral Sentaro Omori. This action, the Battle of Empress Augusta Bay, resulted in a decisive American victory, but the U.S. Navy did not escape unscathed. The destroyer USS *Foote* took a torpedo that blew off the ship's stern and killed 19 men (the only Americans killed in the engagement), wounding another 17. Three other ships were lightly or moderately damaged. The Japanese lost one light cruiser and one destroyer sunk, two cruisers heavily damaged, 25 aircraft shot down, and an unreliably recorded number of men, possibly as high as 658, killed.

THIS MONTH								FRIDAY		NEXT MONTH						
NOVEMBER								**3**		DECEMBER						
S	M	T	W	T	F	S				S	M	T	W	T	F	S
..	..	..	1	2	3	4				..	..	..	..	..	1	2
5	6	7	8	9	10	11				3	4	5	6	7	8	9
12	13	14	15	16	17	18		NOVEMBER		10	11	12	13	14	15	16
19	20	21	22	23	24	25				17	18	19	20	21	22	23
26	27	28	29	30	..	..				24	25	26	27	28	29	30
..	..	..	..	..	..	..				31	..	..	..	..	..	..

1944

On 3 November 1944, the Japanese launched the first of more than 9,300 hydrogen-filled balloon bombs carrying loads varying from a 12-kilogram (26 lb) incendiary device to one 15 kg (33 lb) antipersonnel bomb and four 5 kg (11 lb) incendiary devices. The brainchild of Technical Major Teiji Takada and his colleagues at the Imperial Japanese Army's Ninth Army's Number Nine Research Laboratory, the balloons were designed to travel eastward on the jet stream for three days until they were over Canada and the United States, at which time their control systems would release the bombs.

American aircraft shot down a small number of the balloons, but in the event fewer than 300 reached their destinations.

The U.S. government suppressed reporting of balloon bomb incidents lest the enemy gain the impression that the devices were an effective weapon and build many more of them. They did little harm in any case, but the U.S. Army's 555th Parachute Infantry Battalion suffered one fatality and 22 injuries in fighting bomb-ignited fires.

On Saturday, 5 May 1945, a pregnant woman and five children she was accompanying on a church outing discovered a balloon bomb that had landed in a forest near Bly, Oregon. When its payload exploded, they became the only people known to have been killed in the continental United States by direct enemy action in World War II.

THIS MONTH

NOVEMBER

S	M	T	W	T	F	S
..	..	..	1	2	3	4
5	6	7	8	9	10	11
12	13	14	15	16	17	18
19	20	21	22	23	24	25
26	27	28	29	30	..	..
..	..	..	..	..	..	..

SATURDAY
4
NOVEMBER

1939

NEXT MONTH

DECEMBER

S	M	T	W	T	F	S
..	..	..	..	..	1	2
3	4	5	6	7	8	9
10	11	12	13	14	15	16
17	18	19	20	21	22	23
24	25	26	27	28	29	30
31	..	..	..	..	..	..

On 4 November 1939, the U.S. Congress passed the last of a series of Neutrality Acts intended to keep America out of foreign wars. The Neutrality Act of 1935, which was to expire six months after its enactment, had imposed a general embargo on trading in arms and war materials with all parties in a war and declared that American citizens traveling on the ships of nations at war did so at their own risk.

The Neutrality Act of 1936 renewed the provisions of the 1935 Act, adding a provision that forbade loans or extensions of credit to belligerents.

The Neutrality Act of 1937 included the provisions of the earlier Acts, this time without an expiration date, and extended them to cover civil wars.[1] It also prohibited U.S. ships from carrying any passengers or articles to belligerents, and it forbade U.S. citizens from traveling on belligerent nations' ships.

In a concession to President Roosevelt, the 1937 Act added a provision allowing "cash and carry" sales of materials and supplies to belligerents, who must immediately pay in cash and arrange to transport their purchases without U.S. assistance. (It was thought that since Britain and France were the only nations that controlled the seas, this provision would aid them without aiding Germany.) This "cash and carry" provision expired early in 1939. The Neutrality Act of 1939 reinstated it, thus effectively ending the arms embargo. It also forbade American citizens and ships to enter war zones.

---

1. When the Act was passed in May 1937, the Spanish Civil War had been raging for 10 months. The extension to cover civil wars was included at the request of President Franklin D. Roosevelt, who had in January been rebuffed when he asked American arms manufacturers to impose a moral embargo.

TUESDAY
5
NOVEMBER
1940

On 5 November 1940, the German heavy cruiser ("pocket battleship") *Admiral Scheer* attacked the 37 merchant vessels of Convoy HX-84, bound for Britain from Halifax, Nova Scotia, with Armed Merchant Cruiser HMS *Jervis Bay* for their sole escort. *Jervis Bay*, launched in 1922 as a passenger liner and refitted with seven 1898-vintage 6-inch guns and two 3-inch guns, was hopelessly outgunned and outranged by *Admiral Scheer*'s 280-mm (11-inch) guns, but Captain Edward Fegen ordered the convoy to scatter and set a course straight towards the German, with his guns blazing, to draw its fire. Inevitably, *Jervis Bay* went to the bottom, taking Fegen and all but 66 of his 253 crewmen down with her. *Admiral Scheer* went on to sink five of the convoy's merchant ships, but *Jervis Bay*'s sacrifice bought enough time for the remaining ships to escape and earned Fegen a posthumous Victoria Cross.

THIS MONTH						
NOVEMBER						
S	M	T	W	T	F	S
..	..	..	..	..	..	1
2	3	4	5	6	7	8
9	10	11	12	13	14	15
16	17	18	19	20	21	22
23	24	25	26	27	28	29
30	..	..	..	..	..	..

THURSDAY
6
NOVEMBER

NEXT MONTH						
DECEMBER						
S	M	T	W	T	F	S
..	1	2	3	4	5	6
7	8	9	10	11	12	13
14	15	16	17	18	19	20
21	22	23	24	25	26	27
28	29	30	31	..	..	..

1941

On 6 November 1941, Soviet leader Joseph Stalin addressed his nation's people for only the second time since becoming General Secretary of the Communist Party's Central Committee in April 1922. (He had given his first public address four months earlier, on 3 July.) He announced that although 350,000 Soviet troops had been killed so far in the fight against Germany, the Germans had lost 4.5 million soldiers and that Soviet victory was near. The German body count he reported was a huge exaggeration designed to bolster the people's morale.

THIS MONTH						
NOVEMBER						
S	M	T	W	T	F	S
..	..	1	2	3	4	5
6	7	8	9	10	11	12
13	14	15	16	17	18	19
20	21	22	23	24	25	26
27	28	29	30	..	..	..
..	..	..	..	..	..	..

TUESDAY
7
NOVEMBER
1944

NEXT MONTH						
DECEMBER						
S	M	T	W	T	F	S
..	..	..	..	1	2	3
4	5	6	7	8	9	10
11	12	13	14	15	16	17
18	19	20	21	22	23	24
25	26	27	28	29	30	31
..	..	..	..	..	..	..

On 7 November 1944, the American public went to the polls and returned President Franklin Delano Roosevelt to office for his fourth term. FDR, the only U.S. President to serve more than two terms, would not survive to see the end of the war; he died at Warm Springs, Georgia, in April 1945.

THIS MONTH															NEXT MONTH					
NOVEMBER															DECEMBER					
S	M	T	W	T	F	S									S	M	T	W	T	F	S
1	2	3	4	5	6	7									..	..	1	2	3	4	5
8	9	10	11	12	13	14									6	7	8	9	10	11	12
15	16	17	18	19	20	21									13	14	15	16	17	18	19
22	23	24	25	26	27	28									20	21	22	23	24	25	26
29	30	..	..	..	..	..									27	28	29	30	31	..	..

SUNDAY
8
NOVEMBER
1942

On 8 November 1942, American and British troops of Operation TORCH stumbled ashore at three major landing sites on the north coast of Algeria and Morocco to begin the African campaign that would eventually see the Royal Italian Army and Germany's Afrika Korps defeated in detail. Luck was with the Americans and British in spades: execution of the offensive was confused, clumsy, and fraught with disastrous mistakes, and had the French been well prepared and determined to fight, the Allies would have been thrown back into the sea. French resistance, nonexistent at some points but stiff and quite deadly at others, petered out to end completely on 16 November.

According to historian Rick Atkinson, Operation TORCH "revealed profound shortcomings in leadership, tactics, equipment, martial *élan*, and common sense." Among other problems, the troops who were put ashore were ill trained and utterly unprepared for what they were to face. (One Allied commander remarked that his men appeared to have been taught how to surrender, not how to fight.)

Of the 107,000 Allied troops deployed, casualties numbered 2,225, including 1,100 dead (of whom 337 were American). The French lost about 1,350 killed and about 2,000 wounded. Surprisingly, although the contretemps of war was not forgotten, the traditional American-French amity was quickly restored: when U.S. Rear Admiral Kent Hewitt extended his hand to French Vice Admiral François Michelier and said that the U.S. Navy regretted firing on the Tricolor, Michelier replied, "You had your orders, and you carried them out. I had mine, and I carried them out. Now I am ready to cooperate in every way possible."

THIS MONTH						
NOVEMBER						
S	M	T	W	T	F	S
..	..	..	..	..	..	1
2	3	4	5	6	7	8
9	10	11	12	13	14	15
16	17	18	19	20	21	22
23	24	25	26	27	28	29
30	..	..	..	..	..	..

SUNDAY

9

NOVEMBER

1941

NEXT MONTH						
DECEMBER						
S	M	T	W	T	F	S
..	1	2	3	4	5	6
7	8	9	10	11	12	13
14	15	16	17	18	19	20
21	22	23	24	25	26	27
28	29	30	31	..	..	..
..	..	..	..	..	..	..

On 9 November 1941, Britain's Force K, under the command of Royal Navy Captain W. G. Agnew, attacked Italy's Convoy Beta in the dark morning hours. The convoy, commanded by Captain Ugo Bisciani, comprised two tankers carrying 17,281 tons of fuel and five cargo ships loaded with 389 vehicles, 34,473 tons of munitions and fuel in barrels, and reinforcements for the Italian and German forces in Libya. Force K comprised two light cruisers and two destroyers, while the convoy was escorted by a close force of six destroyers and a distant force of two heavy cruisers and four destroyers. Of the close force, the destroyer *Fulmine* took enough damage that it capsized and sank; the distant force fired a few ineffective rounds but took no other action. In addition to *Fulmine*, Force K sank all seven of the convoy's merchant ships while taking no losses itself; the convoy's destruction left the Italian high command with no choice except to consider Tripoli "practically blockaded."

THIS MONTH						
NOVEMBER						
S	M	T	W	T	F	S
1	2	3	4	5	6	7
8	9	10	11	12	13	14
15	16	17	18	19	20	21
22	23	24	25	26	27	28
29	30	..	..	..	..	..
..	..	..	..	..	..	..

TUESDAY
10
NOVEMBER
1942

NEXT MONTH						
DECEMBER						
S	M	T	W	T	F	S
..	..	1	2	3	4	5
6	7	8	9	10	11	12
13	14	15	16	17	18	19
20	21	22	23	24	25	26
27	28	29	30	31	..	..
..	..	..	..	..	..	..

On 10 November 1942, Germany launched *Fall Anton* (Case Anton), the invasion and occupation of Vichy-controlled southern France. *Fall Anton* was a violation of the Second Compiègne Armistice, signed in June 1940, in which it had been agreed that the Germans would occupy only France's northern and western portions.

The invasion, which had been anticipated by Admiral François Darlan, the French commander in Algiers, should he surrender to the forces of Operation TORCH, was the Nazis' response to an armistice signed by the spineless Darlan, who two days later reneged on his promises under pressure from Vichy and withdrew his cease-fire order. U.S. Major General Mark Clark promptly put Darlan, whose cowardly waffling was almost a household word among Allied commanders, under house arrest and gave his guards a very complete description of his person, ordering them to shoot him if he tried to escape. (As the TORCH campaign progressed, Darlan signed and repudiated two more treaties and had signed and tried to renege on a third before finally bowing to the inevitable.)

Fall Anton was completed when the Germans reached the Mediterranean on the evening of 11 November, with the only active French resistance having consisted of radio broadcasts protesting the Compiègne Armistice.

THIS MONTH						
NOVEMBER						
S	M	T	W	T	F	S
..	..	..	..	..	1	2
3	4	5	6	7	8	9
10	11	12	13	14	15	16
17	18	19	20	21	22	23
24	25	26	27	28	29	30
..	..	..	..	..	..	..

MONDAY
11
NOVEMBER

1940

NEXT MONTH						
DECEMBER						
S	M	T	W	T	F	S
1	2	3	4	5	6	7
8	9	10	11	12	13	14
15	16	17	18	19	20	21
22	23	24	25	26	27	28
29	30	31	..	..	..	..
..	..	..	..	..	..	..

On 11 November 1940, Britain's Royal Navy launched the first all-aircraft ship-to-ship naval attack in history against the battle fleet of Italy's *Regia Marina,* which was at anchor in the harbor at Taranto. At 2100 hours, the aircraft carrier HMS *Illustrious* launched 12 obsolescent Fairey Swordfish biplane torpedo bombers led by Lieutenant Commander M. W. Williamson of No. 815 Squadron, followed 90 minutes later by nine more Swordfish. The aircraft sank the battleship *Conte di Cavour* and damaged the battleships *Caio Duilio* and *Littorio.* The plane whose torpedo did in *Conte di Cavour* was promptly shot down by its target's AA guns and its two-man crew taken prisoner, and one other plane was shot down with the deaths of its crew. In addition to the three battleships, the attack damaged two cruisers and a destroyer as well as several auxiliary vessels. The Italians also lost two aircraft destroyed, 59 men killed, and about 60 men wounded.

The British attack, which had successfully used torpedoes despite the shallow depth of the harbor, was studied carefully by Japanese planners, who were already preparing for the Pearl Harbor attack that would finally come about a year later.

THIS MONTH

NOVEMBER

S	M	T	W	T	F	S
..	..	..	1	2	3	4
5	6	7	8	9	10	11
12	13	14	15	16	17	18
19	20	21	22	23	24	25
26	27	28	29	30	..	..
..	..	..	..	..	..	..

NEXT MONTH

DECEMBER

S	M	T	W	T	F	S
..	..	..	..	..	1	2
3	4	5	6	7	8	9
10	11	12	13	14	15	16
17	18	19	20	21	22	23
24	25	26	27	28	29	30
31	..	..	..	..	..	..

SUNDAY
12
NOVEMBER

1944

On 12 November 1944, the Royal Air Force launched Operation CATE-CHISM. 30 Avro Lancaster heavy bombers from No. 9 and No. 617 Squadrons (accompanied by a film unit aircraft from No. 463 Squadron of the Royal Australian Air Force), each equipped with one 12,000-pound "Tallboy" bomb, attacked the German battleship *Tirpitz*, which was at anchor in Tromsø, Norway. This, the ninth British attempt to sink *Tirpitz*, was successful. At least two bombs struck *Tirpitz*, which suffered a violent internal explosion and capsized. The kill was attributed to the bomb dropped by No. 617 Squadron's commanding officer, Group Captain Willie Tait. Approximately 1,000 of the 1,900 men on board *Tirpitz* were killed or injured, and one No. 9 Squadron Lancaster was damaged by flak but landed safely in neutral Sweden, where it was interned along with its uninjured crew.

THIS MONTH						
NOVEMBER						
S	M	T	W	T	F	S
1	2	3	4	5	6	7
8	9	10	11	12	13	14
15	16	17	18	19	20	21
22	23	24	25	26	27	28
29	30	..	..	..	..	..
..	..	..	..	..	..	..

FRIDAY
13
NOVEMBER
1942

NEXT MONTH						
DECEMBER						
S	M	T	W	T	F	S
..	..	1	2	3	4	5
6	7	8	9	10	11	12
13	14	15	16	17	18	19
20	21	22	23	24	25	26
27	28	29	30	31	..	..
..	..	..	..	..	..	..

On 13 November 1942, two U.S. Navy task forces under the overall command of Rear Admiral Daniel J. Callaghan engaged a Japanese fleet under Vice Admiral Hiroaki Abe in the Naval Battle of Guadalcanal. Fighting continued for three days, yielding an American strategic victory. 13 November, a Friday, is remembered as the day in which the American light cruiser USS *Juneau* was torpedoed and sunk by Japanese submarine *I-26*, leaving only about 100 of *Juneau*'s 697-man crew alive. Left to fend for themselves in the open sea, the survivors numbered only ten when rescued eight days later. Among *Juneau*'s dead were all five sons of Thomas and Alleta Sullivan: George Thomas (aged 27), Francis Henry (26), Joseph Eugene (24), Madison Abel (23), and Albert Leo (20). They had been permitted to serve on the same ship in spite of the U.S. Navy's policy of separating siblings.[2]

---

2. News of the deaths of all five Sullivan brothers became a rallying point for the war effort, with posters and speeches honoring their sacrifice. War bond drives and other patriotic campaigns culminated in the film that inspired *Saving Private Ryan*, 1944's *The Fighting Sullivans*, starring Anne Baxter and Thomas Mitchell. The destroyer USS *The Sullivans* (DD-537) was commissioned on 30 September 1943 and served until 1965.

THIS MONTH								SUNDAY		NEXT MONTH						

THIS MONTH

NOVEMBER

S	M	T	W	T	F	S
..	1	2	3	4	5	6
7	8	9	10	11	12	13
14	15	16	17	18	19	20
21	22	23	24	25	26	27
28	29	30	..	..	..	..
..	..	..	..	..	..	..

SUNDAY
14
NOVEMBER
1943

NEXT MONTH

DECEMBER

S	M	T	W	T	F	S
..	..	..	1	2	3	4
5	6	7	8	9	10	11
12	13	14	15	16	17	18
19	20	21	22	23	24	25
26	27	28	29	30	31	..
..	..	..	..	..	..	..

On 14 November 1943, U.S. President Franklin D. Roosevelt, Generals George Marshall and Henry "Hap" Arnold, Admirals William Leahy and Ernest King, and more than a hundred distinguished politicians and military strategists came under fire while traveling to the Tehran Conference on board the battleship *Iowa*. During a torpedo drill, the destroyer *William D. Porter* accidentally launched a live torpedo while targeting *Iowa*'s No. 2 magazine. *Iowa* immediately executed evasive maneuvers, and the torpedo exploded in wake turbulence 1200 feet aft of the ship. Afterward, General Arnold leaned over to Fleet Commander Admiral King and asked, "Tell me, Ernest, does this happen often in your Navy?"

<table>
<tr><td colspan="7">THIS MONTH</td></tr>
<tr><td colspan="7">NOVEMBER</td></tr>
</table>

THIS MONTH

NOVEMBER

S	M	T	W	T	F	S
1	2	3	4	5	6	7
8	9	10	11	12	13	14
15	16	17	18	19	20	21
22	23	24	25	26	27	28
29	30	..	..	..	..	..
..	..	..	..	..	..	..

SUNDAY

15

NOVEMBER

1942

NEXT MONTH

DECEMBER

S	M	T	W	T	F	S
..	..	1	2	3	4	5
6	7	8	9	10	11	12
13	14	15	16	17	18	19
20	21	22	23	24	25	26
27	28	29	30	31	..	..
..	..	..	..	..	..	..

On 15 November 1942, the Naval Battle of Guadalcanal came to an end with a retreat ordered by the Japanese commander, Vice Admiral Hiroaki Abe. The U.S. Navy suffered the loss of two light cruisers, seven destroyers, 36 aircraft, and 1,732 lives (including Rear Admirals Daniel Callahan and Norman Scott, the only two U.S. Navy admirals to be killed in a surface engagement). The battle, which was a tactical defeat but a strategic victory for the U.S. because it left the Americans in control of the sea around Guadalcanal, had cost the Japanese Imperial Navy two battleships, three destroyers, 11 transports, 64 aircraft, and approximately 1,900 lives.

THIS MONTH						
NOVEMBER						
S	M	T	W	T	F	S
..	..	..	..	..	..	1
2	3	4	5	6	7	8
9	10	11	12	13	14	15
16	17	18	19	20	21	22
23	24	25	26	27	28	29
30	..	..	..	..	..	..

SUNDAY
16
NOVEMBER

NEXT MONTH						
DECEMBER						
S	M	T	W	T	F	S
..	1	2	3	4	5	6
7	8	9	10	11	12	13
14	15	16	17	18	19	20
21	22	23	24	25	26	27
28	29	30	31	..	..	..
..	..	..	..	..	..	..

1941

On 16 November 1941, in the Mediterranean Sea about 50 miles east of Gibraltar, near the location where the aircraft carrier HMS *Ark Royal* had been torpedoed and sunk only days earlier by *U-81*, the British corvette HMS *Marigold*, with Lieutenant J. Renwick in command, engaged U-boat *U-433*, which was commanded by *Oberleutnant* Hans Ey and was on its second patrol of the war. The corvette dropped depth charges, damaging the boat severely and forcing it to the surface, where the Germans opened the scuttling cocks and abandoned ship. *Marigold* shelled and machine-gunned the U-boat as its crew were abandoning it, killing six men. After *U-433* sank, *Marigold* rescued and took prisoner 38 German officers and sailors.

THIS MONTH

NOVEMBER

S	M	T	W	T	F	S
..	..	..	1	2	3	4
5	6	7	8	9	10	11
12	13	14	15	16	17	18
19	20	21	22	23	24	25
26	27	28	29	30	..	..
..	..	..	..	..	..	..

FRIDAY
17
NOVEMBER

1944

NEXT MONTH

DECEMBER

S	M	T	W	T	F	S
..	..	..	..	..	1	2
3	4	5	6	7	8	9
10	11	12	13	14	15	16
17	18	19	20	21	22	23
24	25	26	27	28	29	30
31	..	..	..	..	..	..

On 17 November 1944, after a fierce 20-day battle with German troops, Albanian partisans liberated their capital city, Tirana. Albanian communists, who had formed at Berat in October, attacked the city and took over control, an action that resulted in secure ties with Tito's Yugoslavian communists, who enjoyed British military and diplomatic support, thereby guaranteeing that Belgrade would play a key role in Albania's postwar administration.

THIS MONTH						
NOVEMBER						
S	M	T	W	T	F	S
..	..	..	..	..	1	2
3	4	5	6	7	8	9
10	11	12	13	14	15	16
17	18	19	20	21	22	23
24	25	26	27	28	29	30
..	..	..	..	..	..	..

MONDAY
18
NOVEMBER

NEXT MONTH						
DECEMBER						
S	M	T	W	T	F	S
1	2	3	4	5	6	7
8	9	10	11	12	13	14
15	16	17	18	19	20	21
22	23	24	25	26	27	28
29	30	31	..	..	..	..

1940

On 18 November 1940, the Italian submarine *Maggiore Baracca,* under the command of Lieutenant Commander Enrico Bertarelli, torpedoed and sank the British cargo steamer SS *Lillian Moller,* under Master William Fowler, which had become separated from Convoy SL-53, bound from Sierra Leone to Great Britain. The sinking occurred northwest of Ireland, with the loss of all hands. The *Lillian Moller* was based in Hong Kong and carried a crew of 49. The *Baracca* was named for Italian World War I ace Major Francesco Baracca, whose logo of a prancing horse was adopted by Enzo Ferrari in 1929 as the logo for the *Scuderia Ferrari* racing team and later for his car company.

THIS MONTH								WEDNESDAY		NEXT MONTH						

NOVEMBER

S	M	T	W	T	F	S
..	..	..	..	..	..	1
2	3	4	5	6	7	8
9	10	11	12	13	14	15
16	17	18	19	20	21	22
23	24	25	26	27	28	29
30	..	..	..	..	..	..

WEDNESDAY
19
NOVEMBER
1941

DECEMBER

S	M	T	W	T	F	S
..	1	2	3	4	5	6
7	8	9	10	11	12	13
14	15	16	17	18	19	20
21	22	23	24	25	26	27
28	29	30	31	..	..	..
..	..	..	..	..	..	..

On 19 November 1941, the Australian cruiser HMAS *Sydney* encountered the German Armed Merchant Cruiser *Kormoran*, which was disguised as a Dutch steamer named *Straat Malakka*. *Kormoran* opened fire without warning at 1730 hours, and both ships took serious damage in a 20-minute exchange of torpedoes and 6-inch shells. The Germans abandoned *Kormoran* at about 2100 hours due to raging fires; at midnight, the ship was still afloat and was scuttled with the loss of 82 lives. *Sydney* sank shortly after midnight with the loss of all 645 hands. Various Allied ships rescued many of *Kormoran*'s survivors from lifeboats and rafts, and other craft of the emergency flotilla drifted ashore. A total of 317 survivors became prisoners of war.

THIS MONTH						
NOVEMBER						
S	M	T	W	T	F	S
..	1	2	3	4	5	6
7	8	9	10	11	12	13
14	15	16	17	18	19	20
21	22	23	24	25	26	27
28	29	30	..	..	..	..
..	..	..	..	..	..	..

SATURDAY
20
NOVEMBER
1943

NEXT MONTH						
DECEMBER						
S	M	T	W	T	F	S
..	..	..	1	2	3	4
5	6	7	8	9	10	11
12	13	14	15	16	17	18
19	20	21	22	23	24	25
26	27	28	29	30	31	..
..	..	..	..	..	..	..

On 20 November 1943, after a naval bombardment, troops of the U.S. 2nd Marine Division, the first of an eventual 35,000 American troops to be landed, began an amphibious assault on the Tarawa Atoll in the Gilbert Islands.

Operation GALVANIC had been poorly planned, without proper attention paid to the tides in the area, and most of the landing craft ran aground on an offshore coral reef. Until the tide rose, the only American craft that could approach the shore were the Marines' Amtracs (armored amphibious tractors).

The Japanese defenders, who had planned and fortified well during the year before the Americans arrived, savaged the invaders, using artillery to blow many to bits in their grounded boats and machine-gunning others as they waded through neck-high water to get ashore. The battle raged for 76 hours, ending in a painful U.S. victory, one that cost 1,696 American lives and 2,101 wounded. (During the operation, the jeep carrier USS *Liscombe Bay* was sunk by a submarine torpedo, with the loss of an additional 687 lives.) The Japanese, who had numbered 2,619 troops and 2,200 forced laborers, lost 4,690 lives.

THIS MONTH						
NOVEMBER						
S	M	T	W	T	F	S
..	..	..	..	..	..	1
2	3	4	5	6	7	8
9	10	11	12	13	14	15
16	17	18	19	20	21	22
23	24	25	26	27	28	29
30	..	..	..	..	..	..

FRIDAY
21
NOVEMBER
1941

NEXT MONTH						
DECEMBER						
S	M	T	W	T	F	S
..	1	2	3	4	5	6
7	8	9	10	11	12	13
14	15	16	17	18	19	20
21	22	23	24	25	26	27
28	29	30	31	..	..	..
..	..	..	..	..	..	..

On 21 November 1941, U.S. Secretary of State Cordell Hull and Icelandic Trade Delegation members Vilhjálmur Thór, Ásg Ásgiersson, and Björn Ólaffsson signed into immediate effect an Executive Agreement extending America's Lend-Lease program to provide to Iceland such defense articles, as defined in the Lend-Lease Act of 11 March 1941, as the Government of Iceland might wish to purchase. The Agreement, unlike the original Act, required payment in advance for any articles to be provided under its terms. Also unlike the original Act, the Agreement was open-ended, without a termination date—and it is still in force.

THIS MONTH						
NOVEMBER						
S	M	T	W	T	F	S
..	..	..	..	..	1	2
3	4	5	6	7	8	9
10	11	12	13	14	15	16
17	18	19	20	21	22	23
24	25	26	27	28	29	30
..	..	..	..	..	..	..

FRIDAY
22
NOVEMBER
1940

NEXT MONTH						
DECEMBER						
S	M	T	W	T	F	S
1	2	3	4	5	6	7
8	9	10	11	12	13	14
15	16	17	18	19	20	21
22	23	24	25	26	27	28
29	30	31	..	..	..	..
..	..	..	..	..	..	..

On 22 November 1940, in a major triumph, the Greek army captured the Italian-held Albanian city of Korçë (Koritsa). The city, a commercial and industrial center and the capital of the Korçë region in southeastern Albania, was being used by the Italians as a base for secondary attacks against Thessaloníki (Salonica) and Athens while the main Italian force drove southward along the Ionian Sea coast of the Epirus region. The Greek victory at Korçë yielded about 1,500 Italian prisoners and large quantities of equipment and supplies. The Greeks would hold the city until April 1941, when Nazi Germany intervened to bail out Mussolini's ineptly commanded forces.

THIS MONTH						
NOVEMBER						
S	M	T	W	T	F	S
..	..	..	1	2	3	4
5	6	7	8	9	10	11
12	13	14	15	16	17	18
19	20	21	22	23	24	25
26	27	28	29	30	..	..
..	..	..	..	..	..	..

THURSDAY
23
NOVEMBER

NEXT MONTH						
DECEMBER						
S	M	T	W	T	F	S
..	..	..	..	..	1	2
3	4	5	6	7	8	9
10	11	12	13	14	15	16
17	18	19	20	21	22	23
24	25	26	27	28	29	30
31	..	..	..	..	..	..

1939

On 23 November 1939, German authorities ordered all Polish Jews to wear a yellow fabric Star of David badge bearing the word *Jude* (Jew, in German) or a yellow armband bearing the Star of David and the word *Jude*. This action followed other discriminatory decrees: on 12 October, Jews were forbidden to withdraw more than 200 złotys per week from banks or to have more than 2,000 złotys in cash; on 21 October, Jews were forbidden to deal in textiles or processed leathers; on 22 October, they were forbidden to own radios, go to movie theaters, or teach in Polish schools; on 15 November, Jewish women were forbidden to engage in prostitution; beginning on 17 November a 5 P.M. curfew was imposed on all Jews. More measures would follow, until in late 1940 most Polish Jews were sequestered within ghettoes.

THIS MONTH						
NOVEMBER						
S	M	T	W	T	F	S
..	..	..	1	2	3	4
5	6	7	8	9	10	11
12	13	14	15	16	17	18
19	20	21	22	23	24	25
26	27	28	29	30	..	..
..	..	..	..	..	..	..

FRIDAY
24
NOVEMBER

1944

NEXT MONTH						
DECEMBER						
S	M	T	W	T	F	S
..	..	..	..	..	1	2
3	4	5	6	7	8	9
10	11	12	13	14	15	16
17	18	19	20	21	22	23
24	25	26	27	28	29	30
31	..	..	..	..	..	..

On 24 November 1944, 111 U.S. B-29 Superfortress bombers of the 20th Air Force's 73rd Bombardment Wing, led by Colonel Robert Morgan's *Dauntless Dotty* with mission command pilot General Emmett "Rosie" O'Donnell aboard, took off from Tinian Island in the Solomons chain and executed the first mass raid on Tokyo in history and the first raid of any kind since Jimmy Doolittle's token raid on 18 April 1942. Overcast skies and bad weather made it virtually impossible to hope for any sort of accuracy from aircraft flying at 30,000 feet: even with the use of radar, fewer than 50 bombs struck the primary target, the Nakajima Aircraft Works, and those few did little damage. The high altitude did provide one benefit to the flyers; only one bomber was shot down.

THIS MONTH

NOVEMBER

S	M	T	W	T	F	S
..	..	..	..	..	..	1
2	3	4	5	6	7	8
9	10	11	12	13	14	15
16	17	18	19	20	21	22
23	24	25	26	27	28	29
30	..	..	..	..	..	..

TUESDAY
25
NOVEMBER
1941

NEXT MONTH

DECEMBER

S	M	T	W	T	F	S
..	1	2	3	4	5	6
7	8	9	10	11	12	13
14	15	16	17	18	19	20
21	22	23	24	25	26	27
28	29	30	31	..	..	..

On 25 November 1941, the British Mediterranean Fleet, based in Alexandria, was hunting for Italian convoys headed for Libya. At 1625 hours, as the fleet was 70 miles north of Sidi Barrani, Egypt, German U-boat *U-331*, commanded by *Oberleutnant zur See* Hans-Diedrich Freiherr von Tiesenhausen, attacked the World War I-vintage battleship HMS *Barham* at point-blank range, firing three torpedoes that struck the ship on the port side with what seemed like a single huge explosion abreast her mainmast. Taking on massive quantities of water, *Barham* immediately rolled to port and was on her beam ends in less than two minutes. At that point, her magazines exploded, throwing large chunks of wreckage hundreds of feet. She sank within four minutes of the first explosion, taking with her the lives of 841 men. Her survivors were rescued by the destroyers HMS *Jervis*, HMS *Jackal*, HMS *Nizam*, and HMS *Hotspur*.

U-331 returned to her base at Salamis, where her commander was subsequently promoted to *Kapitänleutnant* and awarded the Knight's Cross of the Iron Cross.

<table>
<tr><td colspan="7">THIS MONTH</td></tr>
<tr><td colspan="7">NOVEMBER</td></tr>
<tr><td>S</td><td>M</td><td>T</td><td>W</td><td>T</td><td>F</td><td>S</td></tr>
<tr><td>1</td><td>2</td><td>3</td><td>4</td><td>5</td><td>6</td><td>7</td></tr>
<tr><td>8</td><td>9</td><td>10</td><td>11</td><td>12</td><td>13</td><td>14</td></tr>
<tr><td>15</td><td>16</td><td>17</td><td>18</td><td>19</td><td>20</td><td>21</td></tr>
<tr><td>22</td><td>23</td><td>24</td><td>25</td><td>26</td><td>27</td><td>28</td></tr>
<tr><td>29</td><td>30</td><td>..</td><td>..</td><td>..</td><td>..</td><td>..</td></tr>
<tr><td>..</td><td>..</td><td>..</td><td>..</td><td>..</td><td>..</td><td>..</td></tr>
</table>

THURSDAY
26
NOVEMBER
1942

<table>
<tr><td colspan="7">NEXT MONTH</td></tr>
<tr><td colspan="7">DECEMBER</td></tr>
<tr><td>S</td><td>M</td><td>T</td><td>W</td><td>T</td><td>F</td><td>S</td></tr>
<tr><td>..</td><td>..</td><td>1</td><td>2</td><td>3</td><td>4</td><td>5</td></tr>
<tr><td>6</td><td>7</td><td>8</td><td>9</td><td>10</td><td>11</td><td>12</td></tr>
<tr><td>13</td><td>14</td><td>15</td><td>16</td><td>17</td><td>18</td><td>19</td></tr>
<tr><td>20</td><td>21</td><td>22</td><td>23</td><td>24</td><td>25</td><td>26</td></tr>
<tr><td>27</td><td>28</td><td>29</td><td>30</td><td>31</td><td>..</td><td>..</td></tr>
<tr><td>..</td><td>..</td><td>..</td><td>..</td><td>..</td><td>..</td><td>..</td></tr>
</table>

On 26 November 1942, violence erupted between American troops and Australian troops and civilians in Brisbane, Australia. There were several causes, including inequities in treatment (American troops were paid better and fed better, received preferential treatment in shops and stores, and were viewed as immoral because of the American custom of "caressing girls in public."); American PXes, forbidden to Australians, were stocked with all sorts of merchandise, food, alcohol, cigarettes, hams, turkeys, ice cream, chocolates, and nylon stockings at low prices—most of which were forbidden or priced virtually out of reach for Australians—while Australian canteens offered only meals, soft drinks, tea, and sandwiches. Each country's troops looked down on the other's, a situation that General Douglas MacArthur exacerbated by reporting American victories or "American and Allied" victories, not mentioning the Australians, who were at that time bearing the brunt of the fighting in New Guinea. The two-day orgy of rioting, which resulted in one Australian death and hundreds of injuries on both sides, was dubbed the "Battle of Brisbane."

NOVEMBER						
S	M	T	W	T	F	S
1	2	3	4	5	6	7
8	9	10	11	12	13	14
15	16	17	18	19	20	21
22	23	24	25	26	27	28
29	30	..	..	..	..	..
..	..	..	..	..	..	..

FRIDAY
27
NOVEMBER
1942

DECEMBER						
S	M	T	W	T	F	S
..	..	1	2	3	4	5
6	7	8	9	10	11	12
13	14	15	16	17	18	19
20	21	22	23	24	25	26
27	28	29	30	31	..	..
..	..	..	..	..	..	..

On 27 November 1942, having declined to join the Allied fleets in North African waters, the Admiralty of Vichy France scuttled the French fleet in Toulon to prevent its capture by German forces during *Unternehmen Lila* (part of *Fall Anton,* the takeover of Vichy France resulting from the French capitulation in Africa). A total of 77 vessels were destroyed, including 3 battleships, 7 cruisers, 15 destroyers, 13 torpedo boats, 6 sloops, 12 submarines, 9 patrol boats, 19 auxiliary ships, 1 school ship, 28 tugs, and 4 cranes. Although the Germans captured 39 small ships, most of them had been sabotaged and disarmed. Some of the major ships burned for quite some time; the cruiser *Marseillaise* took seven days to burn out, and the cruiser *Dupleix* remained afire for ten days.

<table>
<tr><td colspan="7">THIS MONTH</td></tr>
<tr><td colspan="7">NOVEMBER</td></tr>
</table>

			THIS MONTH								SUNDAY						NEXT MONTH		

THIS MONTH

NOVEMBER

S	M	T	W	T	F	S
..	1	2	3	4	5	6
7	8	9	10	11	12	13
14	15	16	17	18	19	20
21	22	23	24	25	26	27
28	29	30	..	..	..	..
..	..	..	..	..	..	..

SUNDAY
28
NOVEMBER

NEXT MONTH

DECEMBER

S	M	T	W	T	F	S
..	..	..	1	2	3	4
5	6	7	8	9	10	11
12	13	14	15	16	17	18
19	20	21	22	23	24	25
26	27	28	29	30	31	..
..	..	..	..	..	..	..

1943

On 28 November 1943, the Tehran Conference began as U.S. President Franklin D. Roosevelt, U.K. Prime Minister Winston Churchill, and USSR Premier Joseph Stalin met in the Soviet Embassy in Tehran, Iran, to discuss strategies for the future conduct of the war against Germany and Japan. The conference would last until 1 December; its most significant outcome was a commitment by the Western Allies to the invasion of Europe whose importance had been acknowledged in 1942. That plan, originally called Operation NEPTUNE and scheduled for 1 May 1944, was later renamed to become Operation OVERLORD. The invasion was launched on the night of 5–6 June 1944, finally giving Stalin the second front for which he had been pleading for years.

THIS MONTH						
NOVEMBER						
S	M	T	W	T	F	S
..	..	..	1	2	3	4
5	6	7	8	9	10	11
12	13	14	15	16	17	18
19	20	21	22	23	24	25
26	27	28	29	30	..	..
..	..	..	..	..	..	..

WEDNESDAY
29
NOVEMBER
1944

NEXT MONTH						
DECEMBER						
S	M	T	W	T	F	S
..	..	..	..	..	1	2
3	4	5	6	7	8	9
10	11	12	13	14	15	16
17	18	19	20	21	22	23
24	25	26	27	28	29	30
31	..	..	..	..	..	..

On 29 November 1944, the 72,000-ton Japanese aircraft carrier *Shinano*, laid down in 1940 as a third *Yamato*-class battleship and respecified in 1942 to become the largest carrier built during the war, was nearly complete and ready for service. Because she had been seen in dry dock at Yokosuka by an American B-29 on a reconnaissance flight, she had been loaded with 50 of the virtually unstoppable *Ohka* rocket-powered suicide aircraft and was being moved to Kure for completion—but unfortunately for the Japanese, American codebreakers had intercepted the order to move her. After consideration as to the best way to intercept and destroy her, however, U.S. Navy admirals concluded that there was no force that they could dispatch to do the job. They and the Japanese failed to count on USS *Archerfish*, a *Balao*-class submarine captained by Commander Joseph F. Enright. *Archerfish*, on station as a rescue boat for downed B-29 crewmen, encountered *Shinano* and went in pursuit. She was able to close on the faster carrier by taking a straight course as the carrier zigzagged along the coast; finally, when *Shinano* zigged into a perfect location for an attack, Enright loosed six torpedoes at her. Four of them struck amidships and detonated. *Shinano*'s commanding officer, Captain Toshio Abe, shrugged off the hits, trusting in his ship's armor. He kept the ship running at top speed, unaware that she had been holed and the pressure of water rushing past the hull at 18 knots was causing *Shinano* to ship millions of gallons of sea water. Her untested watertight doors failed, and several hours after *Archerfish*'s attack she took with her to the bottom 1,435 men and officers, including Captain Abe. Escorts rescued 1,080 men. *Archerfish* crept away unharmed, and the threat of Japan's supercarrier was ended.

THIS MONTH						
NOVEMBER						
S	M	T	W	T	F	S
..	..	..	1	2	3	4
5	6	7	8	9	10	11
12	13	14	15	16	17	18
19	20	21	22	23	24	25
26	27	28	29	30	..	..
..	..	..	..	..	..	..

THURSDAY
30
NOVEMBER
1939

NEXT MONTH						
DECEMBER						
S	M	T	W	T	F	S
..	..	..	..	..	1	2
3	4	5	6	7	8	9
10	11	12	13	14	15	16
17	18	19	20	21	22	23
24	25	26	27	28	29	30
31	..	..	..	..	..	..

On 30 November 1939, 21 Red Army divisions, comprising 450,000 men, invaded Finland while the Soviet Air Force bombed Helsinki. The Soviet government stated that the attack was in response to the unprovoked shelling, three days earlier, of a Soviet border guard post near the Russian village of Mainila, in which four soldiers were reported killed and nine injured. (It is now known that the shelling actually produced no casualties and was carried out by an NKVD unit to provide a pretext for the Soviet Union to withdraw from the 1932 Soviet–Finnish Non-Aggression Pact.)

The Winter War, which Joseph Stalin had actually launched to "correct mistakes" in the drawing of the Russo-Finnish border after the Bolshevik Revolution in 1917, lasted until 13 March 1940 and cost the Soviets far more casualties than had been anticipated (126,875 dead or missing, 188,671 wounded, and 5,572 captured) because Stalin's purges in the 1930s had virtually eliminated experienced field officers in the Soviet military.[3]

Although technically not a theater of action in World War II, the Winter War did arise out of the Soviets' fear of Germany; the NKVD had warned Finland that a war between Germany and the USSR was possible, and Stalin needed an excuse to create a zone of buffer states between the two potential antagonists.

---

3. Stalin had purged the military in response to a series of treasonous letters between Marshal of the Soviet Union Mikhail Tukhachevsky and the German *Wehrmacht*; the letters were actually forged by Reinhard Heydrich, director of the SS intelligence service, the SD, in an attempt to damage the Soviet military. Heydrich believed that he himself was responsible for the purge; but in fact the NKVD, acting under orders from Stalin to fabricate an excuse to dispose of officers who stood between him and absolute power, had instructed a known double agent to leak to the SD hints of a military plot against Stalin.

TUESDAY

1

DECEMBER

1942

DECEMBER						
S	M	T	W	T	F	S
..	..	1	2	3	4	5
6	7	8	9	10	11	12
13	14	15	16	17	18	19
20	21	22	23	24	25	26
27	28	29	30	31	..	..
..	..	..	..	..	..	..

JANUARY						
S	M	T	W	T	F	S
..	..	..	..	..	1	2
3	4	5	6	7	8	9
10	11	12	13	14	15	16
17	18	19	20	21	22	23
24	25	26	27	28	29	30
31	..	..	..	..	..	..

On 1 December 1942, full gasoline rationing began in the United States. Gasoline had been rationed since June; but with virtually the world's entire rubber supply in Axis hands, it became necessary to further curb unnecessary travel in order to conserve critical rubber supplies.

Tires had been rationed since January, with car owners required to register their tires. The system for gasoline rationing cascaded on the tire registration process; in order to obtain ration coupons for gas, an applicant must show that all of his tires, including the spare and any other tires he owned, were properly registered. ("Other" tires could not be automobile tires; any car tires in excess of five were confiscated.) Virtually any car owner could get an A classification, allowing him four gallons a week, while a B classification allowed eight gallons a week. The C classification was reserved for essential war workers, police, doctors, and mail carriers. T was for truck drivers, and the coveted X classification was for "important" people such as politicians.

To further reduce fuel consumption, and thereby preserve rubber, the government established a nationwide speed limit of 35 MPH. For a short time in 1943, rations were reduced further and all pleasure driving was outlawed; but this severely restrictive level of rationing was found to be unacceptable, and it was repealed. Gas rationing ended on 15 August 1945.

THIS MONTH

DECEMBER						
S	M	T	W	T	F	S
..	..	1	2	3	4	5
6	7	8	9	10	11	12
13	14	15	16	17	18	19
20	21	22	23	24	25	26
27	28	29	30	31	..	..
..	..	..	..	..	..	..

WEDNESDAY
2
DECEMBER

1942

NEXT MONTH

JANUARY						
S	M	T	W	T	F	S
..	..	..	..	..	1	2
3	4	5	6	7	8	9
10	11	12	13	14	15	16
17	18	19	20	21	22	23
24	25	26	27	28	29	30
31	..	..	..	..	..	..

On 2 December 1942, working under the aegis of the Manhattan Project, a team of physicists led by Enrico Fermi fired up "Chicago Pile 1," a carefully stacked pile of uranium pellets and graphite bricks in the unheated squash court below the University of Chicago's abandoned football field, Stagg Field, and initiated the world's first sustained nuclear chain reaction. To make their success known to their superiors, they sent to President Roosevelt a message reading, "The Italian navigator has landed in the new world."

THIS MONTH						
DECEMBER						
S	M	T	W	T	F	S
..	..	..	1	2	3	4
5	6	7	8	9	10	11
12	13	14	15	16	17	18
19	20	21	22	23	24	25
26	27	28	29	30	31	..
..	..	..	..	..	..	..

FRIDAY

3

DECEMBER

NEXT MONTH						
JANUARY						
S	M	T	W	T	F	S
..	..	..	..	..	..	1
2	3	4	5	6	7	8
9	10	11	12	13	14	15
16	17	18	19	20	21	22
23	24	25	26	27	28	29
30	31	..	..	..	..	..

1943

On 3 December 1943, CBS Radio correspondent Edward R. Murrow delivered his classic "Orchestrated Hell" broadcast, describing the previous night's Royal Air Force nighttime bombing raid on Berlin, on which he had been a passenger in the Wing Commander's Lancaster, which he identified as "D for Dog." Here is how he ended his broadcast: "Berlin was a kind of orchestrated hell—a terrible symphony of light and flame. It isn't a pleasant kind of warfare. The men doing it speak of it as a job. Yesterday afternoon, when the tapes were stretched out on the big map all the way to Berlin and back again, a young pilot with old eyes said to me, 'I see we're working again tonight.' That's the frame of mind in which the job is being done. The job isn't pleasant; it's terribly tiring. Men die in the sky while others are roasted alive in their cellars. Berlin last night wasn't a pretty sight. In about thirty-five minutes it was hit with about three times the amount of stuff that ever came down on London in a night-long blitz. This is a calculated, remorseless campaign of destruction. Right now the mechanics are probably working on D-Dog, getting him ready to fly again. I return you now to CBS, New York."

THIS MONTH									FRIDAY		NEXT MONTH						

THIS MONTH

DECEMBER

S	M	T	W	T	F	S
..	..	1	2	3	4	5
6	7	8	9	10	11	12
13	14	15	16	17	18	19
20	21	22	23	24	25	26
27	28	29	30	31	..	..
..	..	..	..	..	..	..

FRIDAY
4
DECEMBER

1942

NEXT MONTH

JANUARY

S	M	T	W	T	F	S
..	..	..	..	..	1	2
3	4	5	6	7	8	9
10	11	12	13	14	15	16
17	18	19	20	21	22	23
24	25	26	27	28	29	30
31	..	..	..	..	..	..

On 4 December 1942, the 2nd U.S. Marine Raider Battalion, commanded by Lieutenant Colonel Evans Carlson, completed the "Long Patrol," a 29-day mission in which they attacked and harried Japanese forces under the command of Colonel Toshinari Shōji as the Japanese were escaping from an attempt by the U.S. Marines to encircle them in the Koli Point area on Guadalcanal. As the Japanese fled across the U.S. perimeter in an attempt to rejoin with other units on the island, Carlson's Raiders engaged them in a series of small unit actions, killing 488 Japanese soldiers—and capturing a field gun that was delivering harassing fire on Henderson Field—at the expense of only 16 Marines dead and 19 men wounded despite the ravages of Guadalcanal's pest- and disease-ridden environment. The success of Carlson's Raiders lay largely in the commander's innovative tactical ideas and leadership style: he essentially ignored the class barrier between enlisted personnel and officers, and he reorganized the standard squad into three fire teams that were better able to take independent action should the command chain become disrupted.[1]

---

1. Carlson's egalitarian approach won him few friends among his class-conscious fellow officers. On 22 March 1943, he was relieved as commander of the 2nd Raiders by Lieutenant Colonel Alan Shapley and made executive officer of the 1st Raider Regiment. Within a month Shapley had reorganized the 2nd Raiders into a traditional organization. Carlson's three-fire-team squad organization remained, however, and was soon adopted by the entire U.S. Marine Corps.

THIS MONTH						
DECEMBER						
S	M	T	W	T	F	S
..	1	2	3	4	5	6
7	8	9	10	11	12	13
14	15	16	17	18	19	20
21	22	23	24	25	26	27
28	29	30	31	..	..	..
..	..	..	..	..	..	..

FRIDAY
5
DECEMBER

NEXT MONTH						
JANUARY						
S	M	T	W	T	F	S
..	..	..	..	1	2	3
4	5	6	7	8	9	10
11	12	13	14	15	16	17
18	19	20	21	22	23	24
25	26	27	28	29	30	31
..	..	..	..	..	..	..

1941

On 5 December 1941, the Axis offensive on Moscow came to a halt. As much as anything, the weather had done the Germans in; they were simply not prepared for the record low temperatures, which went as low as −44 degrees Fahrenheit. Soldiers froze to death in their summer uniforms, and vehicles, if they could start at all, had to be warmed for hours before they were usable.

General Heinz Guderian, Germany's leading exponent of armored warfare and commanding officer of the Second Panzer Army, wrote in his journal, "The offensive on Moscow failed. We underestimated the enemy's strength, as well as his size and climate. Fortunately, I stopped my troops on 5 December, otherwise the catastrophe would be unavoidable."

The Germans were 11 miles from Moscow when the offensive was called off. On the same day, the Soviets launched a counteroffensive that German intelligence had thought impossible; starting on the Kalinin Front, the Soviets in the first two days retook Krasnaya Polyana and several other cities in the immediate vicinity of Moscow as well as Kalinin and Klin in the north. Guderian, who had crossed swords several times with Adolf Hitler over Hitler's interference in the management of German campaigns, was relieved of command, along with 40 other general officers including commander-in-chief Walther von Brauchitsch; but Guderian would be recalled in early 1943 as losses in the Panzer corps continued to mount.

<table>
<tr><td>THIS MONTH</td><td>SATURDAY</td><td>NEXT MONTH</td></tr>
</table>

THIS MONTH

DECEMBER

S	M	T	W	T	F	S
..	1	2	3	4	5	6
7	8	9	10	11	12	13
14	15	16	17	18	19	20
21	22	23	24	25	26	27
28	29	30	31	..	..	..
..	..	..	..	..	..	..

SATURDAY
6
DECEMBER

NEXT MONTH

JANUARY

S	M	T	W	T	F	S
..	..	..	..	1	2	3
4	5	6	7	8	9	10
11	12	13	14	15	16	17
18	19	20	21	22	23	24
25	26	27	28	29	30	31
..	..	..	..	..	..	..

1941

On 6 December 1941, British submarine HMS *Perseus,* based in Alexandria and commanded by Lieutenant Commander Edward C. F. Nicolay, was returning to her base from Malta when she struck an Italian mine off Cephalonia, seven miles north of Zakynthos in the Ionian Sea west of the Gulf of Patra. Of the 61 men aboard the submarine when she sank, only one survived, 31-year old Leading Stoker John Capes, who was one of two non-crew members hitching a lift to Alexandria. He and three others escaped from the submarine using the Twill Trunk escape hatch in the engine room and wearing Davis Submerged Escape Apparatus, but only he survived the 170-foot journey to the surface and the five mile swim to the island of Cephalonia. Once there, he was taken into hiding by islanders and remained for 18 months, until he was smuggled to Turkey in a caïque, a sail-rigged fishing boat.

THIS MONTH						
DECEMBER						
S	M	T	W	T	F	S
..	1	2	3	4	5	6
7	8	9	10	11	12	13
14	15	16	17	18	19	20
21	22	23	24	25	26	27
28	29	30	31	..	..	..
..	..	..	..	..	..	..

SUNDAY
7
DECEMBER
1941

NEXT MONTH						
JANUARY						
S	M	T	W	T	F	S
..	..	..	..	1	2	3
4	5	6	7	8	9	10
11	12	13	14	15	16	17
18	19	20	21	22	23	24
25	26	27	28	29	30	31
..	..	..	..	..	..	..

On 7 December 1941, forces of the Imperial Japanese Navy commanded by Admiral Chūichi Nagumo launched a pre-emptive attack, without a declaration of war, against United States forces on the Hawaiian island of Oahu.

Attacks were conducted by fighters and bombers launched from six aircraft carriers, a total of 354 aircraft in two waves. They struck Pearl Harbor, where they damaged all eight U.S. battleships, sinking four; three cruisers, three destroyers, and four other ships were hit as well.

All of the stricken ships except the battleship USS *Arizona* and the training/target ship USS *Utah* were returned to service before the end of the war. Also struck were Army Air Forces bases Hickam and Wheeler Fields, with 188 aircraft destroyed and 159 damaged. 2,402 American personnel were killed and 1,247 were wounded.

The Japanese lost five midget submarines; 29 aircraft; 64 men killed; and Ensign Kazuo Sakamaki, a crew member of one of the midget submarines, captured to become the first Japanese POW of the war.

The attack failed in its primary objective, to destroy the three American aircraft carriers assigned to the Pacific Fleet; USS *Enterprise,* USS *Lexington,* and USS *Saratoga* were all at sea when the Japanese struck.

The famous quotation attributed to Marshal Admiral Isoroku Yamamoto, "I fear all we have done is to awaken a sleeping giant and fill him with a terrible resolve," remains undocumented; the screenwriter of *Tora! Tora! Tora!* supposedly found it in a 1943 letter from Yamamoto to the Admiralty, but no one has ever produced such a letter.

DECEMBER

S	M	T	W	T	F	S
..	1	2	3	4	5	6
7	8	9	10	11	12	13
14	15	16	17	18	19	20
21	22	23	24	25	26	27
28	29	30	31	..	..	..
..	..	..	..	..	..	..

MONDAY
8
DECEMBER

JANUARY

S	M	T	W	T	F	S
..	..	..	..	1	2	3
4	5	6	7	8	9	10
11	12	13	14	15	16	17
18	19	20	21	22	23	24
25	26	27	28	29	30	31
..	..	..	..	..	..	..

1941

On 8 December 1941, Congresswoman Jeanette Rankin of Montana, the first woman elected to the U.S. Congress and a dedicated lifelong pacifist, cast the sole vote against the U.S. declaration of war on Japan. She had also been among those who voted against American entry into World War I. Many citizens had seen her vote in 1917 as evidence that women were not capable of handling the tasks of national leadership. Voted out of office in 1918, she won re-election again in 1940, just in time to face another vote on war.

Knowing that her vote would be political suicide, she nevertheless believed that President Roosevelt had deliberately provoked the Japanese attack in order to bring the U.S. into the war against Germany. After a 40-minute debate on the floor of the House, a roll call vote began. When her turn came, Rankin stood and said, "As a woman, I can't go to war, and I refuse to send anyone else." When the vote was announced outside the House chamber, some patriots threatened to attack her, and she received a police escort from the Capitol building. The press vilified her, accusing her of disloyalty and calling her unkind names, including "Japanette Rankin." She stood her ground and never apologized for her vote.

THIS MONTH

DECEMBER

S	M	T	W	T	F	S
..	..	1	2	3	4	5
6	7	8	9	10	11	12
13	14	15	16	17	18	19
20	21	22	23	24	25	26
27	28	29	30	31	..	..
..	..	..	..	..	..	..

WEDNESDAY

9

DECEMBER

1942

NEXT MONTH

JANUARY

S	M	T	W	T	F	S
..	..	..	..	..	1	2
3	4	5	6	7	8	9
10	11	12	13	14	15	16
17	18	19	20	21	22	23
24	25	26	27	28	29	30
31	..	..	..	..	..	..

On 9 December 1942, having completed the mission assigned to it, the 1st U.S. Marine Division began withdrawing from positions on Guadalcanal, turning over operations on the island to the XIV Corps, which comprised the 2nd Marine Division and the U.S. Army's 25th Infantry and Americal Divisions. U.S. Army Major General Alexander Patch replaced Marine Major General Alexander Vandegrift as commander of Allied forces on Guadalcanal.

Three days later, the Imperial Japanese Navy proposed that Guadalcanal should be abandoned, with support from several staff officers at the Imperial General Headquarters who stated that further efforts to take the island would be in vain. A conference at Rabaul led to a 26 December order to abandon the island. Fighting would continue until 9 February 1943, but Guadalcanal was irretrievably held by the Allies.

THIS MONTH								WEDNESDAY		NEXT MONTH						
DECEMBER								**10**		JANUARY						
S	M	T	W	T	F	S				S	M	T	W	T	F	S
..	1	2	3	4	5	6		DECEMBER		..	..	..	..	1	2	3
7	8	9	10	11	12	13				4	5	6	7	8	9	10
14	15	16	17	18	19	20				11	12	13	14	15	16	17
21	22	23	24	25	26	27				18	19	20	21	22	23	24
28	29	30	31	..	..	..				25	26	27	28	29	30	31
..	..	..	..	..	..	..				..	..	..	..	..	..	..

1941

On 10 December 1941, the Royal Navy's Eastern Fleet task force, Force Z, with a roster of the battleship HMS *Prince of Wales,* the battlecruiser HMS *Repulse,* and four destroyers, was returning to Singapore after having failed to locate and destroy a Japanese invasion fleet north of Malaya. Force Z was traveling without air support, which Fleet Commander Admiral Sir Tom Phillips had declined in favor of maintaining radio silence.

At 0340 hours, Japanese submarine *I-58,* commanded by Lieutenant Mochitsura Hashimoto, was patrolling off the east coast of Malaya when she spotted the British force, which had been reduced by one destroyer when HMS *Tenedos* ran short of fuel on the outward run and was ordered back to Singapore. *I-58* fired five torpedoes at the two capital ships, all of which missed. The British never saw the torpedoes and did not know they had been attacked.

I-58's report of the action reached 22nd Air Flotilla Headquarters at 0315, and ten bombers of the Genzan Air Group were dispatched at 0600.[2] Many more planes of the Genzan, Kanoya, and Mihoro Air Groups, some armed with bombs and some with torpedoes, soon followed. The first wave struck at 1113, concentrating on *Repulse,* but scored only a single hit that did minor damage. The next wave delivered one of eight torpedoes into *Prince of Wales,* causing a list that rendered her unable to fight off low-level attacks by torpedo bombers. She took three more hits and sank at 1318 hours, with 327 lives lost. *Repulse,* meanwhile, had taken four torpedo hits, and she went down at 1233 hours, with 513 killed. The destroyers HMS *Electra,* HMS *Express,* and HMS *Vampire* rescued 1,862 survivors.

Prince of Wales and *Repulse* were the first capital ships ever to be sunk solely by naval air power while actively defending themselves and steaming in the open sea.

---

2. Although Saigon, where the 22nd Air Flotilla Headquarters was located, is east of what was then British Malaya, international time zone boundaries have been drawn such that Saigon is an hour behind Malaya. Thus, Hashimoto's report did not actually arrive before it was sent.

THIS MONTH						
DECEMBER						
S	M	T	W	T	F	S
..	1	2	3	4	5	6
7	8	9	10	11	12	13
14	15	16	17	18	19	20
21	22	23	24	25	26	27
28	29	30	31	..	..	..

THURSDAY
11
DECEMBER

1941

NEXT MONTH						
JANUARY						
S	M	T	W	T	F	S
..	..	..	..	1	2	3
4	5	6	7	8	9	10
11	12	13	14	15	16	17
18	19	20	21	22	23	24
25	26	27	28	29	30	31
..	..	..	..	..	..	..

On 11 December 1941, after aerial bombardment to soften up the defenses, the Japanese South Seas Force launched an amphibious assault at Wake Island. The island's American garrison comprised 450 Marines and 68 Naval personnel under the overall command Navy Commander Winfield S. Cunningham, along with 2,221 civilian contractors.

The Japanese had two cruisers, six destroyers, two destroyers converted to patrol boats, and two troop transport ships carrying 450 SNLF (Special Naval Landing Forces) marines. The Americans had six 5-inch guns that had been removed from the battleship USS *Texas* during 1917 and 1918 refittings; twelve 3-inch antiaircraft guns (with only a single working antiaircraft director); eighteen .50 caliber Browning heavy machine guns; thirty .30 caliber machine guns of various types and in various states of repair; assorted small arm; and four of their original complement of 12 Wildcat fighter planes, the other eight having been destroyed in the bombardment.

After waiting until the enemy's ships were within range of their guns, the Americans opened fire, sinking the destroyer *Hayate* at a distance of 4,000 yards with at least two direct hits to her magazines, which exploded. Within two minutes, she sank in full view of the defenders. Eleven rounds hit the superstructure of the cruiser *Yubari*. The Wildcats sank the destroyer *Kisaragi* by exploding the depth charges stored on her stern with a bomb. Both Japanese destroyers were lost with all hands, with *Hayate* becoming the first Japanese surface warship to be sunk during World War II.

The Japanese had had enough: they withdrew before landing the assault force, suffering their first defeat of the war. The Battle of Wake Island would continue, with no reinforcement or resupply available to the defenders, until 23 December, when the island finally fell to a second, better supported, Japanese amphibious assault.

DECEMBER						
S	M	T	W	T	F	S
..	..	..	..	..	1	2
3	4	5	6	7	8	9
10	11	12	13	14	15	16
17	18	19	20	21	22	23
24	25	26	27	28	29	30
31	..	..	..	..	..	..

TUESDAY
12
DECEMBER

JANUARY						
S	M	T	W	T	F	S
..	1	2	3	4	5	6
7	8	9	10	11	12	13
14	15	16	17	18	19	20
21	22	23	24	25	26	27
28	29	30	31	..	..	..
..	..	..	..	..	..	..

1939

On 12 December 1939, the British destroyer HMS *Duchess,* along with her sisters HMS *Delight,* HMS *Duncan,* and HMS *Dainty,* was escorting the battleship HMS *Barham* back to the U.K. from Gibraltar. At 0400 hours, in the dark of a new moon under foggy conditions off the Mull of Kintyre, the headland at the southwestern tip of Scotland's Kintyre Peninsula, the ships' zigzagging courses crossed and *Barham* collided with *Duchess.* The destroyer capsized, her boilers exploded, and she sank.

The watch had been stood down and sent below, and Ordinary Seaman Ernest Swinhoe, standing at the fore gun, was probably the only man aboard who saw *Barham*'s approach. He dove off the ship and swam a little distance away. After the collision, *Barham* and her escorts lowered boats to rescue the Duchesses,[3] who were mostly half naked as they thrashed in the water. Swinhoe, suffering from hypothermia, heard a coxswain order his crew to cease rowing and be silent; Swinhoe summoned what strength he had and called for help. When he reached *Barham,* he was a "shaking mass" unable to warm himself without help from the corpsmen in sick bay. He was lucky. *Duchess* took with her the lives of 137 of her 160-man crew, including her commanding officer, Lieutenant Commander Robin White.

---

3. British naval tradition refers to members of a ship's crew by the ship's name; thus, crew aboard HMS *Duchess* were known as Duchesses.

THIS MONTH						
DECEMBER						
S	M	T	W	T	F	S
..	..	..	..	..	1	2
3	4	5	6	7	8	9
10	11	12	13	14	15	16
17	18	19	20	21	22	23
24	25	26	27	28	29	30
31	..	..	..	..	..	..

WEDNESDAY
13
DECEMBER

NEXT MONTH						
JANUARY						
S	M	T	W	T	F	S
..	1	2	3	4	5	6
7	8	9	10	11	12	13
14	15	16	17	18	19	20
21	22	23	24	25	26	27
28	29	30	31	..	..	..

1939

On 13 December 1939, lookouts aboard the *Deutschland*-class German cruiser ("pocket battleship") *Admiral Graf Spee,* then cruising off South America, reported sighting a British cruiser and two destroyers. Captain Hans Langsdorff, commanding *Graf Spee,* had already committed his ship to battle when it was discovered that the two destroyers were in fact cruisers, and the Germans were forced into combat with heavy cruiser HMS *Exeter* and light cruisers HMS *Ajax* and HMS *Achilles.* All four ships suffered heavy damage, but *Graf Spee* took the worst of it, as one shell from *Exeter* disabled her fuel cleaning system, leaving the ship with only 16 hours' clean fuel.

To gain time for repairs, Langsdorff put into Montevideo Harbor. Uruguay, then neutral, granted Langsdorff 96 hours before he must leave instead of the 24 hours specified under the rules of war. But on 17 December, misled by false reports of superior British naval forces approaching, Langsdorff ordered his ship scuttled just outside the harbor entrance. It was later partially broken up *in situ,* but portions still remain and can be seen above the surface.

THIS MONTH							THURSDAY	NEXT MONTH						

DECEMBER

S	M	T	W	T	F	S
..	..	..	..	..	1	2
3	4	5	6	7	8	9
10	11	12	13	14	15	16
17	18	19	20	21	22	23
24	25	26	27	28	29	30
31	..	..	..	..	..	..

THURSDAY
14
DECEMBER

JANUARY

S	M	T	W	T	F	S
..	1	2	3	4	5	6
7	8	9	10	11	12	13
14	15	16	17	18	19	20
21	22	23	24	25	26	27
28	29	30	31	..	..	..
..	..	..	..	..	..	..

1939

On 14 December 1939, the League of Nations, formed after World War I with high hopes of preventing another world war but never empowered to back up its decisions with force, expelled the Union of Soviet Socialist Republics in response to the Soviets' 30 November invasion of Finland. Earlier Soviet imperial moves, including the September occupation of eastern Poland and the coercing of alliance pacts on the Baltic States, could be justified as a means of protecting the Ukraine and Byelorussia from the Poles, but the Russo-Finnish War was launched on the flimsiest of fabricated pretexts, the NKVD's shelling of the USSR's own border guard post near Mainila, Russia, on 27 November. Even U.S. President Franklin D. Roosevelt, a Soviet "ally," condemned the invasion, and with almost its dying breath the League pushed the Soviets out the door.

THIS MONTH							MONDAY	NEXT MONTH						
DECEMBER							**15**	JANUARY						
S	M	T	W	T	F	S	DECEMBER	S	M	T	W	T	F	S
..	1	2	3	4	5	6		..	..	..	..	1	2	3
7	8	9	10	11	12	13		4	5	6	7	8	9	10
14	15	16	17	18	19	20		11	12	13	14	15	16	17
21	22	23	24	25	26	27		18	19	20	21	22	23	24
28	29	30	31	..	..	..		25	26	27	28	29	30	31
..	..	..	..	..	..	..		..	..	..	..	..	..	..

1941

On 15 December 1941, after having driven British forces off the Chinese mainland at Kowloon and onto Hong Kong Island itself, and after having unleashed relentless air attacks against Victoria City, the island's business district, and against British vessels in port, Lieutenant General Takashi Sakai, commanding the Imperial Japanese Army's 38th Division, ordered his forces to cross to the island. At 0300 hours, a Japanese reconnaissance party of 300 crossed the Lye Mun Channel from Kowloon to Hong Kong Island. They were seen by British defenders, who slaughtered them as they came ashore. After this repulse, the Japanese bombarded the north shore of Hong Kong for three days to soften up the defenses. Fighting continued until Christmas Day, when the Governor of Hong King, Sir Mark Aitchison, personally executed a surrender document. During the course of the battle, Japanese troops murdered more than 100 defenseless people, most of them civilians, in ten separate non-combat incidents.

DECEMBER

S	M	T	W	T	F	S
..	..	1	2	3	4	5
6	7	8	9	10	11	12
13	14	15	16	17	18	19
20	21	22	23	24	25	26
27	28	29	30	31	..	..
..	..	..	..	..	..	..

WEDNESDAY
16
DECEMBER

1942

JANUARY

S	M	T	W	T	F	S
..	..	..	..	..	1	2
3	4	5	6	7	8	9
10	11	12	13	14	15	16
17	18	19	20	21	22	23
24	25	26	27	28	29	30
31	..	..	..	..	..	..

On 16 December 1942, Adolf Hitler unsheathed against the Roma the claws of his policy to cleanse Germany of "undesirables" when he issued a directive that ordered the purging of the Roma, otherwise known as Gypsies, from Germany. Persons with any amount of Romani blood, however slight, were to be sent to "resettlement" camps in the East, where they would be exterminated along with Jews, homosexuals, and others considered genetically inferior to the mythical "Aryan" race.

THIS MONTH

DECEMBER

S	M	T	W	T	F	S
..	..	..	..	..	1	2
3	4	5	6	7	8	9
10	11	12	13	14	15	16
17	18	19	20	21	22	23
24	25	26	27	28	29	30
31	..	..	..	..	..	..

SUNDAY

17

DECEMBER

1944

NEXT MONTH

JANUARY

S	M	T	W	T	F	S
..	1	2	3	4	5	6
7	8	9	10	11	12	13
14	15	16	17	18	19	20
21	22	23	24	25	26	27
28	29	30	31	..	..	..
..	..	..	..	..	..	..

On 17 December 1944, during the Battle of the Bulge, troops of *Kampfgruppe* Peiper (part of the 1st SS Panzer Division), commanded by Colonel Joachim Peiper, murdered several dozen U.S. prisoners of war near Honsfeld, Belgium. Later the same day, Peiper's troops apparently murdered prisoners at Büllingen; and, still later, at Baugnez, they massacred an additional 84 in a field. The first survivors to return to American lines did so near Malmédy, and the events of the day became known as the Malmédy massacre. Peiper's troops killed at least eight other American prisoners in Ligneuville, and further massacres were reported over the next three days in Stavelot, Cheneux, La Gleize, and Stoumont. In Stavelot, Peiper's men murdered about 100 Belgian civilians. Perpetrators of these related war crimes were brought to trial as part of the Dachau Trials of 1946.

1939

On 18 December 1939, in the first "named" air battle of the Second World War, the Battle of the Heligoland Bight, RAF Bomber Command attempted to follow the scuttling of *Admiral Graf Spee* by destroying another major warship. 24 Wellington bombers of No. 9, No. 37, and No. 149 Squadrons, under the overall command of Wing Commander Richard Kellett, were dispatched to overfly the Heligoland Bight. and specifically the port of Wilhelmshaven, attacking military ships while avoiding other potential targets.

As the British approached, there was perfect visibility, and they were easily spotted by the Germans. At first three AA batteries opened fire; as the bombers flew on, the ground defense passed to five other batteries along with *Scharnhorst, Gneisenau,* and several other naval vessels in the harbor. Little damage was done by either side; but then fighters of *Stab.*/JG 1,[4] commanded by *Generalmajor* Carl-Alfred Schumacher, arrived, and the somewhat disorganized British formation was incapable of mounting an effective defense.

When it was all over, the RAF had lost 12 bombers destroyed and three damaged, with 57 men killed. The *Luftwaffe*'s losses comprised three fighters destroyed, 12 fighters damaged, two pilots dead (one by drowning as he tried to swim ashore after his plane went down), and two pilots wounded.

---

4. In *Luftwaffe* unit identification, JG is the abbreviation for *Jagdgeschwader,* a fighter wing. *Stab.* indicates a headquarters unit within a larger unit, in this case the fighter wing.

THIS MONTH						
DECEMBER						
S	M	T	W	T	F	S
..	1	2	3	4	5	6
7	8	9	10	11	12	13
14	15	16	17	18	19	20
21	22	23	24	25	26	27
28	29	30	31	..	..	..
..	..	..	..	..	..	..

FRIDAY
19
DECEMBER
1941

NEXT MONTH						
JANUARY						
S	M	T	W	T	F	S
..	..	..	..	1	2	3
4	5	6	7	8	9	10
11	12	13	14	15	16	17
18	19	20	21	22	23	24
25	26	27	28	29	30	31
..	..	..	..	..	..	..

On 19 December 1941, the Italian submarine *Scirè* released three "manned torpedoes" (actually midget submarines, each with a crew of two who rode straddling the craft like a horse) just outside the harbor at Alexandria, Egypt. The torpedoes, called *maiali* (pigs) by the Italians, entered the harbor when the British opened their defenses to let three destroyers pass. Luigi Durand de la Penne and Emilio Bianchi pushed their craft, whose engine had failed, to a point beneath the battleship HMS *Valiant* to place their limpet mine. Because Bianchi had been hurt in wrestling the submarine, the men surfaced and were captured. Antonio Marceglia and Spartaco Schergat navigated to the berth of HMS *Queen Elizabeth* and attached their mine; they left the harbor but were captured two days later while posing as French sailors. Unable to find the aircraft carrier that was supposedly in the harbor, Vincenzo Martellotta and Mario Marino attached their mine to the stern of *Sagona,* a Norwegian tanker, and landed safely but were later captured. All three mines exploded as scheduled, doing severe damage to their targets. *Queen Elizabeth* and *Valiant* were sunk in the shallow harbor; both were later raised but were out of action for more than a year. *Sagona* lost her stern, and the destroyer HMS *Jarvis,* alongside *Sagona* for refueling, was badly damaged. Amazingly, only eight men were killed in the attack.

THIS MONTH						
DECEMBER						
S	**M**	**T**	**W**	**T**	**F**	**S**
..	1	2	3	4	5	6
7	8	9	10	11	12	13
14	15	16	17	18	19	20
21	22	23	24	25	26	27
28	29	30	31	..	..	..
..	..	..	..	..	..	..

SATURDAY
20
DECEMBER
1941

NEXT MONTH						
JANUARY						
S	**M**	**T**	**W**	**T**	**F**	**S**
..	..	..	..	1	2	3
4	5	6	7	8	9	10
11	12	13	14	15	16	17
18	19	20	21	22	23	24
25	26	27	28	29	30	31
..	..	..	..	..	..	..

On 20 December 1941, the 1st American Volunteer Group of the Chinese Air Force, nicknamed the Flying Tigers, saw its first combat. The 1st AVG was composed of pilots recruited from the U.S. Army Air Forces, Navy, and Marine Corps under presidential authority and commanded by Claire Lee Chennault. Ground crew and headquarters staff were likewise mostly recruited from the U.S. military, along with some civilians.[5]

All military personnel were required to resign from the U.S. military in order to join the AVG, where they were assigned P-40 Tomahawk aircraft originally built for the Royal Air Force, and trained in Chennault's special tactics that were designed specifically for the P-40.

On 20 December, aircraft of the 1st and 2nd AVG Squadrons intercepted ten unescorted Kawasaki Ki-48 "Lily" bombers of the Imperial Japanese Army's 21st Hikotai as the Japanese were on their way to raid Kunming. The Flying Tigers shot down three of the Japanese bombers and damaged a fourth so severely that it crashed before it could return to its airfield at Hanoi. No P-40s were lost through enemy action, and the bombers jettisoned their loads before reaching their target. As a result of this action, the Japanese launched no further raids against Kunming while the AVG was based there.

---

5. Gregory Boyington, who later became commander of the U.S. Marine Corps' VMF-214, known as the Black Sheep Squadron, flew with the Flying Tigers.

THIS MONTH						
DECEMBER						
S	M	T	W	T	F	S
..	1	2	3	4	5	6
7	8	9	10	11	12	13
14	15	16	17	18	19	20
21	22	23	24	25	26	27
28	29	30	31	..	..	..
..	..	..	..	..	..	..

SUNDAY
21
DECEMBER
1941

NEXT MONTH						
JANUARY						
S	M	T	W	T	F	S
..	..	..	..	1	2	3
4	5	6	7	8	9	10
11	12	13	14	15	16	17
18	19	20	21	22	23	24
25	26	27	28	29	30	31
..	..	..	..	..	..	..

On 21 December 1941, the government of Thailand, under Prime Minister Plaek Phibunsongkhram (known in the West simply as "Phibun"), a field marshal and virtual dictator, signed a treaty of military alliance with Japan, giving Japanese troops passage through Thailand on their way to invade British-held Malaya and Burma. Unlike the puppet state of Manchukuo that the Japanese had established in Manchuria, however, Thailand remained in control of its armed forces and internal affairs; this state of affairs prevailed because the Japanese wanted a bilateral alliance to avoid the bother of pulling the strings of another subject state. On 25 January 1942, acting under Japanese pressure, Phibun declared war on Britain and the United States.

		THIS MONTH								FRIDAY					NEXT MONTH			

THIS MONTH

DECEMBER

S	M	T	W	T	F	S
..	..	..	..	..	1	2
3	4	5	6	7	8	9
10	11	12	13	14	15	16
17	18	19	20	21	22	23
24	25	26	27	28	29	30
31	..	..	..	..	..	..

FRIDAY

22

DECEMBER

1944

NEXT MONTH

JANUARY

S	M	T	W	T	F	S
..	1	2	3	4	5	6
7	8	9	10	11	12	13
14	15	16	17	18	19	20
21	22	23	24	25	26	27
28	29	30	31	..	..	..
..	..	..	..	..	..	..

On 22 December 1944, German armored and artillery forces commanded by *General* Heinrich Freiherr von Lüttwitz had pinned down and surrounded a much smaller contingent from the U.S. 101st Airborne and other units in Bastogne, Belgium, under Brigadier General Anthony McAuliffe. One Airborne trooper is reputed to have remarked, "We're surrounded. We've got 'em right where we want 'em." That the Americans were running dangerously low on ammunition was made obvious by the small volume of fire coming from within the town. Von Lüttwitz sent a truce party into the American lines bearing a politely worded ultimatum the gist of which was that the Americans, unable to be resupplied or reinforced because poor weather was keeping aircraft grounded, had the choice to surrender or be annihilated.

McAuliffe at first misunderstood the contents of the ultimatum as Lieutenant Colonel Harry Kinnard and Lieutenant Colonel Ned Moore explained it to him. When he was made to realize that the Germans were not offering to surrender to him, McAuliffe laughed and said, "Us surrender? Aw, nuts." As McAuliffe's staff was trying to formulate a properly worded reply, Kinnard suggested that McAuliffe's first response summed up the situation pretty well. Colonel Joseph Harper, commander of the 327th Glider Infantry, typed the official reply and delivered it to the truce party. It read as follows:

> To the German Commander.
>
> NUTS!
>
> The American Commander

Confused, the officer commanding the truce party asked what the message meant. Harper replied, "In plain English? Go to hell."

On the next day, the weather started to improve, and Allied air forces began launching resupply and attack sorties.

HEADQUARTERS 101ST AIRBORNE DIVISION
Office of the Division Commander

24 December 1944

What's Merry about all this, you ask? We're fighting - it's cold we aren't home. All true but what has the proud Eagle Division accomplished with its worthy comrades the 10th Armored Division, the 705th Tank Destroyer Battalion and all the rest? Just this: We have stopped cold everything that has been thrown at us from the North, East, South and West. We have identifications from four German Panzer Divisions, two German Infantry Divisions and one German Parachute Division. These units, spearheading the last desperate German lunge, were headed straight west for key points when the Eagle Division was hurriedly ordered to stem the advance. How effectively this was done will be written in history; not alone in our Division's glorious history but in World history. The Germans actually did surround us, their radios blared our doom. Their Commander demanded our surrender in the following impudent arrogance:

December 22nd 1944

"To the U. S. A. Commander of the encircled town of Bastogne.

The fortune of war is changing. This time the U. S. A. forces in and near Bastogne have been encircled by strong German armored units. More German armored units have crossed the river Ourthe near Ortheuville, have taken Marche and reached St. Hubert by passing through Hompre-Sibret-Tillet. Libramont is in German hands.

There is only one possibility to save the encircled U. S. A. Troops from total annihilation: that is the honorable surrender of the encircled town. In order to think it over a term of two hours will be granted beginning with the presentation of this note.

If this proposal should be rejected one German Artillery Corps and six heavy A. A. Battalions are ready to annihilate the U. S. A. Troops in and near Bastogne. The order for firing will be given immediately after this two hour's term.

All the serious civilian losses caused by this Artillery fire would not correspond with the well known American humanity.

The German Commander"

The German Commander received the following reply:
22 December 1944

"To the German Commander:

N U T S !

The American Commander"

Allied Troops are counterattacking in force. We continue to hold Bastogne. By holding Bastogne we assure the success of the Allied Armies. We know that our Division Commander, General Taylor, will say: "Well Done!"

We are giving our country and our loved ones at home a worthy Christmas present and being privileged to take part in this gallant feat of arms are truly making for ourselves a Merry Christmas.

/s/ A. C. McAULIFFE
/t/ McAULIFFE
Commanding.

	THIS MONTH												
	DECEMBER												
S	M	T	W	T	F	S							
..	1	2	3	4	5	6							
7	8	9	10	11	12	13							
14	15	16	17	18	19	20							
21	22	23	24	25	26	27							
28	29	30	31	..	..	..							
..	..	..	..	..	..	..							

TUESDAY
23
DECEMBER

NEXT MONTH						
JANUARY						
S	M	T	W	T	F	S
..	..	..	..	1	2	3
4	5	6	7	8	9	10
11	12	13	14	15	16	17
18	19	20	21	22	23	24
25	26	27	28	29	30	31
..	..	..	..	..	..	..

1941

On 23 December 1941, the Japanese returned to Wake Island in much greater force than they had brought 12 days earlier when they were routed by the Americans. The assault force comprised the aircraft carriers *Soryu* and *Hiryu* (both of which had participated in the Pearl Harbor attack), six cruisers, and six destroyers, with transport barges and two patrol boats carrying 1,500 SNLF (Special Naval Landing Forces) marines.

After a softening-up bombardment by ships and carrier aircraft, troops began landing at 0235 hours. In the fighting on the beach, U.S. Marine Corps pilot Captain Henry Elrod, whose bomb had sunk the destroyer *Kisaragi* on 11 December, was killed; he was posthumously awarded the Medal of Honor.

On nearby Wilkes Island, a force of 70 American Marines wiped out a 100-man force of Japanese SNLF marines, but the small victory was pointless in the face of U.S. Navy Commander Winfield S. Cunningham's surrender of his garrison at 0800 hours.

In the 16-day Battle of Wake Island, the Japanese lost 820 men killed and 333 wounded; two destroyers, two transports, and one submarine sunk; the light cruiser *Yubari* heavily damaged; and approximately 8 aircraft shot down and 20 others damaged. American losses were 120 men dead, 49 wounded, and two missing; all 12 Wildcat fighters destroyed; 433 military personnel and 1,104 civilians taken prisoner, of whom 103 were killed in captivity (98 civilians massacred on 7 October 1943), while another 97 died as POWs.

<table>
<tr><th colspan="7">THIS MONTH</th></tr>
<tr><th colspan="7">DECEMBER</th></tr>
<tr><th>S</th><th>M</th><th>T</th><th>W</th><th>T</th><th>F</th><th>S</th></tr>
<tr><td>..</td><td>1</td><td>2</td><td>3</td><td>4</td><td>5</td><td>6</td></tr>
<tr><td>7</td><td>8</td><td>9</td><td>10</td><td>11</td><td>12</td><td>13</td></tr>
<tr><td>14</td><td>15</td><td>16</td><td>17</td><td>18</td><td>19</td><td>20</td></tr>
<tr><td>21</td><td>22</td><td>23</td><td>24</td><td>25</td><td>26</td><td>27</td></tr>
<tr><td>28</td><td>29</td><td>30</td><td>31</td><td>..</td><td>..</td><td>..</td></tr>
<tr><td>..</td><td>..</td><td>..</td><td>..</td><td>..</td><td>..</td><td>..</td></tr>
</table>

WEDNESDAY
24
DECEMBER

1941

<table>
<tr><th colspan="7">NEXT MONTH</th></tr>
<tr><th colspan="7">JANUARY</th></tr>
<tr><th>S</th><th>M</th><th>T</th><th>W</th><th>T</th><th>F</th><th>S</th></tr>
<tr><td>..</td><td>..</td><td>..</td><td>..</td><td>1</td><td>2</td><td>3</td></tr>
<tr><td>4</td><td>5</td><td>6</td><td>7</td><td>8</td><td>9</td><td>10</td></tr>
<tr><td>11</td><td>12</td><td>13</td><td>14</td><td>15</td><td>16</td><td>17</td></tr>
<tr><td>18</td><td>19</td><td>20</td><td>21</td><td>22</td><td>23</td><td>24</td></tr>
<tr><td>25</td><td>26</td><td>27</td><td>28</td><td>29</td><td>30</td><td>31</td></tr>
<tr><td>..</td><td>..</td><td>..</td><td>..</td><td>..</td><td>..</td><td>..</td></tr>
</table>

On 24 December 1941, there was no repeat of the 1914 Christmas truces.[6] Under relentless pressure from Lieutenant General Masaharu Homma's 14th Imperial Japanese Army, which had invaded the Philippines two days earlier, U.S. Army Forces in the Far East (USAFFE) under General Douglas MacArthur were in the process of executing War Plan ORANGE-3, a prewar plan to defend only Bataan and Corregidor in a delaying action, by retreating into the Bataan Peninsula. Meanwhile, Philippine president Manuel L. Quezon, his family, and the government staff were evacuated to Corregidor along with MacArthur's USAFFE headquarters. USAFFE military personnel were removed from the major urban areas, and MacArthur declared Manila an open city. With the destruction of the U.S. Pacific Fleet at Pearl Harbor, no aid was forthcoming for the Americans and Filipinos, and on 9 April 1942 the Battle of Bataan would end with the largest U.S. surrender since the Battle of Harper's Ferry in the American Civil War.

---

6. In fact, there was no repeat of the Christmas truces during World War I, either. Commanders on both sides were shocked by the events, and they forbade their troops to fraternize with the enemy in the future.

THIS MONTH

DECEMBER

S	M	T	W	T	F	S
1	2	3	4	5	6	7
8	9	10	11	12	13	14
15	16	17	18	19	20	21
22	23	24	25	26	27	28
29	30	31	..	..	..	..
..	..	..	..	..	..	..

NEXT MONTH

JANUARY

S	M	T	W	T	F	S
..	..	..	1	2	3	4
5	6	7	8	9	10	11
12	13	14	15	16	17	18
19	20	21	22	23	24	25
26	27	28	29	30	31	..
..	..	..	..	..	..	..

WEDNESDAY

25

DECEMBER

1940

On 25 December 1940, the German cruiser *Admiral Hipper*, under the command of Admiral Wilhelm Meisel, failed to disrupt British troop convoy WS-5A, then steaming about 700 miles west of Cape Finisterre en route with 20 troop transports from Great Britain to the Middle East. Attacking out of the mist and rain at 0800 hours, *Hipper* shelled the troopship *Empire Trooper*, killing 16 men and inflicting heavy damage. She then attacked the freighter *Arabistan*, narrowly missing an ammunition store, but the corvette HMS *Clematis* chased her off with a single 4-inch gun; shortly thereafter, the cruisers HMS *Berwick*, HMS *Bonaventure*, and HMS *Dunedin* joined the fray. *Hipper* hit *Berwick*'s rear turret, killing four men, and escaped into the mist undamaged. Aircraft from carriers HMS *Argus* and HMS *Furious* searched for the undamaged *Hipper*, by then headed for Brest, but could not find her in the bad weather.

THIS MONTH						
DECEMBER						
S	M	T	W	T	F	S
..	..	..	..	..	1	2
3	4	5	6	7	8	9
10	11	12	13	14	15	16
17	18	19	20	21	22	23
24	25	26	27	28	29	30
31	..	..	..	..	..	..

TUESDAY
26
DECEMBER
1944

NEXT MONTH						
JANUARY						
S	M	T	W	T	F	S
..	1	2	3	4	5	6
7	8	9	10	11	12	13
14	15	16	17	18	19	20
21	22	23	24	25	26	27
28	29	30	31	..	..	..
..	..	..	..	..	..	..

On 26 December 1944, elements of General George "Old Blood and Guts" Patton's Third Army, commanded by Lieutenant Charles P. Boggess, succeeded in punching through to Bastogne, Belgium, from the southwest.

American troops of the 101st Airborne Division, with elements of the 10th Armored Division, the 705th Tank Destroyer Battalion, and other units, had been surrounded in Bastogne since 20 December; yet, with their ammunition and other supplies approaching zero, they had rejected a surrender ultimatum from German forces of the 5th Panzer Army and the XLVII Panzer Corps, who held positions completely encircling the town.

Patton's forces had been some 70 miles to the south and had covered the distance in an incredibly short time. The spearhead reached the lines of the 326th Engineers at approximately 1650 hours on the day after Christmas, and ground communication with American supply dumps was restored on the following day. The siege was broken, and with it Adolf Hitler's last desperate hope for victory in the West. When the news of Bastogne's deliverance reached America, newspapers all over the country referred to the 101st Airborne by the nickname the troopers had given themselves, the "Battered Bastards of Bastogne."

THIS MONTH							SATURDAY	NEXT MONTH						
DECEMBER							**27**	JANUARY						
S	M	T	W	T	F	S		S	M	T	W	T	F	S
..	1	2	3	4	5	6		..	..	..	..	1	2	3
7	8	9	10	11	12	13		4	5	6	7	8	9	10
14	15	16	17	18	19	20	**DECEMBER**	11	12	13	14	15	16	17
21	22	23	24	25	26	27		18	19	20	21	22	23	24
28	29	30	31	..	..	..		25	26	27	28	29	30	31
..	..	..	..	..	..	..		..	..	..	..	..	..	..

1941

On 27 December 1941, British Commandos from four Commando troops, together with a dozen men from Norwegian Independent Company 1, all under the command of Lieutenant Colonel John Durnford-Slater, executed Operation ARCHERY, a raid against German positions on Vågsøy Island, Norway. The action was supported by Royal Navy ships and Royal Air Force bombers and fighter-bombers.

The dawn landing was preceded by a very effective naval bombardment, and all went well except in the town of Måløy, on nearby Måløy Island, where a unit of experienced German mountain rangers from the Eastern Front was on leave. The Germans' experience in sniping and street fighting caused the operation in Måløy to develop into a bitter house-to-house battle. When the fighting was over, the commander of the Norwegians, Captain Martin Linge, had been killed in an attack on the local German headquarters; the Commandos had lost 17 men killed and 53 wounded; the Royal Air Force had lost eight planes; and the Royal Navy had lost four men killed and four wounded.

In addition to at least 120 men killed and 98 taken prisoner, the Germans had lost 10 naval vessels, some of which were scuttled to prevent capture; four factories; the fish-oil stores; ammunition and fuel stores; the telephone exchange; and various military installations—and, perhaps most importantly—a complete copy of the German Naval Code.

DECEMBER

S	M	T	W	T	F	S
1	2	3	4	5	6	7
8	9	10	11	12	13	14
15	16	17	18	19	20	21
22	23	24	25	26	27	28
29	30	31	..	..	..	..
..	..	..	..	..	..	..

SATURDAY
28
DECEMBER

1940

JANUARY

S	M	T	W	T	F	S
..	..	..	1	2	3	4
5	6	7	8	9	10	11
12	13	14	15	16	17	18
19	20	21	22	23	24	25
26	27	28	29	30	31	..
..	..	..	..	..	..	..

On 28 December 1940, as the Greco-Italian War was going badly for the Italians—with the Greeks holding roughly one fourth of Albania, the country from which the Italians had invaded Greece—Benito Mussolini requested military assistance from Germany against the Greeks. Adolf Hitler, not best pleased by the necessity of bailing out his ally, had already observed that the campaign was not going well and had anticipated the necessity for assistance. On 30 October he had issued a directive that included instructions to prepare for an invasion of Greece to be code-named *Unternehmen Marita,* which Germany's military planners scheduled to commence on 6 April 1941.

	THIS MONTH						
	DECEMBER						
S	M	T	W	T	F	S
1	2	3	4	5	6	7
8	9	10	11	12	13	14
15	16	17	18	19	20	21
22	23	24	25	26	27	28
29	30	31	..	..	..	..
..	..	..	..	..	..	..

SUNDAY
29
DECEMBER

1940

	NEXT MONTH						
	JANUARY						
S	M	T	W	T	F	S
..	..	..	1	2	3	4
5	6	7	8	9	10	11
12	13	14	15	16	17	18
19	20	21	22	23	24	25
26	27	28	29	30	31	..
..	..	..	..	..	..	..

On 29 December 1940, a raid by the *Luftwaffe* created the largest contiguous area of Blitz destruction anywhere in Britain. Called the "Second Great Fire of London," the damage was caused by more than 24,000 high explosive bombs and 100,000 incendiary bombs; it stretched south from Islington to the edge of St. Paul's Churchyard, an area greater than that of the Great Fire of London in 1666. The *Luftwaffe* timed the raid to coincide with a particularly low tide on the River Thames, making water difficult to obtain for firefighting. The bombing started more than 1,500 fires, many of which merged to form three major conflagrations that quickly developed into a firestorm, spreading the flames toward St. Paul's Cathedral. At the direction of Prime Minister Winston Churchill, the Cathedral was saved by the London firemen who kept the fire raging in the churchyard from reaching from the Cathedral building and by the volunteer firewatchers of the St. Paul's Watch, who fought to put out the incendiaries on the Cathedral's roof.

THIS MONTH						
DECEMBER						
S	M	T	W	T	F	S
..	1	2	3	4	5	6
7	8	9	10	11	12	13
14	15	16	17	18	19	20
21	22	23	24	25	26	27
28	29	30	31	..	..	..
..	..	..	..	..	..	..

TUESDAY
30
DECEMBER
1941

NEXT MONTH						
JANUARY						
S	M	T	W	T	F	S
..	..	..	..	1	2	3
4	5	6	7	8	9	10
11	12	13	14	15	16	17
18	19	20	21	22	23	24
25	26	27	28	29	30	31
..	..	..	..	..	..	..

On 30 December 1941, the Bethlehem Shipbuilding Corporation completed the fitting-out of the Liberty ship SS *Patrick Henry,* the first of 2,710 Liberty ships to go down the ways, at its Bethlehem-Fairfield Shipyard in Baltimore, Maryland.

SS *Patrick Henry* had been launched on 27 September by President Franklin D. Roosevelt as the first of 14 "Emergency vessels" launched that day at shipyards around the country. The list included SS *John C. Fremont,* SS *Louise Lykes,* SS *Ocean Venture,* SS *Ocean Voice,* SS *Star of Oregon,* and SS *Steel Artisan.* In his speech at the launching, Roosevelt gave the Liberty ships their common moniker when he referred to Patrick Henry's "Give me Liberty, or give me Death!" speech of 23 March 1775, saying that this new class of ships would bring liberty to Europe.

The 441-foot, 14,474-ton Liberty ships were built using an archaic, but thoroughly proven, design, and they were considered hideously ugly. They were welded together rather than riveted, in the first widespread use of the technique. The welded joints proved to be stress risers that encouraged cracking in the low-quality steel used, and several ships were lost to failures of this type. The Liberty ships were nevertheless a triumph of American industry, being built assembly-line style from prefabricated sections made in various places and transported to a shipyard for erection.[7]

SS *Patrick Henry* took 244 days to build, but by 1943 the average time for the three ships being completed each week had fallen to 42 days. As a one-time publicity stunt, SS *Robert E. Peary* was launched in 4 days, 15½ hours from the time her keel was laid.

---

7. SS *Jeremiah O'Brien,* based in San Francisco, and SS *John W. Brown,* based in Baltimore, are the only two surviving fully operational Liberty ships to have served in World War II. Both are operated as living history museums, offering cruises, tours, and other attractions. Of all the ships that participated in the Normandy landings, *Jeremiah O'Brien* alone returned to Normandy for the 50th anniversary events in 1994.

THIS MONTH						
DECEMBER						
S	M	T	W	T	F	S
..	..	1	2	3	4	5
6	7	8	9	10	11	12
13	14	15	16	17	18	19
20	21	22	23	24	25	26
27	28	29	30	31	..	..
..	..	..	..	..	..	..

THURSDAY
31
DECEMBER

1942

NEXT MONTH						
JANUARY						
S	M	T	W	T	F	S
..	..	..	..	..	1	2
3	4	5	6	7	8	9
10	11	12	13	14	15	16
17	18	19	20	21	22	23
24	25	26	27	28	29	30
31	..	..	..	..	..	..

On 31 December 1942, Allied Convoy JW-51B was in the Barents Sea, north of Norway, with 14 merchant ships carrying to the USSR a cargo comprising 202 tanks, 2,046 other vehicles, 87 fighter planes, 33 bombers, and 78,150 tons of fuel and other supplies. Protecting the convoy were the destroyers HMS *Achates, Obdurate, Obedient, Onslow* (escort force commander Captain Robert St. Vincent Sherbrooke's flagship), *Oribi*, and *Orwell*; *Flower*-class corvettes HMS *Rhododendron* and *Hyderabad*; the minesweeper HMS *Bramble*; and trawlers *Vizalma* and *Northern Gem*. Also stationed in the Barents Sea, independently of the convoy, were the cruisers HMS *Sheffield* and HMS *Jamaica*, with two destroyers. These four ships, under the command of Rear Admiral Robert L. Burnett, were designated Force R.

On the previous day, *U-354* (commanded by *Kapitänleutnant* Karl-Heinz Herbschleb) had spotted the convoy and radioed its position. Based at Altafjord in northern Norway was a force commanded by *Admiral* Oskar Kummetz, comprising the heavy cruisers *Admiral Hipper* and *Lützow* and the destroyers *Friedrich Eckholdt, Richard Beitzen, Theodor Riedel, Z29, Z30,* and *Z31.* Kummetz immediately put his force into motion, splitting it into two smaller groups led by *Hipper* and *Lützow*.

The Battle of the Barents Sea was joined at about 0830 hours on the 31st, the shellfire from the area of the convoy attracting the attention of Force R, which rushed into the fray. The area is north of the Arctic Circle, and the entire engagement was fought under polar night. Neither side knew accurately where its own ships, let alone those of the enemy, were, and nobody knew with certainty who was firing at whom. At one point, the German destroyers *Friedrich Eckholdt* and *Richard Beitzen* mistook *Sheffield* for *Admiral Hipper* and tried to form up with her; she fired on them and sent *Friedrich Eckholdt*, broken in two, to the bottom with all hands.

None of the merchant vessels was so much as touched in the engagement, so infuriating Adolf Hitler that he ordered the entire German surface fleet scrapped as being useless. *Admiral* Erich Raeder, supreme commander of the *Kriegsmarine*, resigned. His replacement, U-boat fleet commander Karl Dönitz, saved the surface fleet from the cutter's torch.

	THIS MONTH					
JANUARY						
S	M	T	W	T	F	S
..	1	2	3	4	5	6
7	8	9	10	11	12	13
14	15	16	17	18	19	20
21	22	23	24	25	26	27
28	29	30	31	..	..	..
..	..	..	..	..	..	..

MONDAY
1
JANUARY

1945

	NEXT MONTH					
FEBRUARY						
S	M	T	W	T	F	S
..	..	..	..	1	2	3
4	5	6	7	8	9	10
11	12	13	14	15	16	17
18	19	20	21	22	23	24
25	26	27	28	..	..	..
..	..	..	..	..	..	..

On 1 January 1945, U.S. troops of the 21st Armored Infantry Battalion, 11th Armored Division, massacred some 60 German prisoners of war near the Belgian village of Chenogne. This incident was a virtual duplicate of the German massacre of American prisoners near Malmédy on 17 December 1944: the operation was carried out in cold blood, with the Germans being lined up in fields along the sides of a road and machine-gunned.

Private First Class John Fague, of B Company, recognized that his comrades were committing the same atrocity of which America was accusing the Germans and Japanese. He wrote down an eyewitness account of the murder, ending with the following: "Going back down the road into town I looked into the fields where the German boys had been shot. Dark lifeless forms lay in the snow."

General George Patton, in his diary entry for 4 January, wrote: "The Eleventh Armored is very green and took unnecessary losses to no effect. There were also some unfortunate incidents in the shooting of prisoners. I hope we can conceal this." It is true, however, that the 328th Infantry Regiment had been given orders to shoot prisoners and had carried out those orders, and it is likely that other units had been given similar orders.

THIS MONTH						
JANUARY						
S	M	T	W	T	F	S
..	..	..	1	2	3	4
5	6	7	8	9	10	11
12	13	14	15	16	17	18
19	20	21	22	23	24	25
26	27	28	29	30	31	..
..	..	..	..	..	..	..

THURSDAY
2
JANUARY

1941

NEXT MONTH						
FEBRUARY						
S	M	T	W	T	F	S
..	..	..	..	..	..	1
2	3	4	5	6	7	8
9	10	11	12	13	14	15
16	17	18	19	20	21	22
23	24	25	26	27	28	..
..	..	..	..	..	..	..

On 2 January 1941, at about 0600 hours, German aircraft bombed Dublin, Ireland. They first dropped two bombs in Rathdown Park, Terenure, in south Dublin. The first bomb landed in soft ground and created a large crater but caused little other damage. The second landed behind two houses on Rathdown Park, destroying both and damaging several other nearby houses. They then dropped two more bombs on the corner of Lavarna Grove and Fortfield Road, close to the Kimmage Crossroads. Lavarna Grove was still under construction at this time; the bombs landed on undeveloped land but damaged several nearby houses. There were no deaths from this incident, and only one person was injured. This was the second German bombing of Ireland, and it was followed the next night by a third. It has been surmised that the aircraft that dropped these bombs were seriously lost and off course. Ireland was then, and remained throughout the war, neutral.

THIS MONTH								MONDAY		NEXT MONTH					

THIS MONTH

JANUARY

S	M	T	W	T	F	S
..	..	..	..	..	..	1
2	3	4	5	6	7	8
9	10	11	12	13	14	15
16	17	18	19	20	21	22
23	24	25	26	27	28	29
30	31	..	..	..	..	..

MONDAY

3

JANUARY

1944

NEXT MONTH

FEBRUARY

S	M	T	W	T	F	S
..	..	1	2	3	4	5
6	7	8	9	10	11	12
13	14	15	16	17	18	19
20	21	22	23	24	25	26
27	28	29	..	..	..	..
..	..	..	..	..	..	..

On 3 January 1944, U.S. Marine Corps Major Gregory "Pappy" Boyington, the commander of VMF-214 (known as the Black Sheep Squadron for their unmilitary bearing and behavior), was flying a Vought F4U Corsair as the tactical commander of a 48-plane fighter sweep over Rabaul.

As the Americans got into a furball with approximately 70 Japanese fighters, Boyington shot down his 26th Japanese plane,[1] tying the

---

1. Certain irregularities exist in Boyington's official tally of victories. He claimed six kills while serving with the Flying Tigers, but AVG records document with certainty only 3½ aircraft destroyed, of which some were on the ground and should technically not count as victories.

American record at that time. He in turn was shot down later in the scrap, which lasted for about half an hour, an eternity for dogfighting fighters. His wingman was killed in the action and so could not report what had happened to Pappy.

Boyington had in fact ditched his damaged aircraft and was picked up by a Japanese submarine, spending the rest of the war in Japanese prison camps on Rabaul and Truk, in Ōfuna Prison Camp near Yokohama, and finally in Ōmori Prison Camp near Tokyo.

Boyington's squadron mates assumed that he had been killed; but absent proof of his death, he was listed as missing in action. He asserted in his postwar memoirs that he was never reported as a POW or to the Red Cross. Imperial Japanese Navy Captain Masajiro Kawato, who in 1976 claimed Boyington as a victory, was present in the action on 3 January 1944; but his claim has since been conclusively disproven, and the identity of the pilot or pilots who shot Pappy down remains unknown.

		THIS MONTH				
			JANUARY			
S	M	T	W	T	F	S
..	1	2	3	4	5	6
7	8	9	10	11	12	13
14	15	16	17	18	19	20
21	22	23	24	25	26	27
28	29	30	31	..	..	..
..	..	..	..	..	..	..

THURSDAY
4
JANUARY

1945

		NEXT MONTH				
			FEBRUARY			
S	M	T	W	T	F	S
..	..	..	..	1	2	3
4	5	6	7	8	9	10
11	12	13	14	15	16	17
18	19	20	21	22	23	24
25	26	27	28	..	..	..
..	..	..	..	..	..	..

On 4 January 1945, the Burma Banshees, officially known as the U.S. 10th Air Force's 80th Fighter Group, returned to their original owners several loads of bombs that had been left behind when Imperial Japanese Army Major General Mizukami Genzu withdrew his remaining troops from Myitkyina Airfield in northern Burma to prevent their capture by Merrill's Marauders on 3 August 1944. The bombs, made in Japan, were embellished with greetings along the general lines of this one: "Made in Japan. Returned with 10th Air Force Compliments." The Americans had found the bombs in a concealed Japanese ammunition dump near the airfield. Also left behind were enough fuzes to arm the bombs. The only American contribution, other than the return conveyance and aiming, was an extension bar to allow the bombs to be hung in the regular wing racks of the Banshees' P-47 fighter-bombers.

THIS MONTH						
JANUARY						
S	M	T	W	T	F	S
..	..	..	1	2	3	4
5	6	7	8	9	10	11
12	13	14	15	16	17	18
19	20	21	22	23	24	25
26	27	28	29	30	31	..
..	..	..	..	..	..	..

SUNDAY
5
JANUARY

NEXT MONTH						
FEBRUARY						
S	M	T	W	T	F	S
..	..	..	..	..	..	1
2	3	4	5	6	7	8
9	10	11	12	13	14	15
16	17	18	19	20	21	22
23	24	25	26	27	28	..

1941

On 5 January 1941, the Battle of Bardia came to an end. The battle, begun on 3 January, was the first battle of the war in which an Australian Army formation took part, the first to be commanded by an Australian general (Major General Iven Mackay), and the first to be planned by an Australian staff.

On the first day, Allied forces assaulted the strongly held Italian fortress of Bardia, Libya, with air support and assistance by naval gunfire and the usual preliminary artillery barrage. Sappers used Bangalore torpedoes against barbed-wire defenses and then filled in and broke down the sides of the antitank ditch, paving the way for the infantry and 23 Matilda II tanks to enter the fortress and capture all their objectives, along with 8,000 prisoners. The breach in the Italian perimeter allowed a further advance to a secondary line of defenses named the Switch Line.

On the second day, infantry captured the township of Bardia, cutting the fortress in two and taking thousands of prisoners.

On the third day, 5 January, with the Italians holding only the northern and southernmost parts of the fortress, Allied infantry again advanced, with support from artillery and the remaining six tanks, and captured the southern sector of the fortress while the Italians in the northern sector were surrendering. Allied losses numbered 130 killed and 326 wounded; the Italians lost 1,000 killed, 3,000 wounded, and 36,000 taken prisoner.

This action cleared the way for further Allied advances into Libya, whose end result was that Germany intervened in the African conflict to support its Italian ally. The Battle of Bardia increased the Australian Army's skill and reputation, and it raised confidence in the possibility of an ultimate Allied victory that would lead to the passage of the Lend-Lease Act in the United States.

THIS MONTH						
JANUARY						
S	M	T	W	T	F	S
..	..	..	1	2	3	4
5	6	7	8	9	10	11
12	13	14	15	16	17	18
19	20	21	22	23	24	25
26	27	28	29	30	31	..
..	..	..	..	..	..	..

MONDAY
6
JANUARY

1941

NEXT MONTH						
FEBRUARY						
S	M	T	W	T	F	S
..	..	..	..	..	..	1
2	3	4	5	6	7	8
9	10	11	12	13	14	15
16	17	18	19	20	21	22
23	24	25	26	27	28	..
..	..	..	..	..	..	..

On 6 January 1941, U.S. President Franklin D. Roosevelt delivered his ninth State of the Union address to the combined Houses of Congress. In his speech, he talked about the national security of the United States and the threat to other democracies from the ongoing world war, and in a break with the long-held American tradition of nonintervention, he outlined the role of the United States in helping nations already engaged in the struggle against the Axis. In the context thus established, he said the following:

"In the future days, which we seek to make secure, we look forward to a world founded upon four essential human freedoms.

"The first is freedom of speech and expression—everywhere in the world.

"The second is freedom of every person to worship God in his own way—everywhere in the world.

"The third is freedom from want—which, translated into world terms, means economic understandings which will secure to every nation a healthy peacetime life for its inhabitants—everywhere in the world.

"The fourth is freedom from fear—which, translated into world terms, means a world-wide reduction of armaments to such a point and in such a thorough fashion that no nation will be in a position to commit an act of physical aggression against any neighbor—anywhere in the world.

"That is no vision of a distant millennium. It is a definite basis for a kind of world attainable in our own time and generation. That kind of world is the very antithesis of the so-called new order of tyranny which the dictators seek to create with the crash of a bomb."

Roosevelt's address became known as the Four Freedoms Speech. The theme of the Four Freedoms was also written into the Atlantic Charter, issued in August 1941 by the United States and Great Britain.

In 1943, artist Norman Rockwell took inspiration from the speech to paint four canvases for the *Saturday Evening Post*; each appeared opposite an essay by a prominent thinker of the day. After the war, the theme became an essential part of the charter of the United Nations.

THIS MONTH												NEXT MONTH						
JANUARY								SUNDAY			**FEBRUARY**						

S	M	T	W	T	F	S
..	1	2	3	4	5	6
7	8	9	10	11	12	13
14	15	16	17	18	19	20
21	22	23	24	25	26	27
28	29	30	31	..	..	..
..	..	..	..	..	..	..

SUNDAY
7
JANUARY

S	M	T	W	T	F	S
..	..	..	..	1	2	3
4	5	6	7	8	9	10
11	12	13	14	15	16	17
18	19	20	21	22	23	24
25	26	27	28	29	..	..
..	..	..	..	..	..	..

1940

On 7 January 1940, General Semyon Timoshenko took command of Soviet Army forces in Finland in a last-ditch attempt by Joseph Stalin to break the back of an overwhelming Finnish military superiority. With vastly greater manpower and *matériel,* the Soviets—under the disastrously incompetent leadership of Marshal Kliment Voroshilov—had suffered about 185,000 casualties, three times the number suffered by the Finns, without producing a victory in the war that they had forced on the Finns. Stalin finally jerked the rug out from under Voroshilov; Timoshenko turned things around sufficiently that in March 1940 the Finns were brought to the peace table to sign a treaty in which they ceded more territory than the Soviets had demanded before the war.

THIS MONTH						
JANUARY						
S	M	T	W	T	F	S
..	1	2	3	4	5	6
7	8	9	10	11	12	13
14	15	16	17	18	19	20
21	22	23	24	25	26	27
28	29	30	31	..	..	..
..	..	..	..	..	..	..

MONDAY

8

JANUARY

NEXT MONTH						
FEBRUARY						
S	M	T	W	T	F	S
..	..	..	..	1	2	3
4	5	6	7	8	9	10
11	12	13	14	15	16	17
18	19	20	21	22	23	24
25	26	27	28	29	..	..
..	..	..	..	..	..	..

1940

On 8 January 1940, one day after Joseph Stalin had handed command of his army over to General Semyon Timoshenko, Finnish troops under Colonel Hjalmar Siilasvuo gained a major victory with the annihilation of the Soviet 44th Division in the Battle of Suomussalmi. Over the course of five days, the Finns had employed a tactic known as "motti," by which they divided the Soviet troops into isolated groups and cut them up piecemeal. Also soundly defeating the Soviet 163rd Division, the Finns ended the battle with a loss of about 1,000 men killed or missing and 1,000 wounded; estimates of Soviet casualties range 13,000 to 27,500 killed or missing, as well as 2,100 taken prisoner. After the battle, Finnish troops collected 85 tanks, 437 trucks, 1,620 horses, 52 heavy cannons, 40 field guns, 78 antitank guns, 20 tractors, 13 antiaircraft guns, more than 6,000 rifles, and an enormous amount of ammunition. The Finnish victory prevented the Soviets from capturing the city of Oulu, which is located on Finland's western border and whose fall would have cut Finland in two and forced the Finns to fight on two fronts.

THIS MONTH						
JANUARY						
S	M	T	W	T	F	S
..	1	2	3	4	5	6
7	8	9	10	11	12	13
14	15	16	17	18	19	20
21	22	23	24	25	26	27
28	29	30	31	..	..	..
..	..	..	..	..	..	..

TUESDAY
9
JANUARY
1945

NEXT MONTH						
FEBRUARY						
S	M	T	W	T	F	S
..	..	..	..	1	2	3
4	5	6	7	8	9	10
11	12	13	14	15	16	17
18	19	20	21	22	23	24
25	26	27	28	..	..	..
..	..	..	..	..	..	..

On 9 January 1945, at 0700 hours, against ferocious opposition from *kamikaze* aircraft, Allied ships in the Gulf of Lingayen, to the north of Luzon, began a pre-assault naval bombardment. Promptly one hour later, amphibious American assault forces of the 6th Army, under the command of General Walter Krueger, began landing along a 20-mile stretch of beachfront.

Japanese resistance to the landings was surprisingly light despite the sophisticated and powerful defensive positions the Japanese, commanded by General Tomoyuki Yamashita, had built in the hills surrounding the gulf, and over the next few days approximately 175,000 troops were landed. 15 January saw a second landing 45 miles southwest of Manila. On 31 January, two regiments of the 11th Airborne Division made an airborne assault.

On 3 February, the 1st Cavalry Division captured a bridge across the Tullahan River, gaining access to Manila and entering the city that evening. The battle for Manila began on the next day as the paratroops of the 11th Airborne Division, approaching the city from the south, were brought up short by heavy resistance from the main Japanese defenses there. General Yamashita had ordered his troops to destroy all bridges and other vital installations as soon as the U.S. forces entered the city, and Japanese troops entrenched throughout the city put up stiff resistance. On 11 February, the 11th Airborne Division completed the encirclement of the city, and American troops worked with Filipino guerrillas to root out the remaining Japanese resisters in the following weeks.

By the middle of March, the Allies controlled all strategically and economically important locations on the island, but scattered Japanese resistance continued until mid-August, when Emperor Hirohito ordered the Japanese military to surrender. Of approximately 1,000,000 Allied fighting men committed to the Battle of Luzon, 8,310 were killed and 29,560 were wounded. The Japanese lost 205,535 killed and 9,050 made prisoner.

THIS MONTH

JANUARY

S	M	T	W	T	F	S
..	1	2	3	4	5	6
7	8	9	10	11	12	13
14	15	16	17	18	19	20
21	22	23	24	25	26	27
28	29	30	31	..	..	..
..	..	..	..	..	..	..

WEDNESDAY

10

JANUARY

1940

NEXT MONTH

FEBRUARY

S	M	T	W	T	F	S
..	..	..	..	1	2	3
4	5	6	7	8	9	10
11	12	13	14	15	16	17
18	19	20	21	22	23	24
25	26	27	28	29	..	..
..	..	..	..	..	..	..

On 10 January 1940, *Luftwaffe Major* Erich Hoenmanns, on a flight from an airdrome near Münster to Cologne, lost his bearings in fog and accidentally crossed the Rhine into Dutch and then Belgian airspace. At that point, he somehow cut off the fuel supply inadvertently. The engine quit, and Hoenmanns made a forced landing in a field near Maasmechelen, Belgium. The aircraft he was piloting, a Messerschmitt Bf 108 (a four-seat single-engined sports/touring plane), was destroyed: both wings were ripped off as the craft skidded between two trees, and the engine tore loose from the fuselage.

Hoenmanns was able to walk away, however, and if he had been alone, he would have been interned for landing in a neutral country without permission, but beyond that the incident would have been little more than a trivial blot on the safety record of flying. Unfortunately, with him in the plane was *Major* Hellmuth Reinberger, who was carrying a copy of the plans for *Fall Gelb* (Case Yellow), the invasion of the Low Countries, scheduled to begin one week later, on 17 January. On learning from a farmhand that they were not in Germany, the Germans panicked. While Hoenmanns moved away from the plane as a diversion, Reinberger raced back to recover his briefcase and destroy the documents. His cigarette lighter malfunctioned, and the farmhand was able to provide only a single match, which Reinberger took with him behind a thicket where he could set a fire.

Two Belgian border guards who happened to be passing by saw the smoke, captured the Germans, and took possession of the documents. Belgian intelligence agents quickly realized what they had and notified their superiors; the Belgians notified the French and British, and an immediate crisis ensued but quickly abated when the scheduled dates passed without incident. It has been theorized that the discovery of the documents caused the Germans to make drastic changes in their plans; but in fact *Fall Gelb*, when it did commence on 10 May, unfolded in a form very close to that described in the plans that Reinberger had failed to destroy.

THIS MONTH						
JANUARY						
S	M	T	W	T	F	S
..	1	2	3	4	5	6
7	8	9	10	11	12	13
14	15	16	17	18	19	20
21	22	23	24	25	26	27
28	29	30	31	..	..	..
..	..	..	..	..	..	..

THURSDAY
11
JANUARY
1945

NEXT MONTH						
FEBRUARY						
S	M	T	W	T	F	S
..	..	..	..	1	2	3
4	5	6	7	8	9	10
11	12	13	14	15	16	17
18	19	20	21	22	23	24
25	26	27	28	..	..	..
..	..	..	..	..	..	..

On 11 January 1945, the first convoy moved on the Ledo road. The road, which runs from Ledo, Assam, India to Kunming, Yunnan, China, was

built beginning in December 1942, pursuant to an agreement on 1 December of that year between British General Sir Archibald Wavell, the supreme commander of the Far Eastern Theatre, and American General Joseph Stilwell after the Japanese had cut the Burma Road, forcing the Allies to commence a massive airlift, originally referred to as the "India-China Ferry," to fly cargo over the Himalaya Mountains ("the Hump") to China. The road was renamed the Stilwell Road in early 1945 at the suggestion of Chiang Kai-shek. Complicating construction was the fact that the road could not be engineered in advance because the Japanese controlled most of Burma. The project went forward nevertheless; its construction required 15,000 American soldiers and 35,000 local workers, and the project cost $150,000,000. 1,100 Americans and an undetermined, but much larger, number of local workers died during the construction.

THIS MONTH														NEXT MONTH					
JANUARY														FEBRUARY					

WEDNESDAY

12

JANUARY

1944

S	M	T	W	T	F	S
..	..	..	..	..	..	1
2	3	4	5	6	7	8
9	10	11	12	13	14	15
16	17	18	19	20	21	22
23	24	25	26	27	28	29
30	31	..	..	..	..	..

S	M	T	W	T	F	S
..	..	1	2	3	4	5
6	7	8	9	10	11	12
13	14	15	16	17	18	19
20	21	22	23	24	25	26
27	28	29	..	..	..	..
..	..	..	..	..	..	..

On 12 January 1944, Benito Mussolini's supporters executed Count Galeazzo Ciano, the Italian Foreign Minister and the husband of Mussolini's daughter Edda. The count was among those who had voted at the 24 July 1943 meeting of the Fascist Grand Council to restore King Victor Emmanuel III to the full constitutional powers of which he had been stripped as a result of Mussolini's rise to power. Arrested and imprisoned the next day but rescued on 12 October by the Germans, Mussolini was convinced by Hitler to establish a new regime, the Italian Social Republic (called the Salò Republic after the city where Mussolini settled 11 days after his rescue). The Salò Republic suffered the loss of all the Italian territory controlled by the Allies and by the government of Pietro Badoglio, whom the king had named to succeed Mussolini. In his new role, Mussolini was reduced to the status of a puppet, in effect becoming the *gauleiter* (provincial governor) of Lombardy. Under pressure from Hitler and loyal fascist supporters to strengthen his regime, he orchestrated a series of executions to dispose of some of the fascist leaders who had betrayed him the day before his arrest. One of the victims was Ciano. After his arrest on 11 January, he was tried, convicted of "dissenting against Il Duce's will," and sentenced to death. A Fascist firing squad executed Ciano, Emilio De Bono, Giovanni Marinelli, and others who had voted for Mussolini's ousting. The victims were tied to chairs and shot in the back as a further humiliation. Ciano's last words were "Long live Italy!"

THIS MONTH						
JANUARY						
S	M	T	W	T	F	S
..	..	..	..	1	2	3
4	5	6	7	8	9	10
11	12	13	14	15	16	17
18	19	20	21	22	23	24
25	26	27	28	29	30	31
..	..	..	..	..	..	..

TUESDAY
13
JANUARY

NEXT MONTH						
FEBRUARY						
S	M	T	W	T	F	S
1	2	3	4	5	6	7
8	9	10	11	12	13	14
15	16	17	18	19	20	21
22	23	24	25	26	27	28
..	..	..	..	..	..	..

1942

On or about 13 January 1942, the first five Type IX U-boats participating in *Unternehmen Paukenschlag* (Operation DRUMBEAT) began sinking merchant shipping off the east coast of North America. During the overall operation, which lasted until mid-August, Germany's U-boat fleet sank 609 ships totaling 3.1 million tons, roughly one-fourth of all shipping sunk by U-boats during the entire war, while losing only 22 of their own boats. U-boat commanders referred to this time as the "American shooting season," while their sailors called it the "Second Happy Time," a reference to the first "Happy Time" of 1940–1941.

At first, hunting was exceptionally good along the United States coastline, as no blackout had been imposed, and cities such as Miami and New York presented a perfect "shooting gallery." Boats would stay submerged during the day and surface at night, when they were invisible but could easily see the silhouettes of ships passing up and down the coast with the cities' bright lights behind them.

Once the Americans finally twigged to the danger and instituted the convoy system and coastal blackouts, merchant sinkings began to decline as heightened aerial and surface patrolling began to tell against the U-boats.

Interestingly, the Americans' "Loose Lips Sink Ships" propaganda campaign was not intended so much to prevent damaging information from falling into enemy hands as it was to bolster American civilian morale by reducing communication about how much shipping the Germans were sinking.

THIS MONTH						
JANUARY						
S	M	T	W	T	F	S
..	..	..	..	..	1	2
3	4	5	6	7	8	9
10	11	12	13	14	15	16
17	18	19	20	21	22	23
24	25	26	27	28	29	30
31	..	..	..	..	..	..

THURSDAY
14
JANUARY

NEXT MONTH						
FEBRUARY						
S	M	T	W	T	F	S
..	1	2	3	4	5	6
7	8	9	10	11	12	13
14	15	16	17	18	19	20
21	22	23	24	25	26	27
28	..	..	..	..	..	..
..	..	..	..	..	..	..

1943

On 14 January 1943, the leaders of the Western Allies opened the Casablanca Conference. On the agenda for U.S. President Franklin D. Roosevelt and British Prime Minister Winston Churchill were discussions of the eventual invasion of mainland Europe (which American planners considered to be the only way to defeat Germany), the impending invasion of Sicily and Italy (which British planners insisted would draw Axis forces away from the northern areas and make the later invasion easier), and the policy of requiring unconditional surrender from the Axis powers. When President Roosevelt suddenly announced this surrender condition at Casablanca, he referred to American Civil War General Ulysses S. Grant and the fact that Grant's initials, since the Civil War, had also come to stand for "Unconditional Surrender."

Unconditional surrender is a surrender without conditions, with no guarantees given to the surrendering party, and announcing that it is the only acceptable end to a conflict puts psychological pressure on a weaker adversary. In 1945, Germany did surrender unconditionally; Japan's "unconditional" surrender was given and accepted without clarification of the future status of the emperor, who the Japanese insisted must remain as the head of the Japanese people.

		THIS MONTH							MONDAY			NEXT MONTH				

THIS MONTH

JANUARY

S	M	T	W	T	F	S
..	1	2	3	4	5	6
7	8	9	10	11	12	13
14	15	16	17	18	19	20
21	22	23	24	25	26	27
28	29	30	31	..	..	..
..	..	..	..	..	..	..

MONDAY

15

JANUARY

1945

NEXT MONTH

FEBRUARY

S	M	T	W	T	F	S
..	..	..	..	1	2	3
4	5	6	7	8	9	10
11	12	13	14	15	16	17
18	19	20	21	22	23	24
25	26	27	28	..	..	..
..	..	..	..	..	..	..

On 15 January 1945, the first commercial shipping in five years moved through the English Channel. In May 1940, during the Battle of France, German forces had taken the French ports of Boulogne and Calais, effectively cutting off the British retreat path. Only by dint of desperate fighting, aided by a major tactical error on the part of Hitler, was the port of Dunkirk kept open, allowing the rescue of 336,000 Allied troops in Operation DYNAMO. During the next month, before the Germans established control over ports farther south, the Allies managed to pull out an additional 192,000. Thenceforward, German aircraft, submarines, and E-boats (fast attack boats) made the Channel too hazardous for even major warships, and not until the Normandy landings, by which time the Allies had virtually banished the *Luftwaffe* from the skies and decimated the *Kriegsmarine*'s submarine fleet, did any traffic cross the dangerous waters. (In the run-up to Operation NEPTUNE, the initial landing phase of Operation OVERLORD, E-boats had actually penetrated British waters during a landing exercise and had sunk a troop transport, drowning more than 700 American soldiers.)

THIS MONTH						
JANUARY						
S	M	T	W	T	F	S
..	..	..	..	1	2	3
4	5	6	7	8	9	10
11	12	13	14	15	16	17
18	19	20	21	22	23	24
25	26	27	28	29	30	31
..	..	..	..	..	..	..

FRIDAY
16
JANUARY

NEXT MONTH						
FEBRUARY						
S	M	T	W	T	F	S
1	2	3	4	5	6	7
8	9	10	11	12	13	14
15	16	17	18	19	20	21
22	23	24	25	26	27	28
..	..	..	..	..	..	..

1942

On 16 January 1942, as the Soviet Union's Third Shock Army was in the process of capturing Andreapol, creating a gap between German Army Group North and Army Group Center and opening a path for the starving Red Army to reach the huge German supply dumps at Toropets, Joseph Stalin made public the text of an order that had been issued by *Generalfeld-marschall* Walter von Reichenau, a strong anti-Semite and the commander of the *Wehrmacht*'s Sixth Army, in October 1941. This order, officially called the Severity Order but commonly known as the Reichenau Order, stated that Jews were a subhuman species and were thenceforth to be treated the same as paramilitary partisans. All commanders on the Eastern Front were directed to summarily shoot any and all Jews captured—or if for some reason such as a need for silence, that was not possible, hand them over to the *Einsatzgruppen* execution squads of the *SS-Totenkopfverbände.*

THIS MONTH						
JANUARY						
S	M	T	W	T	F	S
..	..	..	..	..	1	2
3	4	5	6	7	8	9
10	11	12	13	14	15	16
17	18	19	20	21	22	23
24	25	26	27	28	29	30
31	..	..	..	..	..	..

SUNDAY
17
JANUARY

NEXT MONTH						
FEBRUARY						
S	M	T	W	T	F	S
..	1	2	3	4	5	6
7	8	9	10	11	12	13
14	15	16	17	18	19	20
21	22	23	24	25	26	27
28	..	..	..	..	..	..

1943

On 17 January 1943, nearly 200 Lancaster and Halifax heavy bombers of the Royal Air Force conducted the first attack of a two-night bombing campaign against Berlin, the RAF's 54th raid on the German capital. Cloud cover was heavy from England to Germany, but clear patches made it possible for the bombers to drop their entire loads, doing significant damage with the loss of only two aircraft. German radio claimed that residential districts and public buildings, including hospitals, were hit. On the next night, 187 Lancasters and 17 Halifaxes repeated the raid, even following the same routes to the target. This time, the *Luftwaffe*'s night fighters found the bomber stream and shot down 22 bombers. This pair of raids had been an experiment; it was deemed less than successful, and the experiment was discontinued until the advanced H2S airborne ground-scanning radar became available less than a fortnight later.

THIS MONTH						
JANUARY						
S	M	T	W	T	F	S
..	..	..	..	..	1	2
3	4	5	6	7	8	9
10	11	12	13	14	15	16
17	18	19	20	21	22	23
24	25	26	27	28	29	30
31	..	..	..	..	..	..

MONDAY
18
JANUARY
1943

NEXT MONTH						
FEBRUARY						
S	M	T	W	T	F	S
..	1	2	3	4	5	6
7	8	9	10	11	12	13
14	15	16	17	18	19	20
21	22	23	24	25	26	27
28	..	..	..	..	..	..

On 18 January 1943, after almost four months without any deportations, German troops suddenly entered the Warsaw ghetto to restart the "resettlement" operation that had already sent as many as 300,000 Jews to Treblinka and other death camps. The ghetto, covering 1.3 square miles, was "home" to more than 400,000 Jews, of whom those who were not collaborating with their captors, or working as slave laborers, were awaiting their own deportation.

In response to the Germans' incursion, on this day the residents finally acted on the realization that "resettlement" was a lie. Led by the underground ŻOB and ŻZW resistance organizations, they rose against their Nazi masters. ŻOB and ŻZW took control of the ghetto, built shelters and

fighting posts, and struggled against the Germans and Jewish collaborators. Fighting was vicious and deadly, eventually leveling almost all of the
ghetto.

In the end, the spirit of the detainees was no match for the military might
of the Germans; significant resistance ended on 28 April, and the Nazis
officially ended operations with the demolition of the Great Synagogue of
Warsaw on 16 May. According to the official report, at least 56,065 people
were either killed during the fighting or subsequently deported to concentration and death camps.

THIS MONTH

JANUARY

S	M	T	W	T	F	S
..	..	..	1	2	3	4
5	6	7	8	9	10	11
12	13	14	15	16	17	18
19	20	21	22	23	24	25
26	27	28	29	30	31	..
..	..	..	..	..	..	..

SUNDAY
19
JANUARY

NEXT MONTH

FEBRUARY

S	M	T	W	T	F	S
..	..	..	..	..	..	1
2	3	4	5	6	7	8
9	10	11	12	13	14	15
16	17	18	19	20	21	22
23	24	25	26	27	28	..
..	..	..	..	..	..	..

1941

On 19 January 1941, the Indian 4th and 5th Infantry Divisions and other forces under Major General William Platt, the commander of Britain's Sudan Defence Force, launched an offensive against Italian troops in Eritrea. The first action of this campaign was the recapture of Kassala, a vital railway junction on the border between the Sudan and Eritrea. The town's capture was made without resistance, as the Italians, who had originally taken Kassala and the nearby village of Gallabat on 4 January 1940, had evacuated the two municipalities on the night of 17 January as they retreated into Eritrea. Platt's forces continued into Eritrea, and after bitter fighting lasting nearly two months they captured the strategic railway-junction town of Keren. The Italians retreated to Adi Tekelezan, where they found themselves in a much less tenable position than Keren had been, and they finally surrendered on 1 April.

	THIS MONTH										NEXT MONTH					
JANUARY							**TUESDAY**		**FEBRUARY**							
S	M	T	W	T	F	S	**20**	S	M	T	W	T	F	S		
..	..	..	..	1	2	3		1	2	3	4	5	6	7		
4	5	6	7	8	9	10	**JANUARY**	8	9	10	11	12	13	14		
11	12	13	14	15	16	17		15	16	17	18	19	20	21		
18	19	20	21	22	23	24	**1942**	22	23	24	25	26	27	28		
25	26	27	28	29	30	31		..	..	..	..	..	..	..		

On 20 January 1942, senior officials of the Nazi Party met in a villa at 56–58 Am Großen Wannsee, overlooking a bight in the River Havel in Wannsee, a suburb of Berlin, Germany. The Wannsee Conference, hosted by *SS-Obergruppenführer* Reinhard Heydrich, the director of the SS-*Reichssicherheitshauptamt* (Reich Main Security Office, RSHA), was to ensure the cooperation of various government departments in executing the plan to round up, deport, and exterminate the Jewish population of German-occupied Europe.

Reichsmarschall Hermann Göring had placed Heydrich in charge of this plan, the Final Solution to the Jewish Question, on 31 January 1941. Among the 15 attendees were Heydrich himself and *SS-Obersturmbannführer* Adolf Eichmann, whom Heydrich assigned to be his liaison with the departments involved, a position in which Eichmann would oversee the actual carrying-out of the plan.

Heydrich was mortally wounded by an assassination attempt in Prague, Czechoslovakia, on 27 May 1942, dying on 4 June. Eichmann survived the war and escaped capture, living in Austria until 1950. He then moved under a false identity to Argentina, where he lived with his wife Veronika and son Ricardo in a house on Garibaldi Street in San Fernando, a Buenos Aires suburb, until he was captured on 11 May 1960 by a team of agents of Mossad and Shin Bet under the command of Isser Harel. Smuggled to Israel, he stood trial for his part in the murder of some 6 million Jews. He was found guilty of crimes against humanity; war crimes; crimes against Poles, Slovenes, and the Romani people; and membership in three illegal organizations (the SS, the SD, and the Gestapo). Hanged shortly before midnight on 31 May 1962 in the prison at Ramla, Israel, he met his death without having expressed remorse for his actions.

THIS MONTH						
JANUARY						
S	M	T	W	T	F	S
..	1	2	3	4	5	6
7	8	9	10	11	12	13
14	15	16	17	18	19	20
21	22	23	24	25	26	27
28	29	30	31	..	..	..
..	..	..	..	..	..	..

SUNDAY
21
JANUARY
1940

NEXT MONTH						
FEBRUARY						
S	M	T	W	T	F	S
..	..	..	..	1	2	3
4	5	6	7	8	9	10
11	12	13	14	15	16	17
18	19	20	21	22	23	24
25	26	27	28	29	..	..
..	..	..	..	..	..	..

On 21 January 1940, the destroyer HMS *Exmouth*, assigned to carry out patrols and escort convoys in the North Sea, was escorting the merchant ship *Cyprian Prince* through the Moray Firth, off Wick, Scotland, when she was spotted by the German submarine *U-22*, under the command of *Kapitänleutnant* Karl-Heinrich Jenisch. The boat torpedoed *Exmouth*, apparently using several torpedoes to sink her with the loss of her entire 189-man complement. A schoolboy playing hooky discovered 18 bodies that had washed ashore near Wick, and those bodies were buried with full military honors at Wick, with more than 150 relatives of *Exmouth*'s crew in attendance.

Cyprian Prince, which was following at a safe distance behind *Exmouth* and had been warned that the destroyer was hunting submarines, heard multiple muffled explosions before a final, larger, blast after which *Exmouth* disappeared from sight. Captain Benjamin T. Wilson, the master of *Cyprian Prince*, altered course to pass through the waters where *Exmouth* had been and ordered engines stopped to pick up survivors; but he then realized that his virtually irreplaceable cargo of antiaircraft guns, searchlights, and trucks for the defense of the naval base at Scapa Flow was too valuable to risk, and although he had heard voices and seen flashes from hand torches, he ordered his ship onward and maintained radio silence.

When the disaster became known, a debate ensued in the War Cabinet over whether Captain Wilson had done the right thing. The First Lord of the Admiralty settled the question by asserting that the master had followed Admiralty orders and had undoubtedly acted correctly.

THIS MONTH						
JANUARY						
S	M	T	W	T	F	S
..	..	..	..	..	1	2
3	4	5	6	7	8	9
10	11	12	13	14	15	16
17	18	19	20	21	22	23
24	25	26	27	28	29	30
31	..	..	..	..	..	..

FRIDAY
22
JANUARY
1943

NEXT MONTH						
FEBRUARY						
S	M	T	W	T	F	S
..	1	2	3	4	5	6
7	8	9	10	11	12	13
14	15	16	17	18	19	20
21	22	23	24	25	26	27
28	..	..	..	..	..	..
..	..	..	..	..	..	..

On 22 January 1943, the Battle of Buna-Gona came to an end with the main Japanese beachheads in New Guinea, at Buna, Sanananda, and Gona, in Allied hands. The Japanese high command had decided that holding Guadalcanal was more important than holding the New Guinea beachheads and, with Port Moresby in sight of their forces on New Guinea, ordered a withdrawal to the island's northern coast despite the powerful, mutually supporting line of bunkers they had built to block all available approaches.

The battle began on 16 November 1942, with both sides suffering from rampant disease and lacking in even the most basic supplies—some U.S. troops were reduced to part of a C-Ration per day.

Allied intelligence had seriously underestimated the number and determination of the Japanese troops (about 5,500, with an additional 1,000 reinforcements who arrived during the battle) and the strength of their defenses. Allied troops, who were unprepared and ill trained for jungle warfare, made essentially no progress until they were able to build airstrips; with Allied aerial supply and combat support, the tenor of the conflict changed.

Over the course of the two-month engagement, the Australians lost 2,700 men killed, the Americans 798—but there were also about 12,000 Allied wounded. The Japanese lost more than 6,000 killed, 1,200 wounded, and about 200 captured.

THIS MONTH						
JANUARY						
S	M	T	W	T	F	S
..	..	..	..	..	1	2
3	4	5	6	7	8	9
10	11	12	13	14	15	16
17	18	19	20	21	22	23
24	25	26	27	28	29	30
31	..	..	..	..	..	..

SATURDAY
23
JANUARY

NEXT MONTH						
FEBRUARY						
S	M	T	W	T	F	S
..	1	2	3	4	5	6
7	8	9	10	11	12	13
14	15	16	17	18	19	20
21	22	23	24	25	26	27
28	..	..	..	..	..	..
..	..	..	..	..	..	..

1943

On 23 January 1943, forces of the Soviet Army under General Konstantin Rokossovsky recaptured Gumrak Airport in Stalingrad. After the fall of the nearby Pitomnik Airfield on 17 January, Gumrak was the only airfield remaining in German hands as the Soviets drew the noose tighter around the egg-shaped *Kessel* (German for cauldron) in which *General* Friedrich von Paulus' starving and freezing Sixth Army was trapped, and with its capture the last line of supply and escape was cut off. (The very last flight out of the *Kessel*, a Heinkel He III carrying 19 wounded soldiers, departed on 22 January.) Junkers Ju 52 transport aircraft made a few overflights to drop supplies after Gumrak Airport was taken, but for all practical purposes the troops in the *Kessel* were left with no means of direct support. The *Kessel* collapsed eight days later.

THIS MONTH								WEDNESDAY	NEXT MONTH						

JANUARY

S	M	T	W	T	F	S
..	1	2	3	4	5	6
7	8	9	10	11	12	13
14	15	16	17	18	19	20
21	22	23	24	25	26	27
28	29	30	31	..	..	..
..	..	..	..	..	..	..

WEDNESDAY
24
JANUARY

FEBRUARY

S	M	T	W	T	F	S
..	..	..	..	1	2	3
4	5	6	7	8	9	10
11	12	13	14	15	16	17
18	19	20	21	22	23	24
25	26	27	28	..	..	..
..	..	..	..	..	..	..

1945

On 24 January 1945, the Germans executed Associated Press war correspondent Joseph Morton; nine of the 12 OSS agents in the Dawes mission, including team leader Navy Lieutenant Holt Green; and four SOE agents at the Mauthausen-Gusen concentration camp. After the men were interrogated under torture by *Standartenführer* Franz Ziereis, the camp commandant and a known sadist, the execution was carried out under Hitler's Commando Order of 18 October 1942, which ordered the immediate execution, without trial, of all captured Allied commandos or saboteurs, even those in proper uniforms. (Morton was apparently excused from torture.)

The men, all wearing proper uniforms and carrying identification, had been captured on 26 December 1944 by a Nazi counter-partisan unit named "Edelweiss." They had been in a log cabin high on Homolka Mountain in Czechoslovakia, where at that moment 15 Allied intelligence officers, a Slovak officer, a Slovak-American interpreter, two Slovak civilian resistance fighters, and Morton had taken refuge from advancing German troops.

Morton's AP colleagues and his family were not advised of his whereabouts in order not to jeopardize his safety if he had survived. A German radio broadcast on 24 January stated falsely that the men had been tried and found guilty by a military tribunal, and Morton's true fate was not known until the AP launched an investigation after the end of the war. Morton was the only Allied correspondent to be executed by the Axis.

THIS MONTH						
JANUARY						
S	M	T	W	T	F	S
..	1	2	3	4	5	6
7	8	9	10	11	12	13
14	15	16	17	18	19	20
21	22	23	24	25	26	27
28	29	30	31	..	..	..
..	..	..	..	..	..	..

THURSDAY
25
JANUARY

1945

NEXT MONTH						
FEBRUARY						
S	M	T	W	T	F	S
..	..	..	..	1	2	3
4	5	6	7	8	9	10
11	12	13	14	15	16	17
18	19	20	21	22	23	24
25	26	27	28	..	..	..
..	..	..	..	..	..	..

On 25 January 1945, the Battle of the Bulge, the largest and bloodiest battle American forces fought in the war, ended. Begun by a massive German offensive through the supposedly impenetrable Ardennes forest on 16 December 1944, *Unternehmen Wacht am Rhein* (Operation WATCH ON THE RHINE) was aimed at splitting the Allied forces in two and recapturing the port of Antwerp, through which the Allies were moving thousands of tons of supplies.

The battle extended over a bulge of more than 60 miles in the lines and was fought in the worst weather Europe had seen in 50 years, with deep snow and temperatures so cold that weapons had to be maintained

continually and vehicle engines had to be run every half hour to prevent their oil from congealing. (German forces on the Eastern Front had faced similar conditions, with even colder temperatures, but this sort of warfare was new to the Americans.)

More than 700,000 Allied troops were involved; the number of Germans is not known with accuracy but certainly exceeded 350,000. Organized fighting had ended by 22 January, but not until 25 January did the last German troops withdraw to their starting line. The Americans lost approximately 89,500 men (19,000 killed, 47,500 wounded, 23,000 captured or missing) while the British lost 1,408 (200 killed, 969 wounded, and 239 missing). Germany took the hardest blow, losing as many as 100,000 men killed, missing, captured, or wounded.

THIS MONTH						
JANUARY						
S	M	T	W	T	F	S
..	1	2	3	4	5	6
7	8	9	10	11	12	13
14	15	16	17	18	19	20
21	22	23	24	25	26	27
28	29	30	31	..	..	..
..	..	..	..	..	..	..

FRIDAY
26
JANUARY

NEXT MONTH						
FEBRUARY						
S	M	T	W	T	F	S
..	..	..	..	1	2	3
4	5	6	7	8	9	10
11	12	13	14	15	16	17
18	19	20	21	22	23	24
25	26	27	28	..	..	..
..	..	..	..	..	..	..

1945

On 26 January 1945, six tanks and approximately 250 infantrymen of Germany's elite 2nd Mountain Division, determined to wrest the Bois de Riedwihr from American hands, attacked Company B, 15th Regiment, of the U.S. Army's 3rd Infantry Division, on the outskirts of Holtzwihr, France. Company B, participating in the Colmar offensive that was designed to drive the Germans from their last foothold on French soil, had literally been cut to pieces two days earlier, losing every officer killed except the company commander, along with 102 out of 120 enlisted troops either killed or wounded before they even reached their assigned position.

By midnight on 25 January, the remaining 19 men of Company B had penetrated 600 yards into the woods and were in position north of Holtzwihr. Resupplied in the early morning hours, they were ordered to move up to the south end of the woods, facing the village of Holtzwihr, and hold the line until relieved. They reached their assigned position before dawn and tried futilely to dig foxholes in the frozen ground.

At 1400 hours, when the Germans began advancing after an artillery barrage, the company commander ordered his men to fall back to the safety of the forest. He then emptied his MI carbine at the enemy and was preparing to fall back when he spotted a .50-caliber machine gun on the turret of a burning tank destroyer. Realizing that what he was about to do almost certainly meant his own death but knowing that his position had to be held at all costs, he climbed up in the face of bursts of machine-pistol fire and began spraying the oncoming German infantrymen with the heavy machine gun. Some of the German foot soldiers made it to within ten yards of the blazing gun before being cut down.

When two 88-mm shells slammed into the tank destroyer, the American officer was thrown about but managed to retain his composure and continue firing, stopping only to reload or to relay artillery instructions by radio. When American shells began screaming in almost on top of the burning tank destroyer, the Germans realized that their position was no longer tenable. A few crept forward as far as the American 1st Battalion headquarters, but most turned and retreated. Unprotected by infantry, the tanks fled with them.

Carrying field maps that had been shredded by enemy gunfire and bleeding from a wound received in October that had reopened—but otherwise, astonishingly, uninjured—the company commander accepted treatment from a medic but refused to be evacuated. Returning to his company, he helped to organize a counterattack and led his men in an advance that drove the remaining Germans from the area. For his courageous action on this day, First Lieutenant Audie Murphy was awarded the Medal of Honor.

THIS MONTH						
JANUARY						
S	M	T	W	T	F	S
..	..	..	1	2	3	4
5	6	7	8	9	10	11
12	13	14	15	16	17	18
19	20	21	22	23	24	25
26	27	28	29	30	31	..
..	..	..	..	..	..	..

MONDAY
27
JANUARY

NEXT MONTH						
FEBRUARY						
S	M	T	W	T	F	S
..	..	..	..	..	..	1
2	3	4	5	6	7	8
9	10	11	12	13	14	15
16	17	18	19	20	21	22
23	24	25	26	27	28	..
..	..	..	..	..	..	..

1941

On 27 January 1941, Joseph C. Grew, the U.S. Ambassador to Japan, sent a secure telegram from Tokyo to Secretary of State Cordell Hull, warning that Japan was planning a surprise attack on Pearl Harbor:

A member of the Embassy was told by my ------ colleague[2] that from many quarters, including a Japanese one, he had heard that a surprise mass attack on Pearl Harbor was planned by the Japanese military forces, in case of "trouble" between Japan and the United States; that the attack would involve the use of all the Japanese military facilities. My colleague said that he was prompted to pass this on because it had come to him from many sources, although the plan seemed fantastic.

Grew's warning was ignored.

---

2. The colleague in question was later revealed to have been the Peruvian Ambassador.

THIS MONTH										
JANUARY										
S	M	T	W	T	F	S
..	..	..	..	..	1	2
3	4	5	6	7	8	9
10	11	12	13	14	15	16
17	18	19	20	21	22	23
24	25	26	27	28	29	30
31	..	..	..	..	..	..

THURSDAY
28
JANUARY
1943

NEXT MONTH						
FEBRUARY						
S	M	T	W	T	F	S
..	1	2	3	4	5	6
7	8	9	10	11	12	13
14	15	16	17	18	19	20
21	22	23	24	25	26	27
28	..	..	..	..	..	..
..	..	..	..	..	..	..

On 28 January 1943, Germany mobilized its work force for all-out war as the Nazis passed a new law requiring all men between the ages of 16 and 65 and all women between 17 and 50 to register for conscription into the military.

THIS MONTH						
JANUARY						
S	M	T	W	T	F	S
..	..	..	1	2	3	4
5	6	7	8	9	10	11
12	13	14	15	16	17	18
19	20	21	22	23	24	25
26	27	28	29	30	31	..
..	..	..	..	..	..	..

WEDNESDAY
29
JANUARY

1941

NEXT MONTH						
FEBRUARY						
S	M	T	W	T	F	S
..	..	..	..	..	1	2
3	4	5	6	7	8	9
10	11	12	13	14	15	16
17	18	19	20	21	22	23
24	25	26	27	28	..	..
..	..	..	..	..	..	..

On 29 January 1941, Ioannis Metaxas, the titular prime minister (but in actuality the dictator) of Greece, died. Metaxas had been a powerful force in keeping Greece out of war until Mussolini demanded occupation rights in 1940. When the Italian envoy presented Mussolini's demands on 28 October 1940, Metaxas curtly replied in French, "Then it is war." (A popular and enduring legend has it that what he said was simply, "No!" in Greek.) Metaxas' refusal to knuckle under to the Italian dictator was followed within hours by an Italian assault to begin the Greco-Italian War, which the Greeks were winning handily, even after Metaxas' passing, until Mussolini cried to Hitler for help and Germany intervened in April 1941. Metaxas had done all he could to defend his country; the invading Germans had to deal with the "Metaxas Line" of fortifications along the Greco-Bulgarian border.

THIS MONTH															NEXT MONTH						

TUESDAY

30

JANUARY

1945

JANUARY						
S	M	T	W	T	F	S
..	1	2	3	4	5	6
7	8	9	10	11	12	13
14	15	16	17	18	19	20
21	22	23	24	25	26	27
28	29	30	31	..	..	..
..	..	..	..	..	..	..

FEBRUARY						
S	M	T	W	T	F	S
..	..	..	..	1	2	3
4	5	6	7	8	9	10
11	12	13	14	15	16	17
18	19	20	21	22	23	24
25	26	27	28	..	..	..

On 30 January 1945, as the Red Army advanced, the German ship MV *Wilhelm Gustloff* (a former cruise ship built for the KdF[3] movement) was evacuating German civilians, officials, and military personnel from Gotenhafen in occupied Poland. *Wilhelm Gustloff*'s antiaircraft guns were frozen and inoperable, as was the underwater detection equipment on *Löwe*, the escorting torpedo boat; thus, the ship and her escort were defenseless.

Soviet submarine *S-13*, commanded by Captain Aleksandr Marinesko, began following the ships at about 1900 hours. At 2115 hours, she fired three torpedoes at *Wilhelm Gustloff*'s port side. (A fourth torpedo failed to launch and had to be disarmed by the submarine's crew.) The first torpedo struck near the bow, the second hit about midships, and the third struck the engine room, destroying the engines and cutting off electrical power and communications. *Wilhelm Gustloff* took a slight list to port and began settling rapidly by the head.

Many of those who died in the attack were killed by the torpedoes or by drowning in the freezing water. Others were crushed in the initial panic on the stairs and decks, and many jumped into the icy Baltic. Some, realizing

---

3. *Kraft durch Freude* (Strength through Joy, abbreviated KdF), was a state-run leisure/tourism organization that was for a time the largest tourist organization in the world. It was set up to promote the egalitarian benefits of National Socialism, among which was the idea that every German should be able to afford an automobile. Adolf Hitler personally instructed Dr. Ferdinand Porsche to design a *Volkswagen* (people's car), and the vehicle was officially designated the *KdF-Wagen*. The government sold the cars through a savings stamp program. Each week, a worker could buy one stamp and paste it into a booklet. When the booklet was filled, the worker had paid for his car. Only a handful of the cars had been built before war came in 1939, at which time production was converted mostly to military vehicles, primarily the Jeep-like *Kübelwagen* and the amphibious *Schimmwagen*. A few cars were built during the war for high-ranking Nazis.

that their situation was hopeless, used pistols to take their own lives and the lives of their families. The majority of those who perished succumbed to exposure in the freezing water.

Less than 40 minutes after being struck, *Wilhelm Gustloff,* then lying on her side, sank bow first in 144 feet of water, taking with her thousands of people still trapped on the glass-enclosed promenade deck. German ships were able to rescue some of the 10,582 passengers and crew she had been carrying; but the death toll in the sinking of *Wilhelm Gustloff,* 9,343 dead including about 5,000 children, was the largest loss of life in a single sinking in history. Eleven days later, Marinesko and *S-13* repeated their feat, sinking the former liner *Steuben* with two torpedoes only a few miles from where *Wilhelm Gustloff* had gone down. The loss of life in this latter sinking was less; "only" about 5,000 died.

THIS MONTH						
JANUARY						
S	M	T	W	T	F	S
..	..	..	..	..	1	2
3	4	5	6	7	8	9
10	11	12	13	14	15	16
17	18	19	20	21	22	23
24	25	26	27	28	29	30
31	..	..	..	..	..	..

SUNDAY
31
JANUARY

1943

NEXT MONTH						
FEBRUARY						
S	M	T	W	T	F	S
..	1	2	3	4	5	6
7	8	9	10	11	12	13
14	15	16	17	18	19	20
21	22	23	24	25	26	27
28	..	..	..	..	..	..
..	..	..	..	..	..	..

On 31 January 1943, American *Gato*-class submarine USS *Tunny* was patrolling off Formosa. At about 2230 hours, the boat's captain, Lieutenant Commander Elton Watters Grenfell, saw what looked like a worthwhile target, an unidentified Japanese freighter approaching Takao Ko. *Tunny* fired two torpedoes from her bow tubes, but the freighter made a radical change of course, and both fish missed. When the ship counterattacked and dropped two depth charges, *Tunny* broke off the attack and submerged.

Even had the torpedoes found their target, there is more than a little doubt about whether they would have exploded; indeed, two days later, a hit by *Tunny* on another Japanese ship, a tanker, did strike the target with a thud audible to the boat's crew but did not detonate. Ever since the U.S. had entered the war, the Mark XIV torpedo had been so defect ridden that the U.S. Navy's official history of submarine operations says of it, "The only reliable feature of the torpedo was its unreliability." There are records of Japanese ships that returned to port with unexploded Mark XIV torpedoes embedded in holes that they had punched in the ships' sides.

When testing in mid-1943 found that the detonators in seven out of 10 torpedoes dropped 90 feet onto a flat metal plate would fail to trigger but that more than half would work properly if the plate was placed at a 45-degree angle, all boats were ordered to fire their fish at an acute angle instead of at the "textbook-perfect" 90-degree angle. The solution came in the form of modifications to the firing pin; test pins were made in Navy workshops at Pearl Harbor from the propeller blades of Japanese aircraft downed in the 7 December 1941 attack.

THIS MONTH						
FEBRUARY						
S	M	T	W	T	F	S
..	..	..	..	..	..	1
2	3	4	5	6	7	8
9	10	11	12	13	14	15
16	17	18	19	20	21	22
23	24	25	26	27	28	..
..	..	..	..	..	..	..

SATURDAY
1
FEBRUARY

NEXT MONTH						
MARCH						
S	M	T	W	T	F	S
..	..	..	..	..	..	1
2	3	4	5	6	7	8
9	10	11	12	13	14	15
16	17	18	19	20	21	22
23	24	25	26	27	28	29
30	31	..	..	..	..	..

1941

On 1 February 1941, Admiral Husband E. "Kim" Kimmel was appointed Commander-in-Chief (CINCPAC) of the U.S. Navy's Pacific Fleet. Based at Pearl Harbor, Kimmel was the highest-ranking U.S. officer in the Pacific when the Japanese attacked Pearl Harbor on 7 December 1941. He was relieved of command ten days after the attack, while he was planning and executing retaliatory moves, including an effort to relieve and reinforce Wake Island that could have led to an early clash between American and Japanese aircraft carriers. Such an engagement would probably have sealed the fate of the American carriers, whose personnel were woefully unprepared at that time for actual combat.

Kimmel and Lieutenant General Walter Short, commander of the Army's forces in Hawaii, were found by the Roberts Commission to have been guilty of errors of judgment and dereliction of duty in the events leading up to the attack. One of Kimmel's major errors was a failure to ensure that his underlings shared information with their Army counterparts; the Navy had decryption personnel and machinery at Pearl for reading transmissions made in the Japanese "Purple" code but refused to share their decrypts with the Army, whose only access to critical information was via teletype from Washington. Short's performance was no better; at one point, he had flatly refused to allow Army aircraft to be used for long-range surveillance over water, giving the reason that his crews had no training in overwater navigation (an excuse that simply failed to recognize that Navy navigators could work on Army planes as well as on their own).

When he was relieved of command, Kimmel was demoted two stars to the rank of Rear Admiral, and he retired with that rank in 1946.

	THIS MONTH					
FEBRUARY						
S	M	T	W	T	F	S
..	1	2	3	4	5	6
7	8	9	10	11	12	13
14	15	16	17	18	19	20
21	22	23	24	25	26	27
28	..	..	..	..	..	..
..	..	..	..	..	..	..

TUESDAY
2
FEBRUARY

1943

	NEXT MONTH					
MARCH						
S	M	T	W	T	F	S
..	1	2	3	4	5	6
7	8	9	10	11	12	13
14	15	16	17	18	19	20
21	22	23	24	25	26	27
28	29	30	31	..	..	..
..	..	..	..	..	..	..

On 2 February 1943, two days after newly-promoted *Generalfeldmarschall* Friedrich von Paulus had sat in another room while his subordinates surrendered approximately 90,000 men of the German Sixth Army to Soviet forces in Stalingrad, the last organized resistance by forces of the Sixth Army ended in surrender, bringing to a close the 143-day-long battle for Stalin's namesake city. Once the pride of Soviet Russia, the grand and beautiful city on the Volga had been laid waste by aerial bombing, artillery shelling, tank battles, and grenades and other small arms, and it lay totally in ruins. The battle had cost approximately 850,000 Axis casualties and approximately 1,120,000 Soviet casualties, including the deaths of some 40,000 civilians. The Nazi government informed the German people of the disaster, acknowledging for the first time a failure in its war effort.

THIS MONTH						
FEBRUARY						
S	M	T	W	T	F	S
..	..	..	..	1	2	3
4	5	6	7	8	9	10
11	12	13	14	15	16	17
18	19	20	21	22	23	24
25	26	27	28	29	..	..
..	..	..	..	..	..	..

SATURDAY
3
FEBRUARY

1940

NEXT MONTH						
MARCH						
S	M	T	W	T	F	S
..	..	..	..	..	1	2
3	4	5	6	7	8	9
10	11	12	13	14	15	16
17	18	19	20	21	22	23
24	25	26	27	28	29	30
31	..	..	..	..	..	..

On 3 February 1940, three Hawker Hurricanes of B flight, No. 43 Squadron, Royal Air Force, flying from Ackington and piloted by Flight Lieutenant Peter Townsend, Flight Officer "Tiger" Folkes, and Sergeant James Hallowes, shot down the first enemy aircraft to fall on English soil, a Heinkel He III bomber of the *Luftwaffe*'s 4./KG26. The action occurred near Whitby, England. By May of that year, Townsend had claimed two more He IIIs and a sixth share of a third, had been awarded the Distinguished Flying Cross, and had become one of the most capable squadron leaders of the Battle of Britain, serving throughout the battle as commanding officer of No. 85 Squadron, again flying Hurricanes. He was awarded the Distinguished Service Order in April 1941 and later commanded No. 611 Squadron, flying Supermarine Spitfires. He received further honors and promotions during the war, but he is best remembered for his 1950s romance with Princess Margaret, whom he met while he was equerry to her father, King George VI. Despite his distinguished career, his having been divorced in 1952 meant that he had no realistic chance of marriage with the princess, and she eventually renounced him.

THIS MONTH						
FEBRUARY						
S	M	T	W	T	F	S
..	..	..	..	1	2	3
4	5	6	7	8	9	10
11	12	13	14	15	16	17
18	19	20	21	22	23	24
25	26	27	28	..	..	..
..	..	..	..	..	..	..

SUNDAY
4
FEBRUARY
1945

NEXT MONTH						
MARCH						
S	M	T	W	T	F	S
..	..	..	..	1	2	3
4	5	6	7	8	9	10
11	12	13	14	15	16	17
18	19	20	21	22	23	24
25	26	27	28	29	30	31
..	..	..	..	..	..	..

On 4 February 1945, U.S. President Franklin D. Roosevelt, British Prime Minister Winston Churchill, and Soviet Premier Joseph Stalin convened the Yalta Conference, code-named ARGONAUT, in the Livadia Palace near the Black Sea resort town of Yalta in the Crimea. The Soviets really put on the dog, sprucing up the palace and the surrounding towns, bringing in the finest foods and huge quantities of vodka and champagne, and staffing the palace with liveried servants to cater to the Westerners' every whim short of impropriety.

Tops on the conference agenda was Europe's postwar reorganization and what the various Allies' spheres of influence would be. Roosevelt and Churchill, the one in failing health and the other unrealistically optimistic, accepted at face value Stalin's promises of free elections and self-government for Poland, only to be writing each other within two months in a desperate search for a way to put a stop to the first step in a complete Soviet takeover, the wholesale deportations of anti-Soviet Poles.

On the Soviet side, when Foreign Minister Vyacheslav Molotov expressed his concern that the Yalta Agreement's wording might be a problem, Stalin responded, "Never mind. We'll do it our own way later."

THIS MONTH						
FEBRUARY						
S	M	T	W	T	F	S
..	..	..	..	1	2	3
4	5	6	7	8	9	10
11	12	13	14	15	16	17
18	19	20	21	22	23	24
25	26	27	28	29	..	..
..	..	..	..	..	..	..

SATURDAY
5
FEBRUARY

NEXT MONTH						
MARCH						
S	M	T	W	T	F	S
..	..	..	..	..	1	2
3	4	5	6	7	8	9
10	11	12	13	14	15	16
17	18	19	20	21	22	23
24	25	26	27	28	29	30
31	..	..	..	..	..	..

1944

On 5 February 1944, *Oberstleutnant* Egon Mayer, the wing commander of JG 2 "Richthofen," shot down an American P-47 Thunderbolt while flying his Focke Wulf Fw 190A-6 near Arguen. This victory, his 100th, made Mayer the first *Luftwaffe* fighter pilot to claim 100 victories while operating solely over the western (Channel) front. Mayer's total count of victories was 102, including 27 four-engine bombers, 53 Spitfires, and 13 P-47s. He claimed two more P-47s as victories 101 and 102, his last, on the very next day. He was shot down and killed less than a month later, on 2 March, during an attack against a formation of B-17 bombers near Montmédy, France.[1]

---

1. The bombers were being escorted by P-47 fighters of the U.S. 358th Fighter Squadron, led by Major Raymond B. Myers. The P-47s overpowered the German attackers, and Captain Walter V. Gresham shot down Mayer's Fw 190.

FEBRUARY						
S	M	T	W	T	F	S
..	..	..	..	1	2	3
4	5	6	7	8	9	10
11	12	13	14	15	16	17
18	19	20	21	22	23	24
25	26	27	28	..	..	..
..	..	..	..	..	..	..

SATURDAY
6
FEBRUARY
1943

MARCH						
S	M	T	W	T	F	S
..	..	..	..	1	2	3
4	5	6	7	8	9	10
11	12	13	14	15	16	17
18	19	20	21	22	23	24
25	26	27	28	29	30	31
..	..	..	..	..	..	..

On 6 February 1943, beginning in Block 25 at 0330 hours, all female prisoners at Auschwitz II-Birkenau (part of the Auschwitz cluster of concentration camps near Oświęcim, Poland) were gathered in the compound for a general roll call. Dressed inadequately and with no food, they were then marched outside the camp and kept outdoors through the daylight hours. At 1700 hours, "encouraged" by club-swinging female guards and SS men at the gate, the prisoners were ordered to run back to the camp. About 1,000 died during this forced march. Of the survivors, those who were not able to keep up, along with others who were weak, sick, and elderly, were pulled from the ranks with a hook and taken to Block 25 (known familiarly, but not fondly, as the "waiting room for the gas"), whence they were later transported to the gas chambers.

		THIS MONTH				
		FEBRUARY				
S	M	T	W	T	F	S
..	1	2	3	4	5	6
7	8	9	10	11	12	13
14	15	16	17	18	19	20
21	22	23	24	25	26	27
28	..	..	..	..	..	..
..	..	..	..	..	..	..

SUNDAY
7
FEBRUARY

1943

		NEXT MONTH				
		MARCH				
S	M	T	W	T	F	S
..	1	2	3	4	5	6
7	8	9	10	11	12	13
14	15	16	17	18	19	20
21	22	23	24	25	26	27
28	29	30	31	..	..	..
..	..	..	..	..	..	..

On 7 February 1943, the United States government instituted rationing of leather shoes. (Men's rubber shoes, along with many other rubber items, had been rationed since 30 September 1942.) Each man, woman, and child could purchase up to three pairs of leather shoes a year, using designated stamps in War Ration Book One, and later in Books Three and Four. To simplify the system, only six shades of leather were produced.

Even with rationing, however, the supply of leather continued to decrease, and the ration was later decreased to two pairs of leather shoes per year. To make do with less, people took care of the footwear they already had, keeping rubber boots clean, dry, and away from excess heat or cold and repairing shoes and boots whenever possible. Fabric shoes, such as espadrilles, were not rationed; consequently, they suddenly became fashionable.

Theft and black market profiteering were a continuing problem as some people declined to make do. On 3 May 1944, for example, a California man was arrested for stealing seven pairs of shoes. He was convicted and sentenced to six months' imprisonment or a fine of $500.00 (more than $6,000 today).[2]

---

2. Where amounts of money are given in today's dollars, "today" is the date in 2013 or 2014 that corresponds to the date of the entry.

THIS MONTH						
FEBRUARY						
S	M	T	W	T	F	S
..	..	1	2	3	4	5
6	7	8	9	10	11	12
13	14	15	16	17	18	19
20	21	22	23	24	25	26
27	28	29	..	..	..	..
..	..	..	..	..	..	..

TUESDAY
8
FEBRUARY
1944

NEXT MONTH						
MARCH						
S	M	T	W	T	F	S
..	..	..	1	2	3	4
5	6	7	8	9	10	11
12	13	14	15	16	17	18
19	20	21	22	23	24	25
26	27	28	29	30	31	..
..	..	..	..	..	..	..

On 8 February 1944, Allied military planners approved the final plan for Operation OVERLORD, the long-awaited cross-Channel invasion of Europe.

The overall plan comprised several smaller plans; for example, Operation NEPTUNE was the plan for the initial amphibious landings in Normandy on 6 June, while Operation BODYGUARD, including Operations FORTITUDE NORTH and FORTITUDE SOUTH, was the overall deception plan designed to convince the Germans that the main thrust of the invasion would come in Norway or in the Pas de Calais; other plans hinted at the south of France or the Balkans. Some of these operations were further subdivided; for example, Operation COVER was a part of Operation FORTITUDE SOUTH that called for the U.S. Eighth Air Force to bomb transportation and airfield targets and coastal defenses in the Pas de Calais on the four days immediately preceding the actual landing date, while Operation TRANSPORT was a more extensive bombing plan designed to sever widespread rail lines and roads to hamper German reinforcement efforts into Normandy. Operation PLUTO was the plan under which two artificial harbors, code-named Mulberries, were built, floated across the English Channel, and established at Omaha Beach and Arromanches to provide a conduit for the disembarkation of reinforcements and supplies during the early phases of the invasion.

The final plan came together as a result of earlier operations such as Operation POSTAGE ABLE, a December mission that used an X-class midget submarine to collect suitable data for all of the beaches to be assaulted. All of these plans and sub-plans came together in the early morning hours of 6 June 1944 as Allied troops flew, waded, and rode ashore on five beaches in Normandy to begin the process of driving German forces all the way back to Berlin.

THIS MONTH						
FEBRUARY						
S	M	T	W	T	F	S
..	..	..	..	..	..	1
2	3	4	5	6	7	8
9	10	11	12	13	14	15
16	17	18	19	20	21	22
23	24	25	26	27	28	..
..	..	..	..	..	..	..

SUNDAY
9
FEBRUARY
1941

NEXT MONTH						
MARCH						
S	M	T	W	T	F	S
..	..	..	..	..	..	1
2	3	4	5	6	7	8
9	10	11	12	13	14	15
16	17	18	19	20	21	22
23	24	25	26	27	28	29
30	31	..	..	..	..	..

On 9 February 1941, one day after the U.S. Congress passed the Lend-Lease Act, British Prime Minister Sir Winston Churchill, one of modern history's greatest orators, spoke directly to the British people for the first time in five months. In his speech, he provided status updates on the war and praised the people for their steadfastness under the nightly bombing of the Blitz and the military for the gains that it had made in Africa and for wresting air superiority from the Germans.

He then changed his tone, warning of dangers still existing and still to come. The most dire of his warnings came when he said, "Sir John Dill, our principal military adviser, the Chief of the Imperial General Staff, has warned us all that Hitler may be forced, by the strategic, economic and political stresses in Europe, to try to invade these Islands in the near future." Near the end of his allotted time, Churchill made reference to the Americans, quoting a verse of Longfellow that had come to him in a note from U.S. President Roosevelt that was delivered by Wendell Willkie:

. . . Sail on, O Ship of State!
Sail on, O Union, strong and great!
Humanity with all its fears,
With all the hopes of future years,
Is hanging breathless on thy fate!

He then went on to finish: "What is the answer that I shall give, in your name, to this great man, the thrice-chosen head of a nation of a hundred and thirty millions? Here is the answer which I will give to President Roosevelt: Put your confidence in us. Give us your faith and your blessing, and, under Providence, all will be well.

"We shall not fail or falter; we shall not weaken or tire. Neither the sudden shock of battle, nor the long-drawn trials of vigilance and exertion will wear us down. Give us the tools, and we will finish the job."

<table>
<tr><td colspan="7">THIS MONTH</td></tr>
</table>

	THIS MONTH					
		FEBRUARY				

TUESDAY

10

FEBRUARY

1942

NEXT MONTH

MARCH

S	M	T	W	T	F	S
1	2	3	4	5	6	7
8	9	10	11	12	13	14
15	16	17	18	19	20	21
22	23	24	25	26	27	28
..	..	..	..	..	..	..
..	..	..	..	..	..	..

S	M	T	W	T	F	S
1	2	3	4	5	6	7
8	9	10	11	12	13	14
15	16	17	18	19	20	21
22	23	24	25	26	27	28
29	30	31	..	..	..	..
..	..	..	..	..	..	..

On 10 February 1942, while being converted to service as a troop transport, SS *Normandie*, France's largest and fastest passenger ship at the time, caught fire, capsized, and sank while docked at Pier 88 in New York Harbor.

Normandie had been placed in protective custody by the United States Coast Guard after the fall of France on 15 May 1940. Five days after the 7 December 1941 attack on Pearl Harbor, the Americans formally seized the ship under the right of angary and renamed her USS *Lafayette*. The Coast Guard detail aboard took over the duties of the French crew, who were removed at that time, but they abandoned the elaborate fire-prevention system that had been designed to suppress any fire before it became a danger.

On 20 December, President Roosevelt's order for *Normandie*'s transfer to the Navy and conversion to a troopship was recorded. Workers began stripping the ship of everything flammable: all the wood flooring and paneling, cork wall insulation, upholstered furniture and fittings, and linens had to go. At about 1430 hours on 9 February, sparks from a cutting torch being used by a worker named Clement Derrick ignited a stack of kapok life vests that had been stored in the first-class lounge. With the fire-suppression system no longer in operation, the fire spread rapidly and was soon out of control.

The ship's designer, Vladimir Yourkevitch, happened to be in New York at the time, and he proposed that firefighters should enter the ship and open her sea cocks so that she would settle on an even keel into the harbor mud. The authorities' refusal to accept his suggestion spelled the ship's doom. She turned turtle at 0245 hours on 10 February.

THIS MONTH

FEBRUARY

S	M	T	W	T	F	S
..	..	..	..	1	2	3
4	5	6	7	8	9	10
11	12	13	14	15	16	17
18	19	20	21	22	23	24
25	26	27	28	29	..	..
..	..	..	..	..	..	..

SUNDAY
11
FEBRUARY

1940

NEXT MONTH

MARCH

S	M	T	W	T	F	S
..	..	..	..	..	1	2
3	4	5	6	7	8	9
10	11	12	13	14	15	16
17	18	19	20	21	22	23
24	25	26	27	28	29	30
31	..	..	..	..	..	..

On 11 February 1940, German and Soviet representatives in Moscow signed the 1940 German-Soviet Commercial Agreement (also known as Economic Agreement of February 11, 1940, Between the German Reich and the Union of Soviet Socialist Republics). Under the Agreement, the Soviet Union agreed to deliver over the next year, in addition to deliveries under a similar agreement signed in August of the previous year, oil, raw materials and grain to the value of 420 to 430 million Reichsmarks, equivalent to about $2.8 billion in today's U.S. dollars. In exchange, Germany would supply certain raw materials and war *matériel*, including machinery and technologies. The Agreement also provided that the Soviet Union would purchase certain metals and other goods and resell them to Germany; a later addendum to the Agreement provided for the transport through Soviet territory of goods purchased from other countries by Germany.

A further agreement was negotiated in January 1941, and before Hitler launched *Fall Barbarossa* in June 1941, the USSR had delivered to Germany 900,000 tons of oil; 1.6 million tons of grain; and 140,000 tons of manganese ore, estimated to be worth 597.9 million Reichsmarks while German deliveries to the USSR had a combined value of 437.1 million Reichsmarks and included the incomplete *Admiral Hipper*-class naval cruiser *Lützow*, the plans to the battleship *Bismarck*, information on German naval testing, complete machinery for a large destroyer, heavy naval guns and other naval gear, samples of thirty of Germany's latest warplanes, including the Bf 109 fighters, Bf 110 fighters, Ju 88 and Do 215 bombers, oil and electric equipment, locomotives, turbines, generators, diesel engines, ships, machine tools, samples of Germany artillery, tanks, explosives, chemical-warfare equipment, and other items.

THIS MONTH						
FEBRUARY						
S	M	T	W	T	F	S
..	..	..	..	1	2	3
4	5	6	7	8	9	10
11	12	13	14	15	16	17
18	19	20	21	22	23	24
25	26	27	28	29	..	..
..	..	..	..	..	..	..

MONDAY
12
FEBRUARY
1940

NEXT MONTH						
MARCH						
S	M	T	W	T	F	S
..	..	..	..	..	1	2
3	4	5	6	7	8	9
10	11	12	13	14	15	16
17	18	19	20	21	22	23
24	25	26	27	28	29	30
31	..	..	..	..	..	..

On 12 February 1940, German submarine *U-33*, commanded by *Kapitän-leutnant* Hans-Wilhelm Von Dresky, was on a mission to lay mines in the Firth of Clyde near Glasgow, on the western shore of Scotland, a daring task ordered by Adolf Hitler himself. In the very early morning hours, *U-33* was on the surface when her lookouts spotted a ship moving in the opposite direction.

The minesweeper HMS *Gleaner*, with Lieutenant Commander Hugh Price in command, failed to notice the boat lying low in the water and continued on her way; but at 0250 hours the minesweeper's hydrophone operator reported the sound of Diesel engines. Price immediately ordered his ship to reverse course, and *U-33* was caught even as she began a crash dive. Beginning at 0353 hours, the minesweeper attacked with depth charges, seriously damaging the boat. Shortly after the first pattern of depth charges exploded, she hit the bottom and remained there for some time as von Dresky consulted with Friedrich Schilling, the boat's engineer, about his options. (Had von Dresky known that those explosions had also put *Gleaner's* ASDIC (sonar) gear out of action, he could have made his escape; but he was unaware of it, and the opportunity passed.)

At 0522 hours, von Dresky gave the order to blow the boat's tanks, surface, and abandon *U-33*. He also ordered that the fuses be lighted on explosives designed to sink the boat. The British rescued 17 of the boat's crew, including Schilling; the other 25, including von Dresky, were lost. One of the survivors had in his pocket, with orders to cast them into the sea when he was away from the boat, three rotors for the Enigma cipher machine. One of the British sailors involved in the rescue remarked to a fellow sailor that one of the Germans had had what looked like bicycle sprockets on his person; but Price recognized the rotors for what they were and made certain that they were sent to the Government Code and Cypher School (GCCS), the innocuously named facility at Bletchley Park, where Alan Turing's team could study them.

THIS MONTH						
FEBRUARY						
S	M	T	W	T	F	S
..	..	..	..	1	2	3
4	5	6	7	8	9	10
11	12	13	14	15	16	17
18	19	20	21	22	23	24
25	26	27	28	..	..	..
..	..	..	..	..	..	..

TUESDAY
13
FEBRUARY
1945

NEXT MONTH						
MARCH						
S	M	T	W	T	F	S
..	..	..	..	1	2	3
4	5	6	7	8	9	10
11	12	13	14	15	16	17
18	19	20	21	22	23	24
25	26	27	28	29	30	31
..	..	..	..	..	..	..

On 13 February 1945, a three-day period began during which 722 heavy bombers of the Royal Air Force and 527 of the U.S. Army Air Forces dropped more than 3,900 tons of high-explosive bombs and incendiary devices on the city of Dresden, Germany. There were two raids on the night of 13/14 February, one daylight raid on 14 February, and one daylight raid on 15 February (in which Dresden was the secondary target for the weathered-in Böhlen synthetic oil plant near Leipzig). The resulting firestorm destroyed fifteen square miles of the city center and killed between 22,000 and 25,000 people. Conspiracy theorists have argued since the war that Dresden was bombed as revenge for the destruction of Coventry, England, in 1940 and 1941. However, as a communications center, a military manufacturing center staffed largely with slave labor, and a transportation hub, the city was a legitimate strategic target: with 28 troop trains a day passing through its railroad marshaling yard, it was funneling large numbers of military personnel to the Russian front, and additional trains carried huge quantities of arms, armor, and supplies for those troops and the troops already at the front.

		THIS MONTH							

MONDAY

14

FEBRUARY

1944

		FEBRUARY				
S	M	T	W	T	F	S
..	..	1	2	3	4	5
6	7	8	9	10	11	12
13	14	15	16	17	18	19
20	21	22	23	24	25	26
27	28	29	..	..	..	..
..	..	..	..	..	..	..

NEXT MONTH

		MARCH				
S	M	T	W	T	F	S
..	..	..	1	2	3	4
5	6	7	8	9	10	11
12	13	14	15	16	17	18
19	20	21	22	23	24	25
26	27	28	29	30	31	..
..	..	..	..	..	..	..

On 14 February 1944, only six days after the plan for the invasion of Normandy received its final stamp of approval, General Dwight D. Eisenhower, whom President Franklin D. Roosevelt had named in January to be

Supreme Commander of the Allied Expeditionary Force in Europe, established his Supreme Headquarters Allied Expeditionary Force (SHAEF) at Camp Griffiss, Bushy Park, Teddington, London, England. (Chief of Staff General George C. Marshall had been expected, and was hoping, to receive the command; but Roosevelt explained to him that he couldn't get along without Marshall at his side.)

Eisenhower and his headquarters remained in England until the Normandy beachhead was strongly enough established, with sufficient forces in France to justify moving SHAEF to the continent.

When SHAEF relocated, Eisenhower assumed direct command of all land forces in Europe, replacing General Sir Bernard Montgomery, whom he left in command of the British 21st Army Group, which held positions at the eastern end of the beachhead. At that time, to define a parallel command structure, Eisenhower also created the American 12th Army Group, under the command of Lieutenant General Omar Bradley.

THIS MONTH						
FEBRUARY						
S	M	T	W	T	F	S
..	..	..	..	1	2	3
4	5	6	7	8	9	10
11	12	13	14	15	16	17
18	19	20	21	22	23	24
25	26	27	28	..	..	..
..	..	..	..	..	..	..

THURSDAY
15
FEBRUARY

NEXT MONTH						
MARCH						
S	M	T	W	T	F	S
..	..	..	..	1	2	3
4	5	6	7	8	9	10
11	12	13	14	15	16	17
18	19	20	21	22	23	24
25	26	27	28	29	30	31
..	..	..	..	..	..	..

1945

On 15 February 1945, in an investigation prompted by a report from Matthias Langer of Wereth, Belgium, U.S. Army Captain William Everett examined the mutilated bodies of 11 soldiers of the 333rd Field Artillery Battalion.

The 333rd, an all-black unit, had been firing in support of the 106th Infantry Battalion on 16 December 1944, in response to the German onslaught that began the Battle of the Bulge. When the green troopers of the 106th broke and fled, the experienced men of the 333rd continued fighting until their positions were overrun.

All but 11 men of the 333rd were killed or captured. Those 11 men escaped into the woods, avoiding German patrols until, at about 1500 hours the next day, they stumbled across the tiny hamlet of Wereth. Cold, hungry, and exhausted, they knocked on Langer's door, and despite fear of discovery by German sympathizers in the town he unhesitatingly took them in, feeding them and giving them an opportunity to warm themselves.

About an hour later, four men of the 1st SS Division, belonging to *Kampfgruppe* Knittel, pulled up to the house in a *Schwimmwagen*. The Americans quickly surrendered, probably in hopes of sparing the Langer family. The Germans sat them down in the snow while a search of the house was conducted, and they began shivering. Langer asked that the Americans at least be allowed to sit where they could be warm. One of the *Waffen* SS troops responded with a laugh that they'd be plenty warm when they started running.

The Germans then marched the Americans off at a run into the night, following in their vehicle. Villagers heard gunshots shortly thereafter and found the bodies the next morning. Fearing that the Germans might return, they said nothing, and the bodies were buried by new snow. A month later, the villagers directed members of the U.S. 394th Infantry Regiment's Intelligence and Reconnaissance Platoon to the site.

THIS MONTH

FEBRUARY

S	M	T	W	T	F	S
..	..	..	..	1	2	3
4	5	6	7	8	9	10
11	12	13	14	15	16	17
18	19	20	21	22	23	24
25	26	27	28	29	..	..
..	..	..	..	..	..	..

FRIDAY
16
FEBRUARY
1940

NEXT MONTH

MARCH

S	M	T	W	T	F	S
..	..	..	..	..	1	2
3	4	5	6	7	8	9
10	11	12	13	14	15	16
17	18	19	20	21	22	23
24	25	26	27	28	29	30
31	..	..	..	..	..	..

On 16 February 1940, the German tanker *Altmark*, commanded by Captain Heinrich Dau, was returning to Germany carrying as prisoners 299 British merchant sailors who had been picked up from ships sunk by the cruiser *Admiral Graf Spee* before she herself was scuttled.

On her way from the southern Atlantic to Germany, *Altmark* took a circuitous route that passed through the waters of then-neutral Norway. At British insistence, Norwegian naval officers had three times on the preceding day boarded *Altmark*, which was subject to search as the ship of a belligerent in neutral waters. After cursory searches, they finally sent the ship on her way with the torpedo boats HNoMS *Trygg* and HNoMS *Snøgg* as escorts.

Later the same day, British aircraft spotted *Altmark* and alerted the Royal Navy. The destroyer HMS *Cossack*, under the command of Captain Philip Vian, intercepted *Altmark*, and the German went to ground in the Jøssingfjord. On the morning of 16 February, *Cossack* entered the Jøssingfjord. The Norwegians blocked Vian's initial boarding attempts with torpedo tubes aimed at *Cossack*.

Captain Vian then asked the Admiralty for instructions and was ordered by First Lord of the Admiralty Winston Churchill to board *Altmark* unless the Norwegians would escort her to Bergen with a joint British-Norwegian guard aboard. The Norwegians refused to do so, and Vian proceeded with a boarding operation, the Norwegians declining to interfere further. During the action, *Altmark* ran aground, and British sailors boarded her at 2220 hours, killing four German crewmen and wounding five others at the cost of one British seaman wounded. The British searched the ship and freed the captured merchant's men from the hold.

Cossack's action, the last major boarding action fought by the Royal Navy to date, was a violation of Norwegian neutrality, as was the Germans' having brought British merchant sailors into Norwegian waters as prisoners.

THIS MONTH

FEBRUARY

S	M	T	W	T	F	S
..	1	2	3	4	5	6
7	8	9	10	11	12	13
14	15	16	17	18	19	20
21	22	23	24	25	26	27
28	..	..	..	..	..	..
..	..	..	..	..	..	..

NEXT MONTH

MARCH

S	M	T	W	T	F	S
..	1	2	3	4	5	6
7	8	9	10	11	12	13
14	15	16	17	18	19	20
21	22	23	24	25	26	27
28	29	30	31	..	..	..
..	..	..	..	..	..	..

WEDNESDAY
17
FEBRUARY

1943

On 17 February 1943, the legendary Russian fighter pilot Lydia Vladimirovna Litvyak, who was nicknamed the White Lily of Stalingrad by the Soviet news media, received the Order of the Red Banner.

At first turned away for lack of experience, Litvyak then exaggerated her flight experience by 100 hours and was accepted into the all-female 586th Fighter Regiment of the Air Defense Force (586 IAP/PVO) for training on the Yakovlev Yak-1. She was transferred to the 437th IAP, where she was recognized as a born fighter pilot. There she flew her first combat missions in September 1942, downing a Junkers Ju 88 and a Bf 109G-2 flown by *Luftwaffe* ace *Unteroffizier* Erwin Meier on her third mission. Maier parachuted from his aircraft and was captured, and he asked to see the pilot who had outflown him. When he was taken to stand in front of Litvyak, he thought he was being made the butt of a Soviet joke; but when Litvyak described each move of the dogfight to him in perfect detail, he realized that he had been beaten by a woman.

She was later transferred to a squadron that was refitting with the Bell P-39 Airacobra but was from there sent to the 296th IAP, which was still flying the Yak-1. Litvyak, who was shot down and killed in August 1943, is credited with being the deadliest female fighter pilot of all time; there is much dispute about her total number of victories, but the most common tally given is eight solo kills and parts of three team kills.

THIS MONTH

FEBRUARY

S	M	T	W	T	F	S
..	..	..	..	1	2	3
4	5	6	7	8	9	10
11	12	13	14	15	16	17
18	19	20	21	22	23	24
25	26	27	28	29	..	..
..	..	..	..	..	..	..

SUNDAY
18
FEBRUARY

NEXT MONTH

MARCH

S	M	T	W	T	F	S
..	..	..	..	..	1	2
3	4	5	6	7	8	9
10	11	12	13	14	15	16
17	18	19	20	21	22	23
24	25	26	27	28	29	30
31	..	..	..	..	..	..

1940

On 18 February 1940, German submarines illegally sank six merchant ships, all of which had been flying the flags of then-neutral nations: France, Greece, the Netherlands, Norway, Pomerania, and Spain. A total of 40 men were killed on the six vessels. On the same day, German submarine *U-23*, commanded by *Kapitänleutnant* Otto Kretschmer, sank the Royal Navy destroyer HMS *Daring*, which was part of the 14-warship escort for the 26 merchantmen of Convoy HN-12 on its passage from Bergen, Norway, to Methil, Scotland. With her stern blown off by the submarine's torpedo, *Daring* capsized and sank very quickly, taking with her the lives of 157 of the ship's 162-man complement, including her captain, Commander Sydney Alan Cooper. The five surviving Darings were rescued by the submarine HMS *Thistle* which had fortuitously been close enough to witness the attack but, unhappily, not in a position to prevent it.

THIS MONTH								WEDNESDAY		NEXT MONTH						
FEBRUARY								**19**		MARCH						
S	M	T	W	T	F	S				S	M	T	W	T	F	S
..	..	..	..	..	..	1		FEBRUARY		..	..	..	..	..	..	1
2	3	4	5	6	7	8				2	3	4	5	6	7	8
9	10	11	12	13	14	15				9	10	11	12	13	14	15
16	17	18	19	20	21	22				16	17	18	19	20	21	22
23	24	25	26	27	28	..				23	24	25	26	27	28	29
..	..	..	..	..	..	..				30	31	..	..	..	..	..

1941

On 19 February 1941, the *Luftwaffe* began three successive nights of sustained heavy bombing against the snow-covered city of Swansea, South Wales. Swansea, with a population of 205,000, was a manufacturing center for munitions and other war *matériel* and was also the location of a major seaport and an oil refinery, both of which were key to the strategic bombing campaign that the Germans had designed to cripple the area's coal exports, to hamper emergency services, and to demoralize civilians.

After dropping parachute flares to illuminate the targets below, German aircraft delivered a three-night total of 1,273 high-explosive bombs and 56,000 incendiary devices, and by the time the third night's five-hour bombing marathon was over, Swansea's docks and industrial areas were virtually unscathed while 41 acres of the town center, with its markets, cinemas, churches, and railway station, had been nearly obliterated. (11,000 properties were damaged and 857 were destroyed.) Looking at the smoking remains of the 50-year-old Ben Evans department store, residents wondered how the tiny incendiaries, weighing the same as a bag of sugar, could "burn concrete and steel like hell."

The death toll from the 13 hours and 48 minutes of attacks, known as the "three nights Blitz," was 230, with 409 other people injured.

THIS MONTH						
FEBRUARY						
S	M	T	W	T	F	S
1	2	3	4	5	6	7
8	9	10	11	12	13	14
15	16	17	18	19	20	21
22	23	24	25	26	27	28
..	..	..	..	..	..	..

FRIDAY
20
FEBRUARY

1942

NEXT MONTH						
MARCH						
S	M	T	W	T	F	S
1	2	3	4	5	6	7
8	9	10	11	12	13	14
15	16	17	18	19	20	21
22	23	24	25	26	27	28
29	30	31	..	..	..	..
..	..	..	..	..	..	..

On 20 February 1942, Japanese troops under the command of Lieutenant Tadaichi Noda interrogated prisoner of war Captain John R. Gray of the Royal Australian Engineers. Gray was one of 180 Australians who had been captured on 3 February and had already seen an infantry officer, Lieutenant Hatsell G. Garrard, questioned by Noda and an interpreter from the *Kempeitai* (the Imperial Japanese Army's intelligence and counterespionage branch). The Japanese beat Garrard with a heavy stick until he could no longer respond, after which they tied him to a tree and left him to bake in the scorching sun. The particular information Noda wanted was the whereabouts of the Australians' commanding officer, Lieutenant Colonel John J. Scanlan, who was still at large.

The Japanese subsequently murdered all but a very few of the Australians by leading them off into the woods, one after another, and bayoneting them in the back. Eventually the soldiers tired of the sport and began killing their victims in groups of two or three, some with bayonets and others by shooting. Garrard they forced to dig his own grave before they bludgeoned and bayoneted him, finishing by shoving his body into the hole and partially covering it with soil.

Gray was destined for much worse. His captors tied him to a tree and interrogated him under torture for several hours, including dousing him with a handful of biting red ants. They finally untied him; he fell to the ground but arose painfully in a show of defiance. The Japanese then led Gray to a remote spot where a medical doctor named Chikumi, famed for his malevolence and known ironically to the Australians as "Sunshine Sam," administered an injection that put Gray into a stupor. He then cut open Gray's chest and removed his heart while he was still alive in order to observe Gray's reactions. It is not known whether Gray had died before someone administered the *coup de grâce* with a pistol.

Gray had never revealed where Scanlan could be found; in a supremely ironical twist, Scanlan and his party walked up to a *Kempeitai* outpost the next day to surrender themselves.

	THIS MONTH					
FEBRUARY						
S	M	T	W	T	F	S
..	..	1	2	3	4	5
6	7	8	9	10	11	12
13	14	15	16	17	18	19
20	21	22	23	24	25	26
27	28	29	..	..	..	..
..	..	..	..	..	..	..

MONDAY
21
FEBRUARY
1944

	NEXT MONTH					
MARCH						
S	M	T	W	T	F	S
..	..	..	1	2	3	4
5	6	7	8	9	10	11
12	13	14	15	16	17	18
19	20	21	22	23	24	25
26	27	28	29	30	31	..
..	..	..	..	..	..	..

On 21 February 1944, the battleship USS *Alabama* was supporting Fast Carrier Task Force 58.3, which a few days earlier had devastated the Japanese base at Truk, as the carriers laid into the Marianas islands of Tinian, Saipan, and Guam with further heavy attacks to soften the islands up for amphibious assaults. While fighting off one of the frequent Japanese air raids with her twenty long-range 5-inch dual-purpose guns, *Alabama*'s gun director accidentally fired the guns of 5-inch gun mount No. 9 into gun mount No. 5, disabling the turret, killing five sailors and wounding 11.

	THIS MONTH					
		FEBRUARY				
S	M	T	W	T	F	S
..	..	..	..	1	2	3
4	5	6	7	8	9	10
11	12	13	14	15	16	17
18	19	20	21	22	23	24
25	26	27	28	..	..	..
..	..	..	..	..	..	..

THURSDAY
22
FEBRUARY

1940

	NEXT MONTH					
		MARCH				
S	M	T	W	T	F	S
..	..	..	..	1	2	3
4	5	6	7	8	9	10
11	12	13	14	15	16	17
18	19	20	21	22	23	24
25	26	27	28	29	30	31
..	..	..	..	..	..	..

On 22 February 1940, six destroyers of the *Kriegsmarine* became involved in a huge friendly fire incident. The ships were steaming in the North Sea in *Unternehmen Wikinger*, whose purpose was to silence British fishing boats around the Dogger Bank in the belief that they had been reporting the movements of German warships. At about the same time, the *Luftwaffe*'s X *Fliegerkorps* initiated an anti-shipping operation over the North Sea with two squadrons of Heinkel He III bombers.

Because the *Kriegsmarine* had been denied its own air wing, it depended on the *Luftwaffe* for air cover, but communication through the long chain of command was slow, and *Unternehmen Wikinger* was conducted without fighter cover. At about 1900 hours, a Heinkel from 4/KG 26 overflew the destroyer flotilla under a full moon but, uncertain of the ships' status because the squadron had not been informed of friendly ships in the area, made no recognition signals. The absence of signals led the ships to assume that the bomber was British, and they fired on it. The plane returned fire, and the stage was set.

The bomber attacked in earnest, striking the destroyer *Leberecht Maass* with one bomb out of three dropped. The ship lost her steering control and slowed. Except for one ship that was detailed to go alongside to assist, the rest of the flotilla sailed on. The He III made a second run, and the explosions of two bombs broke *Leberecht Maass* in two. The other ships returned to rescue her crew, and at 2000 hours the *Max Schultz* exploded and sank, probably striking a mine.

What happened next was chaos, as nonexistent airplanes, submarines, and torpedoes were all "detected." After half an hour of utter confusion, the flotilla commander ordered the surviving four ships to return home. 578 German sailors had died; the only survivors of the two destroyed ships were 60 men from *Leberecht Maass*.

THIS MONTH

FEBRUARY						
S	M	T	W	T	F	S
1	2	3	4	5	6	7
8	9	10	11	12	13	14
15	16	17	18	19	20	21
22	23	24	25	26	27	28
..	..	..	..	..	..	..
..	..	..	..	..	..	..

NEXT MONTH

MARCH						
S	M	T	W	T	F	S
1	2	3	4	5	6	7
8	9	10	11	12	13	14
15	16	17	18	19	20	21
22	23	24	25	26	27	28
29	30	31	..	..	..	..
..	..	..	..	..	..	..

MONDAY
23
FEBRUARY

1942

On 23 February 1942, the Imperial Japanese Navy submarine *I-17*, under the command of Commander Kozo Nishino, navigated the Santa Barbara Channel, north of Los Angeles, California, while submerged. The sub surfaced at 1910 hours and at 1915 hours, just at sunset, began shelling the Bankline Company oil refinery at Ellwood with her 80-mm deck gun. In the next 20 minutes, *I-17* fired 16 shells, of which 11 fell short into the sea; two overshot and landed on two separate ranches, doing no harm except to make craters; and three struck and destroyed rigging and pumping equipment at a well about 1,000 yards inland. (One man was later wounded while defusing a shell that had failed to explode when it landed on one of the ranches.)

The attack caused a general panic in the area, and air raid sirens were sounded. After the bombardment, *I-17* departed, still on the surface. According to Japanese records, she encountered a destroyer hurrying to the scene, but the Americans did not see the submarine; she continued southward and was observed exiting the channel at 2030 hours. Aircraft gave chase, but she promptly submerged to escape unscathed.

This incident, the war's first bombardment of the United States mainland by Axis forces, triggered fears of a Japanese invasion and provided American officials with an excuse to accelerate the relocation of persons of Japanese ancestry away from the coast to internment camps far inland in accordance with Franklin D. Roosevelt's Executive Order 9066, signed three days earlier.

THIS MONTH							SATURDAY	NEXT MONTH						

<table>
<tr><td colspan="7">THIS MONTH</td><td rowspan="4">SATURDAY

24

FEBRUARY</td><td colspan="7">NEXT MONTH</td></tr>
<tr><td colspan="7">FEBRUARY</td><td colspan="7">MARCH</td></tr>
<tr><td>S</td><td>M</td><td>T</td><td>W</td><td>T</td><td>F</td><td>S</td><td>S</td><td>M</td><td>T</td><td>W</td><td>T</td><td>F</td><td>S</td></tr>
<tr><td>..</td><td>..</td><td>..</td><td>..</td><td>1</td><td>2</td><td>3</td><td>..</td><td>..</td><td>..</td><td>..</td><td>1</td><td>2</td><td>3</td></tr>
<tr><td>4</td><td>5</td><td>6</td><td>7</td><td>8</td><td>9</td><td>10</td><td>4</td><td>5</td><td>6</td><td>7</td><td>8</td><td>9</td><td>10</td></tr>
<tr><td>11</td><td>12</td><td>13</td><td>14</td><td>15</td><td>16</td><td>17</td><td>11</td><td>12</td><td>13</td><td>14</td><td>15</td><td>16</td><td>17</td></tr>
<tr><td>18</td><td>19</td><td>20</td><td>21</td><td>22</td><td>23</td><td>24</td><td>18</td><td>19</td><td>20</td><td>21</td><td>22</td><td>23</td><td>24</td></tr>
<tr><td>25</td><td>26</td><td>27</td><td>28</td><td>..</td><td>..</td><td>..</td><td>25</td><td>26</td><td>27</td><td>28</td><td>29</td><td>30</td><td>31</td></tr>
<tr><td>..</td><td>..</td><td>..</td><td>..</td><td>..</td><td>..</td><td>..</td><td>..</td><td>..</td><td>..</td><td>..</td><td>..</td><td>..</td><td>..</td></tr>
</table>

1945

On 24 February 1945, in the Egyptian Chamber of Deputies, 59-year-old Ahmad Mahir Pasha, the Prime Minister of Egypt, read a decree from King Farouk declaring war on Germany and Japan. (The primary reason for the declaration of war was that it would put Egypt in a position to gain a diplomatic advantage at the end of the war, which the Allies thought imminent.) When Mahir had finished his address, he stepped down to walk to the Senate chamber, and at that moment a 28-year-old lawyer named Mahmoud Essawy stepped forward and shot him four times in the chest, killing him.

Shortly after assuming power in October 1944, Mahir had declared a fatwa against the Muslim Brotherhood. All Muslim Brotherhood candidates for office in the January 1945 elections were defeated, and it was naturally assumed that Essawy was a member of the Brotherhood bent on vengeance for what was thought to have been official malfeasance whereby the elections had been held over two days, allowing the sitting Constitutionalist Liberal Party Cabinet to concentrate police presence against voters of other parties.

Essawy later confessed, however, that he was actually a member of the Wafd Party. Ahmad Mahir and Mahmoud Fahmy Elnokrashy had founded the Saadist Wafd Party in 1938 after their dismissal from the Wafd Party over an internal dispute.

THIS MONTH						
FEBRUARY						
S	M	T	W	T	F	S
..	1	2	3	4	5	6
7	8	9	10	11	12	13
14	15	16	17	18	19	20
21	22	23	24	25	26	27
28	..	..	..	..	..	..
..	..	..	..	..	..	..

THURSDAY
25
FEBRUARY

NEXT MONTH						
MARCH						
S	M	T	W	T	F	S
..	1	2	3	4	5	6
7	8	9	10	11	12	13
14	15	16	17	18	19	20
21	22	23	24	25	26	27
28	29	30	31	..	..	..
..	..	..	..	..	..	..

1943

On 25 February 1943, the Featherston Prisoner-of-War camp in New Zealand was the scene of a deadly incident. The camp, which had been an army camp and was converted in 1942 for POWs, was at the time of the incident under the command of Lieutenant Colonel D.H. Donaldson. It housed about 800 prisoners from the Battle of Guadalcanal, most of them conscripts.

On that unfortunate Thursday, some 240 Japanese POWs, unaware that under the 1929 Geneva Convention camp operators were permitted to require prisoners to perform compulsory labor,[3] staged a sit-in, refusing to work. Lieutenant Toshio Adachi and another officer named Nishimura joined the protesters, refusing to come out of the compound and demanding a meeting with Lieutenant Colonel Donaldson. The camp adjutant, Lieutenant James Malcolm, refused to allow a meeting and instead called in a 47-man armed guard. Some slight scuffles ensued when Lieutenant Malcolm ordered the arrest of the two Japanese officers.

Most of the Japanese maintained relative calm, awaiting the outcome of these minor dust-ups. Then Lieutenant Malcolm fired a warning shot intended to go over their heads. Instead, the bullet struck Lieutenant Adachi, passing through his upper left arm and killing a man behind him. The prisoners responded with a hail of stones. When Malcolm fired again, the prisoners, armed with knives and crude weapons, yelled with rage and charged the guards, who fired on them with rifles and submachine guns. In about thirty seconds' time, the New Zealanders had killed 31 prisoners, mortally wounded another 17, and otherwise wounded a further 74. New Zealand Private Walter Pelvin was killed by a ricochet, and six other guards were wounded.

---

3. Article 27 of the Conventions begins, "Belligerents may utilize the labor of able prisoners of war, according to their rank and aptitude, officers and persons of equivalent status excepted."

A military court of inquiry found that the two Japanese officers had incited their men to riot and exonerated the New Zealanders, citing the fundamental psychological and racial differences between the two sides and the lack of a common language. The Japanese government refused to accept the court's decision.

		THIS MONTH				
		FEBRUARY				
S	M	T	W	T	F	S
..	..	1	2	3	4	5
6	7	8	9	10	11	12
13	14	15	16	17	18	19
20	21	22	23	24	25	26
27	28	29	..	..	..	..
..	..	..	..	..	..	..

SATURDAY
26
FEBRUARY

		NEXT MONTH				
		MARCH				
S	M	T	W	T	F	S
..	..	..	1	2	3	4
5	6	7	8	9	10	11
12	13	14	15	16	17	18
19	20	21	22	23	24	25
26	27	28	29	30	31	..
..	..	..	..	..	..	..

1944

On 26 February 1944, the Battle of the Admin Box in southern Burma came to an official end as Imperial Japanese Army General Tokutaro Sakurai ordered the withdrawal of his forces from around the administration area of the Indian Army's 7th Division. The administration area became a makeshift rectangular defensive position for Major-General Frank Messervy and his staff after their divisional headquarters was overrun on 7 February, two days after Sakurai's troops had begun a counterattack against Indian forces advancing down the coastal plain. Sakurai's plan was intended to repeat the Japanese successes of the previous year and stop the Indian offensive—and perhaps even advance on the port of Chittagong, through which the Indian Army's XV Corps received its supplies.

The Japanese were doing very well, with several small forces holding disused railway tunnels and setting ambushes on the coastal road, along with unexpectedly powerful air support. The situation was recognized as very serious after 7th Division's headquarters were captured, but the Indian 14th Army had worked out counters to the standard Japanese tactics of infiltration and encirclement. The forward divisions of XV Corps were ordered to dig in and hold their positions rather than retreat, while the reserve divisions advanced to their relief. As the defenders closed ranks into the Admin Box, an area roughly 1,200 yards on a side, they were reinforced by other units, including artillery and tanks, but the Japanese soon surrounded them and cut them off from land reinforcement and resupply.

C-47 Dakota aircraft flew a total of 714 sorties, dropping 2,300 tons of supplies and rations to the defenders; the Japanese had not anticipated such a move, and they themselves began to run short of supplies. The fighting became intense and bitter, much of it hand to hand, and the Allies finally took the upper hand as the Japanese, characteristically, were unable to adapt to the new situation that they were facing. The Indians forced the Japanese to retreat and, on the 26th, to withdraw completely. Allied forces suffered 3,506 casualties (killed and wounded) and lost three fighter aircraft, while the Japanese lost 3,106 men killed and 2,229 wounded, along with 65 fighter aircraft.

FEBRUARY

S	M	T	W	T	F	S
1	2	3	4	5	6	7
8	9	10	11	12	13	14
15	16	17	18	19	20	21
22	23	24	25	26	27	28
..	..	..	..	..	..	..
..	..	..	..	..	..	..

FRIDAY
27
FEBRUARY

1942

MARCH

S	M	T	W	T	F	S
1	2	3	4	5	6	7
8	9	10	11	12	13	14
15	16	17	18	19	20	21
22	23	24	25	26	27	28
29	30	31	..	..	..	..
..	..	..	..	..	..	..

On 27 February 1942, 120 troops of the Royal Army's newly-formed 1st Parachute Brigade, under the command of Major John Frost, dropped under ideal conditions of visibility and weather near Bruneval, near Le Havre, France, in Operation BITING, a raid designed to capture intact an example of the Germans' "Würzburg" radar system, a short-range high-precision radar that worked in conjunction with the longer-ranged but rather imprecise "Freya-Meldung-Freya" system to guide German night fighters against night-time raids by British bombers.

The parachute force was divided into four sub-forces, and all but one-half of the "Nelson" force dropped on the edge of their drop zone. As they moved toward the villa housing the radar installation and its operators, the "Jellicoe," "Hardy," and "Drake" forces met no opposition. They surrounded the villa and opened fire with grenades and machine guns. Return fire came from the Germans, one of whom was killed. Two more were taken prisoner, and the others fled. A substantial force remained in an installation near the villa, and troops there were alerted by the small firefight and began firing on the British, killing one paratrooper.

Vehicles could be heard approaching from farther inland, creating a worry for Major Frost, but sappers arrived and began dismantling the radar, placing its components on specially designed carts brought for the purpose. On their arrival at the designated evacuation beach, the paratroopers found out the hard way that the force detailed to clear the beach had not been successful, and additional troops were detached to complete that task while the main force returned to the villa. The Germans had reoccupied the villa and had to be driven out again, with light casualties on both sides.

Returning to the beach, Major Frost found that the German machine gun nest there had been silenced by a flanking operation executed by the small force that had been dropped outside the planned drop zone. Although there was some confusion among the operators of the landing craft assigned to take the raiders off, all the surviving raiders did get away with the complete radar and two prisoners. They had lost a total of two men killed, six wounded, and six captured in exchange for five Germans killed, two wounded, two captured including one of the radar technicians, and three reported missing. When the radar was reassembled in England, British scientists studied it and learned from it how to design countermeasures against it.

FEBRUARY						
S	M	T	W	T	F	S
1	2	3	4	5	6	7
8	9	10	11	12	13	14
15	16	17	18	19	20	21
22	23	24	25	26	27	28
..	..	..	..	..	..	..
..	..	..	..	..	..	..

SATURDAY
28
FEBRUARY
1942

MARCH						
S	M	T	W	T	F	S
1	2	3	4	5	6	7
8	9	10	11	12	13	14
15	16	17	18	19	20	21
22	23	24	25	26	27	28
29	30	31	..	..	..	..
..	..	..	..	..	..	..

On 28 February 1942, Nurse Vivian Bullwinkel (Australian Army Nursing Service) and Private Cecil George Kingsley (British Royal Army Ordnance Corps) were captured and made prisoners of war by Japanese troops.

Bullwinkel was the sole survivor of a massacre perpetrated by the Japanese against Australian nurses and British and Australian servicemen and civilians on Bangka Island, just east of Sumatra, twelve days earlier. The Allied personnel had been traveling on SS *Vyner Brooke*, fleeing the Japanese advance on Malaya. The Japanese bombed and sank the ship; more than 100 survived and made it ashore on Bangka. They discussed their chances and agreed to surrender to the Japanese, in whose control they found the island to be. A ship's officer and the civilian women and children went to find the Japanese and offer their surrender; the military personnel remained behind, and the nurses stayed with them to care for the wounded.

A troop of Japanese arrived and promptly drove all the uninjured and walking wounded men into the brush, where they slaughtered them with rifles and bayonets. The soldiers returned, sat down and cleaned their weapons, and then drove the 22 women into the sea. When the women were waist-deep, the Japanese machine-gunned them from behind. All but Bullwinkel died. The Japanese then dispatched all the stretcher cases with bayonets. Bullwinkel had taken a bullet that passed through her body; it pierced her diaphragm but missed her vital organs. Unconscious, she floated in the water, washing up on shore after the Japanese had left.

When she regained consciousness, she began exploring the area and found Private Kingsley, wounded in another massacre incident on the island. They hid together for twelve days until the Japanese found them on 28 February. Kingsley soon died of his wounds, but Bullwinkel survived. In the prison camp where she was taken, she was reunited with some of the other women who had been on *Vyner Brooke*, and she told them of the massacre. None of them ever mentioned it again until after the war, out of fear that to do so might put the only surviving witness to the atrocity in danger from their captors.

THIS MONTH						
FEBRUARY						
S	M	T	W	T	F	S
..	..	1	2	3	4	5
6	7	8	9	10	11	12
13	14	15	16	17	18	19
20	21	22	23	24	25	26
27	28	29	..	..	..	..
..	..	..	..	..	..	..

TUESDAY
29
FEBRUARY
1944

NEXT MONTH						
MARCH						
S	M	T	W	T	F	S
..	..	..	1	2	3	4
5	6	7	8	9	10	11
12	13	14	15	16	17	18
19	20	21	22	23	24	25
26	27	28	29	30	31	..
..	..	..	..	..	..	..

On 29 February 1944, during the American assault, a group of women, most of whom were "comfort women," took shelter in a dugout behind the naval base on Truk, in the Caroline Islands. ("Comfort women," many of them Korean or Chinese, were women whom the Japanese military forced into prostitution to service the troops.) As defeat loomed, the Imperial Japanese Navy personnel on the island feared that these women would be burdensome and potentially a great embarrassment when the Americans discovered them.

It was decided to make the problem go away by getting rid of them. During a lull in the fighting, three ensigns armed with submachine guns went to the dugout. With the fighting temporarily stopped, a few of the women had come out; these the ensigns gunned down immediately. The men continued into the dugout and fired randomly into the pitch-black interior. Eventually the screams died down, leaving only moans from women who lay wounded.

The ensigns then switched on the electric hand lanterns they were carrying to reveal approximately 70 blood-drenched bodies lying on the floor.

THIS MONTH						
MARCH						
S	M	T	W	T	F	S
..	..	..	1	2	3	4
5	6	7	8	9	10	11
12	13	14	15	16	17	18
19	20	21	22	23	24	25
26	27	28	29	30	31	..
..	..	..	..	..	..	..

WEDNESDAY
1
MARCH

NEXT MONTH						
APRIL						
S	M	T	W	T	F	S
..	..	..	..	..	..	1
2	3	4	5	6	7	8
9	10	11	12	13	14	15
16	17	18	19	20	21	22
23	24	25	26	27	28	29
30	..	..	..	..	..	..

1944

On 1 March 1944, American fighter ace Lieutenant Charles F. "Chuck" Gumm of the 354th Fighter Group stationed at Boxted Airfield in England, who was the first P-51 Mustang pilot to shoot down an enemy plane over Europe, climbed into the cockpit of a P-51B1 Razorback Mustang, serial number 43-12165, to take it up on a check flight.

As the aircraft rose into the sky, its engine failed. According to the testimony of eyewitnesses, including the Reverend Canon W. Wright of St. James' Vicarage, Gumm could have parachuted to safety but, realizing that he was over Nayland village and that if he bailed out, the plane would crash into the town and kill innocent civilians, stayed with the aircraft. He dead-sticked it toward an open field outside the town; as he approached the field, however, he was too low to clear a line of trees at its edge. A wing caught a tree, the aircraft spun, and Gumm was thrown from the cockpit and killed. At the time of his death, he was the group's leading ace, with 7½ victories to his credit. He had also been awarded the Air Medal and three Oak Leaf Clusters. He was awarded posthumously the Silver Star, the Soldiers' Medal, and the Distinguished Flying Cross.

He left behind a brother and two sisters, his wife Muriel, and his infant daughter Toni; and he was related to the entertainer Frances Ethel Gumm, who in 1934 had taken the performing name Judy Garland.

THIS MONTH						
MARCH						
S	M	T	W	T	F	S
..	1	2	3	4	5	6
7	8	9	10	11	12	13
14	15	16	17	18	19	20
21	22	23	24	25	26	27
28	29	30	31	..	..	..
..	..	..	..	..	..	..

TUESDAY
2
MARCH
1943

NEXT MONTH						
APRIL						
S	M	T	W	T	F	S
..	..	..	..	1	2	3
4	5	6	7	8	9	10
11	12	13	14	15	16	17
18	19	20	21	22	23	24
25	26	27	28	29	30	..
..	..	..	..	..	..	..

On 2 March 1943, *SS-Obersturmbannführer* Rudolf Höss, commandant of the Auschwitz-Birkenau concentration camp, received word at 2140 hours that 15,000 Berlin Jews were being transported to the camp.

Höss, who had commanded the camp since its creation in 1940, was determined to do things better than he had seen during his service at Dachau and Sachsenhausen. He expanded the existing facilities, which had been a Polish military barracks, and studied ways to improve the process of human extermination over what he saw when he visited Treblinka.

Höss experimented with different gassing methods, and it was he who in 1941 introduced the lie that arriving prisoners were being taken to showers for delousing, where they were instead poisoned by the most effective method he had discovered, with hydrogen cyanide gas produced from the pesticide Zyklon-B. Under his command, Auschwitz II Birkenau became the most efficiently murderous instrument for human extermination ever devised, with four large gas chambers, each capable of killing 2,000 people at a time, together with the necessary crematoria for disposing of the bodies.

In his affidavit for the Nuremberg trials, Höss estimated that approximately 2,500,000 people were killed at Auschwitz-Birkenau during his tenure there, with another 500,000 dying of other causes. In further testimony he explained that the killing part was quick and easy, that it was the burning that took the most time. He also asserted that residents of the surrounding area knew perfectly well what was going on in the camp because of the awful stench, which could not be suppressed.

The transportees about whom he was notified on 2 March 1943 were some of the "lucky" ones; he ordered that they must all be kept in good health during the journey so that they could work at Auschwitz III Monowitz, the slave labor camp, instead of being mostly sent immediately to be gassed.

Höss was hanged in 1947.

THIS MONTH									NEXT MONTH					
MARCH							**SATURDAY**		APRIL					
S	M	T	W	T	F	S			S	M	T	W	T	F	S
..	..	..	..	..	1	2	**3**		1	2	3	4	5	6	7
4	5	6	7	8	9	10			8	9	10	11	12	13	14
11	12	13	14	15	16	17	**MARCH**		15	16	17	18	19	20	21
18	19	20	21	22	23	24			22	23	24	25	26	27	28
25	26	27	28	29	30	31			29	30	..	..	..	..	..
..	..	..	..	..	..	..			..	..	..	..	..	..	..

1945

On 3 March 1945, during an attack on Meiktila, Burma, Lieutenant William Basil Weston, aged 21, of the Green Howards (Alexandra, Princess of Wales's Own Yorkshire Regiment), was in command of a platoon participating in clearing part of the town of the enemy. In the face of fanatical opposition, he led his men superbly, encouraging them from one bunker position to the next as they used fragmentation grenades and small-arms fire to rout the Japanese. The last bunker he reached was particularly well defended, and as he entered it he fell wounded. Realizing that his men would take heavy casualties in capturing this final position, he pulled the pin out of one of his grenades and deliberately rolled farther into the bunker. The explosion of the grenade killed Weston and all of the enemy troops within the bunker. For his gallantry, Weston was posthumously awarded the Victoria Cross, Britain's highest military honor.

THIS MONTH						
MARCH						
S	M	T	W	T	F	S
..	..	..	..	..	..	1
2	3	4	5	6	7	8
9	10	11	12	13	14	15
16	17	18	19	20	21	22
23	24	25	26	27	28	29
30	31	..	..	..	..	..

TUESDAY
4
MARCH
1941

NEXT MONTH						
APRIL						
S	M	T	W	T	F	S
..	..	1	2	3	4	5
6	7	8	9	10	11	12
13	14	15	16	17	18	19
20	21	22	23	24	25	26
27	28	29	30	..	..	..
..	..	..	..	..	..	..

On 4 March 1941, in the Lotofen Islands, near Narvik, Norway, British landing ships HMS *Queen Emma* and HMS *Princess Beatrix*, escorted by five destroyers of the Sixth Destroyer Flotilla, launched the first large-scale commando raid of the war, landing the elements of a 500-man force comprising Nos. 3 and 4 Commando Battalions, a Royal Engineers Section, and 52 men from the Royal Norwegian Navy. The landing, beginning at 0630 hours, was unopposed, and there was virtually no opposition during the entire action. (The only shots fired by the Germans were four rounds from a gun aboard the armed trawler *Krebs*, which was sunk before she could fire a fifth shot.)

Operation CLAYMORE, as the raid was named, achieved its objectives, including the destruction of the area's fish oil factories and approximately 800,000 Imperial gallons (960,760 U.S. gallons) of oil and glycerin, substances used by the Germans in the manufacture of high explosives. In addition to *Krebs*, naval gunfire and onshore demolition parties sank the merchant ships *Hamburg, Pasajes, Felix, Mira, Eilenau, Rissen, Ando, Grotto,* and *Bernhardt Schultz,* totaling 18,000 tons.

While the raiders were conducting their destructive activities, the Norwegians served ersatz coffee to those who were in a position to accept it. Lieutenant Reginald L. Wills of No. 3 Commando took a few moments to address an impudent telegram to A. Hitler of Berlin. It read, "You said in your last speech German troops would meet the British wherever they landed. Where are your troops?" Brigadier Simon Fraser, 15th Lord Lovat, who was attached to No. 4 Commando, took a bus ride with some of his men to a nearby seaplane base, where their activities earned an ironic rebuke in the form of a letter from the base commander to the *Führer*, complaining about their "unwarlike" behavior.

In addition to bringing back to Britain more than 300 Norwegian volunteers without losing a man, the raiders killed 14 sailors from *Krebs*, including her commander, *Leutnant* Hans Kupfinger, and captured 228 prisoners of war: seven from the *Kriegsmarine*, three from the *Heer*, 15 from the *Luftwaffe*, two from the SS, 147 from the Merchant Navy, and 14 civilians. Operation CLAYMORE was the first of twelve commando raids against Norway, and these raids caused the Germans to increase their presence to the extent that by 1944 there were 370,000 German troops tied up in Norway. The unavailability of the equivalent of more than 20 Royal Army divisions for deployment elsewhere severely hampered the Germans' ability to respond to Allied invasions in French North Africa, Italy, Greece, and France.

The most strategically significant outcome of Operation CLAYMORE, however, was totally unexpected. As the briefly pugnacious *Krebs* went down, *Leutnant* Kupfinger threw the ship's Enigma coding machine overboard before he was killed; but British troops managed to rescue a complete set of coding wheels for the machine as well as a complete set of naval cipher books. Teams at Bletchley Park used these treasures to crack the German codes such that for about five weeks, until the Germans changed their codes, the British had virtually complete information about German naval operations.

THIS MONTH							MONDAY	NEXT MONTH						
MARCH							**5**	APRIL						
S	M	T	W	T	F	S		S	M	T	W	T	F	S
..	..	..	..	1	2	3	**MARCH**	1	2	3	4	5	6	7
4	5	6	7	8	9	10		8	9	10	11	12	13	14
11	12	13	14	15	16	17		15	16	17	18	19	20	21
18	19	20	21	22	23	24		22	23	24	25	26	27	28
25	26	27	28	29	30	31		29	30	..	..	..	..	..
..	..	..	..	..	..	..		..	..	..	..	..	..	..

1945

On 5 March 1945, the Nakajima Aircraft Company completed the first prototype of its Ki-115 *Tsurugi* ("Saber") aircraft. Because the Japanese High Command considered the number of obsolete aircraft available for *kamikaze* attacks to be insufficient, orders were issued to build huge numbers of cheap, simple suicide planes quickly in anticipation of the Allied invasion of Japan. Thus, the intended mission for the *Tsurugi* was to deliver *kamikaze* attacks on Allied shipping, especially the invasion fleet expected to be involved in Operation DOWNFALL, the Allied invasion that was set to begin in October 1945.

Called *Tōka* ("Wisteria Blossom") by the Imperial Japanese Navy, the plane was a single seat, single-engine piston-driven low-wing monoplane built mostly of wood and steel and fitted with a welded steel undercarriage that was to be jettisoned after takeoff and reused on another aircraft. The *Tsurugi* was capable of carrying an 800-kg (1,800 lb) high-explosive bomb powerful enough to split a warship in two, but there was no means for delivering the weapon to its target except by ramming. The aircraft had a top speed of 340 MPH, but its handling and visibility were abysmal, and several *Tsurugi* were involved in fatal crashes during testing and pilot training.

In the end, America's deployment of two atomic bombs and the Soviet Union's entry into the war against Japan, leading to the Japanese surrender on 15 August, obviated the need for the *Tsurugi*. Unlike the rocket-powered Yokosuka MXY7 *Ohka* ("Cherry Blossom") suicide plane (nicknamed *Baka* ("Fool") by American sailors), none of the 104 or 105 *Tsurugi* that were built saw action.

MARCH

S	M	T	W	T	F	S
..	1	2	3	4	5	6
7	8	9	10	11	12	13
14	15	16	17	18	19	20
21	22	23	24	25	26	27
28	29	30	31	..	..	..
..	..	..	..	..	..	..

SATURDAY

6

MARCH

1943

APRIL

S	M	T	W	T	F	S
..	..	..	..	1	2	3
4	5	6	7	8	9	10
11	12	13	14	15	16	17
18	19	20	21	22	23	24
25	26	27	28	29	30	..
..	..	..	..	..	..	..

On 6 March 1943, the 71st *Werfer* Regiment, under the command of *Oberstleutnant* Claus von Stauffenberg, went into action in support of *Unternehmen Capri*, *Generalfeldmarschall* Erwin Rommel's disastrous tank attack on the Eighth Army at Medenine, in Tunisia.

The regiment's weapon, the 15 cm NbW 41 Launcher (*Nebelwerfer*), came into being as a result of the German General Staff's 1930 discovery of a loophole in the 1919 Versailles treaty: Germany was effectively forbidden to develop heavy artillery, but the treaty said nothing about rockets. A new rocket research facility was established at Kummersdorf, near Berlin. One of the facility's projects was to develop a bombardment weapon with a range of 5 to 8 km. A serious problem with small rockets was stability; if the engine burned at all unevenly, it could throw the projectile far off course. (This is why a bottle rocket has a long stick that trails behind the

rocket head; the inertia of the stick keeps the rocket aimed approximately in the right direction.) A team led by Colonel Walther Dornberger solved the problem by mounting the engine at the front of the projectile so that it pulled the payload rather than pushing it, and by spacing 26 small Venturi nozzles around the periphery of the warhead instead of a single central nozzle, canting them so that they applied a spin for further stabilization. The result was one of the most accurate small rockets yet developed.

The final weapon comprised a cluster of six launching tubes mounted on a two-wheeled split-trail carriage originally designed for the *Wehrmacht*'s 37-mm PAK-36 antitank gun. A skilled team could reload and fire all six tubes every 90 seconds, and the *Nebelwerfer* was used to devastating effect on both the Eastern and the Western fronts. American soldiers called the projectiles "screaming meemies" or "moaning meemies," reflecting the sound that they made in flight.

On that day in March, however, the Germans learned a thing or two about deploying rocket weapons as the regiment's three camouflaged batteries were quickly knocked out. The dust that the rockets' exhaust kicked up during launching had served as a targeting beacon for British fighter-bombers.

MARCH

S	M	T	W	T	F	S
..	..	..	..	1	2	3
4	5	6	7	8	9	10
11	12	13	14	15	16	17
18	19	20	21	22	23	24
25	26	27	28	29	30	31
..	..	..	..	..	..	..

WEDNESDAY
7
MARCH

1945

APRIL

S	M	T	W	T	F	S
1	2	3	4	5	6	7
8	9	10	11	12	13	14
15	16	17	18	19	20	21
22	23	24	25	26	27	28
29	30	..	..	..	..	..
..	..	..	..	..	..	..

On 7 March 1945, troops of the U.S. 9th Armored Division advanced from the south into the outskirts of the German city of Remagen, on the Rhine River. Looking down into the city from the ridge they were on, they were stunned to find that the Ludendorff railroad bridge over the Rhine was still standing. When General William Hoge was told that the bridge still stood, he issued orders to advance into the city and capture the bridge intact if possible.

The Germans intended to make certain that the river remained an impassable barrier against any Allied advance into Germany's heartland, and sappers had planted demolition charges on the bridge with orders to blow the charges if an Allied crossing was imminent.

As the Americans fought their way through the town, they learned at about 1515 hours, from German soldiers they captured, that demolition was scheduled for 1600 hours, after all of the Germans who were on the south side of the river would have crossed over to the north bank. As the Americans approached the bridge, the Germans, led by Captain Willi Bratge, first blew a crater in the roadway on the south side of the bridge; but tank dozers quickly filled the crater, and the advance continued. Captain Bratge then threw the switch to destroy the bridge.

The bridge was damaged; but because two Polish conscripts had tampered with the fuses, not all of the charges detonated, and the damage was not irreparable. Lieutenant Hugh Mott, Staff Sergeant John Reynolds, and Sergeant Eugene Dorland, from Company B of the 9th Armored Engineer Battalion, crossed the bridge with the first infantry squad and destroyed the main demolition switch box on the north bank while other members of their company found and removed the remaining explosives. Lieutenant Mott led a team that made hasty repairs, and the first M4 Sherman tanks crossed the Rhine on the Ludendorff bridge at 2200 hours that evening.

In the next few days, as fighting for the city continued, U.S. Engineers constructed three pontoon bridges about 1,000 yards downstream to supplement the damaged railroad bridge, which the Germans continually tried in vain to destroy; it finally collapsed on 17 March, by which time six U.S. Army divisions had crossed to the north side of America's first bridgehead on the Rhine.

	THIS MONTH					
		MARCH				
S	M	T	W	T	F	S
..	..	..	..	..	..	1
2	3	4	5	6	7	8
9	10	11	12	13	14	15
16	17	18	19	20	21	22
23	24	25	26	27	28	29
30	31	..	..	..	..	..

SATURDAY
8
MARCH

1941

	NEXT MONTH					
		APRIL				
S	M	T	W	T	F	S
..	..	1	2	3	4	5
6	7	8	9	10	11	12
13	14	15	16	17	18	19
20	21	22	23	24	25	26
27	28	29	30	..	..	..
..	..	..	..	..	..	..

On 8 March 1941, *Großadmiral* Erich Raeder, commandant of the *Kriegsmarine* and the first to achieve the rank of Grand Admiral since Alfred von Tirpitz, warned Adolf Hitler of a possible American landing in northwest Africa should the United States enter the war. Hitler, who was deep in the planning for *Fall Barbarossa,* to commence in early June, gave no heed to the warning.

In mid-1942, Raeder flew to Hitler's headquarters in Vinniza, Ukraine, where the *Führer* was monitoring the progress of his troops as they advanced on Stalingrad and the Caucasus, to repeat his warning. He called an Allied occupation of northwest Africa "the greatest danger to the overall German war command, now as before." His reasoning was that with a base in northern Africa, the Allies would be in an ideal position both to attack Italy and to endanger German positions in northeastern Africa. Again the warning fell on deaf ears.

Raeder was proven to have been remarkably prophetic when the Allies landed in French North Africa in November 1942 and used the positions gained there to squeeze German forces between two armies, Americans in the west and British in the east, finally driving the Germans out of Africa. They then advanced across the Mediterranean, invading Sicily in July 1943 and mainland Italy in September 1943.

MARCH						
S	M	T	W	T	F	S
..	1	2	3	4	5	6
7	8	9	10	11	12	13
14	15	16	17	18	19	20
21	22	23	24	25	26	27
28	29	30	31	..	..	..
..	..	..	..	..	..	..

TUESDAY
9
MARCH
1943

APRIL						
S	M	T	W	T	F	S
..	..	..	..	1	2	3
4	5	6	7	8	9	10
11	12	13	14	15	16	17
18	19	20	21	22	23	24
25	26	27	28	29	30	..
..	..	..	..	..	..	..

On 9 March 1943, a motley assortment of 14 middle-aged businessmen, veteran members of the Calcutta Light Horse (a regiment originally raised in 1873 that was by 1943 essentially a social club) arrived in Mormugao Harbor at the mouth of the Zuari estuary in Goa, Portuguese India, aboard the disreputable dredging barge *Little Phoebe.*

They had come to execute a covert raid organized by the SOE and code-named Operation BOARDING PARTY, a raid planned and conducted in secret because it was feared that the overt presence of Allied troops in the area could swing neutral Portugal to throw in with Germany.

The primary target was the German merchant ship *Ehrenfels,* which was interned in the harbor under neutrality laws but was using a concealed radio transmitter to send information on Allied ship movements to U-boats prowling the area. The reports she had made up until 9 March had led, or would soon lead, to the sinking of 46 Allied ships in the Arabian Sea in a period of less than six weeks. She and the four other Axis-owned ships in the harbor (three German and one Italian) were to be stolen.

The raiders, who had been given a crash course in Commando operations, boarded *Ehrenfels* and had begun to dismantle her anchor chains when they were discovered by the crew. The Germans, who had previously set incendiary charges to destroy critical documents and parts of the ship in case of attack, set off their charges and opened the ship's sea cocks to scuttle her. The raiders destroyed the radio transmitter and fled to their barge, which quietly sailed away, hugging the coast to avoid searchlights. They then, as planned, notified British intelligence, which dispatched an open message over the wire with a warning of a notional British invasion of Goa. Believing that they had no alternative, the crews of the other interned ships fired their vessels and then scuttled them to prevent their capture.

THIS MONTH						
MARCH						
S	M	T	W	T	F	S
..	..	..	..	1	2	3
4	5	6	7	8	9	10
11	12	13	14	15	16	17
18	19	20	21	22	23	24
25	26	27	28	29	30	31
..	..	..	..	..	..	..

SATURDAY
10
MARCH
1945

NEXT MONTH						
APRIL						
S	M	T	W	T	F	S
1	2	3	4	5	6	7
8	9	10	11	12	13	14
15	16	17	18	19	20	21
22	23	24	25	26	27	28
29	30	..	..	..	..	..
..	..	..	..	..	..	..

On 10 March 1945, after riding the jet stream for some 5,500 miles, one of the last paper balloon bombs launched as part of the Japanese *fūsen bakudan* (*Fu-Go*) program, begun in November 1944, came down near the Manhattan Project's plutonium production complex at the Hanford Engineer Works, code-named "Site W," in the U.S. state of Washington. The bomb fell on electrical power lines that stretched between Bonneville and Grand Coulee Dams, causing a short circuit in the transformer that supplied power to the Hanford complex's nuclear reactor cooling pumps. Fortunately for the Allied war effort, backup generators came on line quickly, restoring power and preventing a meltdown—but although the actual power outage lasted for less than a minute, restoring the reactors to full power took three days, during which time production of the plutonium that would five months later fall on the Japanese city of Nagasaki was halted.

	MARCH							MONDAY		APRIL					

	MARCH					
S	M	T	W	T	F	S
..	..	..	..	..	1	2
3	4	5	6	7	8	9
10	11	12	13	14	15	16
17	18	19	20	21	22	23
24	25	26	27	28	29	30
31	..	..	..	..	..	..

MONDAY
11
MARCH

1940

	APRIL					
S	M	T	W	T	F	S
..	1	2	3	4	5	6
7	8	9	10	11	12	13
14	15	16	17	18	19	20
21	22	23	24	25	26	27
28	29	30	..	..	..	..
..	..	..	..	..	..	..

On 11 March 1940, while the German Type VIIA submarine *U-31*, commanded by *Kapitänleutnant* Johannes Habekost, was undergoing sea trials at Jadebusen in the Heligoland Bight near Wilhelmshaven after a refitting following her fifth patrol, she was attacked by a solo Bristol Blenheim bomber of No. 82 Squadron, RAF Bomber Command. Two of the four 250-lb antisubmarine bombs dropped by Squadron Leader Miles Dewlap's aircraft struck the submarine, sinking her in 50 feet of water and killing all 58 men aboard (48 crew and 10 dock workers). The bomber had just come down through a cloud bank, and it attacked at such a low altitude that the explosions of the bombs caused slight damage to the aircraft.

U-31 was raised before the end of the month, repaired, and sent out on her sixth patrol, under the command of *Korvettenkapitän* Wilfried Prellberg, on 16 September. That patrol ended successfully on 8 October, and *U-31* began her seventh patrol on 19 October. She was not so lucky this time: on 2 November, depth charges from the destroyers HMS *Antelope* and HMS *Achates* forced the boat to the surface, where *Korvettenkapitän* Prellberg and 42 other crew members, all but two who had been killed during the depth charge attack, abandoned ship. Men from HMS *Antelope* attempted to board the unmanned submarine, but the two vessels collided, damaging the destroyer and sinking *U-31*, thereby conferring on her the distinction of being not only the first U-boat sunk in World War II but also the only U-boat to be sunk twice during the war.

\multicolumn{7}{c}{MARCH}						
S	M	T	W	T	F	S
..	..	..	..	1	2	3
4	5	6	7	8	9	10
11	12	13	14	15	16	17
18	19	20	21	22	23	24
25	26	27	28	29	30	31
..	..	..	..	..	..	..

MONDAY
12
MARCH

\multicolumn{7}{c}{APRIL}						
S	M	T	W	T	F	S
1	2	3	4	5	6	7
8	9	10	11	12	13	14
15	16	17	18	19	20	21
22	23	24	25	26	27	28
29	30	..	..	..	..	..
..	..	..	..	..	..	..

1945

On 12 March 1945, RAF Bomber Command dispatched 748 Avro Lancasters, 292 Handley Page Halifaxes, and 68 de Havilland Mosquitos—a total of 1,108 bombers, the greatest number ever launched against a single target—in a daylight raid against the once-beautiful Hanseatic city of Dortmund, in Germany's industrial heartland, the Ruhr.

The British had launched major raids against the city or its environs at least nine times previously, on 18 July 1940; 7 August 1941; 14 and 15 April 1942; 23 March 1943; 4 and 25 May 1943; and 6 and 8 January 1944; and there are records of many smaller raids as well. In the 12 March 1945 bombing, two Lancasters were lost to aircraft failure; there was no enemy activity. All of the other planes returned safely to Britain. The mission also set a record for weight of ordnance, as the aircraft dropped 4,851 tons of bombs through cloud cover onto the city, destroying roughly 90% of the city center and about 70% of all the remaining homes standing in the city. The only information released by the Germans indicated that the bombs fell mostly in the central and southern areas of the city, but civil records later estimated that the raid had caused 6,431 deaths.

After the war, a British team investigating the effects of the bombing attacks on Dortmund concluded, "The final raid carried out against the oil refinery stopped production so effectively that it would have been many months before any substantial recovery could have occurred."

MARCH

S	M	T	W	T	F	S
..	..	..	..	..	1	2
3	4	5	6	7	8	9
10	11	12	13	14	15	16
17	18	19	20	21	22	23
24	25	26	27	28	29	30
31	..	..	..	..	..	..

WEDNESDAY
13
MARCH

1940

APRIL

S	M	T	W	T	F	S
..	1	2	3	4	5	6
7	8	9	10	11	12	13
14	15	16	17	18	19	20
21	22	23	24	25	26	27
28	29	30	..	..	..	..
..	..	..	..	..	..	..

On 13 March 1940, the *Luftwaffe* launched the first, and most severe, of many raids against the Scottish city of Glasgow and the surrounding area, which was a major shipbuilding center. On that night and the next, nearly 250 bombers, based at airfields from Norway to France, caused extensive damage and heavy casualties in the Clydeside shipyard area. In Glasgow itself, 647 people lost their lives, and 6,835 houses suffered serious damage.

There were nine further raids in 1940, some in daylight and others at night, and more followed in the next three years. The 1940 raids were heavily censored: the British media, fearing that civilian morale would suffer, did not publish any photographs that showed the extent of the damage. This policy changed as the war went on; it seems that such images actually served to strengthen the people's resolve.

During the last German raid on Glasgow, on the night of 23 March 1943, an incendiary bomb fell on Queen's Park United Presbyterian Church, the last and most magnificent of the churches designed by the eminent Scottish architect and architectural theorist Alexander "Greek" Thomson, which was completed in 1869. Fueled by the lavish wooden decorative panels within the church, the resulting fire left the building a gaunt skeletal ruin, and the structure had to be demolished.

THIS MONTH							WEDNESDAY	NEXT MONTH						
MARCH							**14**	APRIL						
S	M	T	W	T	F	S		S	M	T	W	T	F	S
..	..	..	..	1	2	3		1	2	3	4	5	6	7
4	5	6	7	8	9	10	MARCH	8	9	10	11	12	13	14
11	12	13	14	15	16	17		15	16	17	18	19	20	21
18	19	20	21	22	23	24		22	23	24	25	26	27	28
25	26	27	28	29	30	31		29	30	..	..	..	..	..
..	..	..	..	..	..	..		..	..	..	..	..	..	..

1945

On 14 March 1945, a four-engined Avro Lancaster B.Mk I (Special) bomber of RAF Bomber Command's No. 617 "Dambusters" Squadron dropped a 22,000-pound Grand Slam bomb on the double-track Schildesche railway viaduct at Bielefeld, Germany.

The Grand Slam was the larger of two "earthquake" or "seismic" bombs developed by the eminent engineer and scientist Sir Barnes Wallis, who also developed the bouncing bombs used to destroy dams. Manufactured in Blochairn, Glasgow, Scotland, by the Vickers, Sheffield Clyde Alloy/Steel Company, the Grand Slam began its development on 18 July 1943, after development of the smaller Tallboy had been completed. These bombs were spin stabilized, and they had a thicker casing than a conventional bomb to allow deeper penetration. The casing had to be very precisely made so that it would be perfectly symmetrical lest unevenness in its shape cause aberrant flight characteristics.

Reaching near-supersonic speeds as it fell, the Grand Slam was capable of penetrating heavy concrete roofs. It was designed to use its seismic effect to weaken or collapse the foundations of hardened target structures; it actually created a cavern under the surface, causing the earth to shift. It was so large that it took a month to cool after the molten Torpex (so called from its original use as a torpedo explosive) was poured into the casing. Because of its high cost, aircrews were instructed to bring the Grand Slam back and land with it if a mission was aborted, rather than jettison it into the sea as was the usual practice to avoid accidental detonations on landing.

The bomb dropped on the Schildesche Viaduct was the first Grand Slam used in combat. Its explosion caused the collapse of two spans, more than 300 feet, of the viaduct. Unfortunately for the Allies, the Germans had foreseen the possibility that the viaduct would be attacked: they had constructed an alternate rail line on earthen fill, thereby turning this first use of the bomb into little more than a full-dress field trial. A total of 46 Grand Slams were used in combat.

	THIS MONTH							WEDNESDAY		NEXT MONTH					

MARCH

S	M	T	W	T	F	S
..	..	..	1	2	3	4
5	6	7	8	9	10	11
12	13	14	15	16	17	18
19	20	21	22	23	24	25
26	27	28	29	30	31	..
..	..	..	..	..	..	..

WEDNESDAY
15
MARCH

1944

APRIL

S	M	T	W	T	F	S
..	..	..	..	..	..	1
2	3	4	5	6	7	8
9	10	11	12	13	14	15
16	17	18	19	20	21	22
23	24	25	26	27	28	29
30	..	..	..	..	..	..

On 15 March 1944, after 58 days of a stalemate battle that had cost tens of thousands of casualties and had already seen the Benedictine abbey atop Italy's Monte Cassino reduced to a ruin, Allied aircraft and artillery blasted the town of Cassino, in the Liri Valley below the abbey.

The abbey, which the Germans had scrupulously not violated, was bombed and shelled because Allied observers convinced their commanders that they had seen Germans within its walls. The resulting destruction turned the massif into a nearly impregnable fortress, and now it was the turn of the town, where the Allies believed about 1,000 German paratroopers were dug in. (The entire population of 22,000 had long since decamped.)

Beginning at 0830 hours, alternating waves of bombers overflew the town at 10- to 20-minute intervals, with B-25 and B-26 medium bombers concentrating on the northern half while heavy B-17s and B-24s worked over the southern half. The first wave, of medium bombers, dropped 800 bombs, which swallowed the town in smoke and flame. The lead bombardier reported, "Target cabbaged real good."

The aerial stonk continued for three and a half hours. At 1212 hours, as the last medium bombers finished their run, a single F-5 aircraft (P-38 photoreconnaissance version)[1] flew over and took photographs that showed buildings reduced to skeletons, with a few peaks still standing but most of the town a vast heap of rubble.

Batteries of artillery continued to paste the town, firing six shells per second; the day's total expenditure of shells reached 200,000. The Allies assumed that nobody could have lived through the horror, but they were wrong. Instead of the thousand Germans thought to have been in the town, there were only about 300, of whom half survived in stone basements and

---

1. The F designation stands for *Fotorecon,* not *Fighter.* The USAAF did not begin changing the designation for fighters from P (for *Pursuit*) to F until after the end of the war.

a few two-man bunkers into which six men managed to squeeze. (It turned out that the fuzes of the aerial bombs had been set to detonate too quickly, so that most of the damage was done above the surface.)

The erstwhile town sat there through the night and into the next day, streets heaped high with rubble and cratered too deeply for tanks to pass, until rain began the process of turning the dust into mud, the craters into pools, and the entire area into a virtually ideal defensive position.

Tying the whole affair up into a not-so-neat package was the fact that fewer than 10% of the bombs had fallen within the town; the rest had come to earth on empty areas, five towns as far afield as 11 miles away, and Allied positions. Lieutenant General Sir Oliver Leese, commanding the British Eighth Army, placed a phone call to U.S. General Mark Clark, the overall theater commander, and inquired coldly, "Tell me, as a matter of interest, is there anything we've done to offend you recently?" Courts martial were instituted against 14 lieutenants, mostly bombardiers, but charges were eventually dropped against all but two, both of whom failed to return from later missions.

MARCH						
S	M	T	W	T	F	S
..	1	2	3	4	5	6
7	8	9	10	11	12	13
14	15	16	17	18	19	20
21	22	23	24	25	26	27
28	29	30	31	..	..	..
..	..	..	..	..	..	..

TUESDAY
16
MARCH
1943

APRIL						
S	M	T	W	T	F	S
..	..	..	..	1	2	3
4	5	6	7	8	9	10
11	12	13	14	15	16	17
18	19	20	21	22	23	24
25	26	27	28	29	30	..
..	..	..	..	..	..	..

On 16 March 1943, the first reports began leaking out of a massacre of Polish nationals in the Katyn Forest, near the Russian villages of Katyn and Gnyozdovo, some 12 miles west of Smolensk.

The killings had been carried out by the NKVD in April and May 1940, after the Politburo signed off on NKVD chief Lavrentiy Beria's proposal to execute all captive members of the Polish Officer Corps, dated 5 March 1940. The NKVD's remit was widened, and other executions were carried out in the Katyn, in Smolensk itself, and in other locations as distant as Byelorussia and the Ukraine. Victims included some 8,000 Polish officers taken prisoner during the 1939 Soviet invasion of Poland and 6,000 police officers; the rest were Polish intelligentsia the Soviets labeled as "intelligence agents, gendarmes, landowners, saboteurs, factory owners, lawyers, officials and priests."

All told, some 22,000 were murdered. The mass graves of some 4,500 Poles were discovered in March 1943 by German troops, and the Nazi government announced the discovery in April in an attempt to discredit and demonize the Russians. When the London-based Polish government-in-exile asked for an investigation by the International Red Cross, Stalin immediately severed diplomatic relations with the Poles.

In 1944, the Soviets retook the Katyn area, exhumed the Polish dead again, and blamed the Nazis. Not until 1989 and the collapse of Soviet power did the Soviet Union, in the person of Premier Mikhail Gorbachev, finally admit that the NKVD had committed the massacres. The official order of March 1940, which Stalin himself had also signed, had ordered the execution of 25,700 Poles, including those found at Katyn and two other sites whose locations Gorbachev revealed.

THIS MONTH									NEXT MONTH					
MARCH							**TUESDAY**		APRIL					
S	M	T	W	T	F	S			S	M	T	W	T	F	S
1	2	3	4	5	6	7	**17**		..	..	..	1	2	3	4
8	9	10	11	12	13	14			5	6	7	8	9	10	11
15	16	17	18	19	20	21			12	13	14	15	16	17	18
22	23	24	25	26	27	28	**MARCH**		19	20	21	22	23	24	25
29	30	31	..	..	..	..			26	27	28	29	30	..	..
..	..	..	..	..	..	..			..	..	..	..	..	..	..

1942

On 17 March 1942, the British U-class submarine HMS *Unbeaten,* under the command of Lieutenant Edward A. "Teddy" Woodward, came one goal shy of a hat trick.

She was patrolling submerged in the area between Sicily and Italy, where she had torpedoed and sunk the German U-boat *U-374* on 12 January. At 0633 hours, while she was off Cape Dell'Armi, *Unbeaten* picked up propeller noises, and two minutes later Lieutenant Woodward, at the periscope, spotted the target that ULTRA decrypts had sent her to attack, the Italian *Brin*-class submarine *Guglielmotti.* At 0640, *Unbeaten* fired four torpedoes; a minute and 40 seconds later an explosion signaled a hit, and *Unbeaten's* hydrophone operator heard the target breaking up. Surfacing at 0720 to look for survivors, the British boat observed "about a dozen" men in the water before the approach of enemy aircraft forced her to dive. At 1005, she heard motor torpedo boats in the area, and over the next 15 minutes three torpedo boats dropped 34 depth charges, all of them too far away to harm the submerged British boat. The Italian boats rescued 12 men from *Guglielmotti,* and *Unbeaten* stole away to return to Malta.

Unfortunately for *Unbeaten,* her name was not proof against injury; on 11 November 1942, while in the Bay of Biscay, she fell victim to friendly fire as she was mistakenly attacked by an RAF Wellington bomber of No. 172 Squadron (Coastal) and sunk with all hands. No other Royal Navy vessel, before or since, has borne the name *Unbeaten.*

MARCH

S	M	T	W	T	F	S
..	..	..	1	2	3	4
5	6	7	8	9	10	11
12	13	14	15	16	17	18
19	20	21	22	23	24	25
26	27	28	29	30	31	..
..	..	..	..	..	..	..

SATURDAY
18
MARCH

APRIL

S	M	T	W	T	F	S
..	..	..	..	..	..	1
2	3	4	5	6	7	8
9	10	11	12	13	14	15
16	17	18	19	20	21	22
23	24	25	26	27	28	29
30	..	..	..	..	..	..

1944

On 18 March 1944, as if the war wasn't enough to deal with, Vesuvius, which had buried the thriving Roman cities of Pompeii and Herculaneum 1,865 years earlier, began an eruption that was to last for several days. Towns and cities as far away as Naples felt the wrath of the mountain as it hurled smoke, ash, and clinker stones from golf-ball size to the size of human heads as high as four miles into the sky. Ash fell as deep as three feet while lava flows as deep as 25 feet coursed down the mountainside, and at least one enterprising Italian made a killing fashioning souvenir ashtrays from the hot rock and selling them to Allied military personnel.

The U.S. 340th Bomb Group, part of the 57th Bomb Wing of the 12th Air Force and the unit to which bombardier and *Catch-22* author Lieutenant Joseph Heller was assigned, was stationed near the village of Pogio Marino, immediately adjacent to the lower slopes of Vesuvius. They quickly decamped to an airfield near Salerno, but that was not far enough from the volcano, and the eruption destroyed eighty-eight of the Group's eighty-nine B-25 Mitchell medium bombers. The only plane to escape the devastation was a "used-up, battle-weary, flak-ridden B-25" that had been signed out a few days before the eruption by Lieutenant Paul Gale and two others of his aircrew, to fly to Cairo, Egypt, for some R&R.

When the eruption subsided after about a week, the volcano had destroyed the villages of San Sebastiano al Vesuvio and Massa di Somma, and part of San Giorgio a Cremano; the death toll, however, was astonishingly low, with only 28 people killed.

THIS MONTH						
MARCH						
S	M	T	W	T	F	S
..	..	..	..	..	1	2
3	4	5	6	7	8	9
10	11	12	13	14	15	16
17	18	19	20	21	22	23
24	25	26	27	28	29	30
31	..	..	..	..	..	..

TUESDAY
19
MARCH

NEXT MONTH						
APRIL						
S	M	T	W	T	F	S
..	1	2	3	4	5	6
7	8	9	10	11	12	13
14	15	16	17	18	19	20
21	22	23	24	25	26	27
28	29	30	..	..	..	..
..	..	..	..	..	..	..

1940

On 19 March 1940, there were serious political rumblings in Great Britain and France, where issues were brought up in the respective Parliaments over the countries' lack of action to aid Finland during the Winter War, a war of Soviet aggression, which had come to an end on 13 March, the day after a Finnish delegation led by Prime Minister Risto Ryti signed the Moscow Peace Treaty.

The British had sold 30 Bristol Blenheim bombers and 10 Hawker Hurricane fighters to Finland; France had sent Morane Saulnier M.S.406 and Caudron-Renault C.714 fighters—but the Hurricanes and C.714s arrived too late to be of use. When it became known that the Finns were negotiating a peace treaty, Britain and France offered to send 50,000 troops, but only if Finland requested the troops before 12 March. Soviet agents in Britain reported this offer to Moscow; Stalin's response was to step up military pressure and press harder to complete the negotiations, and in the end the troops were never requested. The public in both Britain and France had been very much in favor of direct intervention in the war, and the actual aid received by the Finns appeared to be no more than a token.

Members of the British House of Commons debated the issue and criticized Prime Minister Neville Chamberlain, who was already in a poor position due to his actions stretching back to the appeasement doctrine's solidification in 1938 under the Munich Accord. Chamberlain replied that Finland had never officially requested British military aid. In France, the Parliament criticized Premier Édouard Daladier and forced his resignation on 21 March by a vote of no confidence.

	THIS MONTH					
		MARCH				
S	M	T	W	T	F	S
..	..	..	..	..	..	1
2	3	4	5	6	7	8
9	10	11	12	13	14	15
16	17	18	19	20	21	22
23	24	25	26	27	28	29
30	31	..	..	..	..	..

THURSDAY
20
MARCH

1941

	NEXT MONTH					
		APRIL				
S	M	T	W	T	F	S
..	..	1	2	3	4	5
6	7	8	9	10	11	12
13	14	15	16	17	18	19
20	21	22	23	24	25	26
27	28	29	30	..	..	..
..	..	..	..	..	..	..

On 20 March 1941, three Avro Manchester bombers of No. 207 Squadron, based at RAF Waddington in Lincolnshire, took off on a mission to bomb the German submarine pens and, with luck, submarines at Lorient, France. Approximately half an hour after takeoff, one of the planes developed an engine fire. Electing to return to Waddington in an attempt to save the plane, the pilot ordered his crew to abandon the aircraft. Four men obeyed; two were killed and two survived. The pilot and copilot attempted to land the plane, but they were unable to line up in the proper glide path. The plane, with its entire bomb load still aboard, struck a tree and crashed. Both men were killed.

As tongues of flame from the burning engine licked at the wreckage, Aircraftman Second Class Charles L. Wheatley, a ground gunner, realized that the fire threatened to detonate the bombs; he led the fire piquet's rush to fight the fire and battled the blaze from only six feet away, and succeeded in extinguishing it. Wheatley's complete disregard for his own personal safety earned him the George Medal, which King George VI had instituted on 20 September 1940 at the height of the Blitz, saying at the time, "In order that they should be worthily and promptly recognised, I have decided to create, at once, a new mark of honour for men and women in all walks of civilian life. I propose to give my name to this new distinction, which will consist of the George Cross, which will rank next to the Victoria Cross, and the George Medal for wider distribution."

The King awarded Wheatley's medal to him on 4 November 1941, and in February 2012 a building at RAF Waddington was renamed in his honor.

THIS MONTH

MARCH						
S	M	T	W	T	F	S
..	1	2	3	4	5	6
7	8	9	10	11	12	13
14	15	16	17	18	19	20
21	22	23	24	25	26	27
28	29	30	31	..	..	..
..	..	..	..	..	..	..

SUNDAY
21
MARCH

NEXT MONTH

APRIL						
S	M	T	W	T	F	S
..	..	..	..	1	2	3
4	5	6	7	8	9	10
11	12	13	14	15	16	17
18	19	20	21	22	23	24
25	26	27	28	29	30	..
..	..	..	..	..	..	..

1943

On 21 March 1943, *Oberst* Rudolf Christoph Freiherr von Gersdorff aborted an attempt to assassinate Adolf Hitler with a suicide bomb. Von Gersdorff had become close friends with leading Army Group Center conspirator *Oberst* Henning von Tresckow, who brought von Gersdorff into the conspiracy to kill Hitler. After von Tresckow's elaborate plan to assassinate Hitler on 13 March 1943 failed, von Gersdorff declared himself ready to give his life for Germany's sake by becoming one of the earliest known suicide bombers.

On 21 March 1943, Hitler visited the *Zeughaus* Berlin, the old armory on Unter den Linden, to inspect captured Soviet weapons. He was accompanied by *Reichsmarschall* Hermann Göring, Heinrich Himmler, *Generalfeldmarschall* Wilhelm Keitel, *Großadmiral* Karl Dönitz, and other high-ranking Nazis and military officials. As an expert, von Gersdorff was to guide Hitler on a tour of the exhibition.

Moments after Hitler entered the museum, von Gersdorff started two ten-minute delayed fuses on explosive devices hidden in his coat pockets. His plan was to throw himself upon Hitler in a death embrace that would blow them both up. The conspirators had worked out a detailed plan for a coup to follow the assassination and were ready to go; but, contrary to expectations, Hitler raced through the museum in less than ten minutes. After he had left the building, von Gersdorff managed to defuse the devices in a public restroom "at the last second."

Von Gersdorff was immediately transferred back to the Eastern Front, where he managed to evade suspicion.

| THIS MONTH | | | | | | |
| MARCH | | | | | | |
S	M	T	W	T	F	S
1	2	3	4	5	6	7
8	9	10	11	12	13	14
15	16	17	18	19	20	21
22	23	24	25	26	27	28
29	30	31	..	..	..	..
..	..	..	..	..	..	..

SUNDAY
22
MARCH

1942

| NEXT MONTH | | | | | | |
| APRIL | | | | | | |
S	M	T	W	T	F	S
..	..	..	1	2	3	4
5	6	7	8	9	10	11
12	13	14	15	16	17	18
19	20	21	22	23	24	25
26	27	28	29	30	..	..
..	..	..	..	..	..	..

On 22 March 1942, the SS arrested high-ranking *Abwehr* agent Paul Thümmel, an old friend of Heinrich Himmler, in the belief that he was actually a British agent. *Abwehr* chief Admiral Wilhelm Canaris interfered, claiming that Thümmel was actually a double agent working for him, and requested Thümmel's release.

Thümmel's value to Germany was in his connections in Istanbul and the Balkans; Canaris had taken him to Turkey in December 1940, shortly after Hitler had issued his directive for the invasion of the Soviet Union, probably to acquire information about British and Soviet intentions in the Balkans.

Thümmel actually was an agent of the Czechs, not the British, and he was passing information to the Czech government-in-exile in London. The British had assigned to him the code symbol A-54, and it is virtually certain that Canaris was aware that he was spying and that he was secretly committed—as was Canaris himself—to preventing, in whatever way possible, the Nazi domination of Europe. Canaris had at least two paths of contact with MI6, and it is likely that he viewed Thümmel as another possible path; Thümmel also had contacts in the Soviet Union and could be very useful to Canaris in funneling information to or from the Soviets. (Canaris abhorred communism but knew that Soviet arms could only serve to hasten the collapse of the Third Reich.)

In the event, the SS released Thümmel, and he later became the chief of the *Abwehr*'s office in Prague. His activities were eventually discovered, however, and he was executed at the Theresienstadt Concentration Camp on 20 April 1945. Eleven days before Thümmel's execution, Canaris, whose activities included participation in the plot to kill Hitler, was executed at the Flossenbürg Concentration Camp.

THIS MONTH						
MARCH						
S	M	T	W	T	F	S
..	1	2	3	4	5	6
7	8	9	10	11	12	13
14	15	16	17	18	19	20
21	22	23	24	25	26	27
28	29	30	31	..	..	..
..	..	..	..	..	..	..

TUESDAY
23
MARCH

1943

NEXT MONTH						
APRIL						
S	M	T	W	T	F	S
..	..	..	..	1	2	3
4	5	6	7	8	9	10
11	12	13	14	15	16	17
18	19	20	21	22	23	24
25	26	27	28	29	30	..
..	..	..	..	..	..	..

On 23 March 1943, nine B-17 bombers of the U.S. Fifth Air Force attacked the large Japanese base at Rabaul, New Britain, in Papua New Guinea, causing damage to the airfields around the base.

Rabaul is located on the northern side of the eastward-opening Blanche Bay, which lies at the tip of New Britain's Gazelle Peninsula, within the western end of the Rabaul volcanic caldera. The caldera is five miles north to south and nine miles east to west and was formed by a massive eruption about 7,100 years ago. There are several volcanoes on the northern side of Blanche Bay. Recognizing that there had been volcanic activity in the area relatively recently, American planners instructed one of the bombers to drop its full load of heavy bombs into the crater of Rabalanakaia volcano in an attempt to trigger an eruption. The attempt failed; the Americans did not realize that Rabalanakaia was dormant. (Tavurvur, less than two miles from Rabalanakaia, had experienced a minor eruption on 6 June 1941, and there had been frequent earthquakes, which often portend an eruption, between June 1941 and March 1942.)

THIS MONTH								FRIDAY		NEXT MONTH						

<table>
<tr><th colspan="7">MARCH</th></tr>
<tr><th>S</th><th>M</th><th>T</th><th>W</th><th>T</th><th>F</th><th>S</th></tr>
<tr><td>..</td><td>..</td><td>1</td><td>2</td><td>3</td><td>4</td><td>5</td></tr>
<tr><td>6</td><td>7</td><td>8</td><td>9</td><td>10</td><td>11</td><td>12</td></tr>
<tr><td>13</td><td>14</td><td>15</td><td>16</td><td>17</td><td>18</td><td>19</td></tr>
<tr><td>20</td><td>21</td><td>22</td><td>23</td><td>24</td><td>25</td><td>26</td></tr>
<tr><td>27</td><td>28</td><td>29</td><td>30</td><td>31</td><td>..</td><td>..</td></tr>
<tr><td>..</td><td>..</td><td>..</td><td>..</td><td>..</td><td>..</td><td>..</td></tr>
</table>

FRIDAY
24
MARCH

1944

<table>
<tr><th colspan="7">APRIL</th></tr>
<tr><th>S</th><th>M</th><th>T</th><th>W</th><th>T</th><th>F</th><th>S</th></tr>
<tr><td>..</td><td>..</td><td>..</td><td>..</td><td>..</td><td>1</td><td>2</td></tr>
<tr><td>3</td><td>4</td><td>5</td><td>6</td><td>7</td><td>8</td><td>9</td></tr>
<tr><td>10</td><td>11</td><td>12</td><td>13</td><td>14</td><td>15</td><td>16</td></tr>
<tr><td>17</td><td>18</td><td>19</td><td>20</td><td>21</td><td>22</td><td>23</td></tr>
<tr><td>24</td><td>25</td><td>26</td><td>27</td><td>28</td><td>29</td><td>30</td></tr>
<tr><td>..</td><td>..</td><td>..</td><td>..</td><td>..</td><td>..</td><td>..</td></tr>
</table>

On 24–25 March 1944, 76 Allied officers, most of them members of various air forces, escaped from *Stalag Luft* III at Sagan, Germany, in what later became known as the Great Escape.[2] The proposed 200-man escape had been planned and prepared beginning in April 1943 by an escape committee known as X.

The camp had been intentionally located in an area with bright yellow sandy soil that would tend to collapse if tunneled through and would also be easy to spot if dumped on the surface or left on the prisoners' clothing.

The prisoners had dug three tunnels, which they named Tom, Dick, and Harry; the tunnels were two feet square and were dug 30 feet below the surface to avoid detection by seismic microphones. The prisoners installed electric lights, built pumps to provide air to the diggers, and installed trolley carts on rails to speed the movement of men and dirt; and they used more than 2,000 wooden slats taken a few from each man's bed to shore up the tunnels against collapse. A team of "penguins" carried the excavated soil around the compound, scattering it carefully from pouches made from socks and attached inside their pants. Other teams made civilian-type clothing from uniforms, blankets, etc., and a skilled forger created authentic-looking travel and ID papers for the escapees to carry, producing machine-accurate "typescript" entirely by hand. In June 1943, as the Germans caught more of the penguins, X decided to stop work on Harry and Dick, backfilling Harry with the soil taken from Tom.

On 8 September, the Germans found Tom and forced the prisoners to fill it completely. In January 1944, work recommenced on Harry. On the moonless night of 24–25 March, the tunnelers broke through to the surface and were stunned to find that they had come up short of the woods

---

2. The men who escaped were members of the RAF, RAAF, RCAF, RHAF, RNZAF, SAAF, and the British army and navy. Members of the USAAF were involved in the initial stages of the preparation but were moved to another camp seven months before the escape was staged.

surrounding the camp. They nevertheless commenced their escape, one at a time, even during an air raid that temporarily cut power to the lights in the tunnel.

As the 77th man emerged from the tunnel, a camp guard spotted him. A roll call revealed the magnitude of the escape; and when the news was relayed to Berlin, Hitler ordered the execution of all recaptured prisoners but then relaxed this to "only" 50 out of concern for the possible reaction of neutral countries. Over a period of approximately two weeks, 73 of the 76 escapees were recaptured; the Germans shot 50 of them, claiming falsely that they were trying to escape again. Two Norwegians and a Dutchman made it to safety. The High Command removed *Oberst* Fritz von Lindeiner, the camp commandant, replacing him with *Oberst* Franz Braune. The new commandant, appalled by the killings, allowed the prisoners to build a memorial that still stands on the site of the former POW camp. The *Stalag Luft* III killings were among the war crimes charged at the Nuremberg trials.

In 2011, archaeological excavation discovered that after the failed escape, the prisoners had built a fourth tunnel, named George, to be used for concealment if the Germans began murdering the camp's internees as Nazi power crumbled before advancing Soviet forces.

	THIS MONTH										NEXT MONTH				

		MARCH									APRIL				
S	**M**	**T**	**W**	**T**	**F**	**S**			**S**	**M**	**T**	**W**	**T**	**F**	**S**
..	..	..	..	1	2	3			1	2	3	4	5	6	7
4	5	6	7	8	9	10			8	9	10	11	12	13	14
11	12	13	14	15	16	17			15	16	17	18	19	20	21
18	19	20	21	22	23	24			22	23	24	25	26	27	28
25	26	27	28	29	30	31			29	30	..	..	..	..	..
..	..	..	..	..	..	..			..	..	..	..	..	..	..

SUNDAY
25
MARCH

1945

On 25 March 1945, a German V-2 rocket fell out of the sky to land in Whitfield Street in St Pancras, London, England, in the late afternoon. It killed nine people, seriously injured 46, and caused heavy damage to the Whitfield Memorial Chapel at Tottenham Court Road.

The V-2, known to the Germans as the V2, or *Vergeltungswaffe* 2 (Retribution Weapon 2), was the world's first ballistic missile and was the result of a project that had been conceived in the late 1920s and continued through the 1930s, with Wehrner von Braun at its head. Beginning with small rockets that reached heights slightly greater than two miles, the project culminated in the A-4, a liquid-fueled rocket with gyroscopic stabilization, supersonic aerodynamics, and four small vanes that impinged on the rocket exhaust to steer the vehicle. Hitler, who in 1939 considered the rocket nothing more than a bigger artillery shell with a much longer range and a much greater cost, changed his mind in mid-1944 as he began to feel the need for an actual magic bullet, the wonder weapon that Joseph Goebbels had been promising the people for years but which had never materialized.

The V-2, first launched successfully on 3 October 1942, reached speeds of 3,477 miles per hour and was, unlike the V-1 "buzz bomb" cruise missile, unstoppable. It promised to be devastating; the design was rushed to completion at Peenemünde, and V-2s began falling on London on 8 September 1944. The first one landed in Chiswick, in western London, killing three people. By the time the last V-2 landed, on 27 March 1945, the *Wehrmacht* had launched more than 3,100 of the missiles, aiming them at the United Kingdom, France, Belgium, the Netherlands, and Germany (where eleven were used against the bridge and the Allied bridgehead at Remagen). Their explosions caused the deaths of an estimated 9,000 civilian and military personnel. Brutal treatment and inhumane working and living conditions cost the lives of 12,000 of the forced laborers and concentration camp prisoners who built them.

THIS MONTH

		MARCH				
S	M	T	W	T	F	S
..	..	..	..	..	..	1
2	3	4	5	6	7	8
9	10	11	12	13	14	15
16	17	18	19	20	21	22
23	24	25	26	27	28	29
30	31	..	..	..	..	..

NEXT MONTH

		APRIL				
S	M	T	W	T	F	S
..	..	1	2	3	4	5
6	7	8	9	10	11	12
13	14	15	16	17	18	19
20	21	22	23	24	25	26
27	28	29	30	..	..	..
..	..	..	..	..	..	..

WEDNESDAY
26
MARCH

1941

On 26 March 1941, two Italian destroyers of the *Regia Marina*'s *Decima Flottiglia MAS*, named *Crispi* and *Sella*, which had been specially fitted with cranes to operate assault boats, launched six explosive motorboats, each packed with a 300-kg charge in the bow, to attack the British heavy cruiser HMS *York* and two other ships (the Norwegian tanker *Pericles* and another tanker) that were at anchor in Souda Bay, in Crete. (Italian records also mention a cargo ship.)

The boats were to be aimed at their targets from a range of several hundred yards, at which point the drivers would tie the helm down and abandon ship. Three of the boats developed problems of one sort or another and failed to achieve their objectives, but one boat struck *Pericles*, sinking her, and two boats (piloted by MMI Lieutenants Angelo Cabrini and Tullio Tedeschi) rammed *York* amidships. The explosions flooded both of *York*'s boiler rooms and one engine room, killing two British seamen. All six of the Italian boat drivers survived the attack and were captured by the British. *York*'s commanding officer, Captain Reginald Henry Portal, RN, ordered his ship run aground to prevent her from sinking. She was then connected to the submarine HMS *Rover* for electrical power to operate her guns for antiaircraft defense, but she was later severely damaged by air attack and had to be towed away for repairs. On 18 May, German bombers inflicted yet more injury, damaging her beyond repair. Her main guns were wrecked by demolition charges on 22 May 1941, when the Allies began to withdraw from Crete in the face of the Germans' advance.

The question of who had sunk *York* became a source of friction between the *Regia Marina* and the *Luftwaffe*. The matter was resolved by British war records and by the ship's own war log, which the Italians had captured.

<table>
<tr><th colspan="7">THIS MONTH</th><th rowspan="2"></th><th colspan="7">NEXT MONTH</th></tr>
</table>

| THIS MONTH | | | | | | | | NEXT MONTH | | | | | | |

THURSDAY

27

MARCH

1941

MARCH

S	M	T	W	T	F	S
..	..	..	..	..	..	1
2	3	4	5	6	7	8
9	10	11	12	13	14	15
16	17	18	19	20	21	22
23	24	25	26	27	28	29
30	31	..	..	..	..	..

APRIL

S	M	T	W	T	F	S
..	..	1	2	3	4	5
6	7	8	9	10	11	12
13	14	15	16	17	18	19
20	21	22	23	24	25	26
27	28	29	30	..	..	..
..	..	..	..	..	..	..

On 27 March 1941, the following short article appeared in the *Nippu Jiji*, an English-Japanese bilingual newspaper in Honolulu, Hawaii: "Tadashi Morimura, newly appointed secretary of the local Japanese consulate general, arrived here this morning on the *Nitta Maru* from Japan. His appointment was made to expedite the work on expatriation applications and other matters."

Because there was no Tadashi Morimura in the Japanese Foreign Service, this notice should have rung alarm bells among the U.S. intelligence community, but it did not. "Tadashi Morimura," the newly appointed vice consul, was in fact Takeo Yoshikawa, a 1933 graduate of the Imperial Japanese Naval Academy. After his graduation, Yoshikawa served briefly at sea. Late in 1934, he began naval pilot training but was prevented by health problems from completing the course. In 1937 he trained for a career in naval intelligence and was assigned to the IJN headquarters in Tokyo, where by voraciously reading every scrap of information he could lay his hands on, he became an expert on the U.S. Navy. In 1940, he joined the Japanese Foreign Ministry as a junior diplomat.

His expertise on the U.S. Navy earned him a post in Hawaii. On his arrival, he set up shop in a second story apartment that overlooked Pearl Harbor and began spying on the American military. Making no attempt to act covertly, he would wander around the island of Oahu taking notes; he rented light planes at John Rodgers Airport to observe U.S. installations from the air, and he used the gossip among crew members of the Navy's own harbor tugboat as a source of intelligence. He even dove in Pearl Harbor itself, using a hollow reed to breathe, in order to gather information on the topography of the seafloor and the fixtures in the harbor.

The Americans had broken the code Yoshikawa used for his transmissions, but there were so many messages involving ordinary commerce among the traffic between Hawaii and Japan that most of the messages to and from Yoshikawa were "lost in the noise"—including one from Tokyo that divided the harbor into five zones and requested a plot showing the number and locations of all the warships at anchor there. When the coded message arrived indicating that the aerial attack on Pearl Harbor was imminent, Yoshikawa destroyed all the communications, code books, and other potentially incriminating evidence in his possession; and when he was picked up on 7 December, the U.S. authorities could find nothing to tie him to espionage.

He was repatriated in August 1942 as part of an exchange of interned diplomats, and it was some time before the Americans figured out that he had been the chief Japanese spy in Hawaii and, in truth, the man most responsible for the terrible events of 7 December 1941.

| \multicolumn{7}{c|}{THIS MONTH} |||||||
| \multicolumn{7}{c|}{MARCH} |||||||
S	M	T	W	T	F	S
1	2	3	4	5	6	7
8	9	10	11	12	13	14
15	16	17	18	19	20	21
22	23	24	25	26	27	28
29	30	31	..	..	..	..
..	..	..	..	..	..	..

SATURDAY
28
MARCH
1942

| \multicolumn{7}{c|}{NEXT MONTH} |||||||
| \multicolumn{7}{c|}{APRIL} |||||||
S	M	T	W	T	F	S
..	..	..	1	2	3	4
5	6	7	8	9	10	11
12	13	14	15	16	17	18
19	20	21	22	23	24	25
26	27	28	29	30	..	..
..	..	..	..	..	..	..

On 28 March 1942, the Royal Navy and British Commandos, under the auspices of Combined Operations Headquarters, executed Operation CHARIOT, also known as the St. Nazaire Raid. The mission was to destroy, or at least put out of service in some way, the *Normandie* dry dock on the Loire estuary at St. Nazaire, France; with that facility unavailable, any large German warships in need of major repair, such as *Tirpitz*, could no longer be serviced on the Atlantic coast and would be forced to return to German waters.

To accomplish the mission, the British packed the obsolete destroyer HMS *Campbeltown*[3] with explosives fitted with a time-delay fuze and hidden by a casing of steel and concrete. With a fleet of 18 smaller ships, she sailed across the English Channel and through the Bay of Biscay to St. Nazaire, where she rammed the gates of the dry dock. A Commando force landed to destroy machinery and other structures.

The port was well defended, and German gunfire sank or disabled all of the small craft that had been intended to provide return transport for the Commandos, who were thus compelled to fight their way through the town in hopes of escaping overland. When their ammunition ran out, they were forced to surrender. Of the force of 622, 228 men managed to return to Britain. 169 died, and the remaining 215 spent the rest of the war in POW camps.

Campbeltown exploded later in the day, putting the dry dock entirely out of service for the remainder of the war and for several years after the cessation of hostilities. More than 360 Germans died in the action, most of them killed by the explosion of *Campbeltown*.

Paul Wendkos' 1967 Anglo-American film *Attack on the Iron Coast*, featuring Lloyd Bridges and Andrew Keir as the commanders of a bomb-ship attack on a dry dock at the fictional port of Le Clare, was based on Operation CHARIOT.

---

3. *Campbeltown*, formerly USS *Buchanan*, was one of the 50 destroyers transferred to Great Britain by the United States under the Destroyers for Bases Agreement of 2 September 1940.

THIS MONTH						
MARCH						
S	M	T	W	T	F	S
..	1	2	3	4	5	6
7	8	9	10	11	12	13
14	15	16	17	18	19	20
21	22	23	24	25	26	27
28	29	30	31	..	..	..
..	..	..	..	..	..	..

MONDAY
29
MARCH

NEXT MONTH						
APRIL						
S	M	T	W	T	F	S
..	..	..	..	1	2	3
4	5	6	7	8	9	10
11	12	13	14	15	16	17
18	19	20	21	22	23	24
25	26	27	28	29	30	..
..	..	..	..	..	..	..

1943

On 29 March 1943, Air Vice Marshall Sir Ralph A. Cochrane summoned Wing Commander Guy P. Gibson, the commanding officer of No. 617 Squadron RAF, to Group Headquarters, where he gave Gibson a detailed briefing on Operation CHASTISE, which was planned for mid-May.

No. 617 Squadron, having been chosen for the operation, was outfitted with specially modified Avro Lancaster Mk III bombers, each of which could carry one of the special bouncing bombs developed by the eminent engineer and scientist Sir Barnes Wallis for the purpose of destroying dams. The information that Cochrane gave to Gibson included details of the proposed targets, the Möhne and Sorpe Dams in the Ruhr Valley, in Germany's Ruhr industrial heartland.

Gibson was the lead pilot for Operation CHASTISE (better known as the Dambusters Raid), which destroyed both of the main targets and inflicted minor damage on the Edersee dam in the Eder Valley, causing catastrophic flooding in the Ruhr and Eder Valleys and destroying hydroelectric plants, factories, and mines. Collateral damage included the destruction of several villages and the deaths of approximately 1,600 people.

The raid made Gibson famous, but on 19 September 1944 he and Squadron Leader James B. "Paddy" Warwick, his navigator and friend, were killed by friendly fire over Steenbergen, the Netherlands, while returning from a night bombing raid on Rheydt, Germany. At 2319 hours, Sergeant Bernard McCormack, the tail gunner in an Avro Lancaster bomber of No. 61 Squadron, mistook their de Havilland Mosquito for an attacking Junkers Ju 88 and shot it down.[4] Gibson had flown 170 missions and had been

---

4. McCormack realized his mistake during debriefing but said nothing at the time. In 1992, he recorded a confession on a cassette tape, entrusting it to his wife Eunice before his death. The cassette came to light when TV documentary maker James Cutler contacted Mrs. McCormack during research for Peter Jackson's remake of the 1955 film *Dambusters*.

awarded the Distinguished Service Order, the Distinguished Flying Cross, and the Victoria Cross. He was 25. Warwick had flown 27 missions and had been awarded the Distinguished Flying Cross. His age is unknown.

THIS MONTH						
MARCH						
S	M	T	W	T	F	S
..	..	..	..	1	2	3
4	5	6	7	8	9	10
11	12	13	14	15	16	17
18	19	20	21	22	23	24
25	26	27	28	29	30	31
..	..	..	..	..	..	..

FRIDAY

30

MARCH

1945

NEXT MONTH						
APRIL						
S	M	T	W	T	F	S
1	2	3	4	5	6	7
8	9	10	11	12	13	14
15	16	17	18	19	20	21
22	23	24	25	26	27	28
29	30	..	..	..	..	..
..	..	..	..	..	..	..

On 30 March 1945, the staff and guards at the Ravensbrück concentration camp, operating under orders from the camp's commandant, *SS-Hauptsturmführer* Fritz Suhren, were hastily exterminating their prisoners in the face of advancing Soviet troops, with the intention that none would be left alive to testify to what had happened in the camp. A group of Jewish women who were being led to the gas chamber turned against their SS guards. In the *melée*, nine of the women escaped; but they were soon recaptured and were gassed along with the others in the group.

Also killed on that day was a Roman Catholic nun known as *Mère* (Mother) Marie Élisabeth *de l'Eucharistie*. Born in 1890 to a French naval officer in Algeria, Élise Rivet had joined the convent of the medical sisters of Notre Dame de Compassion in Lyon as a young woman, and in 1933 she became the convent's Mother Superior. After France fell to the Germans in 1940, *Mère* Marie Élisabeth began hiding refugees from the Gestapo and eventually used her convent to store weapons and ammunition for the French Resistance.

She was denounced for suspicion of hiding weapons, and on 24 March 1944 the Gestapo arrested her and took her to the prison at Fort Montluc in Lyon. On 28 July she was taken from Fort Montluc to Ravensbrück. There, she was stripped of her religious garments and set to hard labor; it was *Kommandant* Suhren's policy to work his prisoners literally to death by driving them as hard as possible and feeding them as little as possible. In March 1945, she and 1,500 other women were transferred to Uckermark, a subsidiary camp for girls and women near Ravensbrück; by the spring of 1945, Uckermark was known as the last stop before the gas chambers.

On Good Friday, 30 March 1945, *Mère* Marie Élisabeth volunteered to go to the gas chamber in the place of another woman who had children. She was 55. *Kommandant* Suhren survived her by five years; his activities at Ravensbrück earned him a war criminal's death on the gallows, on 12 June 1950.

THIS MONTH						
MARCH						
S	M	T	W	T	F	S
..	..	..	..	1	2	3
4	5	6	7	8	9	10
11	12	13	14	15	16	17
18	19	20	21	22	23	24
25	26	27	28	29	30	31
..	..	..	..	..	..	..

SATURDAY
31
MARCH

NEXT MONTH						
APRIL						
S	M	T	W	T	F	S
1	2	3	4	5	6	7
8	9	10	11	12	13	14
15	16	17	18	19	20	21
22	23	24	25	26	27	28
29	30	..	..	..	..	..
..	..	..	..	..	..	..

1945

On 31 March 1945, a troop of SS men under the command of *SS-Sturmbann-nführer* Heinz Macher attempted to carry out Heinrich Himmler's order to destroy *Schloß* (Castle) Wewelsburg, located in Büren, Germany.

The present castle was completed in 1609, and over the next 300 years it suffered serious damage from both war and natural causes. In 1924, the castle became the property of the town of Büren, which set forth but did not carry through an ambitious plan to renovate the castle, making it into a museum, banquet hall, and cultural center.

In 1933, Heinrich Himmler inspected the castle. Himmler's belief in the occult prophecies surrounding the area led him to order the SS to lease the castle for 100 years at the annual rental of 1 Reichsmark. Between 1934 and 1943, Himmler himself spent 5 million Reichsmarks converting the castle into an "SS Black Camelot"; from 1939 to 1943, the nearby Nieder-hagen concentration camp provided most of the labor, in the persons of about 1,000 Jehovah's Witnesses and Soviet prisoners of war.

With Nazi power crumbling as the *Wehrmacht* was in retreat on all fronts, Himmler ordered the structure demolished so that the devotional objects and important files there should not fall into the hands of the Allies. After the local fire brigade was warned, the attempt to destroy the castle with anti-tank mines proceeded but managed only to damage the southeast tower, which was the least important part of the structure. On Macher's orders, the firemen did not extinguish the fire that the explosions had started, and the flames destroyed most of the rest of the building.

Some 9,000 *SS-Ehrenringe* (SS Honor Rings, unofficially called *Totenkopf-fringe*, Death's Head Rings) had been stored in the castle; Macher removed these treasures and buried them at a secret location in nearby woods. Their present location is unknown.

THIS MONTH						
APRIL						
S	M	T	W	T	F	S
1	2	3	4	5	6	7
8	9	10	11	12	13	14
15	16	17	18	19	20	21
22	23	24	25	26	27	28
29	30	..	..	..	..	..
..	..	..	..	..	..	..

SUNDAY
1
APRIL

1945

NEXT MONTH						
MAY						
S	M	T	W	T	F	S
..	..	1	2	3	4	5
6	7	8	9	10	11	12
13	14	15	16	17	18	19
20	21	22	23	24	25	26
27	28	29	30	31	..	..
..	..	..	..	..	..	..

On 1 April 1945, American forces launched the Allies' largest amphibious landing in the Pacific, Operation ICEBERG, to take the island of Okinawa for use as an advance bombing base and as a jump-off point for Operation DOWNFALL, the invasion of Japan scheduled for September.

Preliminary landings had been made beginning on 26 March by the 77th Infantry Division, who landed in the Kerama Islands, 15 miles west of Okinawa, to secure a protected anchorage for the fleet and eliminate the threat from suicide boats. On 31 March, elements of the Fleet Marine Force Amphibious Reconnaissance Battalion landed without opposition on

Keise Shima, four islets just eight miles west of the Okinawan capital of Naha, bringing with them two battalions of 155 mm "Long Tom" guns of the Army's 420th Field Artillery to cover operations on Okinawa by shelling the main Japanese defensive positions.

The main landing came on April Fools' Day, which was also Easter Sunday, as XXIV Corps and III Amphibious Corps went ashore on the Hagushi beaches on the western coast of Okinawa. The 2nd Marine Division conducted a demonstration off the Minatoga beaches on the southeastern coast to confuse the Japanese about American intentions and impede the movement of reserves to the west side of the island. The Battle of Okinawa lasted until 22 June; during that period, the U.S. 7th, 27th, 77th, and 96th Divisions of the 10th Army and the 1st and 6th Marine Divisions fought on the island with naval and air support from American, British, Australian, and New Zealand forces. The brutally fierce and bloody fighting, intense *kamikaze* attacks on shipping, and the sheer volume of Allied armored vehicles and ships led to the operation's being nicknamed the Typhoon of Steel by the Allies. The Japanese referred to it as *tetsu no ame* ("rain of iron"). The battle produced the greatest number of casualties, for both sides, of all operations in the Pacific Theater. The Allies lost 14,009 killed and more than 38,000 wounded; estimates of total Allied casualties are in the range of 65,000. The Japanese lost 77,166 soldiers killed either in combat or by suicide along with more than 7,000 captured.

While the battle was raging, at least 42,000 and possibly as many as the U.S. military's official count of 142,058 local civilians were killed or forced to commit suicide by the Japanese military. The island's Japanese-run educational system had indoctrinated the Okinawan people that they had to be "more Japanese than the Japanese" and that they were expected to prove it. Japanese propaganda had led the civilians to believe that the Americans would conduct a policy of torture, rape, and murder. Japanese soldiers passed out hand grenades to civilians with instructions to blow themselves up, and some civilians threw themselves and their family members from cliffs at the southern end of the island.

As operations approached the Japanese home islands, the increasing tenacity and ferocity of the Japanese defenders, even when they were completely cut off from reinforcement and supplies, provided a chilling preview of Operation DOWNFALL and probably helped to convince President Harry Truman to use the atomic bombs in August.

		THIS MONTH										NEXT MONTH				

THIS MONTH

APRIL

S	M	T	W	T	F	S
..	..	..	..	..	..	1
2	3	4	5	6	7	8
9	10	11	12	13	14	15
16	17	18	19	20	21	22
23	24	25	26	27	28	29
30	..	..	..	..	..	..

SUNDAY
2
APRIL

1944

NEXT MONTH

MAY

S	M	T	W	T	F	S
..	1	2	3	4	5	6
7	8	9	10	11	12	13
14	15	16	17	18	19	20
21	22	23	24	25	26	27
28	29	30	31	..	..	..
..	..	..	..	..	..	..

On 2 April 1944, the first B-29 Superfortress bomber of the U.S. 20th Air Force's 58th Bombardment Wing landed at Chakulia, near Calcutta, India, to start working up for a new strategic bomber force equipped with B-29 bombers with advance bases in China from which targets in Manchuria and on the home island of Kyushu, Japan, could be attacked.

The 58th Bombardment Operational Training Wing (Heavy) was constituted on 22 April and activated on 1 May 1943 in Kansas to train the first B-29 aircrews and help prepare the new aircraft for operational combat duty. By July, the USAAF had accepted seven YB-29s and had assigned them to the 58th to equip new training squadrons of the 472d Bombardment Group, the Wing's first operational group.

In August 1943, the USAAF's high command decided that 58th Bombardment Wing would be stationed in the CBI Theater (China-Burma-India) by the end of 1943 and would begin attacking Japanese home island targets from bases in China. Delays in the program to ready the bombers slipped the date. As planes came off the Boeing assembly lines, they went to USAAF modification centers located near the assembly plants in Marietta, Georgia, and Omaha, Nebraska, to be refitted with modifications and improvements the need for which had been learned from air combat in Europe.

Finally, in April 1944, the planes—and their crews, who had to undergo an unusually long and arduous training program because of the aircraft's complexity—were considered combat ready and were delivered. The first B-29 bombing raid took place on 5 June 1944, when 98 B-29s took off from bases in eastern India to attack the Makasan railroad yards at Bangkok, Thailand.

Because the Japanese still had command of the seas in the area, all fuel, bombs, spares, and other supplies for the bases in China had to be flown in from India over the Hump. This was a serious logistical problem, especially because the B-29's Wasp R-3350-23 engine had been rushed into production and was singularly unreliable. The aircraft ate engines at a rate that simply could not be sustained with bases in China, and in December 1944 the Joint Chiefs of Staff decided to move the 58th Bombardment wing to bases in the newly captured Marianas Islands of Guam, Saipan, and Tinian. The 58th Bomb Wing flew its last missions in the CBI Theater on 8 February 1945.

THIS MONTH						
APRIL						
S	M	T	W	T	F	S
..	..	..	..	1	2	3
4	5	6	7	8	9	10
11	12	13	14	15	16	17
18	19	20	21	22	23	24
25	26	27	28	29	30	..
..	..	..	..	..	..	..

SATURDAY
3
APRIL
1943

NEXT MONTH						
MAY						
S	M	T	W	T	F	S
..	..	..	..	..	..	1
2	3	4	5	6	7	8
9	10	11	12	13	14	15
16	17	18	19	20	21	22
23	24	25	26	27	28	29
30	31	..	..	..	..	..

On 3 April 1943, American servicemen in the Allied Services' Club, a social center open to all military personnel at 2 Manners Street in Wellington, New Zealand, came to blows with New Zealand servicemen.

No one is sure what the spark was, but the most commonly accepted theory has it that at about 6 P.M., men from the southern United States refused to let some newly arrived Māori servicemen drink in the club because of their skin color. (The U.S. military was segregated until 1948. Māori servicemen said at the time only that "the Yanks" had sought and received preferential treatment.) The Māori insisted, and tempers flared. When the Americans removed their brass-buckled Army service belts and wrapped them around their hands as weapons to emphasize their point of view, Kiwi servicemen, both white and Māori, joined in, and the saloon brawl quickly spread into the street. American MPs arrived to restore order and waded in with their batons swinging.

The donnybrook spread to the A.N.A. Club in Willis Street, where belts and knives were used, to the intersection at James Smith Corner (Manners and Cuba Streets), and as far as the People's Palace, a little less than half a mile distant at 213 Cuba Street.

As fights do, the Battle of Manners Street attracted additional willing participants, including American sailors and Kiwi merchant seamen. The exact number of brawlers is not known, but at least 1,000 servicemen of both nations were involved along with some hundreds of civilians. Conflict around the epicenter subsided after about two hours, but fighting continued up and down the streets until about 10 P.M., when a combination of military police, fatigue, and the American servicemen's fear of missing the last train back to their barracks finally brought the situation under control.

Scores of people had been injured, but a rumor that two Americans were killed was false, and the only military discipline was meted out to one Kiwi soldier. Wartime censorship regulations required state approval to report any military news, and the censors clamped a lid on the story of fisticuffs between men supposedly on the same side. No reference to the ugliest riot in New Zealand's history appeared in local newspapers or on the radio.

	THIS MONTH												NEXT MONTH					

APRIL

S	M	T	W	T	F	S
..	..	..	..	1	2	3
4	5	6	7	8	9	10
11	12	13	14	15	16	17
18	19	20	21	22	23	24
25	26	27	28	29	30	..
..	..	..	..	..	..	..

SUNDAY
4
APRIL

MAY

S	M	T	W	T	F	S
..	..	..	..	..	..	1
2	3	4	5	6	7	8
9	10	11	12	13	14	15
16	17	18	19	20	21	22
23	24	25	26	27	28	29
30	31	..	..	..	..	..

1943

On 4 April 1943, ten Allied prisoners of war escaped from the Davao Penal Colony (known as "Dapecol"), on the island of Mindanao in the Philippines, in the only large-scale escape of Allied POWs from the Japanese in the Pacific Theater.

Established in 1931, Dapecol was the largest prison complex in the country; comprising some 140 acres, it was a maximum-security prison along the lines of Devil's Island and Alcatraz. But instead of water, Dapecol's barrier was a treacherously swampy malarial jungle infested by headhunters, poisonous snakes, crocodiles, and other unpleasant ways to die. During the war, the Imperial Japanese Army took it over for use as a garrison and a POW camp housing some 2,000 prisoners who were forced to work the camp's orchards, fields, and hardwood forest for the benefit of Japan's war effort.

As they did in most POW camps, the Japanese treated their captives cruelly and with evident disdain; the Bushido code equated surrender with treason, effectively casting POWs as less than human. Eighteen POWs are known to have died in the camp before the Japanese abandoned it on 6 June 1944. The ten escapers had been in the camp for a year and were well aware that a death sentence awaited them if they were caught, but they were willing to take the risk in order to tell the world about the atrocities the Japanese were committing against POWs.

Led by 25-year-old USAAF Major William E. "Ed" Dyess, who had transitioned to infantry duty when his squadron ran short of aircraft, and assisted by two Filipino convicts, they spent two months planning and preparing for their breakout—which they accomplished on 4 April 1943 by walking brazenly out through the camp's front gate. Once free, they remained on the run for several weeks.

Finally, they decided to split up; seven joined organized guerrilla forces in northern Mindanao while Major Dyess and two others were evacuated to Australia in July by the submarine USS *Trout*. In addition to delivering information about treatment in Dapecol, the three were the first to break the news of the infamous Bataan Death March to the world. The intelligence they provided prompted increased U.S. military action in the Pacific. Major Dyess was promoted to Lieutenant Colonel and assigned to fly P-38 Lightning fighters. He died in a training accident on 22 December 1943.

THIS MONTH

APRIL

S	M	T	W	T	F	S
..	..	..	..	..	..	1
2	3	4	5	6	7	8
9	10	11	12	13	14	15
16	17	18	19	20	21	22
23	24	25	26	27	28	29
30	..	..	..	..	..	..

WEDNESDAY
5
APRIL

NEXT MONTH

MAY

S	M	T	W	T	F	S
..	1	2	3	4	5	6
7	8	9	10	11	12	13
14	15	16	17	18	19	20
21	22	23	24	25	26	27
28	29	30	31	..	..	..
..	..	..	..	..	..	..

1944

On 5 April 1944, at Los Alamos, New Mexico, Italian physicist Emilio G. Segrè, whom Robert Oppenheimer had brought into the Manhattan Project in 1942 after he had been declared an enemy alien in the wake of the Pearl Harbor bombing, received the first sample of reactor-refined plutonium from Oak Ridge, Tennessee.

The plutonium was intended to be used in a gun-type nuclear device called "Thin Man," but within days Segrè—who for security reasons was working under the false name Earl Seaman—discovered that it would not work in a gun-type device because of the presence of excessive amounts of the isotope Pu-240. Pu-240 has a much shorter half-life than other isotopes, and it raised the spontaneous fission rate of the material to a level five times the rate for cyclotron-refined plutonium (Pu-239). Calculations by Segrè and his team showed that the reactor-refined plutonium would predetonate during the initial phase of critical mass formation, blowing itself apart before a critical mass was achieved.

Segrè's discovery led the Project to switch development on a plutonium device to the far more difficult to engineer implosion design, called "Fat Man," that was tested at Alamogordo to find whether it would actually work and then, when it did, was weaponized and dropped on Nagasaki, Japan.

THIS MONTH									NEXT MONTH						
APRIL									MAY						
S	M	T	W	T	F	S			S	M	T	W	T	F	S
..	..	1	2	3	4	5			..	..	..	..	1	2	3
6	7	8	9	10	11	12			4	5	6	7	8	9	10
13	14	15	16	17	18	19			11	12	13	14	15	16	17
20	21	22	23	24	25	26			18	19	20	21	22	23	24
27	28	29	30	..	..	..			25	26	27	28	29	30	31
..	..	..	..	..	..	..			..	..	..	..	..	..	..

SUNDAY

6

APRIL

1941

On 6 April 1941, the Greco-Italian War suddenly became part of the greater conflict as German, Hungarian, and Italian forces invaded Greece from Bulgaria. The smaller confrontation, set in motion by Mussolini on 28 October 1940 after Greek Prime Minister Ioannis Metaxas refused permission for Italian forces to occupy certain strategic points in his country, was going disastrously for the Italians, and it would have been only a matter of time before the numerically inferior Greeks defeated them.

Mussolini called on Hitler for assistance, and the somewhat annoyed *Führer* gave it to him on 6 April. The Axis forces were slowed (but not stopped) by Greek and British troops at the Metaxas Line. During a nighttime *Luftwaffe* raid on Piraeus, Greece, three bombs dropped at 0315 hours the next morning by Ju 88 bombers of 7. *Staffel,* III./KG 30, led by *Hauptmann* Hajo Hermann, struck the British transport ship SS *Clan Fraser,* which was carrying 350 tons of TNT. The bombs set fire to the ship, which burned for some time before the blaze reached the TNT on board. An ammunition lighter was alongside, and officers from HMAS *Perth* hastily organized some harbor workers to move the lighter away from *Clan Fraser* before her TNT blew.

When the TNT did go, it went up in a huge blast that shattered windows in Athens, seven miles northeast of Piraeus, and was heard 150 miles away. What was left of the ship sank in the harbor. Six of *Clan Fraser*'s crew were killed and nine wounded; the remainder of the crew, including Ship's Master J.H. Giles, had evacuated before the explosion. The ammunition lighter was swamped by the wave generated by the explosion, depositing the Australian naval officers in the drink but leaving them otherwise unharmed. In the light of morning, it was found that the explosion of *Clan Fraser* had devastated the port, putting it completely out of service for 10 days. Further, it had set fire to other transport ships, some of which also exploded, and the end result of the conflagration and explosions was the sinking of 12 ships including *Clan Fraser* herself, along with 50 to 60 smaller craft. A number of fires had also been ignited on shore.

By great good fortune, several officers aboard a neighboring Clan Line ship had taken it upon themselves to evacuate the households near *Clan Fraser*. Taking a street each, they had cleared people from their houses to a distance of about a mile. Some time before *Clan Fraser* went up, they entered a tavern and cleared out its occupants, poured themselves a nightcap, and settled down to sleep.

THIS MONTH						
APRIL						
S	M	T	W	T	F	S
1	2	3	4	5	6	7
8	9	10	11	12	13	14
15	16	17	18	19	20	21
22	23	24	25	26	27	28
29	30	..	..	..	..	..
..	..	..	..	..	..	..

SATURDAY
7
APRIL

1945

NEXT MONTH						
MAY						
S	M	T	W	T	F	S
..	..	1	2	3	4	5
6	7	8	9	10	11	12
13	14	15	16	17	18	19
20	21	22	23	24	25	26
27	28	29	30	31	..	..
..	..	..	..	..	..	..

On 7 April 1945, the largest battleship ever built was sunk.

In March, Japanese military leaders had briefed Emperor Hirohito on their plans to repel the expected Allied invasion of Okinawa, saying that the Imperial Japanese Army was planning extensive air attacks, including the use of *kamikaze*. The emperor was reported to have put the Imperial Japanese Navy on the spot by asking, "But what about the Navy? What are they doing to assist in defending Okinawa? Have we no more ships?" Faced with the necessity for meaningful action, the commanders of the Navy conceived Operation TEN-GO, a suicide mission for their remaining handful of capital ships, including the battleship *Yamato* (whose sister ship, *Musashi*, had been sunk during the Battle of Leyte Gulf, in October 1944).

Following the American invasion of Okinawa on 1 April, preparations went ahead for the operation, and on 6 April, force commander Vice Admiral Seiichi Ito took *Yamato* to sea along with the light cruiser *Yahagi* and eight destroyers. Two American submarines sighted the Japanese force as it passed south through the Bungo Strait. Unable to attack the fast-moving ships, the boats nevertheless shadowed them and sent reports to the U.S. fleet. Soon after dawn on 7 April, American reconnaissance aircraft began shadowing the force, which executed a decoy move westward but at 1130 hours resumed its southward course.

As contact reports came in, Admiral Raymond Spruance, commanding the U.S. 5th Fleet, ordered Task Force 54, which was currently bombarding Japanese shore installations, to intercept and destroy the Japanese ships. Admiral Morton Deyo issued the necessary orders to his force, but he was beaten to the draw by Vice Admiral Marc Mitscher, the commander of Task Force 58, who on his own initiative launched a massive air strike. Beginning at about 1000 hours, eight carriers launched almost 400 aircraft in several waves, including Grumman F6F Hellcat and Vought F4U Corsair fighters, Curtiss SB2C Helldiver dive bombers, and Grumman TBF Avenger torpedo bombers. Learning of Mitscher's launches, Spruance agreed that the air strike could proceed, but he ordered Deyo to assemble a force of six battleships, seven cruisers, and 21 destroyers, readying them for a surface engagement just in case.

At about 1200 hours, Hellcats and Corsairs arrived over the Japanese fleet to deal with the Japanese air cover—and found that there was none. Helldivers and Avengers arriving over the *Yamato* group were thus able to circle the Japanese ship formation just out of antiaircraft range to set up their attacks. At 1232 hours, a lookout on *Yamato*'s bridge spotted the first wave of U.S. aircraft. Two minutes later, *Yamato* opened fire with her 460 mm (18.1-inch) main batteries, firing special antiaircraft shells. The Japanese ships stopped zigzagging, increased speed to 24 knots, began evasive maneuvers, and opened fire with their antiaircraft guns. Including her main batteries, *Yamato* carried almost 200 antiaircraft guns.

The U.S. torpedo airplanes attacked mainly from the port side to increase the probability that a target struck by their torpedoes would capsize in that direction. The aerial attacks, while not neglecting other ships, concentrated on *Yamato*. In the first wave, she took two armor-piercing bombs and one torpedo. In the second wave, at least eight torpedoes and as many as 15 bombs found her. The bombs did extensive topside damage, knocking out her gun directors and forcing crews to aim their guns manually, and also destroying the water damage-control station, making it impossible to counter-flood the ship to counteract a growing list to port. At 1333 hours, working frantically to keep the ship from capsizing, *Yamato*'s damage control team counter-flooded both starboard engine and boiler rooms, mitigating the danger but also drowning several hundred crewmen who were given no warning. A short while later, as *Yamato* was starting a sharp turn to port, three torpedoes ripped into her port side amidships, jamming her auxiliary rudder hard to port. Stuck in a circle and slowed to about 10 knots, she was easy prey for American aircraft that targeted her stern and destroyed her main rudder.

At 1402 hours, with his ship unable to steer and inexorably sinking, Admiral Ito ordered the mission canceled. He ordered the crew to abandon ship and, because *Yamato*'s radios were gone, sent a message by flags to the remaining ships to begin rescuing survivors. At 1405 hours, *Yamato* stopped dead in the water and started to capsize. Admiral Ito and Captain Kosaku Aruga refused to abandon ship. At 1420, she turned turtle and began to sink; three minutes later, her main magazines exploded. The report was heard and the four-mile-high mushroom cloud was seen 120 miles away in Kagoshima, Japan, and it was asserted that the explosion had actually downed some U.S. aircraft that were too close when it occurred.

The final tally of losses stood for the Americans at 10 aircraft destroyed and 10 aircrew killed. The Japanese had lost *Yamato*, the light cruiser *Yahagi*, and four of the eight accompanying destroyers, along with 3,914 lives.

THIS MONTH								WEDNESDAY		NEXT MONTH						
								8								

THIS MONTH

APRIL

S	M	T	W	T	F	S
..	..	..	1	2	3	4
5	6	7	8	9	10	11
12	13	14	15	16	17	18
19	20	21	22	23	24	25
26	27	28	29	30	..	..
..	..	..	..	..	..	..

WEDNESDAY

8

APRIL

1942

NEXT MONTH

MAY

S	M	T	W	T	F	S
..	..	..	..	..	1	2
3	4	5	6	7	8	9
10	11	12	13	14	15	16
17	18	19	20	21	22	23
24	25	26	27	28	29	30
31	..	..	..	..	..	..

On 8 April 1942, the second incarnation of the Royal Navy's Force K stood down with the withdrawal of the light cruiser HMS *Penelope* from Malta.

Allied submarines and aircraft had sunk some Italian ships carrying supplies to Axis forces in North Africa, but most got through. The Royal Navy's next step was to constitute Force K, comprising the light cruisers HMS *Aurora* and *Penelope* along with destroyers HMS *Lance* and *Lively*, on 21 October 1941. Eighteen days later, on 8–9 November, Force K destroyed an entire Axis convoy, an action that led the Italian high command to consider Tripoli "practically blockaded."

On 29 November, Force B sailed into Malta to augment Force K with two more light cruisers, HMS *Neptune* and *Ajax*, and two more destroyers, HMS *Kimberley* and *Kingston*. The combined eight-ship force was so effective that during the next few weeks the Axis supply line suffered 60% losses.

On 19 December, while in pursuit of an Italian convoy, ships from both Forces ran into a minefield, sinking *Neptune* and damaging *Aurora*. The destroyer HMS *Kandahar* also struck a mine while attempting to assist *Neptune* and was herself scuttled the next day by the destroyer *Jaguar*.

Shortly thereafter, the Germans and Italians stepped up their bombardment of Malta, and the Royal Navy withdrew Forces K and B, with the exception of HMS *Penelope*, which was too badly damaged to leave. Remaining in the harbor, *Penelope* drew significant attention from the Axis aircraft, and she was holed so many times that she was unofficially christened "HMS *Pepperpot*." With her withdrawal, Force K was officially disbanded.

		THIS MONTH				
			APRIL			
S	M	T	W	T	F	S
..	..	..	1	2	3	4
5	6	7	8	9	10	11
12	13	14	15	16	17	18
19	20	21	22	23	24	25
26	27	28	29	30	..	..
..	..	..	..	..	..	..

THURSDAY
9
APRIL
1942

		NEXT MONTH				
			MAY			
S	M	T	W	T	F	S
..	..	..	..	..	1	2
3	4	5	6	7	8	9
10	11	12	13	14	15	16
17	18	19	20	21	22	23
24	25	26	27	28	29	30
31	..	..	..	..	..	..

On 9 April 1942, on the Bataan Peninsula, U.S. General Edward P. King surrendered the starving, diseased men under his command, about 12,000 Americans and 63,000 Filipinos, to Japanese General Masaharu Homma. Japanese troops rounded up the Allied soldiers and lined them up four abreast in groups of 100, with four guards assigned to each group, and marched them north under blistering heat toward Camp O'Donnell in Tarlac Province, sixty-five miles away.

As the procession wended its way up the only paved highway that ran down the Bataan Peninsula, a march that took about five days to complete, the prisoners received the absolute minimum amounts of food and water. Guards shot or bayoneted any man who fell, tried to escape, or stopped for water at a roadside spigot or puddle; and they chased off, shot, or bayoneted

any civilians along the way who tried to give food or water to the prisoners. At various points, they singled out prisoners, sometimes in groups, tied them to trees or fences, and shot them dead as examples to the others.

The Japanese killed between 7,000 and 10,000 men during those five days; the exact number is unknown because they kept no records. For the prisoners, to fall down was a signed, sealed, and delivered death certificate unless other prisoners could get the fallen man to his feet and support him as they continued marching.

At Camp O'Donnell, things got even worse. A former Philippine Army camp built to accommodate about 10,000 men, it was suddenly home to about 65,000 sick, starving, exhausted, and largely dispirited American and Filipino prisoners. Food and water were insufficient; prisoners had to line up for as long as six hours to get a drink. There was no medical care, and there were only slit-trench latrines along the sides of the camp for sanitation. The heat was intolerable, and flies were so thick that the prisoners could not keep them away from the food; the insects became a supplement to whatever protein was in the rice balls and watery soup. Malaria, beri beri, dysentery, scurvy, diphtheria, yellow jaundice, and dengue fever swept through the packed men, who before the end of April were dying at the rate of more than four hundred per day. It got so bad that in July the Japanese replaced the camp commander, moved the American prisoners to another camp, and paroled the Filipino prisoners.

The Bataan Death March and its *sequelae* remain among the worst atrocities committed in modern warfare.

		APRIL				
S	M	T	W	T	F	S
..	..	1	2	3	4	5
6	7	8	9	10	11	12
13	14	15	16	17	18	19
20	21	22	23	24	25	26
27	28	29	30	..	..	..
..	..	..	..	..	..	..

THIS MONTH

THURSDAY
10
APRIL
1941

NEXT MONTH

		MAY				
S	M	T	W	T	F	S
..	..	..	..	1	2	3
4	5	6	7	8	9	10
11	12	13	14	15	16	17
18	19	20	21	22	23	24
25	26	27	28	29	30	31
..	..	..	..	..	..	..

On 10 April 1941, the German submarine *U-52*, on her seventh war patrol under *Kapitänleutnant* Otto Salman, was cruising in the North Atlantic, 558 miles southwest of Iceland. Allied Convoy OB-306 was also in the general area, and *U-52* stumbled across the 6,563-ton Dutch merchant ship *Saleier*, whose Master, J. Riedel, had separated her from the Halifax-bound convoy on the previous day. The destinations for her load of coal were Durban, South Africa, and Port Said, Egypt.

At 1912 hours, *U-52* sent two torpedoes into *Saleier* and then surfaced to deliver a *coup de grâce* with her deck gun at 1955 hours. *Saleier* sank 15 seconds after receiving that shot. In the interval between the torpedo hits and the gun shot, *Saleier*'s entire crew of 63, including some wounded men, abandoned ship in three lifeboats. They were sighted the next day by the destroyer USS *Niblack,* commanded by Lieutenant Commander Edward R. Durgin, which picked them up and took them to Reykjavik, Iceland.

En route, *Niblack* picked up a sonar contact that her sonarman identified as a submarine preparing to attack, and under orders from the commanding officer of Division 1, Commander D. R. Ryan, dropped three depth charges. There was no resolution to this action, which is frequently cited as the first military action between the U.S. and Germany in the war. A thorough investigation by the *Kriegsmarine* found that no German submarines had been in the area where *Niblack* put down the first depth charges deployed in anger by a U.S. tin can in the war, and the U.S. Navy concluded that the sonar contact was bogus.

		APRIL				
S	M	T	W	T	F	S
..	..	1	2	3	4	5
6	7	8	9	10	11	12
13	14	15	16	17	18	19
20	21	22	23	24	25	26
27	28	29	30	..	..	..
..	..	..	..	..	..	..

THIS MONTH

FRIDAY
11
APRIL

1941

NEXT MONTH

		MAY				
S	M	T	W	T	F	S
..	..	..	..	1	2	3
4	5	6	7	8	9	10
11	12	13	14	15	16	17
18	19	20	21	22	23	24
25	26	27	28	29	30	31
..	..	..	..	..	..	..

On 11 April 1941, French Army Lieutenant Alain Le Ray became the first of 18 Allied servicemen to escape from *Schloß* Colditz. Located some 90 miles south of Berlin and known in English as Colditz Castle, *Schloß* Colditz was the site of *Oflag* (*Offizierslager*, officers' camp) IV-C, a maximum-security POW camp for officers that the Germans had boasted was escape-proof.

Le Ray was captured after the German invasion of France in 1940 and incarcerated in Colditz. On Good Friday in 1941, he leapt into an old park building as the prisoners marched up a hill after playing soccer. In a 2001 interview, he said, "I was sure they would see me, but there were no shouts, no chase, no dogs." He had prepared well and was wearing homemade civilian clothes under his uniform. Remaining in hiding until after dark, he climbed over a wall and escaped into the woods.

Armed with nothing more than a map of the German railway system that a British prisoner had helped to compile, he made his way to Switzerland. Instead of turning himself in and being interned as a combatant, he made use of his mountaineering skills to avoid discovery while he passed through Switzerland into France, where he became one of the leaders of the French Resistance in the Alpine region of Vercors. After the Normandy invasion of 6 June 1944, he resumed his conventional military career.

THIS MONTH								THURSDAY	NEXT MONTH						

APRIL   **THURSDAY**   **MAY**

S	M	T	W	T	F	S
1	2	3	4	5	6	7
8	9	10	11	12	13	14
15	16	17	18	19	20	21
22	23	24	25	26	27	28
29	30	..	..	..	..	..
..	..	..	..	..	..	..

12
APRIL

S	M	T	W	T	F	S
..	..	1	2	3	4	5
6	7	8	9	10	11	12
13	14	15	16	17	18	19
20	21	22	23	24	25	26
27	28	29	30	31	..	..

1945

On 12 April 1945, Franklin Delano Roosevelt, the thirty-second President of the United States, died suddenly at the age of 63. On 29 March, he had gone to the Little White House at Warm Springs, Georgia, to rest before his anticipated appearance at the founding conference of the United Nations. On the afternoon of 12 April, he said, "I have a terrific pain in the back of my head." He then slumped forward in his chair, unconscious, and was carried into his bedroom, where he died at 1535 hours.

Upon Roosevelt's death, Vice President Harry S Truman stepped into the Presidency.

Roosevelt's death was keenly felt in all quarters, not least because he had made it a practice to keep Truman very much out of the loop, to the extent that the new President was unaware of the existence of the Manhattan Project until 24 April, when he was let in on the secret by Secretary of War Henry Stimson and the project's commanding officer, Major General Leslie Groves.

			THIS MONTH								NEXT MONTH			

			APRIL			
S	M	T	W	T	F	S
..	..	1	2	3	4	5
6	7	8	9	10	11	12
13	14	15	16	17	18	19
20	21	22	23	24	25	26
27	28	29	30	..	..	..
..	..	..	..	..	..	..

SUNDAY
13
APRIL

			MAY			
S	M	T	W	T	F	S
..	..	..	..	1	2	3
4	5	6	7	8	9	10
11	12	13	14	15	16	17
18	19	20	21	22	23	24
25	26	27	28	29	30	31
..	..	..	..	..	..	..

1941

On 13 April 1941, Japanese Foreign Minister Yosuke Matsuoka and Ambassador to the Soviet Union Yoshitsugu Tatekawa sat at a table in Moscow with Soviet Foreign Minister Vyacheslav Mikhailovich Molotov, where the three signed the Soviet–Japanese Neutrality Pact, also known as the Japanese–Soviet Non-Aggression Pact. On the same day, the three also signed a declaration regarding Mongolia and Manchuria in which the Soviet Union pledged to respect the territorial integrity and inviolability of Manchukuo, the puppet state that the Japanese had established in Manchuria, while Japan did the same for the Mongolian People's Republic.

The Soviet–Japanese Neutrality Pact, signed two years after the brief Soviet–Japanese Border War of 1939, was intended to ensure neutrality between the Soviet Union and the Empire of Japan during World War II. Signed before the Japanese attack on Pearl Harbor and Germany's subsequent declaration of war on the U.S.A., it remained in effect until the early morning hours of 9 August 1945, when the Red Army invaded Manchukuo subsequent to the Soviet Union's declaration of war against Japan on 8 August. The Soviets had denounced the Pact, in accordance with its Article III, on 5 April 1945, and their declaration of war and invasion occurred despite the fact that the terms of the treaty stated clearly that it would remain in force for the full five-year term specified in Article III.

When pressed in April 1945 by then-Ambassador Naotake Satō, Molotov confirmed that the treaty would indeed remain in force until April 1946—but that did not stop the Soviets from invading in accordance with the agreement that they had made in Yalta to declare war on Japan within three months of Germany's surrender.

<table>
<tr><td colspan="8" align="center">THIS MONTH</td></tr>
<tr><td colspan="8" align="center">APRIL</td></tr>
<tr><td>S</td><td>M</td><td>T</td><td>W</td><td>T</td><td>F</td><td>S</td></tr>
<tr><td>..</td><td>..</td><td>..</td><td>..</td><td>1</td><td>2</td><td>3</td></tr>
<tr><td>4</td><td>5</td><td>6</td><td>7</td><td>8</td><td>9</td><td>10</td></tr>
<tr><td>11</td><td>12</td><td>13</td><td>14</td><td>15</td><td>16</td><td>17</td></tr>
<tr><td>18</td><td>19</td><td>20</td><td>21</td><td>22</td><td>23</td><td>24</td></tr>
<tr><td>25</td><td>26</td><td>27</td><td>28</td><td>29</td><td>30</td><td>..</td></tr>
<tr><td>..</td><td>..</td><td>..</td><td>..</td><td>..</td><td>..</td><td>..</td></tr>
</table>

WEDNESDAY
14
APRIL

1943

<table>
<tr><td colspan="8" align="center">NEXT MONTH</td></tr>
<tr><td colspan="8" align="center">MAY</td></tr>
<tr><td>S</td><td>M</td><td>T</td><td>W</td><td>T</td><td>F</td><td>S</td></tr>
<tr><td>..</td><td>..</td><td>..</td><td>..</td><td>..</td><td>..</td><td>1</td></tr>
<tr><td>2</td><td>3</td><td>4</td><td>5</td><td>6</td><td>7</td><td>8</td></tr>
<tr><td>9</td><td>10</td><td>11</td><td>12</td><td>13</td><td>14</td><td>15</td></tr>
<tr><td>16</td><td>17</td><td>18</td><td>19</td><td>20</td><td>21</td><td>22</td></tr>
<tr><td>23</td><td>24</td><td>25</td><td>26</td><td>27</td><td>28</td><td>29</td></tr>
<tr><td>30</td><td>31</td><td>..</td><td>..</td><td>..</td><td>..</td><td>..</td></tr>
</table>

On 14 April 1943, the U.S. Navy's Fleet Radio Unit, Pacific Fleet, intercepted and decrypted a Japanese Navy message enciphered in the supposedly unbreakable JN-25 code. It contained details of an inspection visit to Bougainville, in the Solomon Islands, scheduled for 18 April, four days hence. Making the inspection would be Admiral Isoroku Yamamoto, commander-in-chief of the Imperial Japanese Navy's Combined Fleet. The message included Yamamoto's itinerary together with his planned arrival and departure times from the various locations as well as descriptions of the number and types of aircraft that would transport and accompany him. The decrypt was duly forwarded to Admiral Chester Nimitz, commander-in-chief of the U.S. Navy Pacific Fleet, who immediately decided to launch a mission to kill Yamamoto en route.

After receiving the necessary approval from the White House via Navy Secretary Frank Knox, Nimitz assigned the task to Admiral William "Bull" Halsey, whose forces were in the Solomon Islands area.

On the morning of 18 April, with Admiral Yamamoto seated in the left front seat of the passenger compartment, a converted Hasegawa G4M2 "Betty" bomber took off from Rabaul at 0600 hours. Yamamoto's chief of staff, Vice Admiral Matome Ugaki, was in a second Betty. Six Mitsubishi A6M Zero fighters provided a fighter escort. For the intercept mission, the USAAF equipped eighteen P-38G Lightning fighters of the 339th Fighter Squadron with two 165-gallon drop tanks each for the 1,000-mile round trip from Kukum Field on Guadalcanal (600 miles out via a circuitous wave-hopping course under radio silence to avoid detection, and 400 miles straight back).

Planned by Major John Mitchell, the American mission was code-named Operation VENGEANCE in recognition that the date was the first anniversary of the Doolittle Raid. The longest fighter-intercept mission of the war, it was executed flawlessly: Mitchell's force arrived at the intercept point one minute early, at 0934 hours, just as the Japanese aircraft were descending through haze over Bougainville in preparation for landing at

Balalae. The remainder of the American force had ascended to 18,000 feet to serve as top cover, leaving the four P-38s that had been designated as the "killer flight" to jettison their auxiliary tanks, turn to the right to parallel the bombers, and begin a full power climb to intercept them.

The tanks on Lieutenant Besby F. Holmes' fighter failed to detach, forcing Holmes and his wingman, Lieutenant Raymond K. Hine, to retire. This left only Captain Thomas G. Lamphier, Jr., and Lieutenant Rex T. Barber to accomplish the mission. Barber attacked the bombers, while Lamphier turned to go after the escorting fighters. As Barber strafed the bombers repeatedly, one .50 caliber round struck Yamamoto's shoulder and another entered the left side of his jaw and exited near the temple on the right side of his head, probably killing him instantly. Shortly afterward, Barber's guns found the left engine of Yamamoto's plane; it began to trail heavy black smoke, and the plane rolled to the left and fell away to crash in the jungle.

Not knowing which of the bombers carried the high-ranking officer who was the target, Barber then went after the second Betty and spotted it over the water trying to evade an attack by Lieutenant Holmes, who had damaged the bomber's right engine after his P-38's tanks had finally dropped. Barber tore into the Betty, causing it to shed chunks of metal that damaged his own aircraft before it crashed into the water. Vice Admiral Ugaki survived this attack.

At some point, Lieutenant Hine's P-38 disappeared, and he was never seen again. He was the only American lost in the attack. The Japanese government kept Yamamoto's death under wraps until 21 May; when it was announced, American newspapers published a story that civilian Coastwatchers had seen Yamamoto boarding a bomber in the area. The Japanese apparently bought the story, failed to realize that their naval code had been broken, and so did not change the code.[1]

---

1. The Japanese actually did guess that the Americans had broken one of their codes but concluded that it could not have been JN-25 that had been breached, and the code remained in use.

APRIL

S	M	T	W	T	F	S
..	..	..	1	2	3	4
5	6	7	8	9	10	11
12	13	14	15	16	17	18
19	20	21	22	23	24	25
26	27	28	29	30	..	..
..	..	..	..	..	..	..

WEDNESDAY
15
APRIL

MAY

S	M	T	W	T	F	S
..	..	..	..	..	1	2
3	4	5	6	7	8	9
10	11	12	13	14	15	16
17	18	19	20	21	22	23
24	25	26	27	28	29	30
31	..	..	..	..	..	..

1942

On 15 April 1942, troops of Great Britain's I Burma Corps began to destroy the infrastructure of the Yenangyaung oil fields. Situated on the Irrawaddy River in Burma, Yenangyaung (in English, literally "stream of oil") had been an active oil-producing area since at least 1755. During World War II it was the location of a strategically and tactically important oil refinery.

With the startling speed and success of the Japanese advance through Burma during the Burma Campaign and the Battle of Yenangyaung (begun on 11 April), retreating British forces were forced to blow up the oil fields and refinery to prevent the Japanese from capturing them intact. (One of Japan's primary purposes in capturing Burma and the Dutch East Indies was to obtain the oil and rubber it needed to fuel its war machine.) The task of demolition was assigned to a small group of experienced men, some of whom had served as sappers with the British Indian Army's Bombay Pioneers in World War I. The group included Captain (acting Major) Arthur H. Virgin of the 20th Burma Rifles, who later became commanding officer of the Indian Pioneer Corps, part of the Fourteenth Army under Field Marshal Sir William Slim. They completed their work of destruction at 2200 hours on 16 April and then had to swim across the Irrawaddy River because the only bridge had been blown up to delay the Japanese advance. Their escape took them on foot through enemy-held territory and eventually nearly 1,000 miles to Imphal and Kohima in India.

\multicolumn{7}{c}{THIS MONTH}						

APRIL

S	M	T	W	T	F	S
..	..	1	2	3	4	5
6	7	8	9	10	11	12
13	14	15	16	17	18	19
20	21	22	23	24	25	26
27	28	29	30	..	..	..
..	..	..	..	..	..	..

WEDNESDAY
16
APRIL

MAY

S	M	T	W	T	F	S
..	..	..	..	1	2	3
4	5	6	7	8	9	10
11	12	13	14	15	16	17
18	19	20	21	22	23	24
25	26	27	28	29	30	31
..	..	..	..	..	..	..

1941

On 16 April 1941, at 0500 hours, the first of two large German bombing raids that came to be called the Belfast Blitz came to an end. Belfast, Northern Ireland, a major manufacturing center, was the home of Harland and Wolff, one of the largest shipbuilding yards in the world, which employed more than 30,000 people and had by the date of the raid built 136 ships of the Royal Navy, including the aircraft carriers HMS *Formidable* and *Unicorn*. Other industries included aircraft manufacturer Short Brothers, builders of the Sunderland flying boat and the Stirling bomber as well as the Handley-Page Hereford bomber; James Mackie & Sons, producers of ammunition for the Bofors antiaircraft gun; and a host of smaller manufacturers.

In this raid, which had commenced at 2300 hours the previous evening, 200 Heinkel He 111s, Junkers Ju 88s, and Dornier Do 17s dropped 203 tons of high-explosive bombs, 80 parachute mines, and 800 incendiary bombs. In the belief that they might damage RAF fighters, the city's seven ground-based antiaircraft ceased firing—but the RAF had not responded, and the raiders were unopposed. The deaths of 758 people on the ground constituted the greatest loss of life caused by any bombing raid outside London; another 1,500 were injured. In addition to many public buildings and 13 churches, 56,000 homes, roughly half the housing in the city, were destroyed, leaving some 100,000 people homeless.

		APRIL				
S	M	T	W	T	F	S
..	..	..	1	2	3	4
5	6	7	8	9	10	11
12	13	14	15	16	17	18
19	20	21	22	23	24	25
26	27	28	29	30	..	..
..	..	..	..	..	..	..

THIS MONTH

FRIDAY

17

APRIL

1942

NEXT MONTH

		MAY				
S	M	T	W	T	F	S
..	..	..	..	..	1	2
3	4	5	6	7	8	9
10	11	12	13	14	15	16
17	18	19	20	21	22	23
24	25	26	27	28	29	30
31	..	..	..	..	..	..

On 17 April 1942, French General Henri Giraud claimed a twofer, having escaped from German prison camps in both World Wars.

On 10 May 1940, Giraud became commander of the French 7th Army and was sent to the Netherlands to delay German troops at Breda on 13 May. On 19 May, he was at the front with a reconnaissance patrol as his troops attempted to stop a German assault through the Ardennes, and he was captured at Wassigny. The Germans court-martialed him for ordering the execution of two German saboteurs who had been caught wearing civilian clothes, but he was acquitted and taken to *Schloß* Königstein, a castle fortress situated on a mesa overlooking the town of Königstein, near Dresden, that was being used as a high-security prisoner-of-war camp.

He planned his escape carefully over the next two years, teaching himself German and memorizing a map of the area. He wove a 150-foot rope out of twine, torn bedsheets, and copper wire that friends had smuggled into the prison for him. He devised a code to use in his letters home, so that he could advise his family of his plans.

On 17 April 1942, he lowered himself down the wall of the mesa. He had shaved off his distinctive mustache, and wearing a Tyrolean hat he traveled about 500 kilometers to Schandau, near the Czechoslovakian border, to meet an SOE contact who provided him with new clothes, money, and identity papers. From Schandau he traveled to the Swiss border by train. By that time, the Germans had published an alert for him, so to avoid border guards he walked through the mountains until he was stopped by two Swiss soldiers. He eventually made it into Vichy France, where he tried to convince Premier Philippe Pétain that Germany would lose and that France must resist the German occupation. His views were rejected, and Minister of State Pierre Laval tried to persuade him to return to Germany, where he would have faced almost certain execution. (Heinrich Himmler had ordered the Gestapo to assassinate him.)

Yet while remaining loyal to Pétain and the Vichy government, Giraud refused to cooperate with the Germans. He was secretly contacted by the

Allies, who gave him the code name KINGPIN. General Dwight Eisenhower had him brought secretly to Gibraltar and asked him to take command of Vichy French troops in North Africa during Operation TORCH, a position from which he could direct them to join the Allies. After the duplicitous François Darlan was assassinated, Giraud attained the desired post. Later, he participated in the Casablanca Conference. In May 1944, unable to come to terms with the political ego of "Deux Mètres," Charles de Gaulle, with whom he had been named co-president of the *Comité français de la Libération Nationale* and the FFI, the Free French Forces, Giraud declined the post of Inspector General of the Army and instead took his retirement.

THIS MONTH						
APRIL						
S	M	T	W	T	F	S
..	..	..	1	2	3	4
5	6	7	8	9	10	11
12	13	14	15	16	17	18
19	20	21	22	23	24	25
26	27	28	29	30	..	..
..	..	..	..	..	..	..

SATURDAY

18

APRIL

NEXT MONTH						
MAY						
S	M	T	W	T	F	S
..	..	..	..	..	1	2
3	4	5	6	7	8	9
10	11	12	13	14	15	16
17	18	19	20	21	22	23
24	25	26	27	28	29	30
31	..	..	..	..	..	..

1942

On 18 April 1942, sixteen specially modified B-25 Mitchell bombers under the command of Lieutenant Colonel James Doolittle took off from the deck of the aircraft carrier USS *Hornet* on a mission planned by Doolittle, to bomb Tokyo, Japan.

The initial plan accepted that the planes would not be able to return to *Hornet*; they were to fly to China. The American ships were discovered too early, however, and the planes were forced to take off farther out to sea than planned, leaving them with insufficient fuel to complete their mission. They went anyway, dropping 16 tons of bombs on Tokyo and killing some 50 people.

The purposes of the raid were to bolster American morale and to cause the Japanese, who had been told that Japan was invulnerable to attack, to begin doubting their leadership. Both goals were achieved.

After bombing Tokyo, the planes flew as far as they could before their fuel ran out. Four crash-landed, 11 crews bailed out, and three of the Raiders died. Eight were captured; three were executed, and one died of starvation in a Japanese POW camp. One crew made it to Russia. The Doolittle Raid sent a loud, clear message to America's enemies: "We will fight. And whatever it takes, we will win."

THIS MONTH						
APRIL						
S	M	T	W	T	F	S
..	..	..	..	1	2	3
4	5	6	7	8	9	10
11	12	13	14	15	16	17
18	19	20	21	22	23	24
25	26	27	28	29	30	..
..	..	..	..	..	..	..

MONDAY
19
APRIL
1943

NEXT MONTH						
MAY						
S	M	T	W	T	F	S
..	..	..	..	..	..	1
2	3	4	5	6	7	8
9	10	11	12	13	14	15
16	17	18	19	20	21	22
23	24	25	26	27	28	29
30	31	..	..	..	..	..

On 19 April 1943, on the eve of Passover, German police and SS auxiliary forces under the command of *SS-Oberführer* Ferdinand von Sammern-Frankenegg entered the Jewish ghetto in Warsaw, Poland, to deport all Jews within to the Treblinka death camp, an operation they expected to take three days. Organized Jewish resistance developed, as insurgents attacked with Molotov cocktails, hand grenades, and small arms. Outside the ghetto, Polish nationalists rose in arms, further complicating the situation.

Unable to contain the uprising, von Sammern-Frankenegg was relieved and replaced by *SS-Brigadeführer* Jürgen Stroop, who led a better organized and supported attack. After several days' fighting, Stroop delivered an ultimatum to surrender. It was rejected, and the Germans commenced to destroy the ghetto, burning down houses and blowing up basements and sewers. Fighting ultimately lasted until the Germans subdued the insurgency on 16 May. According to Nazi records, the Germans lost 17 killed and 93 wounded (not including Jews coerced into collaboration), while approximately 13,000 Jews and Poles were killed and 56,885 were deported to concentration and death camps, principally Treblinka.

APRIL

S	M	T	W	T	F	S
1	2	3	4	5	6	7
8	9	10	11	12	13	14
15	16	17	18	19	20	21
22	23	24	25	26	27	28
29	30	..	..	..	..	..
..	..	..	..	..	..	..

FRIDAY
20
APRIL

1945

MAY

S	M	T	W	T	F	S
..	..	1	2	3	4	5
6	7	8	9	10	11	12
13	14	15	16	17	18	19
20	21	22	23	24	25	26
27	28	29	30	31	..	..
..	..	..	..	..	..	..

On 20 April 1945, having taken up residence in the *Führerbunker* 8.5 meters below the *Reichskanzlei* (the Reich Chancellery) three months earlier, Adolf Hitler celebrated his 56th birthday. Depressed and unwell, no longer garrulous but taciturn and prone to violent rages, with nervous tics, a pasty complexion, and a left arm that had degenerated to virtual uselessness due to Parkinson's Disease, the *Führer* ventured to the surface for the last time. In the blasted garden of the *Reichskanzlei*, with publicity cameras rolling, he awarded Iron Crosses to a small troop of *Hitlerjugend* (Hitler Youth) to honor their heroism in the ongoing Battle of Berlin, during which thousands of them, armed boys and girls as young as eight years of age, wearing adult-sized uniforms and helmets that flopped around on their heads as they fought with rifles, *Panzerfausts*, and even 88-mm guns, were killed by Soviet troops or committed suicide to avoid capture.

THIS MONTH						
APRIL						
S	M	T	W	T	F	S
..	..	1	2	3	4	5
6	7	8	9	10	11	12
13	14	15	16	17	18	19
20	21	22	23	24	25	26
27	28	29	30	..	..	..
..	..	..	..	..	..	..

MONDAY
21
APRIL

1941

NEXT MONTH						
MAY						
S	M	T	W	T	F	S
..	..	..	..	1	2	3
4	5	6	7	8	9	10
11	12	13	14	15	16	17
18	19	20	21	22	23	24
25	26	27	28	29	30	31
..	..	..	..	..	..	..

On 21 April 1941, with retreat cut off by German forces that had secured the vital Metsovon Pass and captured Ioannina on 19 April to trap some 223,000 Greek troops in Albania, Greek General Georgios Tsolakoglou surrendered to the Germans. He and several of his colleagues had realized on 20 April that further resistance was useless.

With the agreement of Lieutenant General Panagiotis Demestichas, commander of I Corps; Lieutenant General Georgios Bakos, commander of II Corps; and Spyridon Vlachos, the metropolitan of Ioannina, Tsolakoglou relieved Lieutenant General Ioanis Pitsikas, commander of the Army of Epirus. He immediately sent messengers to the Germans proposing surrender, and on the same day he signed a surrender protocol with the commander of the *Leibstandarte SS Adolf Hitler* brigade, *General der Waffen-SS* Josef "Sepp" Dietrich.

The Greek commander-in-chief, Alexandros Papagos, ordered that Tsolakoglou be relieved immediately and that resistance should continue to the last, but the surrender was formalized on 21 April at Larissa, with Tsolakolglou signing the unconditional surrender of the Hellenic Army to the Germans.

The surrender protocol intentionally omitted any mention of Italy, which the Greeks considered that they had beaten and wanted to deny the pleasure of a victory that it had not earned. The petulant Benito Mussolini made so much noise, however, that a third ceremony was held on 23 April, with the inclusion of Italian representatives.

On 30 April, Tsolakoglou was appointed Prime Minister of the collaborationist Greek government, but he was dismissed from that position on 2 December 1942.

THIS MONTH						
APRIL						
S	M	T	W	T	F	S
..	..	..	..	..	..	1
2	3	4	5	6	7	8
9	10	11	12	13	14	15
16	17	18	19	20	21	22
23	24	25	26	27	28	29
30	..	..	..	..	..	..

SATURDAY
22
APRIL
1944

NEXT MONTH						
MAY						
S	M	T	W	T	F	S
..	1	2	3	4	5	6
7	8	9	10	11	12	13
14	15	16	17	18	19	20
21	22	23	24	25	26	27
28	29	30	31	..	..	..

On 22 April 1944, under a heavily overcast sky that was dispensing an intermittent light drizzle, the U.S. 24th and 41st Infantry Divisions, commanded by Lieutenant General Robert Eichelberger, landed at Tanahmerah Bay and Humboldt Bay, respectively, near Hollandia in Dutch New Guinea, in Operation RECKLESS.

Commencing at 0600 hours, Naval Task Force 58, comprising aircraft carriers, cruisers, and lesser ships, delivered a 45-minute pre-landing barrage, and supporting fighter aircraft had been aloft since daybreak despite the weather. No Japanese aircraft rose in defense, and there was only light and scattered resistance on shore. The landing itself was a virtual nightmare, however, as planners had misread aerial photographs; where they had expected solid land at Red Beach 2, the troops encountered a swampy morass that mired guns, trucks, and tanks up to their axles and was impassable by anything larger or heavier than single infantrymen bearing only small arms. Fortunately, Red Beach 1 was solid, and the adjacent area was more spacious than had been anticipated; logistics were nonetheless painful because Red Beach 1 was fronted by a reef that would allow only shallow-draft craft over it.

On the same day, in Operation PERSECUTION, about 140 miles farther east, at Aitape, the U.S. 41st Infantry Division's 163rd Regimental Combat Team (detached) and the No. 62 Works Wing of the Royal Australian Air Force landed together under the command of Brigadier General Jens A. Doe, in the Australian Territory of New Guinea. This landing went very smoothly. The two landings, carried out deep in Japanese-held territory, involved 80,000 troops and were supported by 217 ships for transport and protection. The mission was to isolate the Japanese 18th Army at Wewak, preventing it from moving westward towards Hollandia, to secure Tadji Airfield (which was located a few miles southeast of Aitape) for support to the Hollandia landings after the carriers of Task Force 58 departed, and to establish light naval facilities at Aitape to support further operations. Action at Aitape, against light resistance as most of the 1,000 Japanese garrisoned there fled into the hills, was essentially completed by 1300 hours. Aircraft were using Tadji airfield by 24 April as the troops of Operation RECKLESS pushed inland. By 1115 hours on 23 April, the 41st Division's 162d Infantry had captured Hollandia town, which offered no resistance at all.

THIS MONTH						
APRIL						
S	M	T	W	T	F	S
..	..	1	2	3	4	5
6	7	8	9	10	11	12
13	14	15	16	17	18	19
20	21	22	23	24	25	26
27	28	29	30	..	..	..
..	..	..	..	..	..	..

WEDNESDAY
23
APRIL

NEXT MONTH						
MAY						
S	M	T	W	T	F	S
..	..	..	..	1	2	3
4	5	6	7	8	9	10
11	12	13	14	15	16	17
18	19	20	21	22	23	24
25	26	27	28	29	30	31
..	..	..	..	..	..	..

1941

On 23 April 1941, at an America First Committee meeting in New York City, Charles A. Lindbergh publicly called for the United States to stay out of the European war. Lindbergh, an active participant in the Noninterventionist movement, had spent several years in Europe, including an extended visit to Germany, where as the guest of *Generalfeldmarschall* Hermann Göring he personally flew state-of-the-art warplanes and received the Service Cross of the German Eagle for his contributions to aviation. He was greatly impressed by the unity and will of the German people and by what the Nazis had done to revitalize Germany, and because he saw a Nazi victory in the European war as inevitable, he agreed with the original Four Principles of the America First Committee:

The United States must build an impregnable defense for America.

No foreign power, nor group of powers, can successfully attack a prepared America.

American democracy can be preserved only by keeping out of the European war.

"Aid short of war" weakens national defense at home and threatens to involve America in war abroad.

Lindbergh's view of the European war differed substantially from that of the Roosevelt administration and the so-called interventionists in the United States. He did not see the conflict as basically a war for democracy or morality, and he did not place blame for it entirely on Hitler and the Axis. He distrusted the ideology and moral righteousness of the British and French, and he saw the war not as a clash to the death between implacable foes with irreconcilable differences but rather as almost an internecine squabble like those between ancient Athens and Sparta—but nonetheless a squabble that could destroy Western civilization. He was racist (and anti-Semitic) and feared that "Asiatic hordes" could also destroy Western civilization. He had worked with the French Nobel laureate Dr. Alexis Carrel and was in accord with Carrel's promotion of euthanasia for criminals, the insane, and anyone else who, in Carrell's view, weakened the foundation of civilization.

On 7 December 1941, everything changed. The very next day, Lindbergh offered his services to his country but was refused by President Franklin D. Roosevelt himself, who said, "You can't have an officer leading men who thinks we're licked before we start." Lindbergh thereupon went to work as a private consultant to Henry Ford, whose company was building B-24 bombers at its plant in Willow Run, Michigan.

In 1943, Lindbergh convinced United Aircraft, whose Pratt & Whitney, Vought, and Sikorsky subsidiaries built engines, fighter planes, and helicopters, respectively, to send him to the Pacific as an observer, where he did rather more than merely observe. He flew more than 50 combat missions and shot down one enemy fighter. At 42 years of age, he often bested men half his age in feats demanding intense physical ability. His greatest contribution to the war effort might have been his success in teaching other pilots how to conserve fuel and extend their flying range by up to 500 miles.

	APRIL					
S	M	T	W	T	F	S
..	..	..	1	2	3	4
5	6	7	8	9	10	11
12	13	14	15	16	17	18
19	20	21	22	23	24	25
26	27	28	29	30	..	..
..	..	..	..	..	..	..

FRIDAY
24
APRIL

1942

	MAY					
S	M	T	W	T	F	S
..	..	..	..	..	1	2
3	4	5	6	7	8	9
10	11	12	13	14	15	16
17	18	19	20	21	22	23
24	25	26	27	28	29	30
31	..	..	..	..	..	..

On 24 April 1942, in one of a 20-month series of raids on Port Moresby, in Australian Papua on the island of New Guinea, twelve Mitsubishi A6M2 Zeros of the Tainan Kokutai, based at Rabaul, New Britain, attacked the Seven Mile Airfield near Port Moresby. Six of the Japanese aircraft took on several Curtiss P-40 Kittyhawks of the RAAF's No. 75 Squadron, and when they returned to base they claimed five P-40s shot down. They actually shot down three. (Overclaiming, sometimes to an astonishing degree, was common on both sides; the confusion in a dogfight frequently caused multiple pilots to claim the same victim.) The other six Zeros went after other aircraft, primarily bombers on the ground. This group claimed one Bell P-39 Airacobra and two Martin B-26 Marauders but actually failed to destroy the P-39. They did, however, damage one Consolidated PBY flying boat moored in Fairfax Harbor.

On the same day, Joseph Rochefort's cryptanalytic team, based at Pearl Harbor, intercepted Japanese Navy radio messages mentioning the existence of task forces bearing names such as MO Covering Force, MO Attack Force, RZP Occupation Force, RXB Occupation Force, and so on. Rochefort, who later would identify the Japanese codegroup AF as referring to the American base at Midway Island and whose work laid the foundation for the Japanese defeat there, concluded that these task forces were being prepared for an attack in the Port Moresby area. The invasion fleet for that attack, commanded by Vice Admiral Shigeyoshi Inoue, was turned back in early May in the Battle of the Coral Sea, when it lost 92 of the 127 carrier aircraft it was carrying at the hands of an American task force under Vice Admiral Frank Jack Fletcher.

THIS MONTH						
APRIL						
S	M	T	W	T	F	S
1	2	3	4	5	6	7
8	9	10	11	12	13	14
15	16	17	18	19	20	21
22	23	24	25	26	27	28
29	30	..	..	..	..	..
..	..	..	..	..	..	..

WEDNESDAY
25
APRIL
1945

NEXT MONTH						
MAY						
S	M	T	W	T	F	S
..	..	1	2	3	4	5
6	7	8	9	10	11	12
13	14	15	16	17	18	19
20	21	22	23	24	25	26
27	28	29	30	31	..	..
..	..	..	..	..	..	..

On 25 April 1945, First Lieutenant Albert G. Kotzebue, commanding officer of Company G of the 273rd Infantry Regiment, an element of the U.S. 69th Infantry Division, took Russian-speaking Tech/5 Stephen Kowalski and 34 other men from his regiment's Intelligence and Reconnaissance platoon on a recon patrol across the Mulde River near Strehla, Germany. In the course of their exploration, they met German soldiers who were desperate to surrender to anyone other than the Red Army, as well as Allied POWs who were still a little dazed by their sudden release from captivity.

In the village of Leckwicz, the patrol met a mounted trooper from a Soviet Guards rifle regiment of the First Ukrainian Front, under the

command of Lieutenant Colonel Alexander Gardiev. The Soviet soldier was also conducting a scouting mission and was, as Lieutenant Kotzebue described him during debriefing, "reserved, aloof, suspicious, not enthusiastic."Later on the same day, another patrol under Second Lieutenant William Robertson, with Frank Huff, James McDonnell, and Paul Staub met a Soviet patrol commanded by Lieutenant Alexander Silvashko on the destroyed Elbe bridge of Torgau, southwest of Berlin.

These two meetings were the first contact between troops of the Western Allies and troops of the Soviet Union. In the West, 25 April was referred to as Elbe Day, while the Soviets called it "Encounter at the Elbe."On 26 April, the commanders of the 69th Infantry Division of the U.S. First Army and the 58th Guards Rifle Division of the Soviet 5th Guards Army met at Torgau to make arrangements for the formal "Handshake of Torgau" between Robertson and Silvashko in front of photographers on 27 April. The two stood for their photograph, with hands clasped and Silvashko's arm draped around Robertson's shoulders, in front of American and Soviet flags and a hurriedly made poster reading EAST MEETS WEST.

THIS MONTH						
APRIL						
S	M	T	W	T	F	S
..	..	..	1	2	3	4
5	6	7	8	9	10	11
12	13	14	15	16	17	18
19	20	21	22	23	24	25
26	27	28	29	30	..	..
..	..	..	..	..	..	..

SUNDAY
26
APRIL
1942

NEXT MONTH						
MAY						
S	M	T	W	T	F	S
..	..	..	..	..	1	2
3	4	5	6	7	8	9
10	11	12	13	14	15	16
17	18	19	20	21	22	23
24	25	26	27	28	29	30
31	..	..	..	..	..	..

On 26 April 1942, the old four-stack destroyer USS *Sturtevant* departed Key West, Florida, at 1520 hours to make rendezvous with a convoy sailing from New Orleans. She was a day behind schedule, and her captain, Lieutenant Commander C. L. Weigle, ordered the ship to proceed at 27 knots, just short of flank speed, as soon as she cleared the sea buoy.

At about 1720 hours, when *Sturtevant* was 18 miles north of Key West, a violent explosion lifted her stern from the water. There was no apparent harm to the ship's seaworthiness, but the explosion had damaged *Sturtevant*'s sonar and communications gear, leaving her partially blind and unable to call for backup. Captain Weigle assumed that his ship was under attack by a submarine; he ordered General Quarters, reduced speed, and turned back to engage the enemy. Two depth charges were dropped immediately, and two more were dropped soon after.

About a minute after the second pair rolled off the racks, a second blast rocked the ship. Something was definitely amiss as she began to settle rapidly, although she did remain on an even keel. Minutes later, a third explosion ripped her keel apart beneath the after deckhouse, causing Number 3 stack to collapse and Captain Weigle to order the crew to abandon ship. The midships section sank very quickly, and the stern portion of the vessel settled soon thereafter. The bow, oddly, remained above water for several hours. Finally, however, all but the crow's nest disappeared beneath the waves. Thirteen men went to the bottom with *Sturtevant*; 136 survivors were rescued after a Coast Guard patrol plane radioed in a distress message and rescue ships got under weigh, arriving at the scene at about 2230 hours. The ship's fuel tanks had ruptured; there was a huge slick of Bunker C on the water, and four of the rescued men died later from the oil coating their skin.

The cause of *Sturtevant*'s destruction was three mines in a minefield that had been laid by her berthmate in Key West, the minelayer USS *Miantonomah*. In the hush-hush atmosphere that had arrived with the war, the locations—and even the existence—of minefields were considered Secret, and *Sturtevant* had not been informed of the minefield that killed her. The lesson was not learned, however; between 26 April and 2 July, three friendly merchant ships went to the bottom in America's defensive minefields. There is no record that any of these minefields sank, or even damaged, even one enemy vessel.

	THIS MONTH							MONDAY		NEXT MONTH						
		APRIL						**27**				MAY				

<table>
<tr><th colspan="7">APRIL</th></tr>
<tr><th>S</th><th>M</th><th>T</th><th>W</th><th>T</th><th>F</th><th>S</th></tr>
<tr><td>..</td><td>..</td><td>..</td><td>1</td><td>2</td><td>3</td><td>4</td></tr>
<tr><td>5</td><td>6</td><td>7</td><td>8</td><td>9</td><td>10</td><td>11</td></tr>
<tr><td>12</td><td>13</td><td>14</td><td>15</td><td>16</td><td>17</td><td>18</td></tr>
<tr><td>19</td><td>20</td><td>21</td><td>22</td><td>23</td><td>24</td><td>25</td></tr>
<tr><td>26</td><td>27</td><td>28</td><td>29</td><td>30</td><td>..</td><td>..</td></tr>
<tr><td>..</td><td>..</td><td>..</td><td>..</td><td>..</td><td>..</td><td>..</td></tr>
</table>

MONDAY
27
APRIL
1942

<table>
<tr><th colspan="7">MAY</th></tr>
<tr><th>S</th><th>M</th><th>T</th><th>W</th><th>T</th><th>F</th><th>S</th></tr>
<tr><td>..</td><td>..</td><td>..</td><td>..</td><td>..</td><td>1</td><td>2</td></tr>
<tr><td>3</td><td>4</td><td>5</td><td>6</td><td>7</td><td>8</td><td>9</td></tr>
<tr><td>10</td><td>11</td><td>12</td><td>13</td><td>14</td><td>15</td><td>16</td></tr>
<tr><td>17</td><td>18</td><td>19</td><td>20</td><td>21</td><td>22</td><td>23</td></tr>
<tr><td>24</td><td>25</td><td>26</td><td>27</td><td>28</td><td>29</td><td>30</td></tr>
<tr><td>31</td><td>..</td><td>..</td><td>..</td><td>..</td><td>..</td><td>..</td></tr>
</table>

On 27 April 1942, at Pearl Harbor, Hawaii, Joseph Rochefort's crypt-analytic team reported two critical pieces of information: first, that the Imperial Japanese Navy had changed the call signs of some major warships, possibly indicating that a big operation was in the works; and second, that IJN Second Fleet commander Vice Admiral Nobutake Kondō had sent to Tokyo a request for navigation charts of the Aleutian Islands area and the latest intelligence on AOE and KCN (Dutch Harbor and Kodiak). These two messages presaged an operation against the Aleutians, and that operation materialized simultaneously with the attack on Midway Island, commencing with the 3 June bombing of the Dutch Harbor Naval Operating Base on Unalaska Island.

Often thought to have been a diversion to draw American forces away from Midway (AF), the Aleutian attack, planned by Admiral Isoroku Yamamoto and commanded by Vice Admiral Boshiro Hosogaya, was actually intended to gain control of the Pacific Great Circle routes, about which U.S. General Billy Mitchell stated to the U.S. Congress in 1935, "I believe that in the future, whoever holds Alaska will hold the world. I think it is the most important strategic place in the world." The Japanese believed correctly that by controlling the Aleutians they would be in a superb position to prevent the U.S. from attacking Japan across the northern Pacific; the Americans, conversely, feared that control of the islands would give the Japanese the ability to establish airfields from which they could attack the U.S. West Coast.

The Aleutian Campaign, sometimes called the "Forgotten Battle," continued until 15 August 1943, when elements of the U.S. Seventh Army landed unopposed on the island of Kiska. The Japanese had completed their evacuation of Kiska 17 days earlier after having lost Attu, the westernmost island in the Aleutian chain, in a bloody campaign during May 1943. The Aleutian Campaign cost the U.S. 2,121 men killed and missing, 3,416 wounded, and 8 captured; 225 aircraft destroyed, and three warships sunk. The Japanese lost 4,350 killed and 28 captured; and 16 ships sunk. Staff Sergeant John A. Hauck, my father-in-law, served on Kiska.

THIS MONTH						
APRIL						
S	M	T	W	T	F	S
..	..	..	..	..	..	1
2	3	4	5	6	7	8
9	10	11	12	13	14	15
16	17	18	19	20	21	22
23	24	25	26	27	28	29
30	..	..	..	..	..	..

FRIDAY
28
APRIL

1944

NEXT MONTH						
MAY						
S	M	T	W	T	F	S
..	1	2	3	4	5	6
7	8	9	10	11	12	13
14	15	16	17	18	19	20
21	22	23	24	25	26	27
28	29	30	31	..	..	..
..	..	..	..	..	..	..

On 28 April 1944, Allied forces were in the second day of Exercise Tiger, one in a series of large-scale rehearsals for the impending Normandy invasion. These exercises were conducted in Lyme Bay, near Slapton, Devon, England, because the beach, Slapton Sands, was similar in character to the beaches chosen for the Normandy assault.

Failures to communicate can have tragic consequences, and the first of these had come during the pre-landing naval bombardment on the morning of 27 April. To accustom the infantrymen to the sights, sounds, and smells of an actual landing, the British heavy cruiser HMS *Hawkins* shelled the beach with live ammunition from H−60 to H−30. Because some of the landing ships were delayed, the officer in charge delayed H-hour for 60 minutes. *Hawkins* received the message, but several of the landing craft did not receive it and went in on the original schedule. Instead of having half an hour for the beachmasters to inspect the beach and declare it safe, American troops were landing as the bombardment took place. According to the only ship's log recovered from this incident, the troops proceeded past a white tape placed on the beach to mark the line beyond which they should not go while the firing was in progress. 308 men were lost to friendly fire.

An even more serious incident, however, occurred on 28 April. Convoy T-4 consisted of eight LSTs[2] that were scheduled to land a follow-up force and equipment after a beachhead was established. Two warships were assigned to protect the convoy, but the destroyer HMS *Scimitar* had been holed above the waterline in a collision the day before with one of the LSTs. *Scimitar*'s captain took his ship out of the exercise, steaming off to Plymouth for repair and leaving the convoy covered only by the corvette HMS *Azalea*.

---

2. LST is the abbreviation for "Landing Ship, Tank"; but the vessels, with a flank speed of only 12 knots, were commonly known to their crews as "Large Slow Targets."

Due to a typographical error in the orders, the Americans and British were operating on different radio frequencies, and the LSTs were not notified of *Scimitar*'s absence.

During the night of 27–28 April, other British ships sighted nine German fast torpedo boats (*S-Boote*, or *Schnellboote*, called E-boats by the Allies) of the 5th and 9th *Schnellboote Flotillen*, based at Cherbourg. They notified *Azalea*, whose captain did not relay the information to the convoy because he assumed that they had been notified as he was. British warships and shore batteries at Salcombe, to the south of Slapton Sands, were instructed not to fire on the Germans to avoid letting them know that the area was defended.

At about 0200 hours, the Germans attacked the convoy, which first realized the danger at 0204 when *LST-507* was struck by a torpedo and burst into flame. All surviving personnel were ordered to abandon ship. *LST-531* took a fish shortly thereafter and sank in six minutes. *LST-289* opened fire at the boats and received a torpedo in her stern, but she was able to reach port. The remaining LSTs and two British destroyers fired at the E-boats, which laid a smoke screen and escaped at high speed without loss.

Ten BIGOTed[3] officers were reported missing, raising a serious concern that the plan for the invasion might be fatally compromised and that the operation should be canceled. This disastrous attack, known as the Battle of Lyme Bay, cost 749 Allied lives: 198 Navy personnel and 551 Army personnel. (All ten of the BIGOTs' bodies were recovered, and the decision was made to proceed.)

To conceal the purpose of the exercises, the Allies clamped a lid on the incident, instructing medical personnel treating the wounded to ask no questions, act as though they were veterinarians treating sick and injured animals, and keep no records. The incident was not made public until 5 August, when SHAEF released statistics on the casualties associated with the Normandy Invasion, including information about the E-Boat attack on 28 April.

Although it would be cold comfort to the families of the dead, Allied commanders learned valuable lessons like those learned at Dieppe, and the disaster produced changes in procedures that may have ensured the success of the Normandy landings on 6 June.

---

3. The word BIGOT, an acronym for "British Invasion of German Occupied Territories," was applied to personnel who were privy to information at the highest levels, including knowledge of ULTRA, the cracking of the Germans' Enigma code, and access to its decrypts.

THIS MONTH

APRIL

S	M	T	W	T	F	S
1	2	3	4	5	6	7
8	9	10	11	12	13	14
15	16	17	18	19	20	21
22	23	24	25	26	27	28
29	30	..	..	..	..	..
..	..	..	..	..	..	..

SUNDAY

29

APRIL

1945

NEXT MONTH

MAY

S	M	T	W	T	F	S
..	..	1	2	3	4	5
6	7	8	9	10	11	12
13	14	15	16	17	18	19
20	21	22	23	24	25	26
27	28	29	30	31	..	..
..	..	..	..	..	..	..

On 29 April 1945, Eva Anna Paula Braun, dressed in a dark blue or black silk dress under a gray fur cape, stood next to Adolf Hitler in the conference room in the *Führerbunker* beneath the *Reichskanzlei* in Berlin as Walter Wagner, a fiftyish lawyer and notary who was also a low-ranking official in the Propaganda Ministry but was then serving in the *Volkssturm*, led the couple through the vows of a civil marriage.

When summoned by Joseph Goebbels on 28 April, Wagner had discovered that the necessary paperwork was not available. He secured the proper documentation and proceeded to perform the ceremony in the early morning hours of the 29th, just after midnight. In compliance with Nazi regulations, he asked both members of the couple whether they were of pure Aryan blood and free from hereditary diseases. The official witnesses were Martin Bormann and Joseph Goebbels.

When signing the marriage certificate, Eva wrote "Eva B," then stopped, crossed out the B, and finished writing her name as "Eva Hitler, *geboren* Braun." Afterward, the 33-year-old bride and her 56-year old husband hosted a small champagne-breakfast reception. Adolf Hitler remained with the party for only about half an hour; then he withdrew to his study with Frau Traudl Junge, his private secretary, to dictate his political testament and his personal will.

On the next day, the *Führer* held his final staff conference. He had lunch as usual at 1400 hours and then supervised the poisoning of his beloved German Shepherd Blondi and her puppies. Shortly after 1500 hours, the Hitlers bade farewell to the staff and retired to their private room, where they bit into thin glass vials of cyanide. Adolf at the same instant also shot himself in the head with a 7.65 mm Walther pistol. Hitler's valet, Heinz Linge, and Hitler's SS adjutant, Otto Günsche, entered the study shortly thereafter and found the bodies.

In accordance with the terms of Adolf Hitler's will, the corpses were carried up the stairs and through the bunker's emergency exit to the ruined garden behind the *Reichskanzlei*, where they were placed in a shell crater, doused with gasoline, and set ablaze. A few days later, Soviet troops found the charred remains. So that Hitler's final resting place should not become a shrine for Nazis in the future, the remains were removed to be secretly buried at the SMERSH compound in Magdeburg along with the bodies of Joseph and Magda Goebbels and their six children.

On 4 April 1970, a Soviet KGB team with detailed burial charts secretly dug up the five wooden boxes of remains. The team burned the remains thoroughly, crushed them to powder, and threw the ashes into the Biederitz river.

THIS MONTH						
APRIL						
S	M	T	W	T	F	S
..	..	..	..	1	2	3
4	5	6	7	8	9	10
11	12	13	14	15	16	17
18	19	20	21	22	23	24
25	26	27	28	29	30	..
..	..	..	..	..	..	..

FRIDAY
30
APRIL

1943

NEXT MONTH						
MAY						
S	M	T	W	T	F	S
..	..	..	..	..	..	1
2	3	4	5	6	7	8
9	10	11	12	13	14	15
16	17	18	19	20	21	22
23	24	25	26	27	28	29
30	31	..	..	..	..	..

On 30 April 1943, the British submarine HMS *Seraph*, under the command of Lieutenant Norman "Bill" Jewell, surfaced off Huelva, Spain, and lowered Captain (acting Major) William Martin, Royal Marines, into the water. Major Martin was dead at the time, and in fact he had never lived. His dunking was the culmination of a deception scheme devised by Lieutenant Commander Ewen Montagu, RN, who based it on a suggestion by Flight Lieutenant Charles Cholmondeley, RAF, that the British dump a body in a badly opened parachute with a working radio set in France for the Germans to find. Reasoning that the Allies would not know the radio was captured, Cholmondeley said, the Germans would put it into service as though the spy had landed safely, and the Allies could thereby feed misinformation to the enemy.

Cholmondeley's suggestion, a variation of a technique known as the Haversack Ruse, was at first dismissed; but it was later taken up for use in the run-up to Operation HUSKY, the invasion of Sicily. The plan was to create a military officer's persona to go with an unclaimed body, seed the body with false documents, and set it adrift near Huelva, where the British knew that the prevailing ocean currents would drive it inshore and that there was an *Abwehr* agent who was friendly with the Spanish authorities. Exhibiting a macabre sense of humor, for his project Montagu chose from the list of available names the somewhat grisly—but appropriate—name Operation MINCEMEAT.

After consultation with a noted pathologist followed by weeks of effort to find a body that would appear to have died by drowning, Montagu and his team located the body of a man in his mid-30s and received permission from his family to use it in the war effort. They then went to work to create Major Martin and the documents he was to carry. Since it was obvious to one and all that Sicily would be the next target after French North Africa, the documents needed to convey convincingly that such was not the case.

One of the documents was a letter in which Lieutenant General Sir Archibald Edward Nye explained to Lieutenant General Harold Alexander that Sicily could not be used as the cover target for the notional Operation BRIMSTONE because it had already been chosen as the cover target for Operation HUSKY.

The second piece of the puzzle was a letter from Lord Louis Mountbatten to Admiral of the Fleet Sir Andrew Cunningham, in which was a hint that Sardinia was the target of Operation HUSKY in the form of a heavy-handed joke asking Cunningham to see that Major Martin brought some sardines back to England, as they were "on points" (rationed) there. This letter also mentioned a secondary operation in the Peloponnese.

There was also a copy of a real propaganda booklet that was ostensibly being sent to General Dwight Eisenhower for his approval.

Major Martin was described as an expert on landing craft, a specialty that combined with Nye's and Lord Louis' letters to more than justify his being sent to Africa by air with those documents in his possession. All the little things were thought of, including love letters and a photo of the notional major's notional fiancée Pam as well as letters from his father and a solicitor; the finishing touch was a pair of theatre ticket stubs "proving" that Major Martin had been in London as late as 24 April.

On 19 April, *Seraph* set sail from Scotland with her cargo, labeled as optical equipment, sealed in a large canister and preserved in an atmosphere of carbon dioxide. When Major Martin was set adrift, he was accompanied by (but not attached to) an overturned life raft with only one paddle, evidence that he had come from a downed airplane. His documents were in a briefcase attached to him by a sleeve chain.

The Spanish found the body and, as expected, turned the documents over to the German agent, who opened, photographed, and resealed them (but not so well that the British were unable to determine that he had indeed opened them). He then returned them to the Spanish, who handed them over to the British consul. The copies went to Berlin to receive a proper intelligence appreciation. The Germans bought the lie, all the way up to Hitler, who ordered the transfer of forces away from Sicily to both Sardinia and the Peloponnese. Operation MINCEMEAT was not the sole reason for the success of Operation HUSKY, but, like the troops and support personnel in the assault, it did its part.

MAY						
S	M	T	W	T	F	S
..	..	1	2	3	4	5
6	7	8	9	10	11	12
13	14	15	16	17	18	19
20	21	22	23	24	25	26
27	28	29	30	31	..	..
..	..	..	..	..	..	..

TUESDAY
1
MAY

JUNE						
S	M	T	W	T	F	S
..	..	..	..	..	1	2
3	4	5	6	7	8	9
10	11	12	13	14	15	16
17	18	19	20	21	22	23
24	25	26	27	28	29	30
..	..	..	..	..	..	..

1945

On 1 May 1945, Joseph Goebbels, whom Adolf Hitler's will named to succeed Hitler as Reich Chancellor, dispatched the Chief of the Army General Staff, *General der Infanterie* Hans Krebs, accompanied by *Oberst* Theodor von Dufving, under a white flag to deliver a letter to Lieutenant General Vasily Ivanovich Chuikov, commander of the Soviet 8th Guards Army and overall commander of Soviet forces in central Berlin. The letter contained terms for the surrender of Berlin that were acceptable to Goebbels.

Krebs and von Dufving arrived at Chuikov's command post shortly before 0400 hours. Krebs spoke Russian, and he informed Chuikov that Adolf and Eva Hitler had suicided in the *Führerbunker*. Chuikov was not aware of the *Führerbunker*'s existence or that Hitler was married, but he dissembled, saying calmly that he already knew all of this. As had been agreed in 1943 at the Casablanca Conference, the Soviets were not prepared to accept anything short of unconditional surrender, and Chuikov was therefore not willing to negotiate with Krebs—who in fact was not in a position to negotiate so long as Goebbels was alive. The meeting came to nought, and the Germans returned to the *Führerbunker*, Krebs appearing, according to Traudl Junge, "worn out, exhausted."

Goebbels himself removed the obstacle to unconditional surrender when, at about 2000 hours, he and his wife Magda killed their six children and then went up to the same garden where the Hitlers' charred bodies remained in a shell crater. There, they bit into cyanide capsules and either immediately shot themselves or were given a *coup de grâce* by Goebbels' SS adjutant, Günther Schwägermann. Their bodies, but not those of the children, were then delivered to the flames as had the Hitlers' bodies been the previous day.

With Krebs no longer in any emotional state to handle the surrender, the task fell to *General der Artillerie* Helmuth Weidling, the commander of the Berlin Defense Area. No longer bound by Goebbels' order prohibiting unconditional surrender, Weidling executed a document of capitulation with Chuikov on 2 May. When Chuikov asked, "Where is Krebs?"

Weidling replied, "I saw him yesterday in the Reich Chancellery. I thought he would commit suicide…" Krebs was last seen alive as most of the others in the *Führerbunker* were making their escape in the early morning hours of 2 May; Frau Junge reported later that when she approached him to say good-bye, he straightened up and smoothed his uniform before greeting her. He and several others in high positions remained in the bunker, and Soviet troops found their bodies later, each with a self-inflicted gunshot wound to the head.

THIS MONTH							FRIDAY	NEXT MONTH						
MAY							**2**	JUNE						
S	M	T	W	T	F	S	MAY	S	M	T	W	T	F	S
..	..	..	..	..	1	2		1	2	3	4	5	6	7
4	5	6	7	8	9	10		8	9	10	11	12	13	14
11	12	13	14	15	16	17		15	16	17	18	19	20	21
18	19	20	21	22	23	24		22	23	24	25	26	27	28
25	26	27	28	29	30	31		29	30	..	..	..	..	..
..	..	..	..	..	..	..		..	..	..	..	..	..	..

FRIDAY 2 MAY

1941

On 2 May 1941, British forces at RAF Habbaniya, between Ramadi and Fallujah, Iraq, launched pre-emptive air strikes against besieging Iraqi forces of the rebel government of Rashid Ali, beginning the Anglo-Iraqi War. The Iraqis had occupied the plateau to the south of the RAF Habbaniya air base on 30 April, informing the base commander, Air Vice Marshal Harry G. Smart, that all British air activity must cease immediately.

RAF Habbaniya and RAF Shaibah, near Basra, had remained after 1937, when the British effectively ended the governing role established for them under a treaty brokered by the League of Nations. The Anglo-Iraqi Treaty of 1930 had stirred up serious resentment because it required Iraq to allow continued British use of certain bases to protect Britain's petroleum interests and maintain a link in the air route between Egypt and India.

The British planned and executed their 2 May response well, and within only four days they had destroyed much of the Iraqi air force. On 6 May, suffering continual bombardment and with no meaningful air support, the Iraqi ground forces withdrew. The Anglo-Iraqi war, however, lasted until 31 May; at its conclusion, the British had reoccupied Iraq and returned the ousted pro-British regent, the Hashemite Prince 'Abd al-Ilah, to power. The campaign did nothing to calm Iraqi nationalist resentment against the British-supported monarchy, but it did leave Great Britain able to continue using Iraqi bases through the Second World War.

THIS MONTH						
MAY						
S	M	T	W	T	F	S
..	1	2	3	4	5	6
7	8	9	10	11	12	13
14	15	16	17	18	19	20
21	22	23	24	25	26	27
28	29	30	31	..	..	..
..	..	..	..	..	..	..

WEDNESDAY
3
MAY

NEXT MONTH						
JUNE						
S	M	T	W	T	F	S
..	..	..	..	1	2	3
4	5	6	7	8	9	10
11	12	13	14	15	16	17
18	19	20	21	22	23	24
25	26	27	28	29	30	..
..	..	..	..	..	..	..

1944

On 3 May 1944, Viktor Andreevich Kravchenko, who had served as a captain in the Red Army until his posting to Washington, DC, as a member of the Soviet Lend-Lease Purchasing Commission, abandoned his post and requested political asylum in the United States. Soviet authorities demanded the defector's immediate extradition, calling him a traitor. U.S. Ambassador to the Soviet Union Joseph E. Davies appealed directly to President Franklin D. Roosevelt on behalf of Stalin to have Kravchenko returned, but the appeal failed and Kravchenko was granted asylum.

Because he feared assassination by agents of the NKVD (later the KGB), Kravchenko lived the remainder of his life under a false name. He fell in love with Cynthia Kuser-Earle, an American, but the two never married because public records could increase the chances that Soviet agents might discover his whereabouts. They had two sons, Anthony and Andrew, whose birth certificates were registered under their mother's name (Earle). The sons remained unaware of their father's real identity until 1965, only months before he died of a gunshot to the head on 26 February 1966. His death was ruled a suicide, but President Lyndon B. Johnson, who had taken an interest in Kravchenko's case, instructed the FBI to determine whether his suicide note was authentic or a Soviet fabrication. The FBI ruled that it was authentic. Some details concerning Kravchenko's last days remain questionable, however, and his son Andrew believes that the KGB could have succeeded in assassinating him.

THIS MONTH						
MAY						
S	M	T	W	T	F	S
. .	. .	. .	. .	. .	1	2
3	4	5	6	7	8	9
10	11	12	13	14	15	16
17	18	19	20	21	22	23
24	25	26	27	28	29	30
31	. .	. .	. .	. .	. .	. .

MONDAY
4
MAY
1942

NEXT MONTH						
JUNE						
S	M	T	W	T	F	S
. .	1	2	3	4	5	6
7	8	9	10	11	12	13
14	15	16	17	18	19	20
21	22	23	24	25	26	27
28	29	30	. .	. .	. .	. .
. .	. .	. .	. .	. .	. .	. .

On 4 May 1942, U.S. Task Force 17, under Rear Admiral Frank Jack Fletcher, made the first carrier strike of the Battle of the Coral Sea, as USS *Yorktown* launched 12 TBD Devastator and 28 SBD Dauntless aircraft at 0700 hours against newly established Japanese positions at Tulagi in the Solomon Islands. Reaching the target at 0850 hours, the aircraft found that Rear Admiral Aritomo Gotō's Covering Force had already, according to plan, withdrawn to support an operation to take Port Moresby on the island of Papua New Guinea. The American attack did light damage to minelayer *Okinoshima* and destroyer *Kikuzuki*. At 1210 hours, a second attack wave hit Tulagi, sinking minesweepers *WA-1* and *WA-2*, damaging mine-sweeper *Tama Maru,* and killing 87 Japanese personnel. USS *Yorktown* lost three aircraft, but all aircrew were rescued. The Japanese withdrew from Tulagi temporarily, but would very soon return to complete the construction of a seaplane base. During the following two days, although at one time the two carrier fleets were less than 100 miles apart, reconnaissance flights from both nations searched unsuccessfully for each other's ships.

THIS MONTH						
MAY						
S	M	T	W	T	F	S
..	..	..	..	..	1	2
3	4	5	6	7	8	9
10	11	12	13	14	15	16
17	18	19	20	21	22	23
24	25	26	27	28	29	30
31	..	..	..	..	..	..

TUESDAY
5
MAY
1942

NEXT MONTH						
JUNE						
S	M	T	W	T	F	S
..	1	2	3	4	5	6
7	8	9	10	11	12	13
14	15	16	17	18	19	20
21	22	23	24	25	26	27
28	29	30	..	..	..	..
..	..	..	..	..	..	..

On 5 May 1942, British forces launched Operation IRONCLAD to open the Battle of Madagascar, whose object was to capture the Vichy French-controlled island before Japanese forces, which were known to be on the way there, could occupy it. The 29th Infantry Brigade and No. 5 Commando landed in assault craft at Courrier and Ambararata Bays, just west of Diego Suarez, the major port at the northern end of the island. In the follow-up waves were Royal Marines and two brigades of the 5th Infantry Division.

A diversionary attack was staged to the east. Fairey Albacore and Swordfish torpedo bombers, supported by Grumman Martlets (the British version of the F4F Wildcat), attacked Vichy shipping. The South African Air Force, which had carried out pre-assault reconnaissance, also provided a small number of aircraft.

The defending Vichy forces, commanded by Governor General Armand Léon Annet, numbered about 8,000 troops, and their defense was highly effective in the beginning, bringing the main Allied force to a halt by the morning of 6 May. The British broke the deadlock by a daring maneuver in which the destroyer HMS *Anthony* dashed straight into the harbor at Diego Suarez and landed 50 Royal Marines in the rear of the French. The Marines did what they do best, creating a "disturbance in the town out of all proportion to their numbers," and the French surrendered Diego Suarez on 7 May.

Japanese submarines *I-10, I-16,* and *I-20* arrived 29 May. *I-10*'s reconnaissance plane spotted the battleship HMS *Ramillies* at anchor in Diego Suarez harbor; the next day, *I-20* and *I-16* launched *tokkotai* (midget submarines, known as special attack units), one of which managed to enter the harbor and fire its two torpedoes while under depth charge attack from two corvettes. One torpedo seriously damaged *Ramillies* but caused no casualties, and the second sank the oil tanker *British Loyalty,* killing six men in the engine room. HMS *Ramillies* was later repaired in Durban and then sailed to Plymouth for more extensive repair.

On 10 September, the British launched Operation STREAMLINE JANE, to seize the entire island. Fighting continued until an armistice was signed on 6 November.

The British lost 107 men killed and 280 wounded, with a further 233 men dying from disease. The French lost 146 men killed and 500 wounded. All four members of the two Japanese midget submarines' crews were killed: two in a firefight, one by drowning, and the fourth, whose body was never found, probably also by drowning. (Crewmembers of the midget submarines understood that "special attack unit" meant "suicide boat" even though the mother submarines would attempt to rendezvous after the midgets completed their assignments.) One British ship was damaged and one was sunk; both Japanese midget submarines were lost.

THIS MONTH												
MAY						
S	M	T	W	T	F	S
..	..	..	..	1	2	3
4	5	6	7	8	9	10
11	12	13	14	15	16	17
18	19	20	21	22	23	24
25	26	27	28	29	30	31
..	..	..	..	..	..	..

TUESDAY
6
MAY

1941

JUNE						
S	M	T	W	T	F	S
1	2	3	4	5	6	7
8	9	10	11	12	13	14
15	16	17	18	19	20	21
22	23	24	25	26	27	28
29	30	..	..	..	..	..
..	..	..	..	..	..	..

On 6 May 1941, the Republic P-47 Thunderbolt took its maiden flight. The P-47 was designed by Alexander de Seversky and Alexander Kartveli, both immigrants to the U.S. from Georgia in the Soviet Union. The U.S. Army Air Corps reviewed the first prototype in June 1940, liked what it saw, and placed an order in September 1940 for the all-metal fighter.

The plane's advanced features included self-sealing fuel tanks, an air-conditioned cockpit, and a huge turbocharged Pratt & Whitney radial engine. The result was an amazingly robust airplane but one that was extremely large for a fighter and also heavier than any other fighter aircraft used during World War II. When he was introduced to his new airplane, Second Lieutenant Paul L. Van Cleef, of the 365th Fighter Group, said, "Wow!!! That's *big!* Does it fly?"

Because of its size, the P-47 proved relatively ineffective as a high-altitude interceptor; but it soon found its perfect role as a ground-attack fighter. In the hands of Soviet Air Force pilots on the Eastern Front, it became a formidable tank buster.

In July 1943, the XP-47K prototype was completed; its bubble canopy improved pilot visibility tremendously, and the canopy design very quickly appeared on the P-47D, replacing the earlier Razorback design. By the end of its production lifespan, a total of 15,683 P-47s had been built.

		MAY						THURSDAY			JUNE				
S	M	T	W	T	F	S			S	M	T	W	T	F	S
..	..	..	..	..	1	2	**7**		..	1	2	3	4	5	6
3	4	5	6	7	8	9			7	8	9	10	11	12	13
10	11	12	13	14	15	16	MAY		14	15	16	17	18	19	20
17	18	19	20	21	22	23			21	22	23	24	25	26	27
24	25	26	27	28	29	30			28	29	30	..	..	..	..
31	..	..	..	..	..	..			..	..	..	..	..	..	..

THIS MONTH — NEXT MONTH

1942

On 7 May 1942, Japanese search planes over the Coral Sea in support of Operation MO, the invasion of Papua New Guinea to secure Port Moresby as a base, had spent two fruitless days looking for the American fleet when they spotted fleet oiler USS *Neosho* and destroyer USS *Sims*, which in order to refuel *Sims* had retired from Admiral Frank Jack Fletcher's Task Force 17 into what should have been safer waters.

With less than optimal visibility, the Japanese observers mistook the ships for an aircraft carrier and a cruiser. Vice Admiral Takeo Takagi, commander of the Port Moresby operation's carrier task force (comprising the fleet carriers *Shōkaku* and *Zuikaku* with their cover and support ships), believed his searchers had at last found Fletcher's main force. He ordered a full-on attack by both his carriers, sinking *Sims* and damaging *Neosho* seriously enough that she had to be scuttled. Thus distracted, however, the Japanese failed to locate the bulk of Fletcher's carrier force.

The Americans were not immune from such observational mistakes; observers reported spotting two carriers and four cruisers but had actually seen only two cruisers and two destroyers. While pursuing the mythical carriers, attack aircraft from the fleet carriers USS *Lexington* and USS *Yorktown* stumbled over light carrier *Shōhō* and sank her. Their radio report, "Scratch one flattop," became common parlance among U.S. personnel.

Alarmed by the loss of *Shōhō*, Vice Admiral Shigeyoshi Inoue issued orders to the invasion group north of the Louisiades to hold its position until the American carriers could be found and destroyed. On 8 May, the battle continued as American aircraft damaged *Shōkaku* heavily. In return, the Japanese did critical damage to *Lexington*, necessitating her scuttling, and also damaged *Yorktown*.

At that point, the two fleet commanders disengaged from each other and retired. With insufficient aircraft remaining to cover the invasion, Admiral Inoue recalled the Port Moresby invasion fleet. From a tactical standpoint, with *Lexington* sunk, the Battle of the Coral Sea was a Japanese victory; but in the long run, the Americans had emerged victorious because they had demonstrated that they could stop a major Japanese seaborne attack and because they had incapacitated *Zuikaku* and *Shōkaku* to the extent that the two carriers could not participate in the Battle of Midway a month later.

The Battle of the Coral Sea was history's first naval engagement in which neither combatant's ships sighted any ships of the enemy. There was no surface-to-surface action; all action was air to air or air to surface.

THIS MONTH						
MAY						
S	M	T	W	T	F	S
..	..	1	2	3	4	5
6	7	8	9	10	11	12
13	14	15	16	17	18	19
20	21	22	23	24	25	26
27	28	29	30	31	..	..
..	..	..	..	..	..	..

TUESDAY
8
MAY

NEXT MONTH						
JUNE						
S	M	T	W	T	F	S
..	..	..	..	..	1	2
3	4	5	6	7	8	9
10	11	12	13	14	15	16
17	18	19	20	21	22	23
24	25	26	27	28	29	30
..	..	..	..	..	..	..

1945

On 8 May 1945, the war in Europe came to an official end.

On the previous day, in the war room at General Dwight Eisenhower's Forward Headquarters at Reims, France, the Third Reich had surrendered unconditionally to the Allies. Signing the surrender instrument for Germany at 0241 hours was *Generaloberst* Alfred Jodl, Chief of the *Wehrmacht* and Chief of Staff to *Reichspräsident* Karl Dönitz, who was serving in a Weimar Republic office that Hitler had abolished in 1934 but resurrected for Dönitz in his will rather than name anyone to the position of *Führer*. Below Jodl's signature were those of Lieutenant General Walter Bedell "Beetle" Smith, chief of staff to the Supreme Allied Commander; General Ivan Suslaparov, head of the Soviet mission to France; and General François Sevez of France.

The ceremony took all of five minutes; General Eisenhower, preferring not to associate with the Germans, declined to participate and remained in a separate room with his Deputy Supreme Commander, Air Chief Marshal Sir Arthur Tedder. Waiting for the Germans as they left was General Eisenhower. With no exchange of salutes, the Germans stood at attention before Eisenhower as he asked them, "Do you understand the terms of this unconditional surrender and are you ready to comply with them?" The question was translated, and Jodl clicked his heels and gave an affirmative bow of his head. Two minutes later, the Germans were gone.

But the European war did not end on 7 May. On 8 May, Soviet troops captured the Reichstag and planted atop it the famous red flag. And at the insistence of Joseph Stalin, who refused to accept the signatures given at Reims, the Third Reich again surrendered unconditionally to the Allies, this time in a more elaborate ceremony at the seat of the Soviet Military Administration in Berlin-Karlshorst. Signing for Germany on this occasion, at 2301 hours, were *Generalfeldmarschall* Wilhelm Keitel, Chief of the General Staff of the German Armed Forces; *Generaladmiral* Hans-Georg von Friedeburg, Commander-in-Chief of the *Kriegsmarine*; and *Generaloberst* Hans-Jürgen Stumpff, representing the *Luftwaffe*. (Von Friedeburg had been present at Reims as well, along with *Major* Wilhelm Oxenius, but had not signed the 7 May surrender document.) Signing for the allies were Marshal Georgiy Zhukov on behalf of the Supreme High Command of the Red Army; Air Chief Marshal Sir Arthur Tedder, Deputy Supreme Commander of the Allied Expeditionary Force; General Carl Spaatz, Commander of the United States Strategic Air Forces; and General Jean de Lattre de Tassigny, Commander of the First French Army.

After the Germans had left the building, the Allied officers present enjoyed a sumptuous banquet that ended only when the party had to break up at 0600 hours on 9 May so the various personnel could be flown back to their units. This time, V-E Day had really arrived.

THIS MONTH						
MAY						
S	M	T	W	T	F	S
..	..	..	..	1	2	3
4	5	6	7	8	9	10
11	12	13	14	15	16	17
18	19	20	21	22	23	24
25	26	27	28	29	30	31
..	..	..	..	..	..	..

FRIDAY

9

MAY

1941

NEXT MONTH						
JUNE						
S	M	T	W	T	F	S
1	2	3	4	5	6	7
8	9	10	11	12	13	14
15	16	17	18	19	20	21
22	23	24	25	26	27	28
29	30	..	..	..	..	..

On 9 May 1941, amid heavy convoy losses as the Battle of the Atlantic continued to rage, the Type IXB U-boat *U-110* was on her second patrol of the war under the command of *Kapitänleutnant* Fritz-Julius Lemp. She had departed Lorient on 15 April, and on 27 April she sank the British merchant steamer *Henri Mory*.

Lemp then went after Convoy OB-318, at that time east of Cape Farewell (Greenland). She sank the merchant ships *Esmond* and *Bengore Head*, but she did not do so unnoticed. The corvette HMS *Aubretia*, commanded by Lieutenant Commander Vivian Funge Smith, located the U-boat with ASDIC. *Aubretia* and destroyer HMS *Broadway*, under Lieutenant Commander Thomas Taylor, then laid a blanket of depth charges that did serious damage to *U-110*.

Broadway and destroyer HMS *Bulldog*, under Commander Addison J. Baker-Cresswell, maintained contact with the submarine; *Broadway* set herself on a ramming course; but instead of ramming, Funge Smith ordered a last-second evasive turn and the dropping of two depth charges set to detonate beneath the boat, with the intent of forcing her to remain surfaced so that her crew might abandon her before scuttling. In making his turn, the helmsman failed to take into account the projection of *U-110*'s fins, and the destroyer was holed as one of the fins scraped along her side.

At that point, Lemp had had enough, and he announced, "Last stop, everybody out." As the boat's crew swarmed out through the deck hatch, the crew of *Bulldog*—assuming that the Germans intended to use the deck gun—fired on them, killing 14 men. As soon as he realized that the boat was being abandoned, Baker-Cresswell ordered his men to cease firing. The Germans had opened the scuttling valves and lit the scuttling charges' fuses; Lemp ordered radio operator Heinz Wilde to leave the codebooks and Enigma machine and get out; he then followed Wilde out of the boat.

Lemp was in the water, swimming away from the boat, when he realized that the scuttling charges must have failed to detonate. He turned back to destroy the codebooks and Enigma machine but disappeared from view and was never seen again.

The 32 surviving German sailors were captured. Sub-lieutenant David Balme of *Bulldog* took eight men as a boarding party; as they boarded the submarine, their whaleboat was smashed against the hull by a wave and destroyed. They continued into the U-boat, closed the scuttling valves, and took everything portable, including the codebooks, the Enigma machine, and a massive hoard of additional secret documents; and a second whaler was sent to retrieve them.

By radio, the Admiralty immediately named the action Operation PRIMROSE, and it was held as top secret; the United States was let in on the secret when Winston Churchill briefed Franklin D. Roosevelt in January 1942.

Broadway took *U-110* in tow back toward Britain, but by the next morning she was visibly down by the stern. She soon sank, stern dropping and bow rising until she stood like a pillar as she slipped into the depths.

After the war, the Germans claimed that a British sailor had put a rifle bullet into *Kapitänleutnant* Lemp as he was returning to his U-boat, but British personnel, including Sub-lieutenant Balme, vigorously denied such claims. The documents and Enigma machine captured from *U-110* helped Bletchley Park codebreakers solve the *Reservehandverfahren* cipher.

THIS MONTH						
MAY						
S	M	T	W	T	F	S
..	..	..	..	1	2	3
4	5	6	7	8	9	10
11	12	13	14	15	16	17
18	19	20	21	22	23	24
25	26	27	28	29	30	31
..	..	..	..	..	..	..

SATURDAY
10
MAY

NEXT MONTH						
JUNE						
S	M	T	W	T	F	S
1	2	3	4	5	6	7
8	9	10	11	12	13	14
15	16	17	18	19	20	21
22	23	24	25	26	27	28
29	30	..	..	..	..	..
..	..	..	..	..	..	..

1941

On 10 May 1941, Rudolf Hess, Deputy *Führer* and second in line to succeed Adolf Hitler after *Reichsmarschall* Hermann Göring, went flying over the British Isles.

Hess was an avid and skilled pilot, having been taught to fly near the end of World War I and competed in air races in the 1920s. When the Germans invaded Poland, Hess asker Hitler for permission to join the *Luftwaffe*, but Hitler forbade him to do so and ordered him to cease flying until the end of the war. Hess convinced the *Führer* to reduce the term of his ban to one year, and by May 1941 he was officially permitted to fly although his duties kept him on the ground.

As the war progressed, Hitler became more and more involved in foreign affairs and the conduct of the war, and Martin Bormann managed to usurp Hess' position at the side of his beloved leader. Hess, now sidelined, decided to undertake a peace mission on his own, and to that end he took off at 1745 hours on 10 May from the airfield at Augsburg-Haunstetten in his personal twin-engined Messerschmitt Bf 110-1/N fighter, which he had ordered modified by the addition of a radio compass and extra-large fuel tanks, and flew to Scotland. He had previously attempted to make contact with Douglas Douglas-Hamilton, the Duke of Hamilton, a British flyer whom he had never met; but MI5 had intercepted the letter written for Hess in November 1940 by Albrecht Haushofer, who mistakenly believed that Douglas-Hamilton, his own personal friend, was involved with an opposition party that was opposed to war with Germany, and Douglas-Hamilton had not seen it until March 1941.

As Hess flew over Scotland at treetop level, his aircraft was detected and identified as a Bf 110, and pursuit was launched. Hess climbed to 6,000 feet and bailed out, injuring his foot either in bailing out or upon landing. He landed near Eaglesham and was discovered still struggling with his parachute by local farmer David McLean. Hess gave his name as *Hauptmann* (Captain) Alfred Horn and said he had an urgent message for the Duke of Hamilton. McLean called the local Home Guard, who escorted Hess to the police station at Giffnock, confiscated his possessions, and questioned him. He was then taken to Maryhill Barracks in Glasgow, where his injured foot was treated.

Despite his continued assertions that he was Alfred Horn, his identity was already suspected, and when Douglas-Hamilton arrived the next morning, he freely admitted who he really was. No peace negotiations, however, were forthcoming, and Hess became a prisoner of war. Radio Munich announced on 12 May that he had gone missing in the air but did not mention his mission (described in a letter he had left for Hitler) or his destination. On 13 May, Joachim von Ribbentrop was sent to deliver the bad news in person to Benito Mussolini; the British press announced Hess' capture the same day. Hess' wife Ilse learned that her husband was alive on 14 May, when German radio broadcast the news to the German people.

With typical British irreverence, music-hall performer Arthur Askey was soon singing a comedy song titled, "Thanks for Dropping In, Mr Hess."

THIS MONTH						
MAY						
S	M	T	W	T	F	S
..	..	1	2	3	4	5
6	7	8	9	10	11	12
13	14	15	16	17	18	19
20	21	22	23	24	25	26
27	28	29	30	31	..	..
..	..	..	..	..	..	..

FRIDAY
11
MAY

1945

NEXT MONTH						
JUNE						
S	M	T	W	T	F	S
..	..	..	..	..	1	2
3	4	5	6	7	8	9
10	11	12	13	14	15	16
17	18	19	20	21	22	23
24	25	26	27	28	29	30
..	..	..	..	..	..	..

On 11 May 1945, the Target Committee of the Manhattan Project, led by Dr. Robert Oppenheimer, finished a two-day meeting at which the agenda included discussion of the heights at which the two types of bombs should be detonated; weather; jettisoning of an unused bomb before landing (decided against); the status of targets; psychological factors to be considered in target selection; use of the bombs against military targets (decided that such targets should be associated with cities to maximize the psychological effect of a detonation); dealing with the radiation released by a bomb; coordination with other air operations such as a follow-up incendiary raid; the necessity for thorough rehearsals; and operating requirements for the safety of participating aircraft.

Dr. Joyce C. Stearns had surveyed possible targets, and he offered (in order) Kyoto, Hiroshima, Yokohama, Kokura, and Niigata. The committee discussed the possibility of bombing the palace of Emperor Hirohito and decided that recommending such an action was not within the committee's purview.

In the event, Hiroshima was chosen for the first bomb on 6 August, with a secondary target of Kokura. Kyoto was passed over because of its symbolic value as the historical capital of Japan and also because it was the location of too many irreplaceable shrines and other works of art. On 9 August, Kokura was advanced to be the primary target; but bad weather prevented deployment of the second bomb there, and the bomb was dropped on Nagasaki, the secondary target.

THIS MONTH						
MAY						
S	M	T	W	T	F	S
..	..	..	..	..	1	2
3	4	5	6	7	8	9
10	11	12	13	14	15	16
17	18	19	20	21	22	23
24	25	26	27	28	29	30
31	..	..	..	..	..	..

TUESDAY
12
MAY
1942

NEXT MONTH						
JUNE						
S	M	T	W	T	F	S
..	1	2	3	4	5	6
7	8	9	10	11	12	13
14	15	16	17	18	19	20
21	22	23	24	25	26	27
28	29	30	..	..	..	..
..	..	..	..	..	..	..

On 12 May 1942, German U-boat *U-553*, commanded by *Kapitänleutnant* Karl Thurmann, torpedoed and sank the British passenger/cargo steamer SS *Nicoya*, killing six of the 88 people on board, a few miles south of Anticosti Island, near the mouth of the St. Lawrence River. She followed this exploit a few hours later by sinking the Dutch freighter SS *Leto* eight nautical miles north of Cap-de-la-Madeleine, Quebec, killing 12 of the 53 crew. The U-boat then returned to her regular patrol in the North Atlantic. These two sinkings, which signaled the beginning of the Battle of the St. Lawrence, were the first fatal casualties inflicted by a foreign power in Canada's inland waters since the War of 1812.

The Royal Canadian Navy immediately supplemented the four ships guarding the area (a minesweeper, two motor launches, and an armed yacht) by deploying five Flower-class corvettes, but this reinforcement was still far from adequate. Several escort ships from the Royal Navy were attached to the RCN for some months, and the Royal Canadian Air Force conducted regular patrols over the river and gulf.

On 6 July, *Kapitänleutnant* Ernst Vogelsang took *U-132* into the Gulf; and within the space of half an hour, he torpedoed the British freighter SS *Dinaric* (killing four of her 38 crew), the Belgian freighter SS *Hainaut* (killing one of her 45 crew), and the Greek freighter SS *Anastassios Pateras* (killing three of her 28 crew). *Anastassios Pateras* and *Hainaut* sank immediately; *Dinaric* remained afloat until 9 July before sinking. Working together with four Curtiss P-40 Warhawks from No. 130 Squadron RCAF, the *Bangor*-class minesweeper HMCS *Drummondville*, commanded by Lieutenant James P. Fraser, damaged *U-132*'s ballast pumps, caused her to leak more than 1,000 gallons of fuel, and drove her to the bottom, where she hid silently for 12 hours before fleeing the gulf for repairs.

In September, three U-boats made a joint raid on the St. Lawrence. U-517 sank nine ships and damaged another in a two-week period, escaping attacks by escort vessels each time and sinking the Flower-class corvette

HMCS *Charlottetown* on 11 September. *U-165* was less successful against merchant shipping, but she sank the armed yacht HMCS *Raccoon*.

Eastern Air Command positioned itself to better defend the remaining convoys by establishing a Special Submarine Hunting Detachment of No. 113 Squadron RCAF in Chatham, New Brunswick. They made their first U-boat attack on 9 September, when Pilot Officer R.S. Keetley dove on *U-165*, about 20 miles south of Anticosti Island. He did not do much damage to the submarine, but subsequent naval and air activity in the area frustrated the U-boat's efforts to attack other convoys.

Within 24 hours of 24 September, crews from 113 Squadron registered seven sightings and three attacks on *U-517*. Flying Officer M.J. Bélanger, an experienced 23-year old Québec native who came to the squadron from duty as a flying instructor, made two of the attacks. Neither sank the U-boat. Aircraft continued to harry the submarine as it cruised the Gulf. Bélanger was in the cockpit for another attack on *U-517* on 29 September. Although his depth charges exploded all around the submarine's hull, she survived yet again. Still, Bélanger's attacks had badly damaged the boat and injured some of her crew.

Because of the continuing submarine activity, the river and gulf were closed to transatlantic ships until early 1944, remaining open only to coastal craft. After the U.S. Navy entered the fray, U-boat losses began climbing; this, coupled with a steady decline in Germany's ability to build boats to replace those lost, caused the *Kriegsmarine* to redeploy its U-boat fleet to the primary Atlantic convoy routes to disrupt the Allied war resupply effort, effectively ending the Battle of the St. Lawrence by the end of November 1942.

THIS MONTH						
MAY						
S	M	T	W	T	F	S
..	..	..	1	2	3	4
5	6	7	8	9	10	11
12	13	14	15	16	17	18
19	20	21	22	23	24	25
26	27	28	29	30	31	..
..	..	..	..	..	..	..

MONDAY
13
MAY

NEXT MONTH						
JUNE						
S	M	T	W	T	F	S
..	..	..	..	..	..	1
2	3	4	5	6	7	8
9	10	11	12	13	14	15
16	17	18	19	20	21	22
23	24	25	26	27	28	29
30	..	..	..	..	..	..

1940

On 13 May 1940, as Dutch Queen Wilhelmina was fleeing her country for asylum in the United Kingdom, as the Germans were defeating the Dutch at the Battle of Grebbeberg, and as the ministers of the Dutch government were establishing a government-in-exile in London, Winston Spencer Churchill entered the House of Commons to deliver his first speech as the new British Prime Minister, having been appointed on the evening of the previous Friday by King George VI upon the resignation of Neville Chamberlain. In the final two paragraphs of his speech, he said:

"Sir, to form an Administration of this scale and complexity is a serious undertaking in itself, but it must be remembered that we are in the preliminary stage of one of the greatest battles in history, that we are in action at many points in Norway and in Holland, that we have to be prepared in the Mediterranean, that the air battle is continuous and that many preparations have to be made here at home. In this crisis I hope I may be pardoned if I do not address the House at any length today. I hope that any of my friends and colleagues, or former colleagues, who are affected by the political reconstruction, will make all allowances for any lack of ceremony with which it has been necessary to act. I would say to the House, as I said to those who have joined the government: 'I have nothing to offer but blood, toil, tears and sweat.'

"We have before us an ordeal of the most grievous kind. We have before us many, many long months of struggle and of suffering. You ask, what is our policy? I will say: It is to wage war, by sea, land and air, with all our might and with all the strength that God can give us; to wage war against a monstrous tyranny, never surpassed in the dark and lamentable catalogue of human crime. That is our policy. You ask, what is our aim? I can answer in one word: victory; victory at all costs, victory in spite of all terror, victory, however long and hard the road may be; for without victory, there is no survival. Let that be realized; no survival for the British Empire, no survival for all that the British Empire has stood for, no survival for the urge and impulse of the ages, that mankind will move forward towards its goal. But I take up my task with buoyancy and hope. I feel sure that our cause will not be suffered to fail among men. At this time I feel entitled to claim the aid of all, and I say, 'Come then, let us go forward together with our united strength.'"

THIS MONTH						
MAY						
S	M	T	W	T	F	S
..	..	..	..	..	1	2
3	4	5	6	7	8	9
10	11	12	13	14	15	16
17	18	19	20	21	22	23
24	25	26	27	28	29	30
31	..	..	..	..	..	..

THURSDAY
14
MAY

1942

NEXT MONTH						
JUNE						
S	M	T	W	T	F	S
..	1	2	3	4	5	6
7	8	9	10	11	12	13
14	15	16	17	18	19	20
21	22	23	24	25	26	27
28	29	30	..	..	..	..

On 14 May 1942, Pearl Harbor-based cryptanalyst Lieutenant Commander Joseph Rochefort presented his theory that Japan was going to attack the American air base at Midway Atoll to Captain Lynde McCormick, the war plans officer for Admiral Chester Nimitz, the U.S. Navy's supreme commander in the Pacific. McCormick went with Rochefort to the cryptanalyst's office in the windowless basement of "The Dungeon," where over the course of several hours Rochefort showed him the trail of evidence that had led to the formation of the theory.

McCormick was convinced that Rochefort was probably right, and he took the theory to Nimitz, whom he convinced to act on the theory. From a series of decrypts, Rochefort's team knew that a Japanese invasion against an American island base was imminent; the question was, what island was it? The key to the puzzle was Rochefort's guess that AF, a code group that appeared in the stream of intercepted Japanese communications, referred to Midway. How to find out if his guess was right?

Rochefort's team came up with a way to test his theory. They sent a message to Midway, by courier instead of radio to ensure that it could not be intercepted, instructing the air base there to transmit a radio message saying that its water purification plant had broken down. (Because all of Midway's clean water had to be shipped in or extracted from seawater, a failure of its water plant would be very serious.) When a Japanese message showed up saying that AF was having problems with its water supply, Rochefort knew he had struck gold. Admiral Ernest King, Chief of Naval Operations in Washington, remained skeptical; but Nimitz and his staff nevertheless proceeded to formulate a plan to lay a trap for the Japanese invasion force, and the stage was set for the battle that changed the course of the war in the Pacific.

THIS MONTH							MONDAY		NEXT MONTH						
MAY							**15**		JUNE						
S	M	T	W	T	F	S	MAY		S	M	T	W	T	F	S
..	1	2	3	4	5	6			..	..	..	..	1	2	3
7	8	9	10	11	12	13			4	5	6	7	8	9	10
14	15	16	17	18	19	20			11	12	13	14	15	16	17
21	22	23	24	25	26	27			18	19	20	21	22	23	24
28	29	30	31	..	..	..			25	26	27	28	29	30	..
..	..	..	..	..	..	..			..	..	..	..	..	..	..

1944

On 15 May 1944, German concentration camp authorities began a three-day process of transferring 7,503 prisoners from Theresienstadt, in Czechoslovakia, to Auschwitz, in Poland. A principal reason for this move was to relieve the overcrowding at Theresienstadt before an impending visit by the International and Danish Red Cross organizations.

Under public pressure after about 470 Jews were deported from Denmark to Theresienstadt, the Germans had agreed to admit two delegates from the International Red Cross and one from the Danish Red Cross to visit the camp in June. Theresienstadt served a special purpose for the Nazis; it was kept as a "model ghetto," mitigating to some extent the stories of the Nazis' genocide. Prisoners in Theresienstadt lived under a Jewish administration that was subordinate to the Germans but did coordinate

housing, electricity, water, police, judicial, and postal services, as well as labor detachments, kitchen work, cleaning of the barracks, and nursing. The inmates wore civilian clothing and enjoyed a vibrant cultural life through the efforts of the thousands of artists, both amateur and professional, who were interned there, who produced concerts, theatrical performances, artworks, literary readings, and new musical compositions. The highly anomalous conditions within Theresienstadt also reinforced its propaganda value for the Nazis.

The prisoner transfer was only part of the elaborate measures taken to disguise conditions and to portray an atmosphere of normality. Prisoners were forced to plant gardens and renovate barracks. The members of the Red Cross delegation, when they arrived, were accompanied by *SS-Sturmbannführer* Karl Rahm, the camp commandant, and *SS-Obergruppenführer und General der Polizei* Ernst Kaltenbrunner, the senior Nazi Security Police official in the occupied Czech lands, as well as SS officers from Berlin. Among the attractions presented to dupe the delegation was a performance of Verdi's *Requiem* by an unwilling choir of Jewish prisoners under Czech Jewish inmate Rafael Schächter. The prisoners also treated them to a soccer game in the camp square, complete with staged cheering crowds, and a performance of the children's opera *Brundibár* in a community hall built for the occasion.

It was all fake. The day after the visit, the Germans resumed deportations from Theresienstadt to Auschwitz, including Schächter and most of his chorus.

THIS MONTH							THURSDAY	NEXT MONTH						
MAY							**16**	**JUNE**						
S	M	T	W	T	F	S		S	M	T	W	T	F	S
..	..	..	1	2	3	4	**MAY**	..	..	..	..	..	..	1
5	6	7	8	9	10	11		2	3	4	5	6	7	8
12	13	14	15	16	17	18		9	10	11	12	13	14	15
19	20	21	22	23	24	25		16	17	18	19	20	21	22
26	27	28	29	30	31	..		23	24	25	26	27	28	29
..	..	..	..	..	..	..		30	..	..	..	..	..	..

1940

On 16 May 1940, as it became clearer and clearer that war was on the horizon for America, President Roosevelt delivered an address to Congress in which he stated that the American people must recast their thinking about national protection, that the world had changed. He described how motorized armies could sweep through enemy territories at the rate of 200 miles a day; how paratroops were being dropped from airplanes in large numbers behind enemy lines; and how airborne troops were being landed from aircraft in open fields, on wide highways, and at local civil airports. The speed of war had become so great that the Atlantic and Pacific Oceans were no longer a barrier to enemy fleets. Fifth columnists could pose as peaceful visitors while actively working to destroy an enemy's country from within.

Roosevelt made it clear that modernization of America's armed forces was inevitable and urgent and that it had the approval of the American people. He asked Congress to appropriate $546,000,000 ($9,245,808,000 today) for the Army (including the Army Air Corps), $250,000,000 ($4,233,428,570 today) for the Navy, and US Marine Corps, and $100,000,000 ($1,693,371,430 today) for his own office for national defense purposes. He also requested authorization for the military and his own office to issue contracts in the amount of $186,000,000 and $100,000,000, respectively.

He closed by saying, "Our ideal, our objective is still peace—peace at home and peace abroad. Nevertheless, we stand ready not only to spend millions for defense but to give our service and even our lives for the maintenance of our American liberties. Our security is not a matter of weapons alone. The arm that wields them must be strong, the eye that guides them clear, the will that directs them indomitable. These are the characteristics of a free people, a people devoted to the institutions they themselves have built, a people willing to defend a way of life that is precious to them all, a people who put their faith in God."

On the same day, he responded to Prime Minister Churchill's telegram from the previous day, pointing out that any military aid to Britain must have authorization from the U.S. Congress and that the U.S. fleet would remain concentrated at Pearl Harbor for the time being.

THIS MONTH							MONDAY	NEXT MONTH						
MAY							**17**	JUNE						
S	M	T	W	T	F	S		S	M	T	W	T	F	S
..	..	..	..	..	..	1		..	..	1	2	3	4	5
2	3	4	5	6	7	8		6	7	8	9	10	11	12
9	10	11	12	13	14	15	MAY	13	14	15	16	17	18	19
16	17	18	19	20	21	22		20	21	22	23	24	25	26
23	24	25	26	27	28	29		27	28	29	30	..	..	..
30	31	..	..	..	..	..		..	..	..	..	..	..	..

1943

On 17 May 1943, Lieutenant Colonel Robert M. Stillman, commander of the 8th Air Force's 322nd Bombardment Group (Medium), based at RAF Rattlesden Airfield in England, led an 11-plane flight of twin-engined Martin B-26B Marauders on the 322nd's second low-level mission to the Netherlands.

The first mission, which was the first combat action seen by the B-26, had attacked an electrical generating plant near Ijmuiden three days earlier.

The second mission was sent to Haarlem and Ijmuiden. Captain R. D. Stephens' aircraft turned back 33 miles from the Dutch coast with a power failure in the top turret and incorrect boost readings from the right engine, leaving the rest of the planes to proceed. As the first flight crossed the Dutch coast at an altitude of 50 feet, it was met by a hail of 20 mm flak that hit the lead plane, which was piloted by Colonel Stillman, and killed the copilot, Lieutenant Ellis J. Resweber. With its flight control cables severed, the plane did an uncontrolled snap roll and crashed. Stillman and two of his crew survived to be captured and spent the next two years as prisoners of war.

The second flight, about a mile south of the first, encountered more defenders, and Lieutenant Vincent S. Garrambone's lead plane was also hit and went down; Garrambone and three of his crew survived and were captured. Of the remaining eight planes, five were shot down (three by flak, two by Focke Wulf Fw 190s), two collided in mid-air, and the last went down after it was hit by debris from the two that had collided.

In the course of 39 minutes, German defenders had taken all 10 bombers out of the war. 24 men became POWs, 23 were killed, 11 were listed as missing and were never found, and two escaped capture and were able to return to territory under Allied control. One of the POWs, Sergeant Lester F. Miller, was repatriated by the Germans, and another, Sergeant Kleber L. Jones, suicided while in captivity.

In turning back, Captain Stephens had followed the established protocol, climbing to 1,000 feet to give the crew sufficient altitude to bail out should it be necessary; while a POW, Colonel Stillman expressed a belief that Stephens' plane had been spotted by enemy radar, thus alerting the Germans to the presence of the aircraft that continued the mission.

Stillman's replacement, assigned on 19 May, was Colonel Glenn C. Nye, who had commanded the 322nd in the first few months after it was constituted in mid-1942. Nye had the misfortune to be in command when on 29 May one of the 322nd's aircraft crashed on the airfield, killing all six of its crew, damaging a hangar, and causing a certain decline in morale.

As a result of the 17 May disaster, the 322nd was stood down, and the B-26 program was put on temporary hold. It appeared that it was suicidal to fly the B-26 at low level, so tactics were rethought and the 322nd was retrained for medium-altitude operations for several weeks before returning to combat on 17 July.

For its overall combat performance from 14 May 1943 to 24 July 1944, which helped to prove the efficacy of medium bombers, the 322nd received a Distinguished Unit Citation.

THIS MONTH							THURSDAY	NEXT MONTH						

<table>
<tr><th colspan="7">MAY</th><th rowspan="4" style="text-align:center">THURSDAY

18

MAY</th><th colspan="7">JUNE</th></tr>
<tr><th>S</th><th>M</th><th>T</th><th>W</th><th>T</th><th>F</th><th>S</th><th>S</th><th>M</th><th>T</th><th>W</th><th>T</th><th>F</th><th>S</th></tr>
<tr><td>..</td><td>1</td><td>2</td><td>3</td><td>4</td><td>5</td><td>6</td><td>..</td><td>..</td><td>..</td><td>..</td><td>1</td><td>2</td><td>3</td></tr>
<tr><td>7</td><td>8</td><td>9</td><td>10</td><td>11</td><td>12</td><td>13</td><td>4</td><td>5</td><td>6</td><td>7</td><td>8</td><td>9</td><td>10</td></tr>
<tr><td>14</td><td>15</td><td>16</td><td>17</td><td>18</td><td>19</td><td>20</td><td></td><td>11</td><td>12</td><td>13</td><td>14</td><td>15</td><td>16</td><td>17</td></tr>
<tr><td>21</td><td>22</td><td>23</td><td>24</td><td>25</td><td>26</td><td>27</td><td></td><td>18</td><td>19</td><td>20</td><td>21</td><td>22</td><td>23</td><td>24</td></tr>
<tr><td>28</td><td>29</td><td>30</td><td>31</td><td>..</td><td>..</td><td>..</td><td></td><td>25</td><td>26</td><td>27</td><td>28</td><td>29</td><td>30</td><td>..</td></tr>
<tr><td>..</td><td>..</td><td>..</td><td>..</td><td>..</td><td>..</td><td>..</td><td></td><td>..</td><td>..</td><td>..</td><td>..</td><td>..</td><td>..</td><td>..</td></tr>
</table>

1944

On 18 May 1944, the 123-day Battle of Monte Cassino came to an end with an Allied victory. Begun on 17 January, the battle consisted of a series of four assaults as the Allies attempted to breach the Germans' Winter Line and break through to Rome.

The first three assaults were costly failures. On the morning of 15 February, after the second failure, 142 Boeing B-17 Flying Fortresses heavy bombers, followed by 47 North American B-25 Mitchell and 40 Martin B-26 Marauder medium bombers, laid waste to the abbey overlooking the town with 1,150 tons of ordnance, reducing the top of Monte Cassino to a smoking mass of rubble and killing 230 Italian civilian refugees but not one German. Between bomb runs, II Corps artillery pounded the mountain. That same afternoon and the next day, 59 fighter-bombers and more artillery barrages dropped yet more explosive on the rubble. German positions above and behind the monastery were untouched.

A continuation of the second assault again failed; the destruction of the abbey—whose sanctity the Germans had before the bombing scrupulously respected—had provided the Germans with excellent positions for observation and artillery siting.

The third battle began on 15 March with the leveling of the town of Cassino itself. After a 31/2 hour bombardment with 750 tons of 1,000-pound bombs fitted with delayed action fuzes, New Zealand troops advanced behind a creeping artillery barrage from 746 artillery tubes. 150 German paratroopers, the survivors of the 300 who had been alive before the bombing and artillery barrage, rallied to the defense more quickly than anticipated, and by the time the Allies could mount a follow-up wave, it was too late.

The fourth assault opened at 2300 hours on 11 May with a massive bombardment from 1,660 artillery tubes manned by British, Americans, Poles, New Zealanders, South Africans, and Frenchmen. Within an hour and a half the attack was in motion in all four sectors. By daylight only the

French had achieved their objectives and were rolling up the German positions between themselves and the British Eighth Army.

In the mountains above Cassino, the Poles took Monte Calvario, only to have German paratroopers take it back. For three days the Poles and Germans slugged it out, both sides taking heavy losses until the Polish commander called the attacks off. On 17 May, the Poles were back, clawing at Monte Cassino under constant artillery and mortar fire and with little natural cover for protection. Fighting was fierce and at times hand to hand.

With their line of supply threatened by the Allied advance in the Liri valley, the Germans decided to withdraw. In the early hours of 18 May, the 78th Division and Polish II Corps linked up in the Liri valley two miles west of the rubble of what had been the town of Cassino. On the Cassino high ground the survivors of the second Polish offensive were so battered that "it took some time to find men with enough strength to climb the few hundred yards to the summit." A patrol from the 12th Podolian Polish Cavalry Regiment finally struggled to the heights and raised the red and white flag of Poland over the ruins of the abbey.

The only Germans remaining were a group of thirty wounded men who had been unable to move. The Allies had poured 240,000 men, 1,900 tanks, and 4,000 aircraft into the campaign, and they lost 55,000 men killed, missing, and wounded. The Germans had replied with about 140,000 men and an unknown number of tanks and aircraft, and they lost about 20,000 men killed, wounded, or captured.

THIS MONTH

		MAY				
S	M	T	W	T	F	S
..	..	..	..	1	2	3
4	5	6	7	8	9	10
11	12	13	14	15	16	17
18	19	20	21	22	23	24
25	26	27	28	29	30	31
..	..	..	..	..	..	..

MONDAY
19
MAY

1941

NEXT MONTH

		JUNE				
S	M	T	W	T	F	S
1	2	3	4	5	6	7
8	9	10	11	12	13	14
15	16	17	18	19	20	21
22	23	24	25	26	27	28
29	30	..	..	..	..	..
..	..	..	..	..	..	..

On 19 May 1941, a little more than a month in advance of the launch of *Fall Barbarossa,* German military authorities established a set of official "Guidelines for the behavior of the troops in Russia." The guidelines demanded that German troops take "ruthless and energetic action" against "the Bolshevik mortal enemy of the National Socialist German people." This category included "agitators, francs-tireurs [irregular guerrilla units], saboteurs, and Jews."

Essentially, the guidelines called for summary judgment without specific evidence of guilt, providing a convenient way to liquidate anyone and everyone in the path of the German march to Moscow, including not only the military's political commissars and the entire Jewish population of areas through which the Germans moved, but also Communist party officials who had been so careless or naïve as to fail to flee. In Estonia, German police arrested 14,500 Communists. 4,070 of those arrested were killed out of hand, 5,500 were sent to concentration camps, and several thousand "fellow travelers" were released.

While the systematic arrests and killings served to eliminate potential opposition and to maintain security, they also "cleansed" areas that were considered to be future *Lebensraum* (living space) for Germans who would be allowed to migrate into the conquered lands after the war was over.

The ordained measures were carried out as instructed: ruthlessly and vigorously—and this criminally brutal treatment of the Soviet peoples engendered in them a primal hatred and an unquenchable thirst for revenge that came back to claw viciously at military and civilian Germans alike as the tide of war turned and the Red Army pushed the *Wehrmacht* backward across the western Soviet Union and Poland and into Germany, killing with no quarter, looting even the poorest towns and villages, and raping virtually every human female they could get their hands on, from ancient crones to barely pubescent girls, in a relentlessly vindictive campaign that finally came to a bitter and bloody culmination with the planting of the Soviet flag on the roof of the Reichstag in Berlin.

THIS MONTH						
MAY						
S	M	T	W	T	F	S
..	1	2	3	4	5	6
7	8	9	10	11	12	13
14	15	16	17	18	19	20
21	22	23	24	25	26	27
28	29	30	31	..	..	..
..	..	..	..	..	..	..

SATURDAY

20

MAY

NEXT MONTH						
JUNE						
S	M	T	W	T	F	S
..	..	..	..	1	2	3
4	5	6	7	8	9	10
11	12	13	14	15	16	17
18	19	20	21	22	23	24
25	26	27	28	29	30	..
..	..	..	..	..	..	..

1944

On 20 May 1944, a V-2 ballistic missile on a test flight fell on the swampy bank of the Bug River near the village of Sarnaki, south of Siemiatycze in eastern Poland.

In 1943, several parts of fired V-2s had been captured by members of the Polish Underground, called the *Armia Krajowa* (Home Army, abbreviated AK), who watched launches, figured out where the test landing sites were, and strove to arrive at the landing sites before the Germans. In late 1943, in cooperation with British intelligence, the AK had concerted a plan called Operation MOST III, whose object was to capture a complete V-2 and transport it to Britain. At that time, one group within the British intelligence community believed the AK's reports about the V-1 and V-2 while a second group, highly skeptical, argued that launching a rocket of the size reported by the AK was impossible using any known fuel.

In March 1944, Polish Lieutenant Colonel Kazimierz Iranek-Osmecki, an AK member whose code name was MAKARY, crawled up to the Blizna railway line and saw on a flatcar heavily guarded by SS troops "an object which, though covered by a tarpaulin, bore every resemblance to a monstrous torpedo."

On 20 May, members of the AK beat the Germans to the landing site and, finding the virtually undamaged rocket sticking out of the swamp, shoved it down far enough to conceal it beneath the surface of the water. The Germans, failing to find the rocket, gave it up as a bad job and departed. The Poles dug up their prize, dismantled it, smuggled the parts across Poland, loaded them onto a C-47 Dakota, and shipped them to England.

The skeptical party was left with no choice but to accept that the 13-ton, 46-foot-long V-2 rocket was a reality. On 12 June, when a radio message from Polish Intelligence reported that the Germans were using liquid oxygen, the British and Polish intelligence communities both realized that discovering the nature of the actual fuel used by the rockets (a mixture of 75% ethyl alcohol and 25% water) was crucial.

	THIS MONTH							SUNDAY		NEXT MONTH					

MAY

S	M	T	W	T	F	S
..	1	2	3	4	5	6
7	8	9	10	11	12	13
14	15	16	17	18	19	20
21	22	23	24	25	26	27
28	29	30	31	..	..	..
..	..	..	..	..	..	..

SUNDAY
21
MAY

JUNE

S	M	T	W	T	F	S
..	..	..	..	1	2	3
4	5	6	7	8	9	10
11	12	13	14	15	16	17
18	19	20	21	22	23	24
25	26	27	28	29	30	..

1944

On 21 May 1944, First Lieutenant Joseph Heller, author of the milestone antiwar novel *Catch-22* (published in 1961 and never since out of print), arrived on the island of Corsica for duty with the 340th Bombardment Group (Medium), part of the USAAF's 12th Air Force. Heller flew 60 combat missions as a bombardier in twin-engined North American B-25 Mitchell bombers, and *Catch-22* is based largely on his and others' experiences as members of the 340th.

The title of *Catch-22* has an interesting history: originally, Heller titled the book *Catch-18*, but with the recent publication of Leon Uris' *Mila 18*, about the German occupation of Warsaw, Heller's publisher requested that he change the title to avoid confusion.

In the novel, Catch-22 was invoked when a man tried to get out of flying the ever-increasing number of missions required to earn rotation back to the U.S.; the only way to get out was to be certified crazy, but asking the group's medical officer to certify you crazy was proof that you weren't crazy. The phrase has entered the English language to describe any such paradoxically irresolvable situation.

THIS MONTH								SATURDAY		NEXT MONTH						
MAY								**22**		JUNE						
S	M	T	W	T	F	S				S	M	T	W	T	F	S
..	..	..	..	..	..	1				..	..	1	2	3	4	5
2	3	4	5	6	7	8		MAY		6	7	8	9	10	11	12
9	10	11	12	13	14	15				13	14	15	16	17	18	19
16	17	18	19	20	21	22				20	21	22	23	24	25	26
23	24	25	26	27	28	29				27	28	29	30	..	..	..
30	31	..	..	..	..	..				..	..	..	..	..	..	..

1943

On 22 May 1943, a working prototype of the most advanced fighter aircraft to be deployed in World War II was rolled out at Lechfeld, München-Oberbayern, in Bavaria, and demonstrated for Adolf Hitler, Erhard Milch, Adolf Galland, Willy Messerschmitt, and other top Nazi officials. The product of a research and development program that had begun in 1938, the Messerschmitt Me 262 *Schwalbe* (Swallow) was the first operational jet-powered combat aircraft in history.

The performance on this day was marred by minor mechanical failures, but Hitler was nonetheless impressed. His enthusiasm, as was often the case, would be misplaced; this aircraft was exactly what Germany needed to counter the increasing threat from new Allied fighters and bombers, but Hitler—relying on his vaunted military genius—demanded that the design be used for a *Schnellbomber* (light fast bomber), not for fighters. His intransigence in this regard sent Messerschmitt's engineers back to the drawing board, slowing further development and delaying the aircraft's

eventual introduction into combat. Recognizing the *Schwalbe*'s potential as a high-performance fighter-interceptor, Albert Speer and others went behind Hitler's back and pulled the appropriate strings to continue the jet fighter program.

The first Me 262s were deployed to France in April 1944, and they were a stunning shock to Allied aircrews, who later recalled their horror at seeing enemy fighters moving so quickly. On 1 September 1944, Lieutenant General Carl Spaatz, commander of Strategic Air Forces in Europe, expressed his fear that these new jet fighters would inflict heavy losses on Allied bombing missions.

As it happened, there were too few to do a thorough job, but they did demonstrate what sort of havoc they could have created if Hitler had not gotten in the way: on 18 March 1945, for example, 37 Me 262s intercepted a force of 1,221 bombers and 632 escorting fighters on a mission to Berlin. Although they were hugely outnumbered, the jets shot down 13 bombers and six fighters for the loss of only two of their own.

German fighter ace *Generalleutnant* Adolf Galland, in a bit of wishful thinking, later stated that had the deployed numbers been greater, the Allies would never have achieved air superiority over the French coast, and the Normandy invasion would have been delayed or even averted; but on 10 April 1945, Allied aircraft shot down at least 14 Me 262s, nearly half of the of the jets from Galland's *Jagdverband* 44 that rose against them over Oranienberg, and destroyed another 25 Me 262s on the ground. This single day, which became known as the "day of the great jet massacre," proved fatal to the *Luftwaffe*, which as a result abandoned the defense of Berlin.

THIS MONTH							THURSDAY	NEXT MONTH						
MAY							**23**	JUNE						
S	M	T	W	T	F	S		S	M	T	W	T	F	S
..	..	..	1	2	3	4		..	..	..	..	..	..	1
5	6	7	8	9	10	11	**MAY**	2	3	4	5	6	7	8
12	13	14	15	16	17	18		9	10	11	12	13	14	15
19	20	21	22	23	24	25		16	17	18	19	20	21	22
26	27	28	29	30	31	..		23	24	25	26	27	28	29
..	..	..	..	..	..	..		30	..	..	..	..	..	..

1940

On 23 May 1940, British authorities arrested Sir Oswald Ernald Mosley, 6th Baronet of Ancoats. Mosley, the leader of the British Union of Fascists (BUF), was at that time mostly focused on advocating for a negotiated peace; but fascism was on the outs in Britain, and along with most of the other active fascists in Britain, he was interned under Defence Regulation 18B. The BUF was proscribed later that year.

Mosley's wife, the astonishingly beautiful Diana Mitford, the Honourable Lady Mosley, the third daughter of David Bertram Ogilvy Freeman-Mitford, 2nd Baron Redesdale, was interned on 29 June 1940, eleven weeks after the 13 April birth of her fourth son, Max. The Mosleys lived together for most of their internment in a house in the grounds of Holloway prison, and in later life the irrepressible Lady Mosley remarked that she never again grew woodland strawberries that tasted as good as those she had cultivated in the prison garden.

Mosley used the time to read extensively on classical civilizations and refused visits from most BUF members, but on 18 March 1943 Dudley and Norah Elam (both prominent fascists, who had been released by then) accompanied Unity Mitford to see her sister Diana. Mosley agreed to the visit because he thought (mistakenly) that Lady Redesdale, Diana's and Unity's mother, would be accompanying Unity.

Later that year, Mosley, who had served with the Royal Flying Corps in World War I and had been invalided out with a leg injury suffered in a plane crash, developed a serious case of phlebitis in the leg that had been injured. Under pressure from Winston Churchill, Herbert Morrison, the Home Secretary and the man in charge of prisons, ordered the couple's release from Holloway Prison on 20 November 1943. They spent the rest of the war under house arrest.

The war ended what remained of Mosley's political reputation; but he was persuaded to return to politics and form the Union Movement, which called for a single nation-state to cover the continent of Europe, and he later attempted to launch a National Party of Europe to this end. The

Union Movement's meetings were often physically disrupted, largely by the same opponents who had disrupted BUF meetings before the war, and Mosley became disillusioned. Remarking, "You don't clean up a dungheap from underneath it," he moved to Ireland in 1951, later moving to France, where he spent most of the rest of his life.

THIS MONTH						
MAY						
S	M	T	W	T	F	S
..	..	..	..	1	2	3
4	5	6	7	8	9	10
11	12	13	14	15	16	17
18	19	20	21	22	23	24
25	26	27	28	29	30	31
..	..	..	..	..	..	..

SATURDAY
24
MAY
1941

NEXT MONTH						
JUNE						
S	M	T	W	T	F	S
1	2	3	4	5	6	7
8	9	10	11	12	13	14
15	16	17	18	19	20	21
22	23	24	25	26	27	28
29	30	..	..	..	..	..
..	..	..	..	..	..	..

On 24 May 1941, the German battleship *Bismarck* was at sea for the only offensive operation of her career, code-named *Rheinübung* (RHINE EXERCISE). Escorted by the heavy cruiser *Prinz Eugen,* her senior in the service by 23 days, the squeaky clean new battleship was to break into the Atlantic, beginning on 18 April, and raid Allied shipping between North America and Great Britain. Aboard *Bismarck* was *Admiral* Günther Lütjens, *Flottenchef* (Fleet Chief) of the *Kriegsmarine.*

The British detected the two ships off Scandinavia and deployed forces to find and block them. On 24 May, *Bismarck* and *Prinz Eugen* engaged the battlecruiser HMS *Hood* and the battleship HMS *Prince of Wales* in the Battle of the Denmark Strait. Less than 10 minutes after the British ships opened fire, a shell from *Bismarck* struck *Hood* near her aft magazines. *Hood* exploded very soon thereafter, sinking within three minutes and taking with her all but three of her crew. *Prince of Wales* continued to exchange fire with *Bismarck* but soon broke off the engagement and retired due to malfunctions in her main armament.

Bismarck had taken three hits during the battle and was leaking oil from her forward fuel tanks but suffered no casualties while costing the British one battlecruiser, 1,428 men killed, and nine men wounded. Despite having won a brilliant tactical victory, she was unable to continue her mission.

Two days later, pursued into the North Atlantic by forces of the Royal Navy and the Royal Air Force, *Bismarck* was brought to bay by "obsolete" Fairey Swordfish three-seat biplane torpedo bombers of No. 818 Naval Air Squadron, off the carrier HMS *Ark Royal.* The aircraft located her in almost total darkness, at around 2100 hours, by searching with airborne ASV II radar, and immediately launched an attack. A single hit by the torpedo from the Swordfish piloted by Lieutenant Commander John Moffat (with J. D. "Dusty" Miller, Observer, and A. J. Hayman, Telegraphist/Air Gunner) crippled the ship's steering gear and jammed her rudder 15° to port.

The next morning, HMS *King George V* and HMS *Rodney,* two British battleships that had been pursuing *Bismarck* from the west, opened fire at 0847 hours. *Bismarck* returned fire, but she could not steer, was listing to port, and could achieve a speed of only 11 knots. Not only was it impossible to bring much of her armament to bear, but *Bismarck* was also an easy target for the British, who could see her clearly as she was silhouetted by the morning sun. In less than 30 minutes, the two battleships, with an assist from heavy cruisers HMS *Norfolk* and HMS *Dorsetshire,* had silenced all of *Bismarck*'s heavy guns. Because Lütjens refused to strike her ensign, the British continued to pound her, and in an engagement lasting about 70 minutes longer they did so much damage that *Bismarck*'s commanding officer, *Kapitän zur See* Otto Ernst Lindemann, elected to scuttle his ship.

In an astonishing reversal, the *Kriegsmarine* lost one battleship, about 2,100 men killed (including *Admiral* Lütjens and *Kapitän* Lindemann), and 114 men captured while only three British sailors were wounded, all by friendly fire.

In 1960, American country/rockabilly singer Johnny Horton recorded a rousing novelty song called "Sink the *Bismarck*," describing (with more than a little artistic license) the events of these four days. The song rose to the Number 3 position on popular music charts.

THIS MONTH						
MAY						
S	M	T	W	T	F	S
..	..	..	..	..	..	1
2	3	4	5	6	7	8
9	10	11	12	13	14	15
16	17	18	19	20	21	22
23	24	25	26	27	28	29
30	31	..	..	..	..	..

TUESDAY
25
MAY

1943

NEXT MONTH						
JUNE						
S	M	T	W	T	F	S
..	..	1	2	3	4	5
6	7	8	9	10	11	12
13	14	15	16	17	18	19
20	21	22	23	24	25	26
27	28	29	30	..	..	..
..	..	..	..	..	..	..

On 25 May 1943, the German authorities at Auschwitz-Birkenau gassed 1,035 Sinti and Roma people—507 men and 528 women, mostly from Białystok and Austria—of the *Zigeunerfamilienlager*, the "Gypsy family camp," in Birkenau. Several hundred of these people had been ill, many with typhus, due to the conditions within the camp, which included overcrowded barracks, unsatisfactory sanitary conditions, and a hospital barracks full of patients. These inmates' sickness gave the camp commandant, Rudolf Höss, an excuse to write their deaths off as having been due to natural causes.

Five days later, having been appointed chief physician of the *Zigeunerfamilienlager*, Dr. Josef Mengele arrived at the camp to take up his position. From then until the Allies were approaching the camp, Mengele was in charge of the selection process, deciding which of the new arrivals standing on the selection ramp would live (for a while, at least), and which would go directly to the gas chambers. He sent approximately 20,000 people to their deaths each month. Of those whom he did not condemn immediately, some were so unfortunate as to fall into his clutches for "medical" experiments. Mengele was particularly interested in people who had eyes of two colors, and he once sewed two children together, back to back, in an attempt to create Siamese twins. Several survivors of Birkenau alleged that he had 300 children burned alive in an open fire. He took all of his research papers with him when he fled before the Allies liberated the camp. His papers later fell into the hands of the Allies and are currently being held in a vault in Israel; they have never been published.

THIS MONTH						
MAY						
S	M	T	W	T	F	S
..	..	..	1	2	3	4
5	6	7	8	9	10	11
12	13	14	15	16	17	18
19	20	21	22	23	24	25
26	27	28	29	30	31	..
..	..	..	..	..	..	..

SUNDAY
26
MAY

1940

NEXT MONTH						
JUNE						
S	M	T	W	T	F	S
..	..	..	..	..	..	1
2	3	4	5	6	7	8
9	10	11	12	13	14	15
16	17	18	19	20	21	22
23	24	25	26	27	28	29
30	..	..	..	..	..	..

On 26 May 1940, the British nation launched Operation DYNAMO, an attempt to extract from France more than 300,000 Allied troops whom German forces under *Generalfeldmarschall* Gerd von Rundstedt had trapped in Dunkirk, France. While the Battle of Dunkirk raged, hundreds of British watercraft, ranging from fishing smacks to transport ships, struggled across the English Channel to rescue the trapped troops.

Operation DYNAMO would have been forestalled had Hitler not listened to the self-important but utterly incompetent *Reichsmarschall* Hermann Göring, who insisted that the *Luftwaffe* could take care of the Allied troops without assistance from ground forces. Believing that Göring could make good on his boast, Hitler ordered von Rundstedt to stop his attack, thereby making it possible for the rag-tag British fleet to carry out the rescue operation.

The rescue effort lasted until 3 June, saving 224,686 British and 121,445 French and Belgian troops from the Germans at a cost of approximately 11,000 men killed and 40,000 captured, and 50,000 vehicles, nine destroyers, 200 other watercraft, and 177 aircraft. The Germans lost between 20,000 and 30,000 men killed or wounded, about 100 tanks, and 240 aircraft.

THIS MONTH						
MAY						
S	M	T	W	T	F	S
..	..	..	..	..	1	2
3	4	5	6	7	8	9
10	11	12	13	14	15	16
17	18	19	20	21	22	23
24	25	26	27	28	29	30
31	..	..	..	..	..	..

WEDNESDAY
27
MAY
1942

NEXT MONTH						
JUNE						
S	M	T	W	T	F	S
..	1	2	3	4	5	6
7	8	9	10	11	12	13
14	15	16	17	18	19	20
21	22	23	24	25	26	27
28	29	30	..	..	..	..

On 27 May 1942, *SS-Obergruppenführer* and *General der Polizei* Reinhard Heydrich, head of the *Reichssicherheitshauptamt* (the combined security services of Nazi Germany) and acting *Reichsprotektor* of the Protectorate of Bohemia and Moravia, left his home in Panenské Břežany, Czechoslovakia, at 1030 hours on his daily commute to Prague Castle.

Waiting for him by the tram stop at a tight curve near Bulovka Hospital in Prague were Warrant Officer Jozef Gabčík, Staff Sergeant Jan Kubiš, and Sergeant Josef Valčík. The three paratroopers had been prepared and trained by Britain's Special Operations Executive for the execution of Operation ANTHROPOID, a plan to assassinate Heydrich, who was commonly known as the Butcher of Prague. As Heydrich's green, open-topped Mercedes 320 Convertible B reached the curve, Gabčík stepped in front of the vehicle and tried to open fire with his Sten submachine gun, but the gun jammed. Heydrich ordered his driver, *SS-Oberscharführer*[1] Johannes Klein, to stop the car. When Heydrich stood up to shoot Gabčík with his pistol, Kubiš threw a briefcase containing a modified anti-tank grenade at the car. Although the missile failed to land in the car, the detonation of the grenade hurled shrapnel fragments through the right rear bumper, embedding shrapnel and bits of upholstery in Heydrich's body. The shrapnel also injured Kubiš.

After the grenade exploded, Gabčík and Kubiš fired at Heydrich with handguns, but they had been shaken by the explosion and scored no hits. Heydrich appeared not to know that he had been struck by shrapnel; he staggered out of the car with his own pistol blazing and tried to give chase but, bleeding heavily, soon collapsed. He ordered Klein to pursue Gabčík on foot. (Kubiš had fled on a bicycle.) The chase led to a butcher shop, where Gabčík shot Klein twice, wounding him in the leg, and then escaped to a local safe house.

---

1. Equivalent to an American staff sergeant

Gabčík and Kubiš were initially convinced that the attack had failed; but in fact Heydrich had been mortally wounded. He died on 4 June. His assassination had a tremendous impact, leading to the immediate dissolution of the Munich Agreement that had been signed in 1938 by Great Britain, France, Germany, and Italy. Britain and France agreed that after the Nazis were defeated, the Sudetenland would be restored to Czechoslovakia. The assassination also led to a wave of merciless reprisals by SS troops, including the burning and leveling of the village of Lidice, the burning of the village of Ležáky, and the killing of some 5,000 civilians.

Operation ANTHROPOID was the only successful government-organized assassination of a top-ranking Nazi official, but the attackers did not live to see the fruits of their labors. On 18 June, SS troops cornered them in Karel Boromejsky Church in Prague, and they all died in a firefight.

MAY						
S	M	T	W	T	F	S
..	..	..	1	2	3	4
5	6	7	8	9	10	11
12	13	14	15	16	17	18
19	20	21	22	23	24	25
26	27	28	29	30	31	..
..	..	..	..	..	..	..

TUESDAY
28
MAY

JUNE						
S	M	T	W	T	F	S
..	..	..	..	..	..	1
2	3	4	5	6	7	8
9	10	11	12	13	14	15
16	17	18	19	20	21	22
23	24	25	26	27	28	29
30	..	..	..	..	..	..

1940

On 28 May 1940, William C. Bullitt, the United States Ambassador to France, sent an urgent telegram to the United States, asking his close friend President Roosevelt to dispatch a cruiser to Bordeaux, France, to bring arms and ammunition urgently required by the French police to quell a feared "communist uprising" as German forces neared Paris and other industrial centers, and to take away the French and Belgian gold reserves. "If you cannot send a cruiser of the *San Francisco* class to Bordeaux," he begged, "please order the *Trenton* at Lisbon to take on fuel and supplies at once for a trip to America, and order her today to Bordeaux." In response to Bullitt's plea, Roosevelt ordered the *New Orleans*-class heavy cruiser USS *Vincennes,* with destroyers USS *Truxton* and USS *Simpson,* to set course for the Azores on the first leg of a voyage to Bordeaux to attend to Bullitt's second request.

THIS MONTH

MAY

S	M	T	W	T	F	S
..	..	..	1	2	3	4
5	6	7	8	9	10	11
12	13	14	15	16	17	18
19	20	21	22	23	24	25
26	27	28	29	30	31	..
..	..	..	..	..	..	..

WEDNESDAY

29

MAY

1940

NEXT MONTH

JUNE

S	M	T	W	T	F	S
..	..	..	..	..	..	1
2	3	4	5	6	7	8
9	10	11	12	13	14	15
16	17	18	19	20	21	22
23	24	25	26	27	28	29
30	..	..	..	..	..	..

On 29 May 1940, No. 264 Squadron RAF, based at Manston, England, and commanded by Squadron Leader Philip A. Hunter, claimed 37 kills in two sorties, including 19 Junkers Ju 87 *Stuka* dive bombers, nine Messerschmitt Bf 110 heavy fighters, eight Messerschmitt Bf 109 fighters, and one Junkers Ju 88 bomber, while suffering no losses themselves (although one plane did come back minus both ailerons and its rudder).

The squadron was equipped with the new two-seat Boulton Paul P.82 Defiant turret fighter that had been designed to maul enemy bombers, which the RAF had assumed would be attacking *en masse* with no long-range fighter escort because the Germans had no such fighters. (The British had failed to realize that *Blitzkrieg* warfare would quickly deliver into German hands airfields close enough to the United Kingdom that long-range fighters would not be necessary.) The P.82 was fitted with an electro-hydraulically powered turret housing quad electrically fired 7.7-millimeter Browning machine guns. There were no fixed forward-firing weapons, but the gunner could rotate the turret directly forward and transfer firing control to the pilot. This design made up to some extent for the lack of forward-firing guns; but when the turret was facing forward, its guns were aimed 19 degrees upward. With no associated gunsight, it was difficult for the pilot to fire the guns accurately. On this occasion, the *Luftwaffe* fighter pilots mistook the Defiant fighters for Hawker Hurricane fighters and dove on the supposedly defenseless British fighters. Their surprise can only be imagined as they were welcomed to the party by a withering concentration of fire.

As German fighter pilots learned over the next few weeks to identify them with accuracy, however, Defiants became extremely vulnerable to attack from the front or below. In late August, with losses mounting, they were retired from daytime service and were transferred to night fighter units, where they were very effective.

THIS MONTH						
MAY						
S	M	T	W	T	F	S
..	..	..	..	..	1	2
3	4	5	6	7	8	9
10	11	12	13	14	15	16
17	18	19	20	21	22	23
24	25	26	27	28	29	30
31	..	..	..	..	..	..

SATURDAY
30
MAY

1942

NEXT MONTH						
JUNE						
S	M	T	W	T	F	S
..	1	2	3	4	5	6
7	8	9	10	11	12	13
14	15	16	17	18	19	20
21	22	23	24	25	26	27
28	29	30	..	..	..	..
..	..	..	..	..	..	..

On 30 May 1942, Air Marshal Arthur ("Bomber") Harris dispatched history's first "thousand-bomber raid" against Köln (Cologne), Germany. Weather conditions over Germany combined with limitations on the range of the RAF's new ground-based GEE navigational system to force Harris to choose Köln instead of his preferred target of Hamburg.

Harris had earlier said, "The Nazis entered this war under the rather childish delusion that they were going to bomb everyone else, and nobody was going to bomb them. At Rotterdam, London, Warsaw and half a hundred other places, they put their rather naïve theory into operation. They sowed the wind, and now they are going to reap the whirlwind."

He had lobbied repeatedly for larger raids in the belief that such large raids might be devastating enough to knock Germany out of the war or, if not, at least be shocking enough to have a serious impact on German morale. The actual count of aircraft participating in Operation MILLEN-NIUM was 1,012 (including 131 Halifaxes, 79 Hampdens, 46 Manchesters, 88 Stirlings, 602 Wellingtons, and 28 Whitleys)—but in order to achieve the massive force he wanted, Harris was forced to augment the otherwise insufficient number of planes by including 369 aircraft from training squadrons.

This raid marked the introduction of a new British tactic: the "bomber stream," a long, narrow formation in which all the bombers followed the same course, with each assigned to an altitude and a space in the stream. The bomber stream replaced the technique of sending each aircraft individually, to plot and follow its own route into Germany and out again. The German defensive strategy was laid out in what was called the Kammhuber Line, consisting of three layers of zones ("cells") about 20 miles north to south and 12½ miles east to west. Two German night fighters were assigned to each cell, and they received ground-directed guidance from their own *Himmelbelt* controller. The *Himmelbelt* control center could handle only two fighters; this was adequate for dealing with the older British tactic, but the bomber stream, with the bombers using the GEE system to fly down the center of a cell, overwhelmed the German system.

In the event, 868 aircraft bombed the main target and 15 aircraft struck other targets. The total tonnage dropped was 1,455 tons, of which one third was high-explosive bombs and the other two thirds were incendiaries. The British recorded that the raid killed between 469 and 486 people, of whom 58 were military personnel; injured 5,027, and left 45,132 home-less. Forty-three British aircraft failed to return. The German govern-ment estimated that Köln received 900 tons of high explosive and 110,000 incendiary bombs, and that about 400 were killed.

THIS MONTH						
MAY						
S	M	T	W	T	F	S
..	..	..	..	..	1	2
3	4	5	6	7	8	9
10	11	12	13	14	15	16
17	18	19	20	21	22	23
24	25	26	27	28	29	30
31	..	..	..	..	..	..

SUNDAY
31
MAY

NEXT MONTH						
JUNE						
S	M	T	W	T	F	S
..	1	2	3	4	5	6
7	8	9	10	11	12	13
14	15	16	17	18	19	20
21	22	23	24	25	26	27
28	29	30	..	..	..	..
..	..	..	..	..	..	..

1942

On 31 May 1942, *Generalfeldmarschall* Albert Kesselring ("Uncle Albert" to his troops, and "Smiling Albert" to the Allies) could count only 83 serviceable aircraft available to him in the Mediterranean. This dismal state was due to the success of Operations BOWERY and LB, combined Anglo-American operations to deliver Spitfire fighters to Malta.

The seaborne missions, called "club runs," were covered by Force H, based at Gibraltar (called "The Club" because it was considered to be an exclusive club of the most efficient warships in the Royal Navy). The technique was to embark the required fighters on aircraft carriers, make certain shipboard modifications at Gibraltar, and then transport the planes to within flight range of Malta and launch them. The Axis developed tactics to combat the club runs, at first going after the aircraft in the air and then targeting them on the ground before they could refuel and rearm, and later going after the carriers. The British lost HMS *Ark Royal* on a club run, and the U.S. assigned USS *Wasp* to the project during April and May 1942.

Spitfires were urgently required to counter the more modern German fighters that were appearing and which outclassed the tough but outdated Hurricanes that had been delivered by several earlier ferry operations. In mid-April, Operation CALENDAR had delivered 48 Spitfires, but the Germans had been forewarned, and all 48 of the planes were destroyed, most of them on the ground, within 48 hours of their arrival on 20 April. Operations BOWERY and LB succeeded in delivering a total of 78 Spitfires to Malta, with the result that the Germans and Italians were themselves suddenly outclassed.

JUNE						
S	M	T	W	T	F	S
1	2	3	4	5	6	7
8	9	10	11	12	13	14
15	16	17	18	19	20	21
22	23	24	25	26	27	28
29	30	..	..	..	..	..
..	..	..	..	..	..	..

SUNDAY
1
JUNE

JULY						
S	M	T	W	T	F	S
..	..	1	2	3	4	5
6	7	8	9	10	11	12
13	14	15	16	17	18	19
20	21	22	23	24	25	26
27	28	29	30	31	..	..
..	..	..	..	..	..	..

1941

On 1 June 1941, as a shortage of basic clothing materials developed, the government of the United Kingdom introduced clothing rationing. Each British subject received a Clothing Book containing 60 differently colored coupons; the coupons in the book were designed to permit the person to buy one completely new set of clothes over the course of a year's time. (Children's books contained 70 coupons, to allow for growing out of some clothes during the year.)

Coupons of any given color were not available for use until the government issued one of its periodic announcements saying that coupons of such-and-such a color could be used; this scheme prevented the people from snapping up the supply by blowing all their coupons at once. If a person did not need or want to buy clothes at the time a given set of coupons became available, he or she could save the coupons and use them with a later set to buy more at that time. Every item of clothing was given a "value" in coupons; for example, a man's overcoat was worth 16 coupons, a woman's wool dress 11, a dress of cotton or other material seven, pajamas eight, a nightdress six, underpants four, and a pair of socks or stockings two. Handkerchiefs came in at two for one coupon. Children's items cost less; a man's cotton shirt was worth five coupons, but a boy's cotton shirt was worth only four.

To make a purchase, the person chose the item or items desired and handed over the coupon book to the shopkeeper, who would cut out the appropriate number of coupons. The customer could then hand over the money to make the actual purchase.

Later in the war, as shortages continued and got more severe, the ration was reduced to 48 coupons for adults and 58 for children.

THIS MONTH						
JUNE						
S	M	T	W	T	F	S
..	..	..	..	..	1	2
3	4	5	6	7	8	9
10	11	12	13	14	15	16
17	18	19	20	21	22	23
24	25	26	27	28	29	30
..	..	..	..	..	..	..

SATURDAY
2
JUNE

1945

NEXT MONTH						
JULY						
S	M	T	W	T	F	S
1	2	3	4	5	6	7
8	9	10	11	12	13	14
15	16	17	18	19	20	21
22	23	24	25	26	27	28
29	30	31	..	..	..	..
..	..	..	..	..	..	..

On 2 June 1945, Grumman F6F-5 fighters of VF-87, part of Air Group 87, off USS *Ticonderoga*, made the first of three fighter sweeps against airfields on Kyushu, the southernmost of the Japanese Home Islands, in an attempt to stop special attack aircraft from taking off to attack Allied forces engaged in Operation ICEBERG, the battle for Okinawa.

"Special attack aircraft" was a polite euphemism used by the Japanese to refer to *kamikaze* aircraft. On 2 June, and again on 3 June, the targets of the Hellcats were Ronchi and Kokubu airfields, at the head of Kagoshima. Planes from other carriers of Task Force 38 attacked other airfields in southern Kyushu. The targeted airfields and others had already been subjected to thousands of sorties by B-29s that should have been bombing industrial complexes and war *matériel* factories, but the high-altitude bombing had been ineffective. On all of these sweeps, the primary targets were the aircraft dispersed in an intricate system of dispersal areas and revetments adjacent to the airfields. The Americans strafed and dropped fragmentation bombs, and at Kanoya (8 June) the bombs were fitted with VT (proximity) fuzes for the first time.

The Americans found it extremely difficult to pick targets in their dives and to assess the damage they were causing because the Japanese had been very clever, concealing their aircraft in covered revetments and mixing dummy planes with the real ones. The three days of raiding produced eleven confirmed aircraft destroyed and a substantial number believed to have been damaged.

THIS MONTH													NEXT MONTH					

TUESDAY

3

JUNE

1941

JUNE
S	M	T	W	T	F	S
1	2	3	4	5	6	7
8	9	10	11	12	13	14
15	16	17	18	19	20	21
22	23	24	25	26	27	28
29	30	..	..	..	..	..
..	..	..	..	..	..	..

JULY
S	M	T	W	T	F	S
..	..	1	2	3	4	5
6	7	8	9	10	11	12
13	14	15	16	17	18	19
20	21	22	23	24	25	26
27	28	29	30	31	..	..

On 3 June 1941, a twin-engine de Havilland DH.84 Dragon II "Rapide" biplane aircraft, owned by Great Western & Southern Airlines Ltd and operated by Olley Air Services, disappeared after leaving St. Mary's in the Scilly Isles on a flight to Land's End, at the westernmost tip of Cornwall.

The Dragon, registration number G-ACPY, had been the first aircraft operated by Aer Lingus, which had sold it in 1938. It was piloted by Captain William D. Anderson and was carrying John Leggitt, Secretary of the Anglo-Egyptian Chamber of Commerce, his wife Sheelagh, and their children Jeannie and Romalita, who had been vacationing at Penzance; and Mrs. Georgina Griffith. An immediate search turned up the body of one of the passengers, washed up near Portreath; the other five were never found.

Later investigation established that a Heinkel He 111H-4 bomber returning to France at a low altitude from a raid over the north of England had fired on the Dragon with its single nose-mounted machine gun; with its port engine in flames, the passenger plane crashed into the sea and sank. The *Luftwaffe*'s explanation of the incident was that the Dragon, a model that was also in use by the British military, had been considered a legitimate target.

Passenger air service from the Scilly Isles was suspended until 27 October of the same year, at which time officials established a system of contact with a radar station to confirm that no enemy aircraft were near enough to pose a danger.

THIS MONTH						
JUNE						
S	M	T	W	T	F	S
..	1	2	3	4	5	6
7	8	9	10	11	12	13
14	15	16	17	18	19	20
21	22	23	24	25	26	27
28	29	30	..	..	..	..
..	..	..	..	..	..	..

THURSDAY
4
JUNE
1942

NEXT MONTH						
JULY						
S	M	T	W	T	F	S
..	..	..	1	2	3	4
5	6	7	8	9	10	11
12	13	14	15	16	17	18
19	20	21	22	23	24	25
26	27	28	29	30	31	..
..	..	..	..	..	..	..

On 4 June 1942, American forces commanded by Admiral Chester Nimitz engaged Japanese forces under the overall command of Admiral Isoroku Yamamoto in the Battle of Midway.

The Japanese operation, a major invasion of Midway Atoll planned by Yamamoto and named Operation MI, with the invasion fleet under the command of Vice Admiral Chūichi Nagumo, was supported by four fleet carriers (*Akagi, Kaga, Hiryu,* and *Soryu*) and was intended to lure out of Pearl Harbor the American aircraft carriers that had been at sea on 7 December 1941 so that they could be destroyed in a decisive battle. (The outdated Japanese naval strategy was built around the concept of a major "decisive battle," which had won the naval component of the Russo-Japanese war for them in 1905, at the Battle of Tsushima.)

The plan had serious flaws: it was based on faulty assumptions about potential American reactions, and the disposition of ships was not made wisely. Because Joseph Rochefort's cryptanalytic team had broken the Japanese codes and tricked the Japanese into revealing the target, the U.S. Navy was forewarned and laid a three-carrier trap, setting Vice Admiral William Halsey's Task Force 16, led by the carriers USS *Enterprise* and USS *Hornet* (commanded by Rear Admiral Raymond Spruance because Halsey was stricken with psoriasis and confined to the base at Pearl Harbor) in one location and, in a separate location 10 miles to the north, Task Force 17, led by USS *Yorktown* under Admiral Frank Jack Fletcher.

Yorktown had taken considerable damage in the Coral Sea, and inspectors at Pearl Harbor calculated that she would need at least two weeks of repairs. Instead, she was rushed through three days and nights of repairs to ready her for Midway, and she was still carrying frantically busy personnel from a repair ship as she steamed out of Pearl. When battle was joined, Japanese naval commanders momentarily believed they had mistaken *Yorktown* for another ship; they thought that she had been sunk in the Coral Sea—yet here she was.

At Midway, as at the Coral Sea, neither combatant's ships saw any of the other's ships; all action was air to air or air to surface, in which the Americans lost about 150 aircraft, the Japanese 248. In addition to the aircraft, the Americans lost *Yorktown* (for real this time) and the destroyer USS *Hammann* sunk, and 307 lives. The Japanese lost all four of the carriers in the battle fleet as well as the cruiser *Mikuma* sunk, and 3,057 lives. (Another Japanese cruiser, *Mogami*, was heavily damaged, with nearly all of her superstructure reduced to a useless tangle of smoking metal.)

The American victory, which was certainly decisive but hardly according to Yamamoto's wishes, ended the six-month string of stinging U.S. defeats that had marked America's entry into the war (except for the Coral Sea, which was a slight tactical victory for the Japanese but cost them ships and aircraft that might have swayed the course of the battle at Midway). Midway was the turning point in the Pacific naval war; although there would still be terrible sea battles costing both sides many thousands of lives, Japanese shipbuilding and pilot training were on the decline while American construction and training were on the rise, and never again would the Imperial Japanese Navy pose a major threat to the Allies.

THIS MONTH						
JUNE						
S	M	T	W	T	F	S
..	..	..	..	1	2	3
4	5	6	7	8	9	10
11	12	13	14	15	16	17
18	19	20	21	22	23	24
25	26	27	28	29	30	..
..	..	..	..	..	..	..

MONDAY
5
JUNE

1944

NEXT MONTH						
JULY						
S	M	T	W	T	F	S
..	..	..	..	..	..	1
2	3	4	5	6	7	8
9	10	11	12	13	14	15
16	17	18	19	20	21	22
23	24	25	26	27	28	29
30	31	..	..	..	..	..

On 5 June 1944, after a massively bloody campaign starting in Sicily and moving to the Italian mainland with landings at the toe of the "boot" and at Salerno, American forces of Lieutenant General Mark Clark's Fifth Army and Commonwealth and Allied forces of General Sir Bernard Montgomery's Eighth Army entered Rome, the first of the Axis capitals to fall to the Allies in World War II.

The Italian campaign was statistically the most costly single campaign in the European Theater of Operations, with the Allies losing some 60,000 troops killed and about 260,000 wounded, captured, or missing; and the Germans suffering about 50,000 deaths and about 286,000 wounded,

captured, or missing (not including those who entered captivity when an armistice was signed on 29 April 1945).

The handsome and vainglorious Clark, who had an outsized personal press entourage and who permitted photographs of his profile to be taken only from his "good side," expected Rome's fall to make his name a household word, featured in newspapers and on radio around the Allied world; but he was doomed to bitter disappointment the very next morning as the Normandy invasion stole his thunder.

Cover designed by
Richard F. Binder
using Cutright Regular (Waldenfonts)
and Kododa (Waldenfonts).

Interior typeset in Mrs Eaves (Emigre)
and Grotesk (URW)
by

PROSPECT HILL
PUBLISHING SERVICES

Nashua, New Hampshire

18356108R00264

Made in the USA
Middletown, DE
03 March 2015